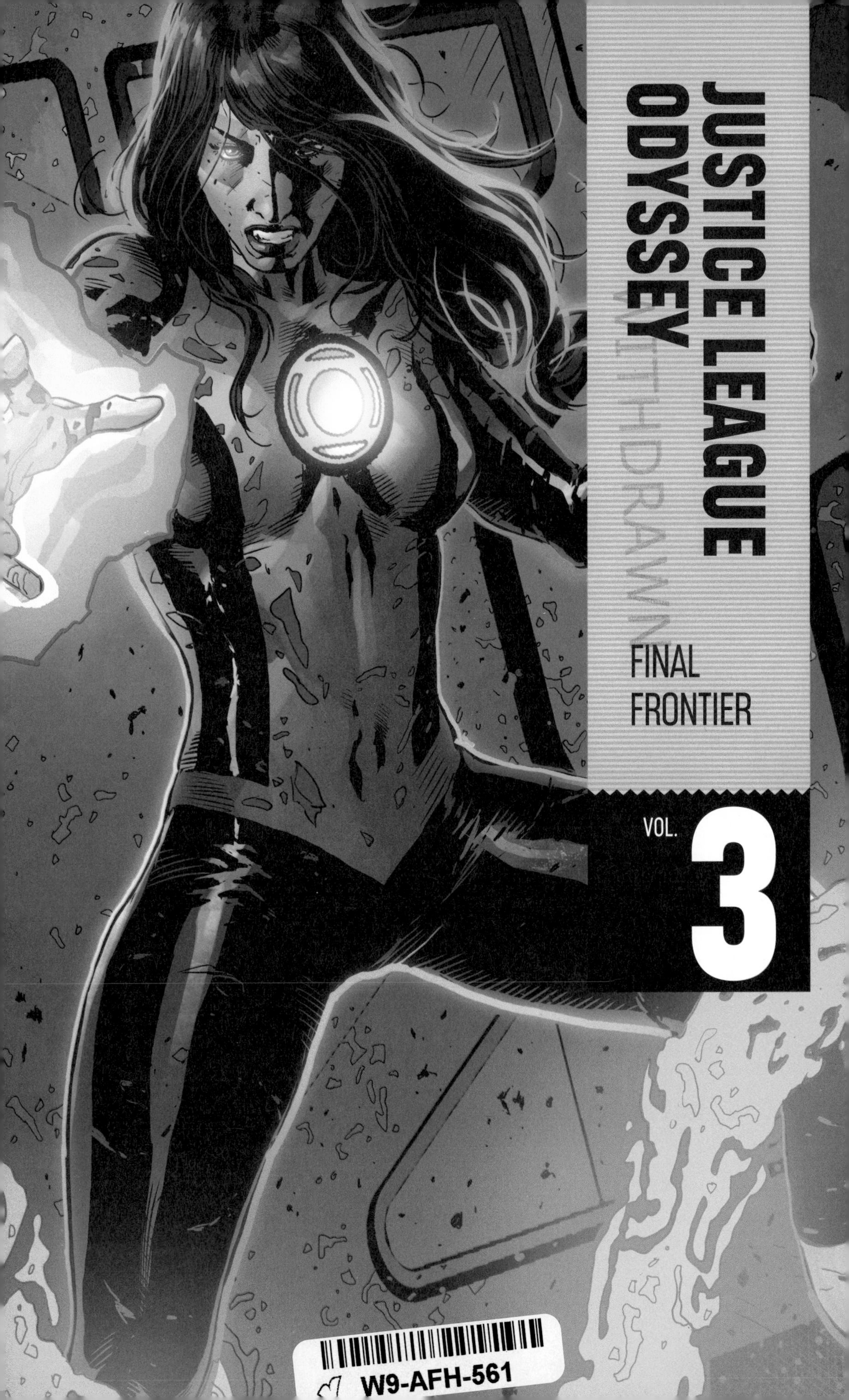

JUSTICE LEAGUE ODYSSEY

FINAL FRONTIER

VOL. 3

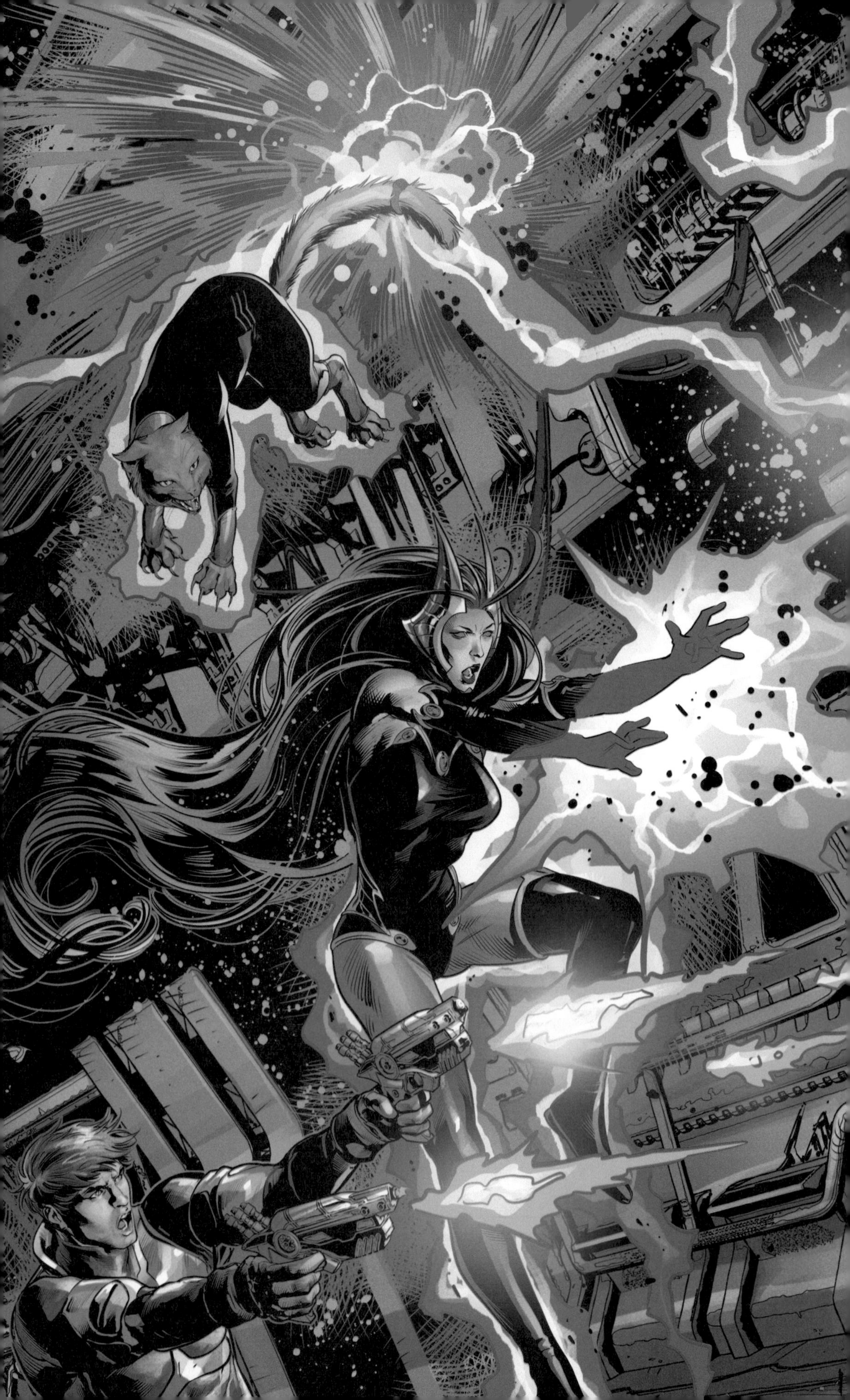

JUSTICE LEAGUE ODYSSEY

FINAL FRONTIER

writer

DAN ABNETT

artists

WILL CONRAD
CLIFF RICHARDS
CHRISCROSS
LE BEAU UNDERWOOD
DANNY MIKI
SCOTT HANNA

colorists

RAIN BEREDO
PETE PANTAZIS

letterer

ANDWORLD DESIGN

collection cover art

WILL CONRAD and
RAIN BEREDO

VOL.

3

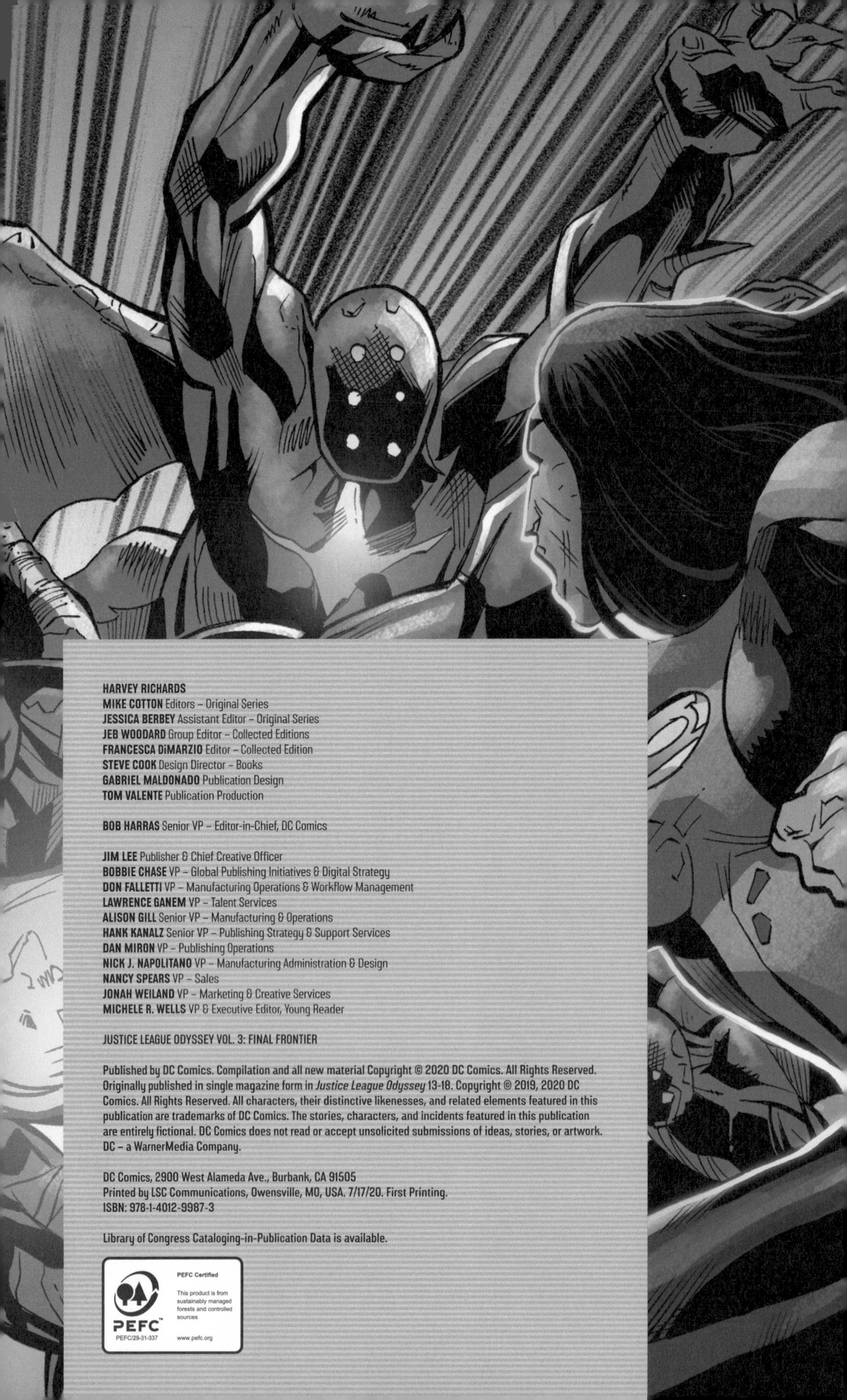

HARVEY RICHARDS
MIKE COTTON Editors – Original Series
JESSICA BERBEY Assistant Editor – Original Series
JEB WOODARD Group Editor – Collected Editions
FRANCESCA DiMARZIO Editor – Collected Edition
STEVE COOK Design Director – Books
GABRIEL MALDONADO Publication Design
TOM VALENTE Publication Production

BOB HARRAS Senior VP – Editor-in-Chief, DC Comics

JIM LEE Publisher & Chief Creative Officer
BOBBIE CHASE VP – Global Publishing Initiatives & Digital Strategy
DON FALLETTI VP – Manufacturing Operations & Workflow Management
LAWRENCE GANEM VP – Talent Services
ALISON GILL Senior VP – Manufacturing & Operations
HANK KANALZ Senior VP – Publishing Strategy & Support Services
DAN MIRON VP – Publishing Operations
NICK J. NAPOLITANO VP – Manufacturing Administration & Design
NANCY SPEARS VP – Sales
JONAH WEILAND VP – Marketing & Creative Services
MICHELE R. WELLS VP & Executive Editor, Young Reader

JUSTICE LEAGUE ODYSSEY VOL. 3: FINAL FRONTIER

DC Comics, 2900 West Alameda Ave., Burbank, CA 91505
Printed by LSC Communications, Owensville, MO, USA. 7/17/20. First Printing.
ISBN: 978-1-4012-9987-3

Library of Congress Cataloging-in-Publication Data is available.

PEFC Certified
This product is from sustainably managed forests and controlled sources
www.pefc.org
PEFC/29-31-337

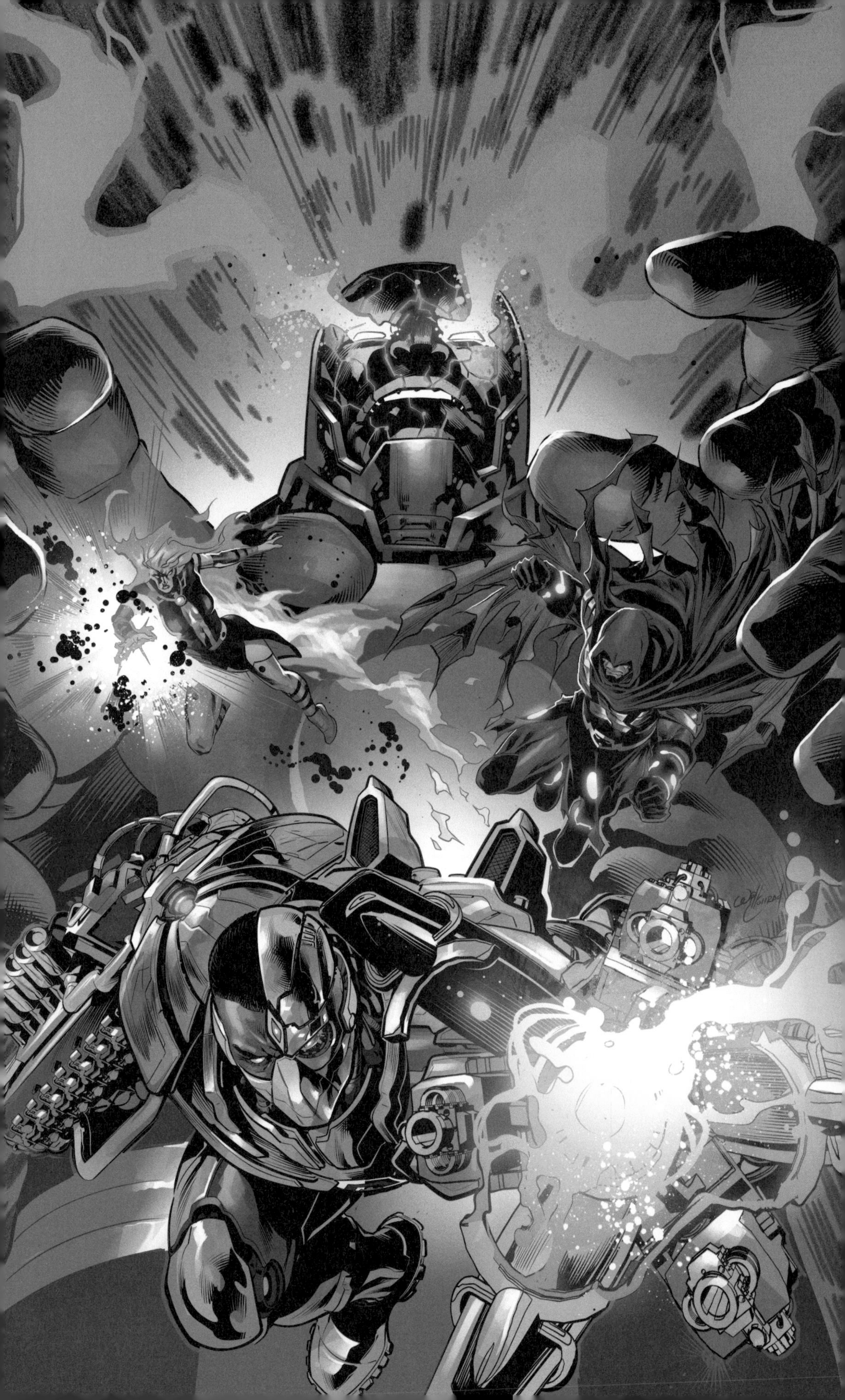

Justice League Odyssey **#13** variant cover by
LUCIO PARRILLO

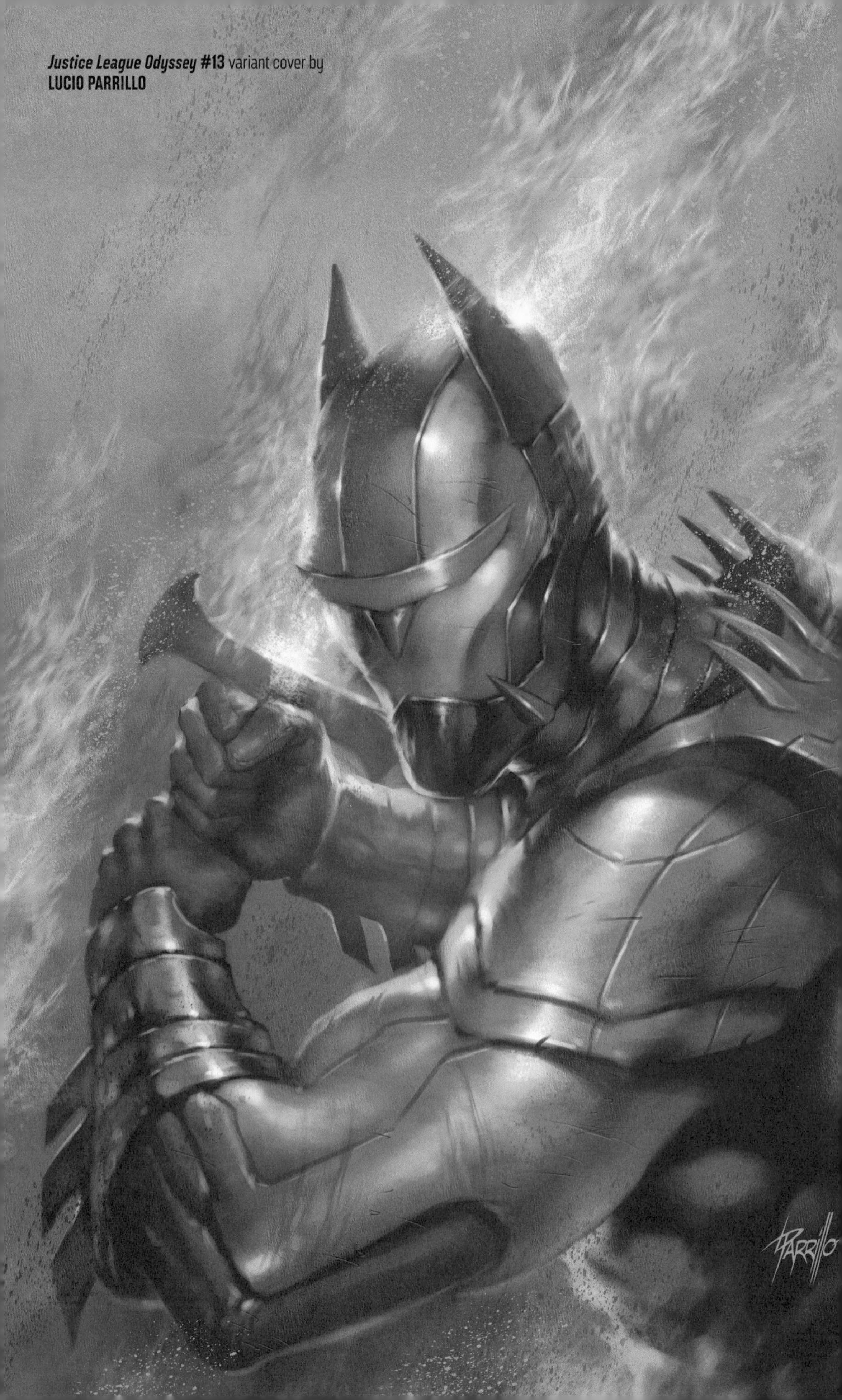

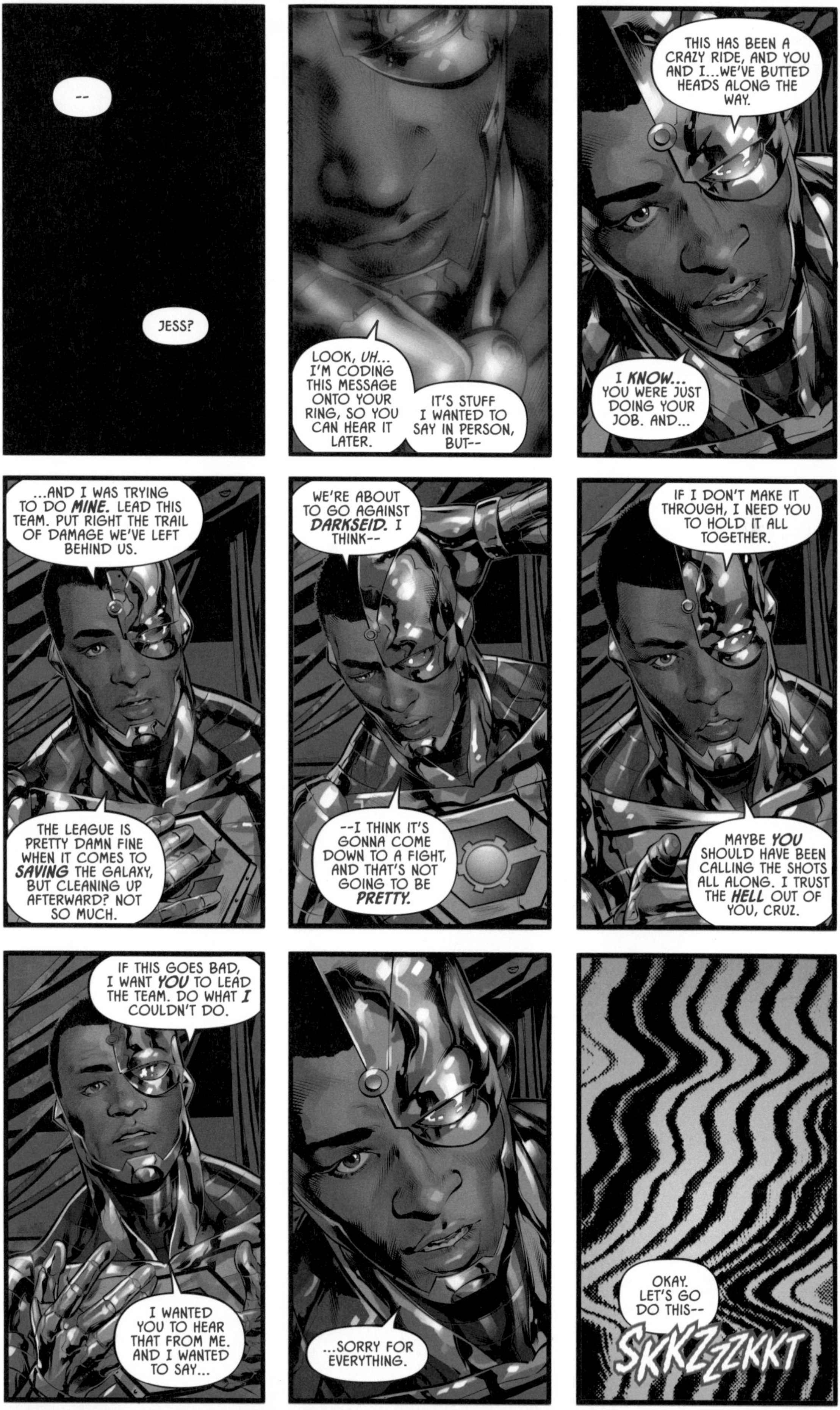
--
JESS?
LOOK, UH... I'M CODING THIS MESSAGE ONTO YOUR RING, SO YOU CAN HEAR IT LATER.
IT'S STUFF I WANTED TO SAY IN PERSON, BUT--
THIS HAS BEEN A CRAZY RIDE, AND YOU AND I...WE'VE BUTTED HEADS ALONG THE WAY.
I KNOW... YOU WERE JUST DOING YOUR JOB. AND...
...AND I WAS TRYING TO DO MINE. LEAD THIS TEAM. PUT RIGHT THE TRAIL OF DAMAGE WE'VE LEFT BEHIND US.
THE LEAGUE IS PRETTY DAMN FINE WHEN IT COMES TO SAVING THE GALAXY, BUT CLEANING UP AFTERWARD? NOT SO MUCH.
WE'RE ABOUT TO GO AGAINST DARKSEID. I THINK--
--I THINK IT'S GONNA COME DOWN TO A FIGHT, AND THAT'S NOT GOING TO BE PRETTY.
IF I DON'T MAKE IT THROUGH, I NEED YOU TO HOLD IT ALL TOGETHER.
MAYBE YOU SHOULD HAVE BEEN CALLING THE SHOTS ALL ALONG. I TRUST THE HELL OUT OF YOU, CRUZ.
IF THIS GOES BAD, I WANT YOU TO LEAD THE TEAM. DO WHAT I COULDN'T DO.
I WANTED YOU TO HEAR THAT FROM ME. AND I WANTED TO SAY...
...SORRY FOR EVERYTHING.
OKAY. LET'S GO DO THIS--
SKKZZZKKT

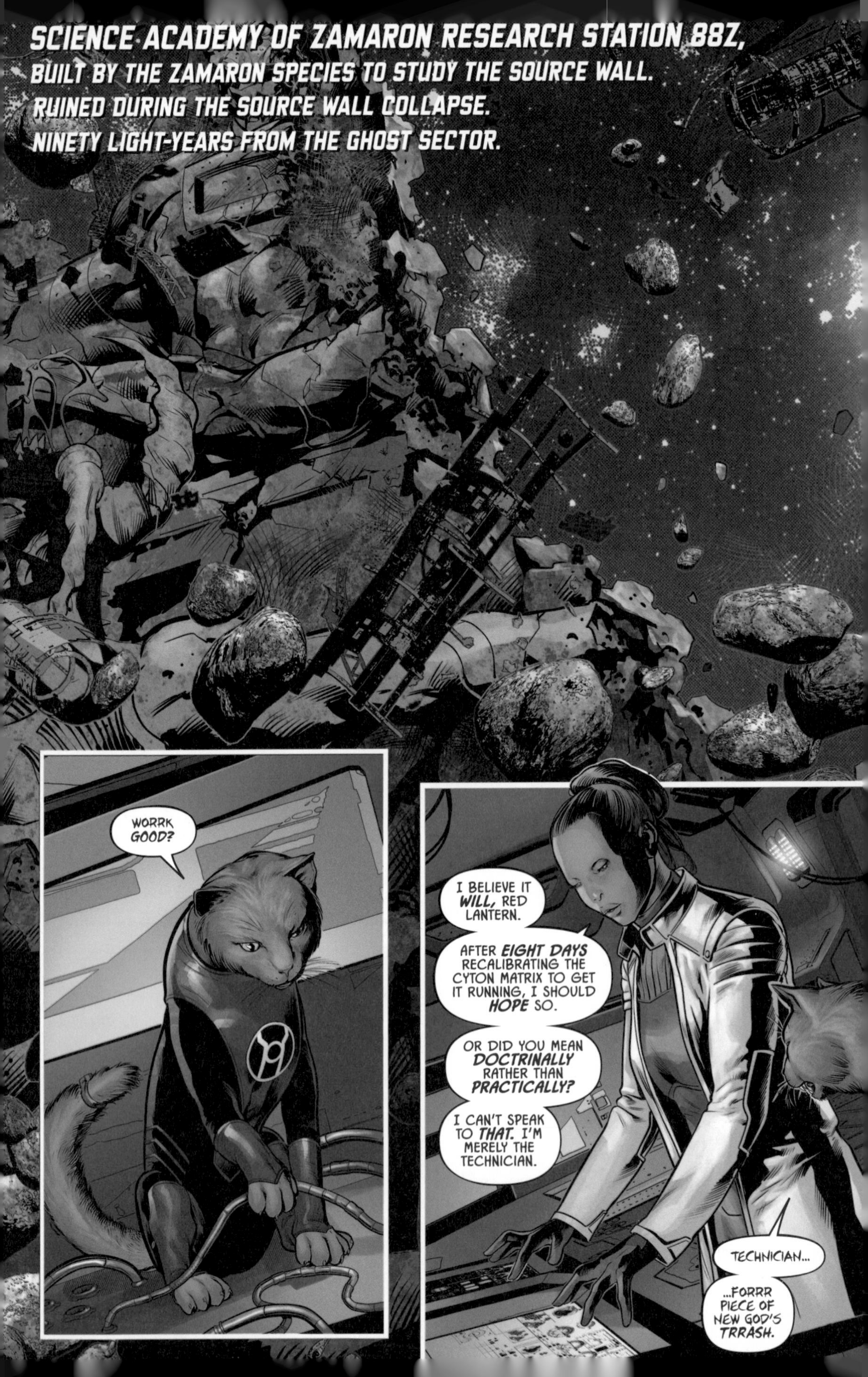

SCIENCE ACADEMY OF ZAMARON RESEARCH STATION 88Z,
BUILT BY THE ZAMARON SPECIES TO STUDY THE SOURCE WALL.
RUINED DURING THE SOURCE WALL COLLAPSE.
NINETY LIGHT-YEARS FROM THE GHOST SECTOR.
WORRK GOOD?
I BELIEVE IT WILL, RED LANTERN.
AFTER EIGHT DAYS RECALIBRATING THE CYTON MATRIX TO GET IT RUNNING, I SHOULD HOPE SO.
OR DID YOU MEAN DOCTRINALLY RATHER THAN PRACTICALLY?
I CAN'T SPEAK TO THAT. I'M MERELY THE TECHNICIAN.
TECHNICIAN...
...FORRR PIECE OF NEW GOD'S TRRASH.

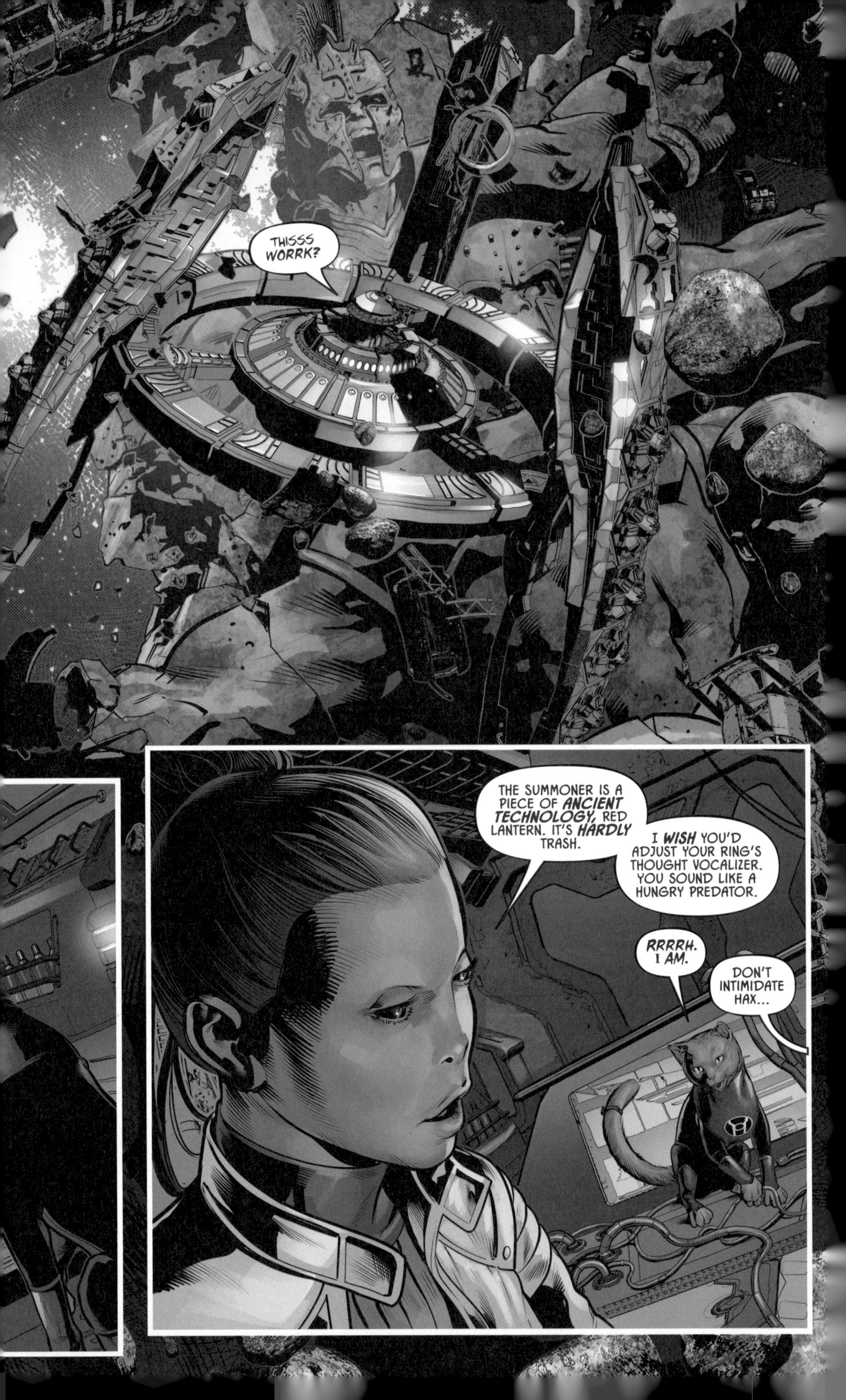
THISSS WORRK?
THE SUMMONER IS A PIECE OF ANCIENT TECHNOLOGY, RED LANTERN. IT'S HARDLY TRASH.
I WISH YOU'D ADJUST YOUR RING'S THOUGHT VOCALIZER. YOU SOUND LIKE A HUNGRY PREDATOR.
RRRRH. I AM.
DON'T INTIMIDATE HAX...

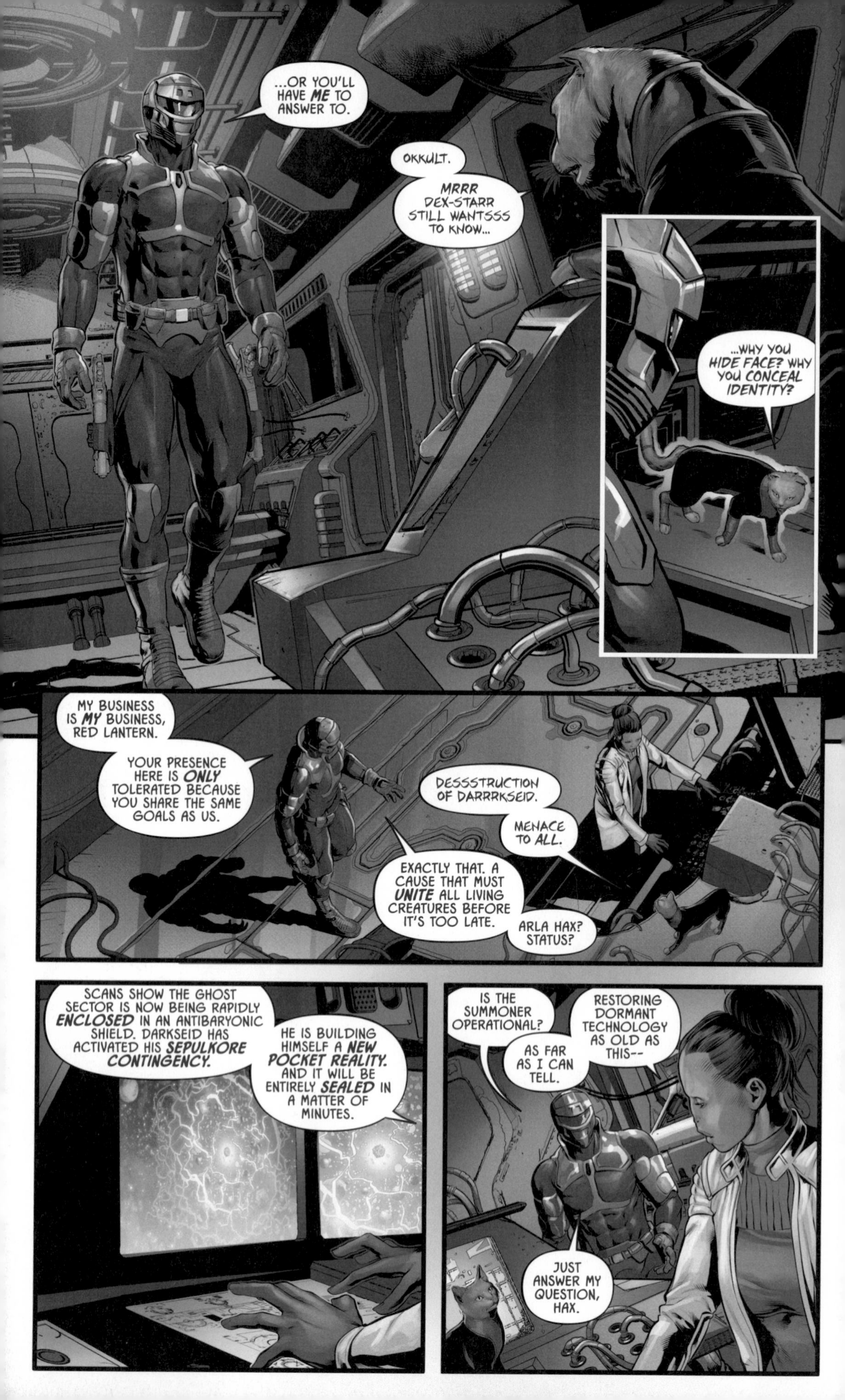
...OR YOU'LL HAVE ME TO ANSWER TO.
OKKULT.
MRRR DEX-STARR STILL WANTSSS TO KNOW...
...WHY YOU HIDE FACE? WHY YOU CONCEAL IDENTITY?
MY BUSINESS IS MY BUSINESS, RED LANTERN.
YOUR PRESENCE HERE IS ONLY TOLERATED BECAUSE YOU SHARE THE SAME GOALS AS US.
DESSSTRUCTION OF DARRRKSEID.
MENACE TO ALL.
EXACTLY THAT. A CAUSE THAT MUST UNITE ALL LIVING CREATURES BEFORE IT'S TOO LATE.
ARLA HAX? STATUS?
SCANS SHOW THE GHOST SECTOR IS NOW BEING RAPIDLY ENCLOSED IN AN ANTIBARYONIC SHIELD. DARKSEID HAS ACTIVATED HIS SEPULKORE CONTINGENCY.
HE IS BUILDING HIMSELF A NEW POCKET REALITY. AND IT WILL BE ENTIRELY SEALED IN A MATTER OF MINUTES.
IS THE SUMMONER OPERATIONAL?
RESTORING DORMANT TECHNOLOGY AS OLD AS THIS--
AS FAR AS I CAN TELL.
JUST ANSWER MY QUESTION, HAX.

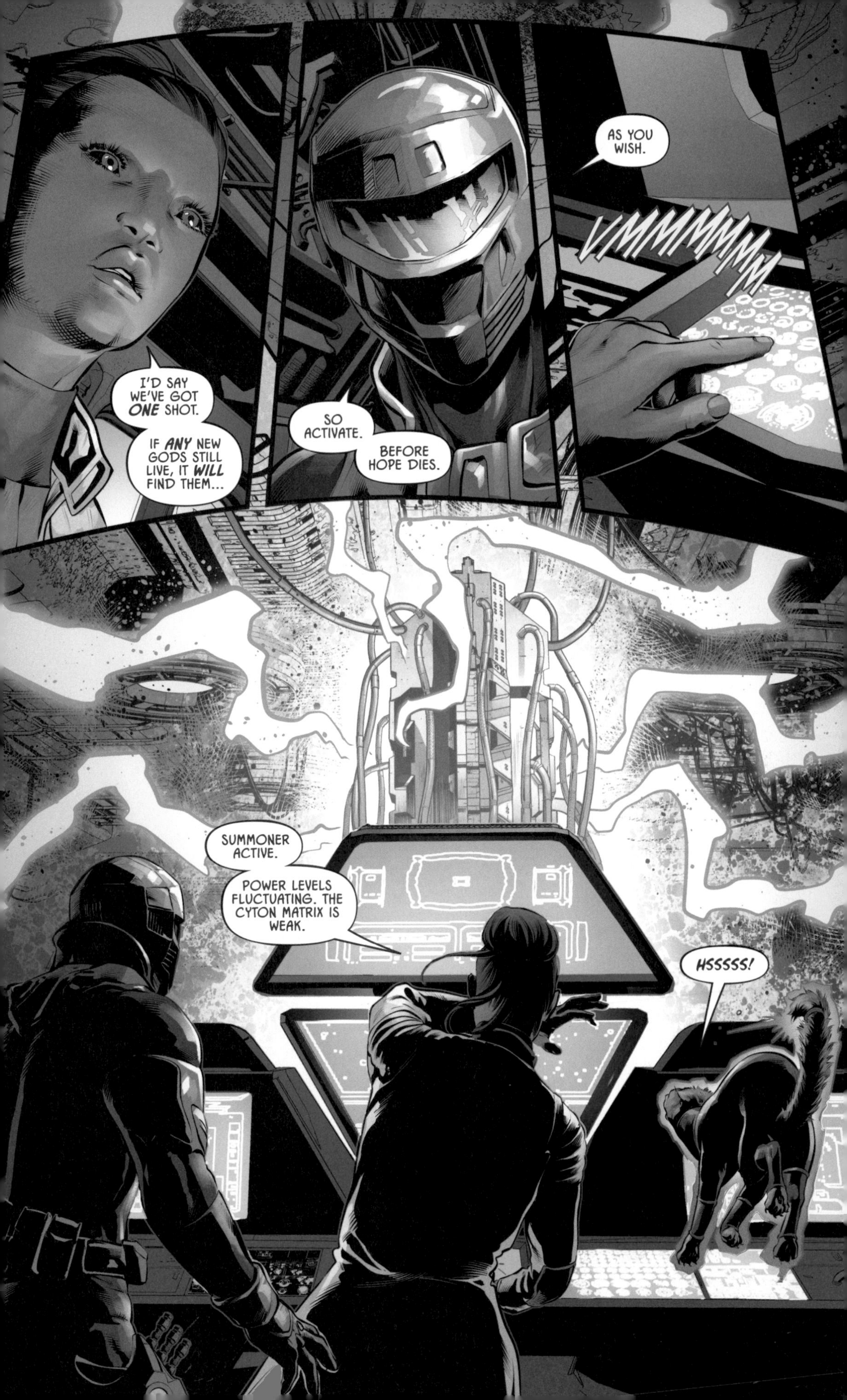
I'D SAY WE'VE GOT ONE SHOT.
IF ANY NEW GODS STILL LIVE, IT WILL FIND THEM...
SO ACTIVATE.
BEFORE HOPE DIES.
AS YOU WISH.
VMMMMMMM
SUMMONER ACTIVE.
POWER LEVELS FLUCTUATING. THE CYTON MATRIX IS WEAK.
HSSSSS!

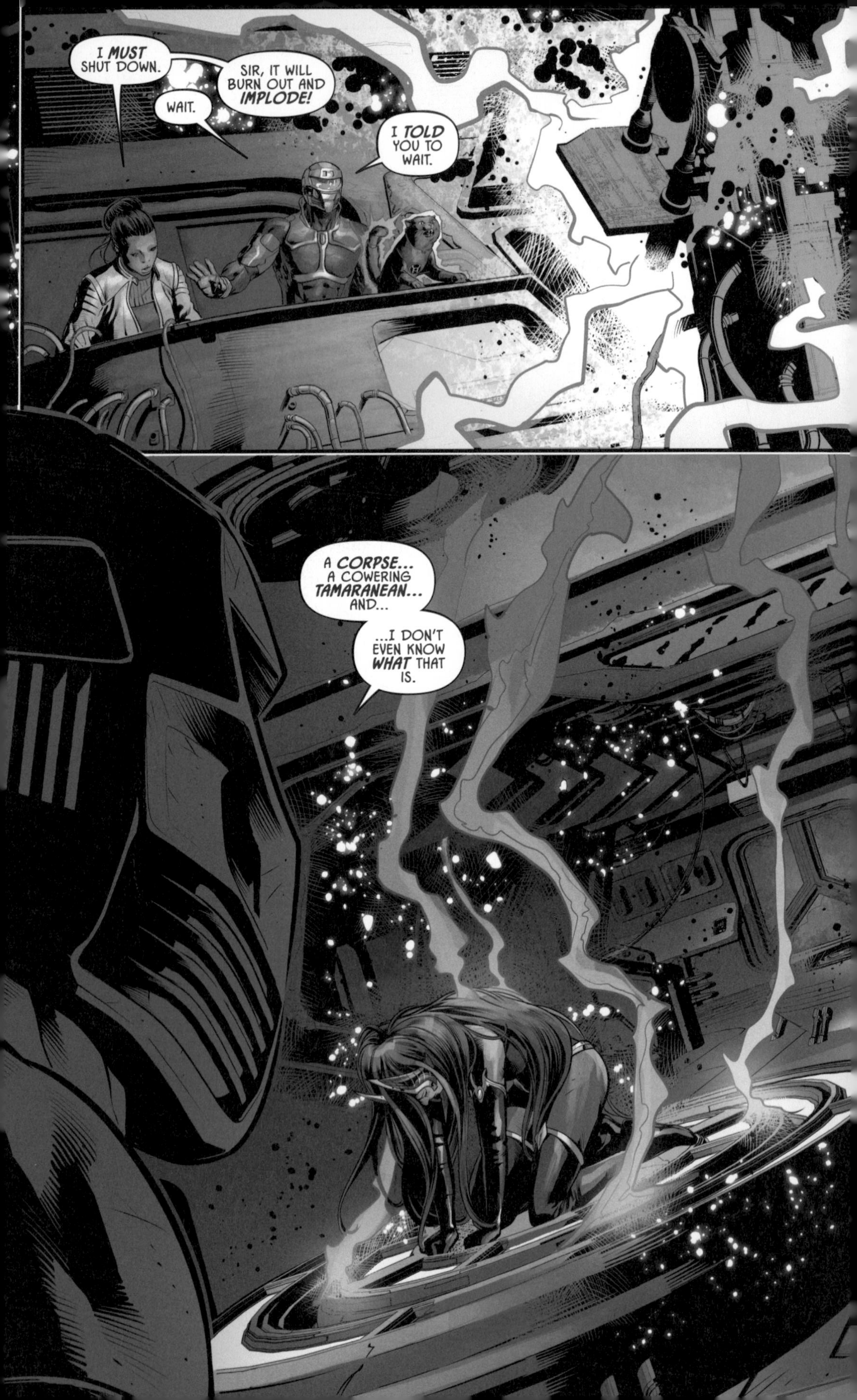

I MUST SHUT DOWN.
SIR, IT WILL BURN OUT AND IMPLODE!
WAIT.
I TOLD YOU TO WAIT.
A CORPSE... A COWERING TAMARANEAN... AND...
...I DON'T EVEN KNOW WHAT THAT IS.

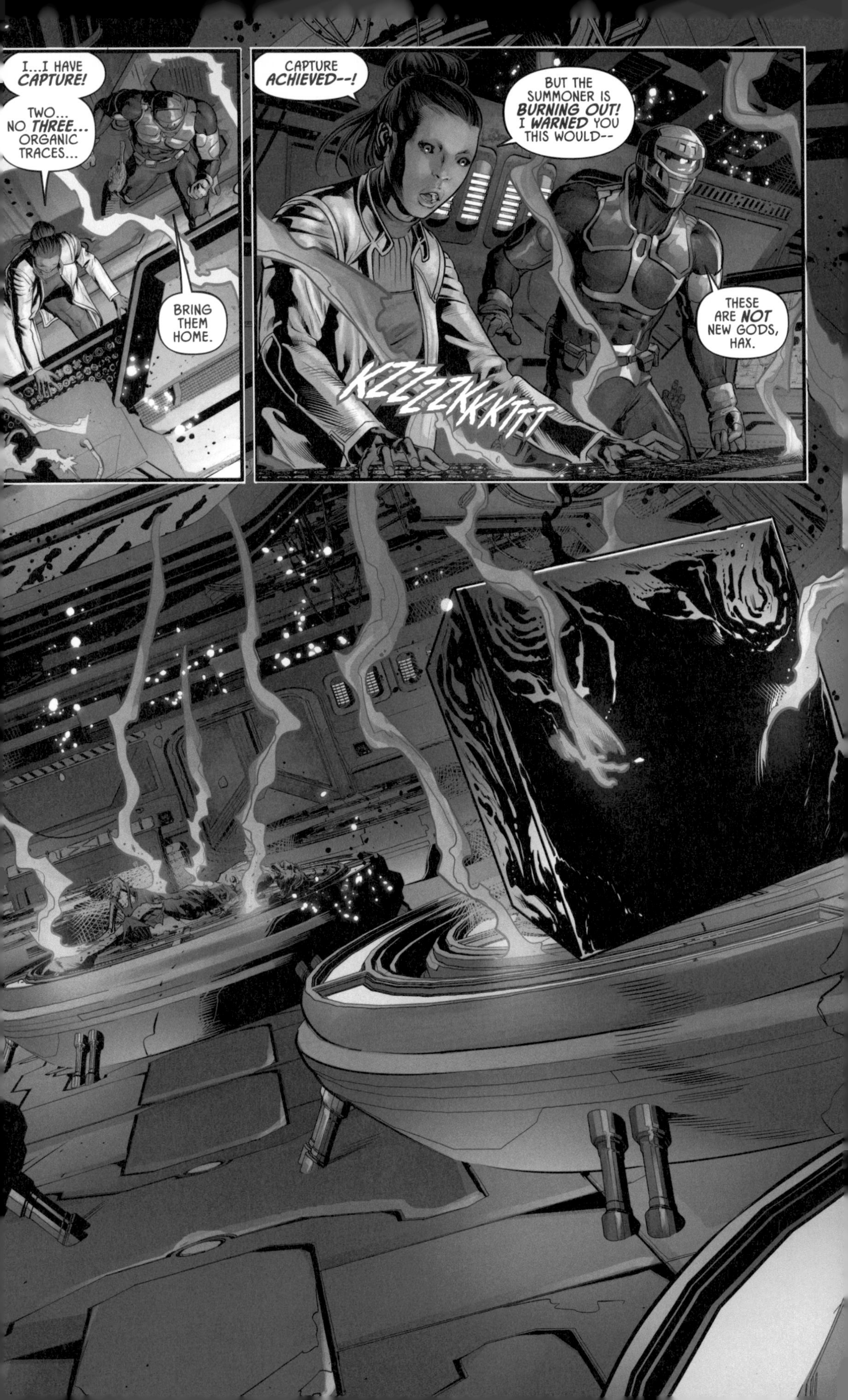

I...I HAVE CAPTURE!
TWO... NO THREE... ORGANIC TRACES...
BRING THEM HOME.
CAPTURE ACHIEVED--!
BUT THE SUMMONER IS BURNING OUT! I WARNED YOU THIS WOULD--
THESE ARE NOT NEW GODS, HAX.
KZZZZKKKTTT

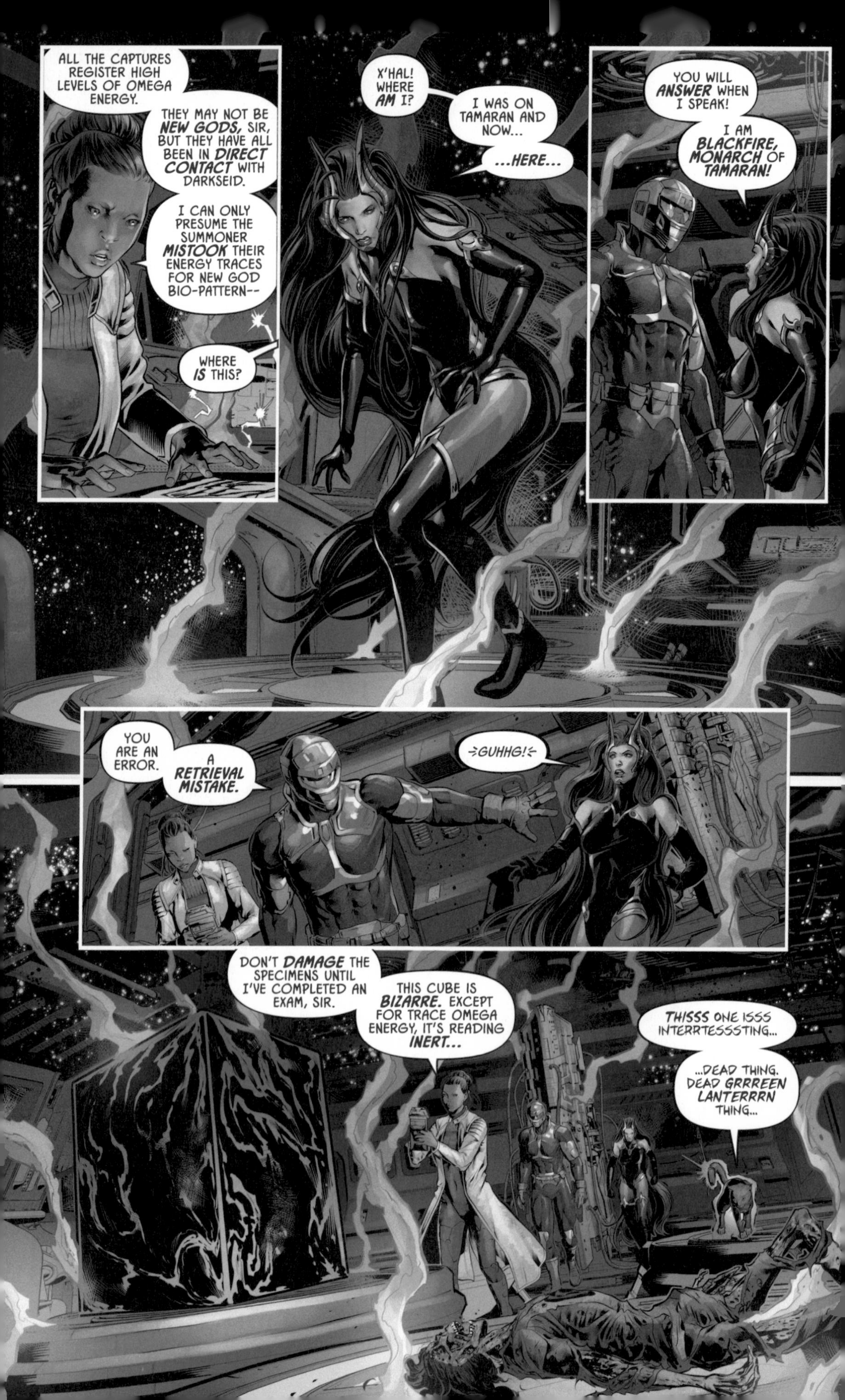
ALL THE CAPTURES REGISTER HIGH LEVELS OF OMEGA ENERGY.
THEY MAY NOT BE NEW GODS, SIR, BUT THEY HAVE ALL BEEN IN DIRECT CONTACT WITH DARKSEID.
I CAN ONLY PRESUME THE SUMMONER MISTOOK THEIR ENERGY TRACES FOR NEW GOD BIO-PATTERN--
WHERE IS THIS?
X'HAL! WHERE AM I?
I WAS ON TAMARAN AND NOW...
...HERE...
YOU WILL ANSWER WHEN I SPEAK!
I AM BLACKFIRE, MONARCH OF TAMARAN!
YOU ARE AN ERROR.
A RETRIEVAL MISTAKE.
GUHHG!
DON'T DAMAGE THE SPECIMENS UNTIL I'VE COMPLETED AN EXAM, SIR.
THIS CUBE IS BIZARRE. EXCEPT FOR TRACE OMEGA ENERGY, IT'S READING INERT...
THISSS ONE ISSS INTERRTESSSTING...
...DEAD THING. DEAD GRRREEN LANTERRRN THING...

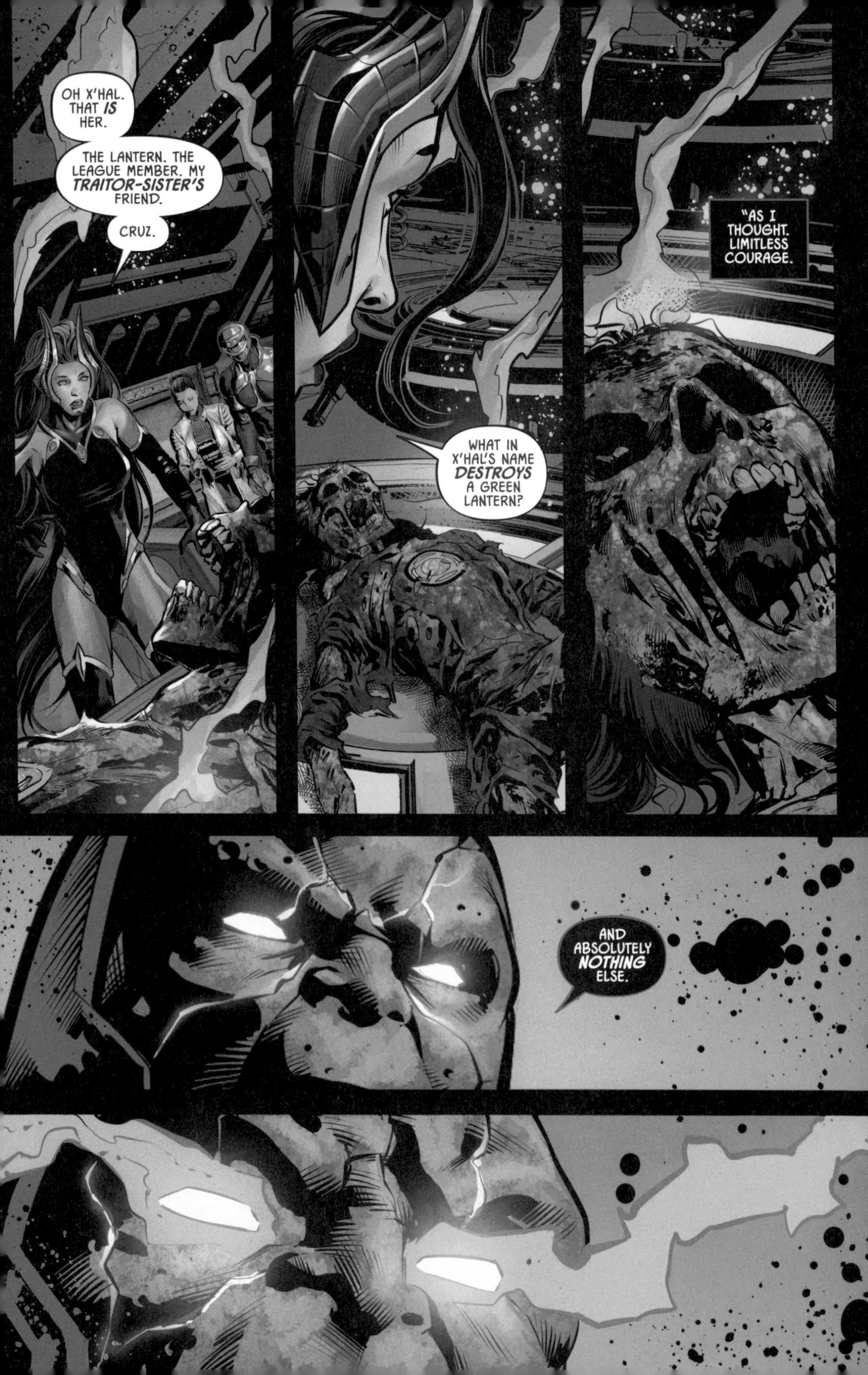
OH X'HAL. THAT IS HER.
THE LANTERN. THE LEAGUE MEMBER. MY TRAITOR-SISTER'S FRIEND.
CRUZ.
WHAT IN X'HAL'S NAME DESTROYS A GREEN LANTERN?
"AS I THOUGHT. LIMITLESS COURAGE.
AND ABSOLUTELY NOTHING ELSE.

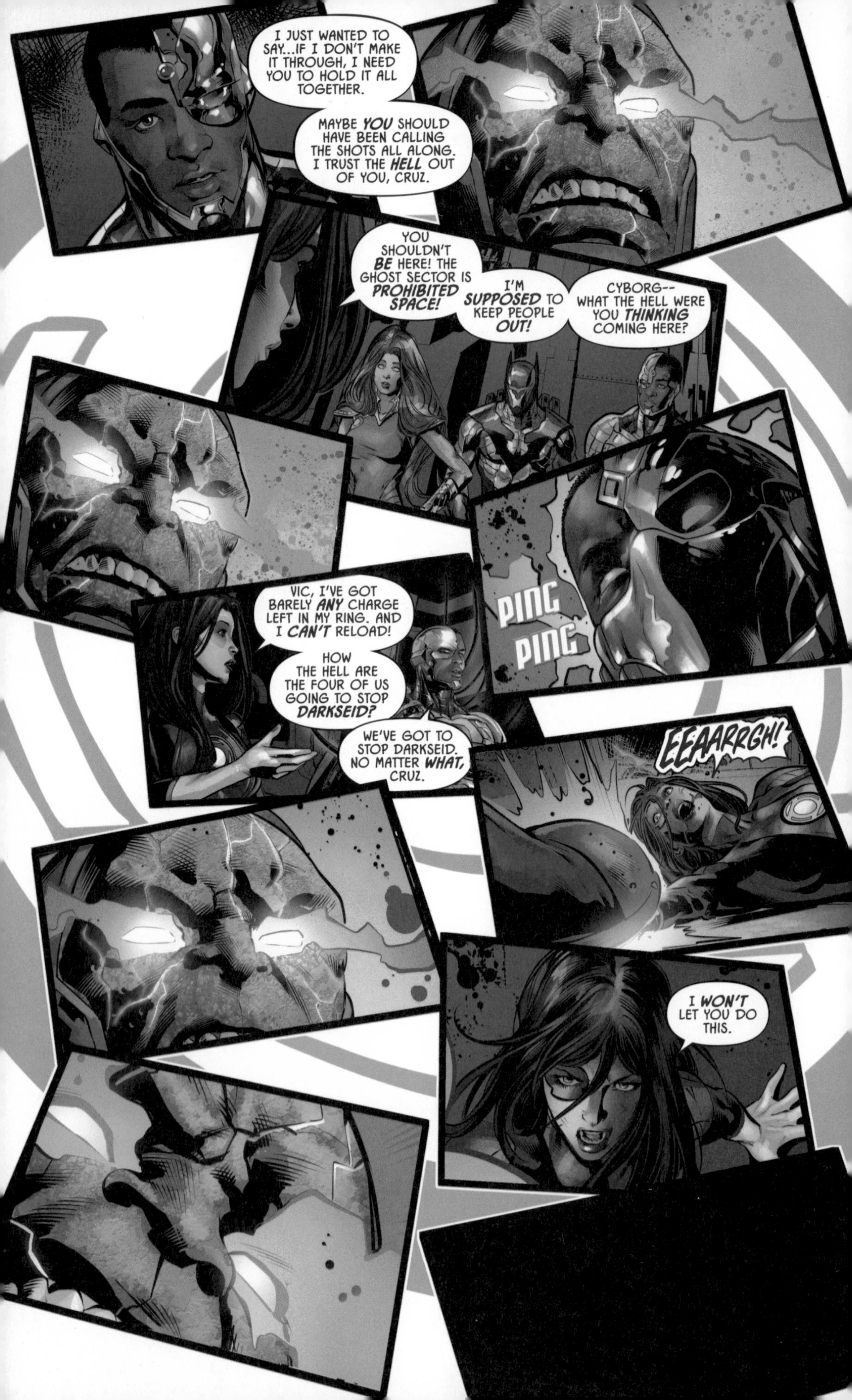
I JUST WANTED TO SAY...IF I DON'T MAKE IT THROUGH, I NEED YOU TO HOLD IT ALL TOGETHER.
MAYBE YOU SHOULD HAVE BEEN CALLING THE SHOTS ALL ALONG. I TRUST THE HELL OUT OF YOU, CRUZ.
YOU SHOULDN'T BE HERE! THE GHOST SECTOR IS PROHIBITED SPACE!
I'M SUPPOSED TO KEEP PEOPLE OUT!
CYBORG-- WHAT THE HELL WERE YOU THINKING COMING HERE?
PING
PING
VIC, I'VE GOT BARELY ANY CHARGE LEFT IN MY RING. AND I CAN'T RELOAD!
HOW THE HELL ARE THE FOUR OF US GOING TO STOP DARKSEID?
WE'VE GOT TO STOP DARKSEID. NO MATTER WHAT, CRUZ.
EEAARRGH!
I WON'T LET YOU DO THIS.

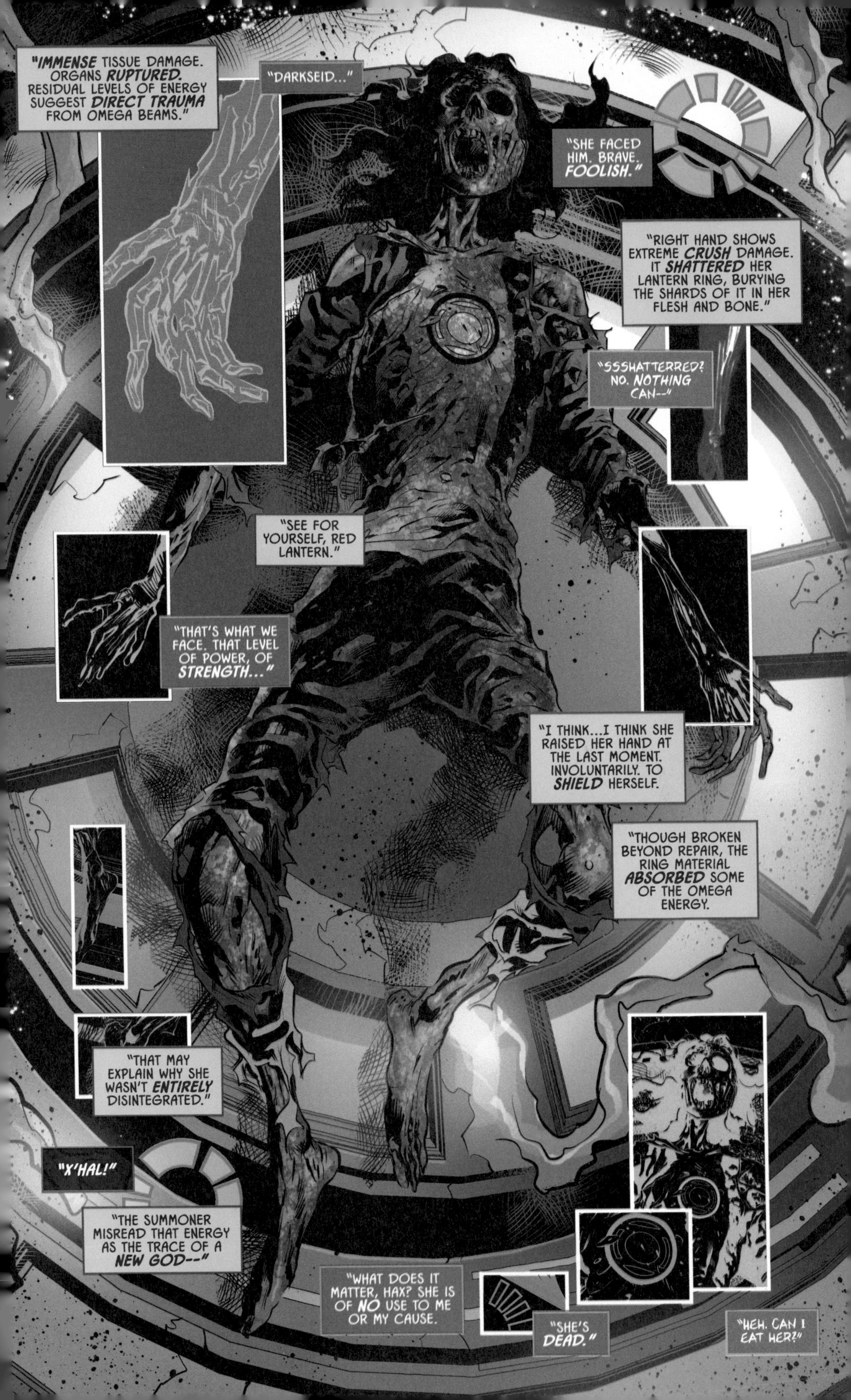
"IMMENSE TISSUE DAMAGE. ORGANS RUPTURED. RESIDUAL LEVELS OF ENERGY SUGGEST DIRECT TRAUMA FROM OMEGA BEAMS."
"DARKSEID..."
"SHE FACED HIM. BRAVE. FOOLISH."
"RIGHT HAND SHOWS EXTREME CRUSH DAMAGE. IT SHATTERED HER LANTERN RING, BURYING THE SHARDS OF IT IN HER FLESH AND BONE."
"SSSHATTERRED? NO. NOTHING CAN--"
"SEE FOR YOURSELF, RED LANTERN."
"THAT'S WHAT WE FACE. THAT LEVEL OF POWER, OF STRENGTH..."
"I THINK...I THINK SHE RAISED HER HAND AT THE LAST MOMENT. INVOLUNTARILY. TO SHIELD HERSELF.
"THOUGH BROKEN BEYOND REPAIR, THE RING MATERIAL ABSORBED SOME OF THE OMEGA ENERGY.
"THAT MAY EXPLAIN WHY SHE WASN'T ENTIRELY DISINTEGRATED."
"X'HAL!"
"THE SUMMONER MISREAD THAT ENERGY AS THE TRACE OF A NEW GOD--"
"WHAT DOES IT MATTER, HAX? SHE IS OF NO USE TO ME OR MY CAUSE.
"SHE'S DEAD."
"HEH. CAN I EAT HER?"

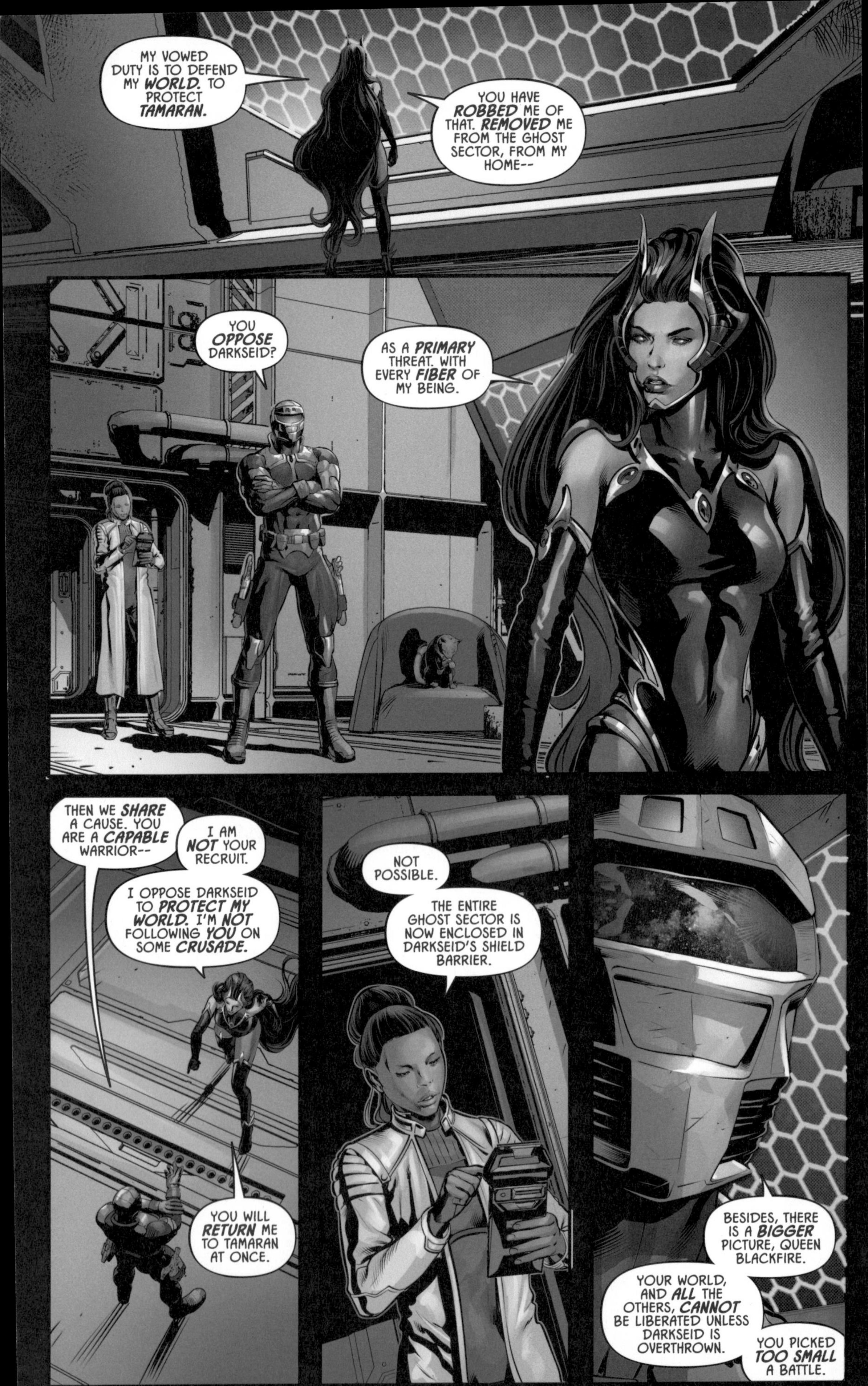
MY VOWED DUTY IS TO DEFEND MY WORLD. TO PROTECT TAMARAN.
YOU HAVE ROBBED ME OF THAT. REMOVED ME FROM THE GHOST SECTOR, FROM MY HOME--
YOU OPPOSE DARKSEID?
AS A PRIMARY THREAT. WITH EVERY FIBER OF MY BEING.
THEN WE SHARE A CAUSE. YOU ARE A CAPABLE WARRIOR--
I AM NOT YOUR RECRUIT.
I OPPOSE DARKSEID TO PROTECT MY WORLD. I'M NOT FOLLOWING YOU ON SOME CRUSADE.
YOU WILL RETURN ME TO TAMARAN AT ONCE.
NOT POSSIBLE.
THE ENTIRE GHOST SECTOR IS NOW ENCLOSED IN DARKSEID'S SHIELD BARRIER.
BESIDES, THERE IS A BIGGER PICTURE, QUEEN BLACKFIRE.
YOUR WORLD, AND ALL THE OTHERS, CANNOT BE LIBERATED UNLESS DARKSEID IS OVERTHROWN.
YOU PICKED TOO SMALL A BATTLE.

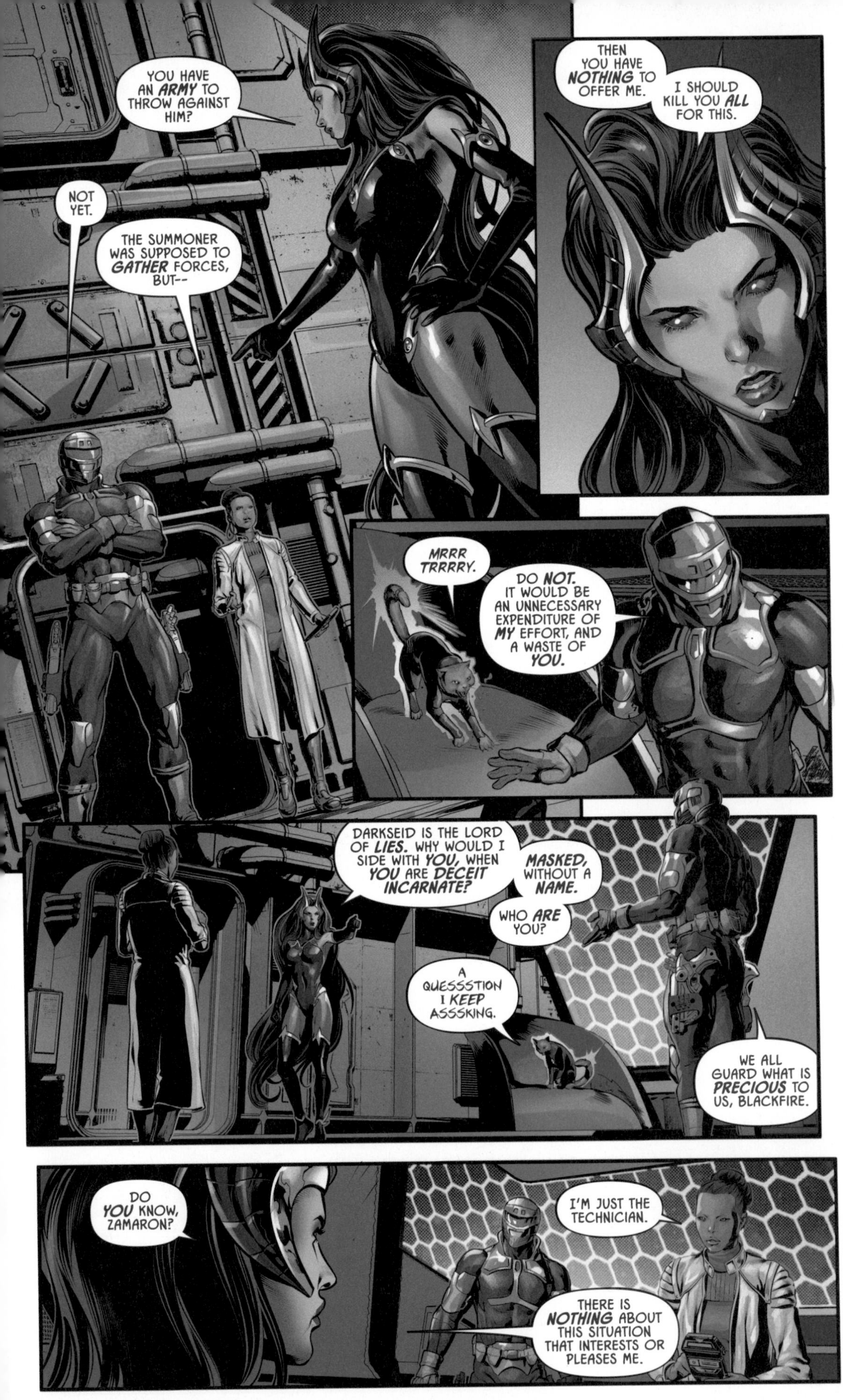

YOU HAVE AN ARMY TO THROW AGAINST HIM?
NOT YET.
THE SUMMONER WAS SUPPOSED TO GATHER FORCES, BUT--
THEN YOU HAVE NOTHING TO OFFER ME.
I SHOULD KILL YOU ALL FOR THIS.
MRRR TRRRRY.
DO NOT. IT WOULD BE AN UNNECESSARY EXPENDITURE OF MY EFFORT, AND A WASTE OF YOU.
DARKSEID IS THE LORD OF LIES. WHY WOULD I SIDE WITH YOU, WHEN YOU ARE DECEIT INCARNATE?
MASKED, WITHOUT A NAME.
WHO ARE YOU?
A QUESSSTION I KEEP ASSSKING.
WE ALL GUARD WHAT IS PRECIOUS TO US, BLACKFIRE.
DO YOU KNOW, ZAMARON?
I'M JUST THE TECHNICIAN.
THERE IS NOTHING ABOUT THIS SITUATION THAT INTERESTS OR PLEASES ME.

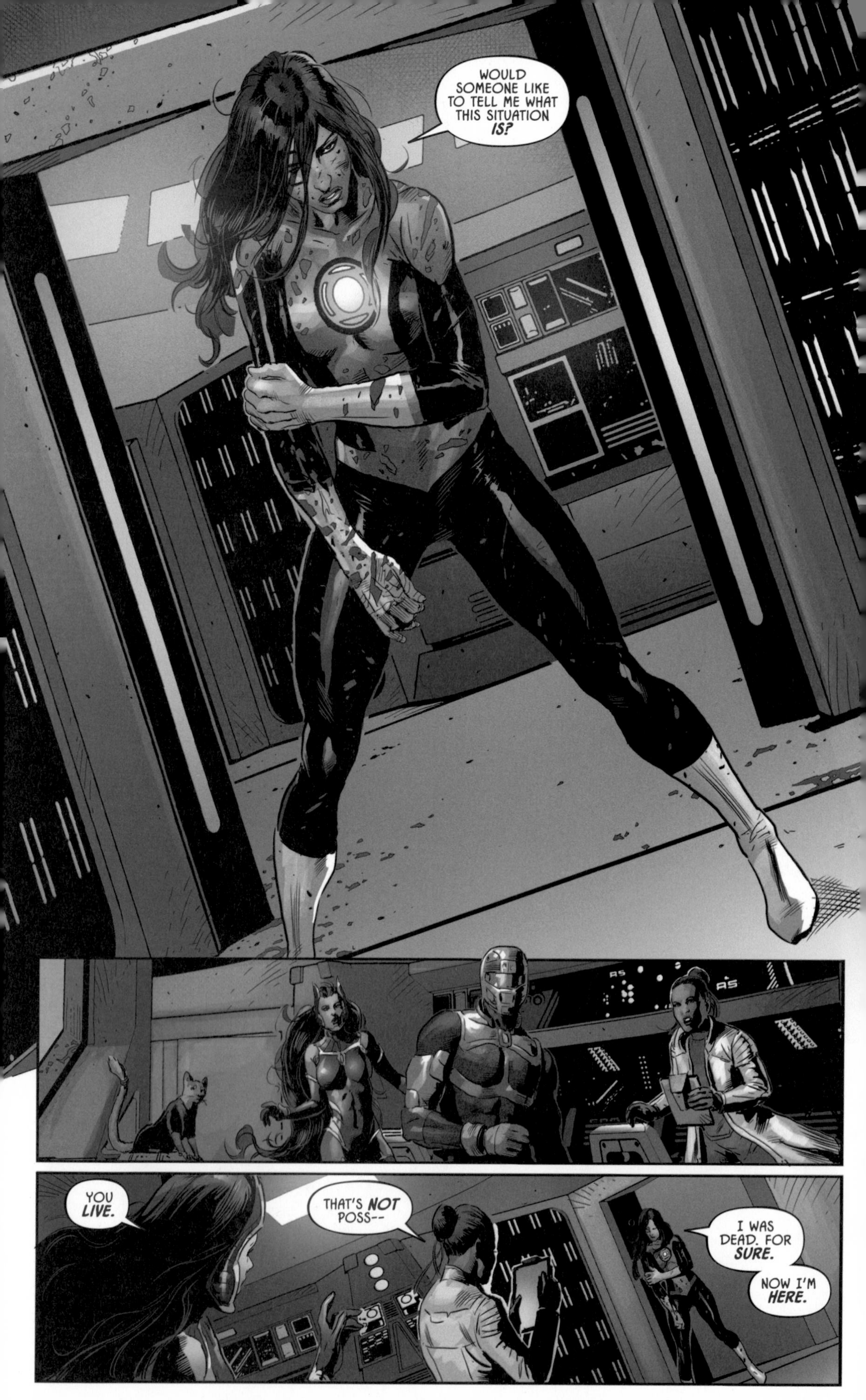
WOULD SOMEONE LIKE TO TELL ME WHAT THIS SITUATION *IS?*
YOU *LIVE.*
THAT'S *NOT* POSS--
I WAS DEAD. FOR *SURE.*
NOW I'M *HERE.*

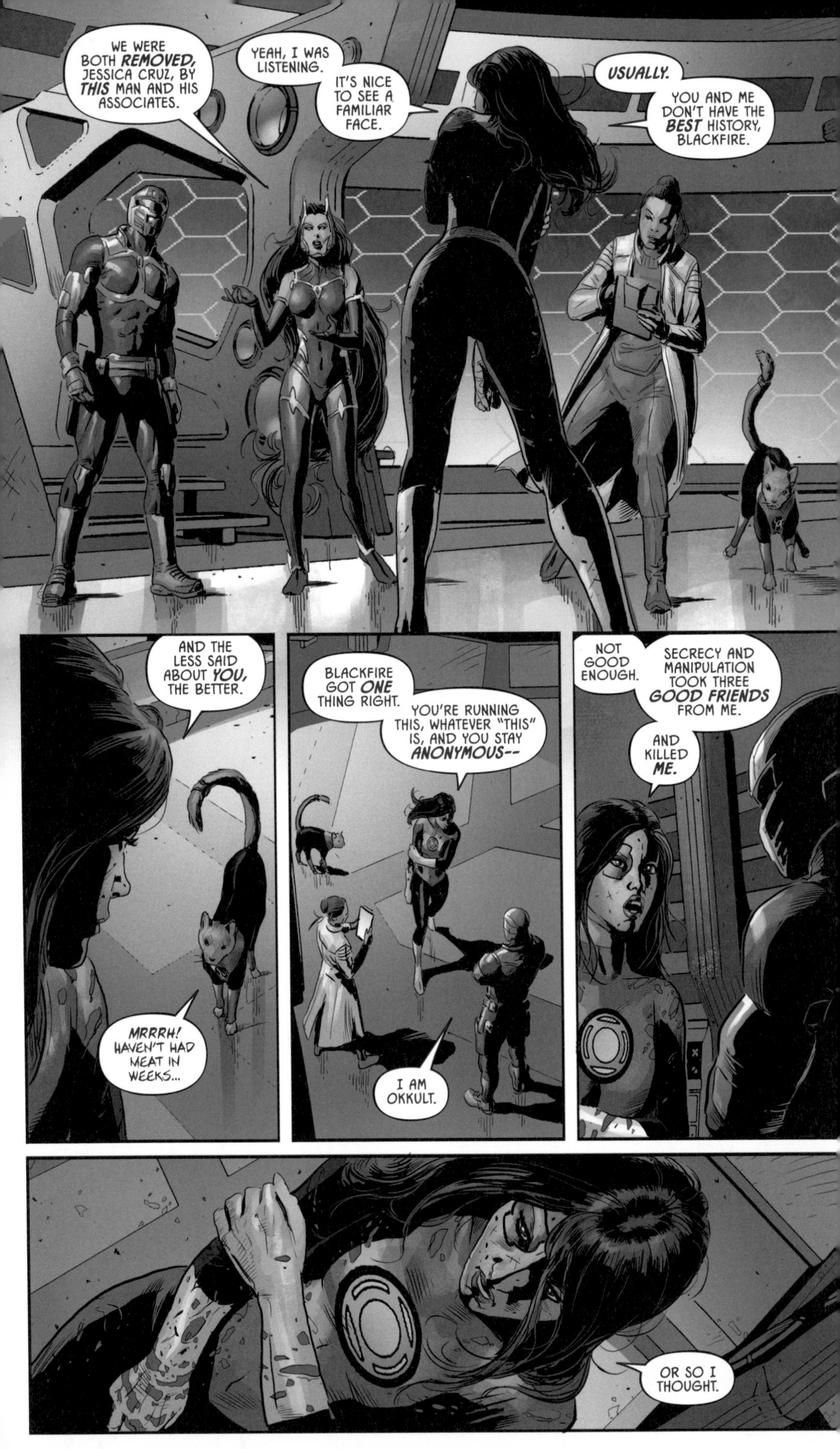
WE WERE BOTH REMOVED, JESSICA CRUZ, BY THIS MAN AND HIS ASSOCIATES.
YEAH, I WAS LISTENING.
IT'S NICE TO SEE A FAMILIAR FACE.
USUALLY.
YOU AND ME DON'T HAVE THE BEST HISTORY, BLACKFIRE.
AND THE LESS SAID ABOUT YOU, THE BETTER.
MRRRH! HAVEN'T HAD MEAT IN WEEKS...
BLACKFIRE GOT ONE THING RIGHT.
YOU'RE RUNNING THIS, WHATEVER "THIS" IS, AND YOU STAY ANONYMOUS--
I AM OKKULT.
NOT GOOD ENOUGH.
SECRECY AND MANIPULATION TOOK THREE GOOD FRIENDS FROM ME.
AND KILLED ME.
OR SO I THOUGHT.

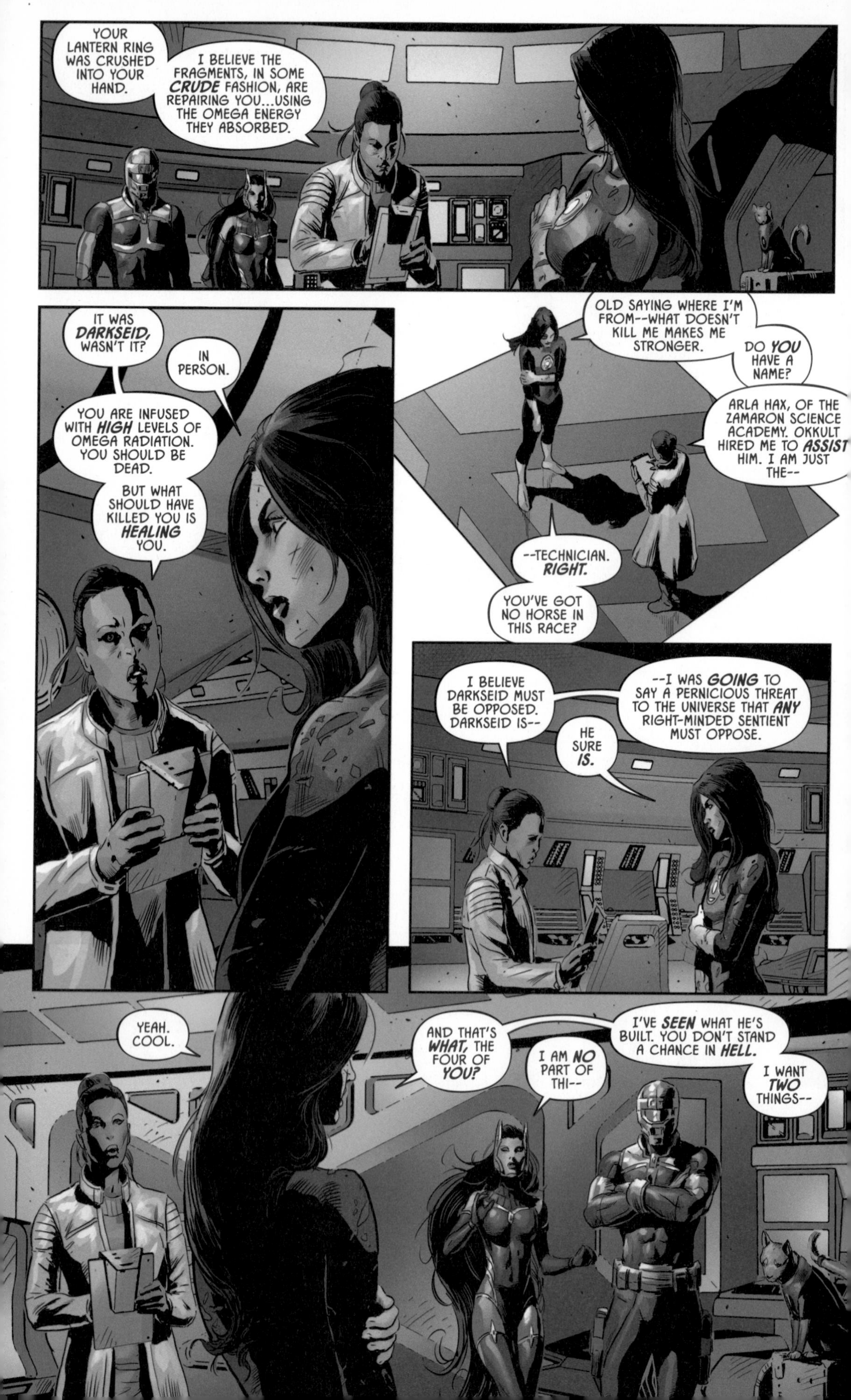

YOUR LANTERN RING WAS CRUSHED INTO YOUR HAND.
I BELIEVE THE FRAGMENTS, IN SOME CRUDE FASHION, ARE REPAIRING YOU...USING THE OMEGA ENERGY THEY ABSORBED.
IT WAS DARKSEID, WASN'T IT?
IN PERSON.
YOU ARE INFUSED WITH HIGH LEVELS OF OMEGA RADIATION. YOU SHOULD BE DEAD.
BUT WHAT SHOULD HAVE KILLED YOU IS HEALING YOU.
OLD SAYING WHERE I'M FROM--WHAT DOESN'T KILL ME MAKES ME STRONGER.
DO YOU HAVE A NAME?
ARLA HAX, OF THE ZAMARON SCIENCE ACADEMY. OKKULT HIRED ME TO ASSIST HIM. I AM JUST THE--
--TECHNICIAN. RIGHT.
YOU'VE GOT NO HORSE IN THIS RACE?
I BELIEVE DARKSEID MUST BE OPPOSED. DARKSEID IS--
HE SURE IS.
--I WAS GOING TO SAY A PERNICIOUS THREAT TO THE UNIVERSE THAT ANY RIGHT-MINDED SENTIENT MUST OPPOSE.
YEAH. COOL.
AND THAT'S WHAT, THE FOUR OF YOU?
I AM NO PART OF THI--
I'VE SEEN WHAT HE'S BUILT. YOU DON'T STAND A CHANCE IN HELL.
I WANT TWO THINGS--

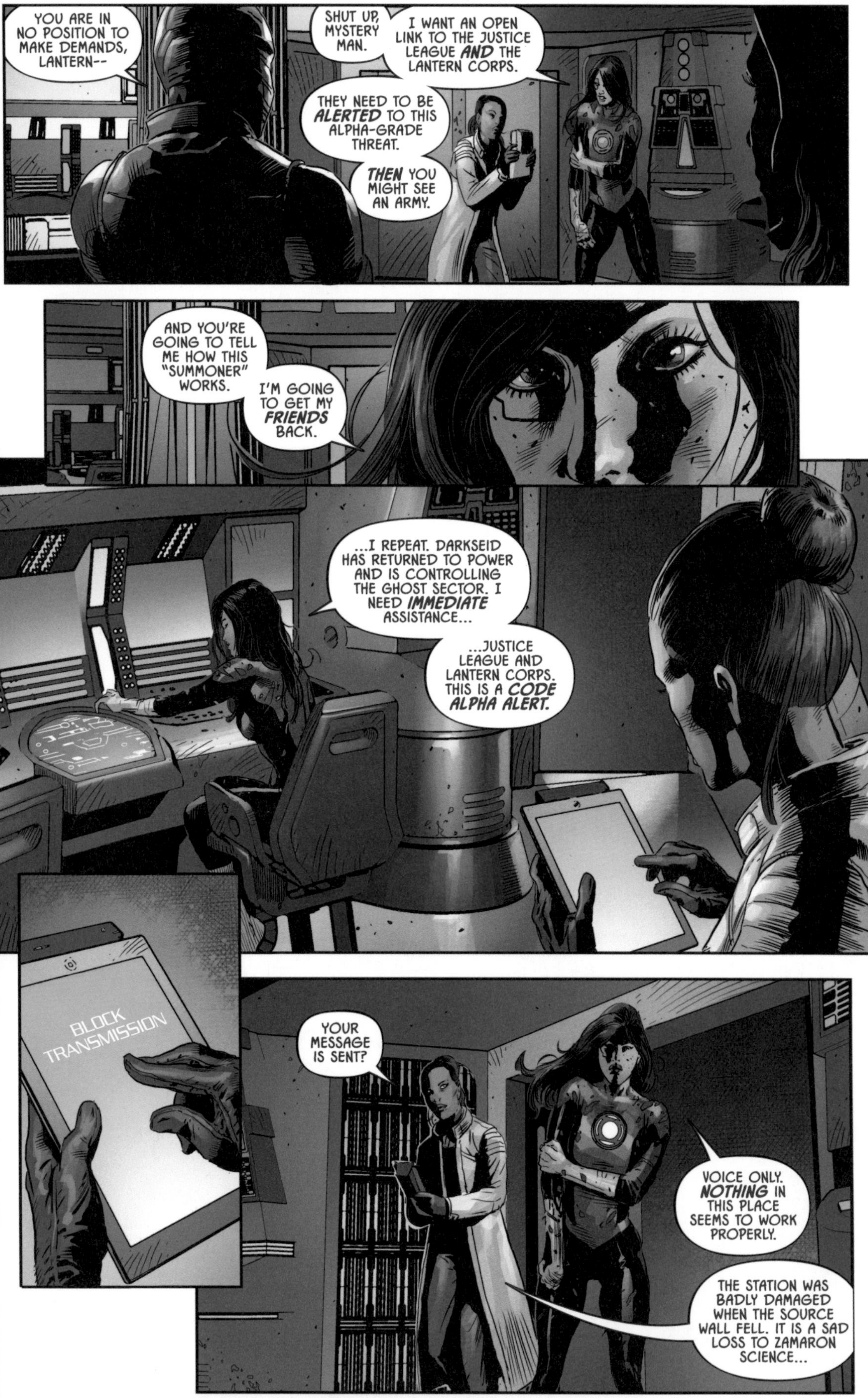
YOU ARE IN NO POSITION TO MAKE DEMANDS, LANTERN--
SHUT UP, MYSTERY MAN.
I WANT AN OPEN LINK TO THE JUSTICE LEAGUE AND THE LANTERN CORPS.
THEY NEED TO BE ALERTED TO THIS ALPHA-GRADE THREAT.
THEN YOU MIGHT SEE AN ARMY.
AND YOU'RE GOING TO TELL ME HOW THIS "SUMMONER" WORKS.
I'M GOING TO GET MY FRIENDS BACK.
...I REPEAT. DARKSEID HAS RETURNED TO POWER AND IS CONTROLLING THE GHOST SECTOR. I NEED IMMEDIATE ASSISTANCE...
...JUSTICE LEAGUE AND LANTERN CORPS. THIS IS A CODE ALPHA ALERT.
BLOCK TRANSMISSION
YOUR MESSAGE IS SENT?
VOICE ONLY. NOTHING IN THIS PLACE SEEMS TO WORK PROPERLY.
THE STATION WAS BADLY DAMAGED WHEN THE SOURCE WALL FELL. IT IS A SAD LOSS TO ZAMARON SCIENCE...

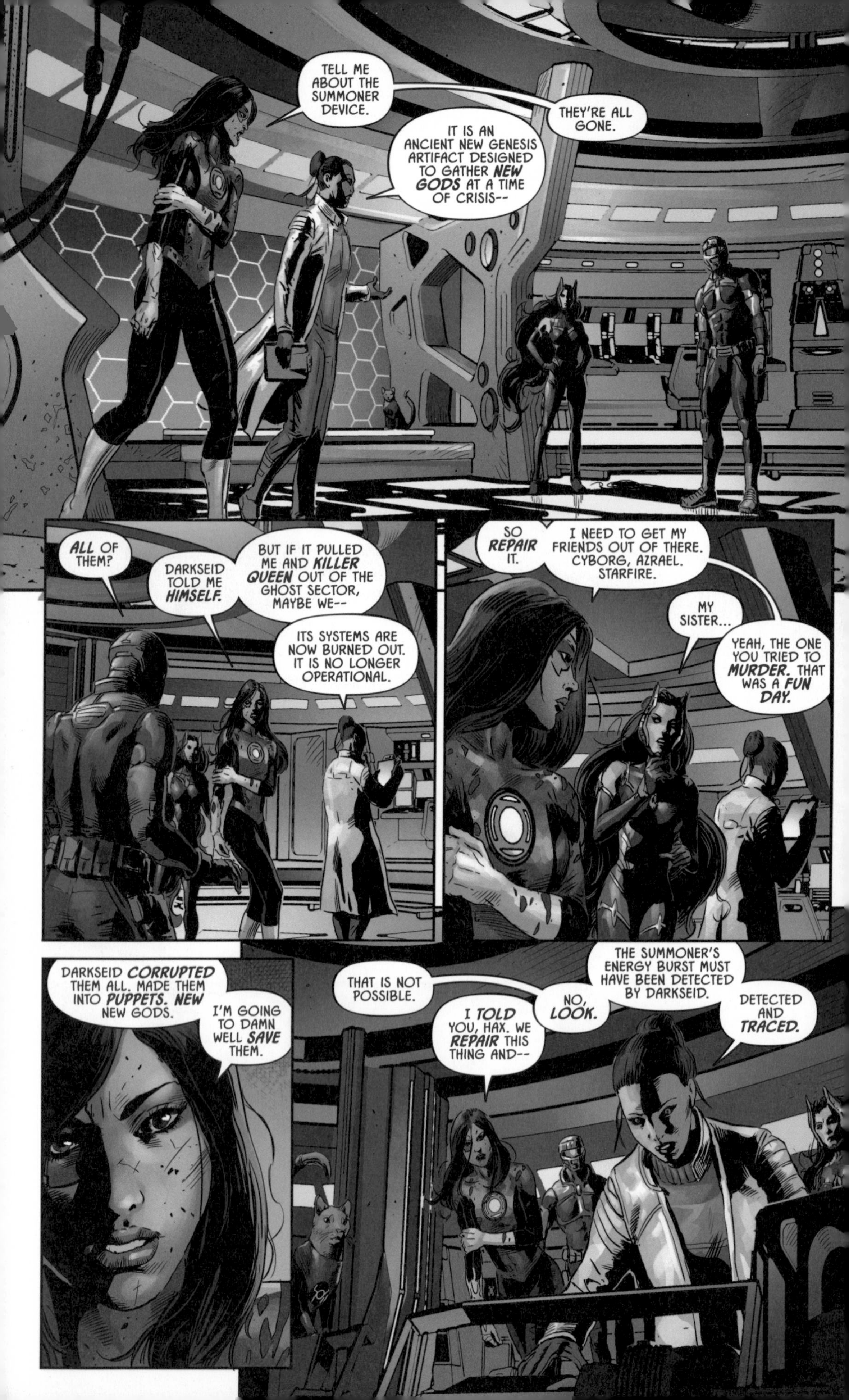
TELL ME ABOUT THE SUMMONER DEVICE.
IT IS AN ANCIENT NEW GENESIS ARTIFACT DESIGNED TO GATHER NEW GODS AT A TIME OF CRISIS--
THEY'RE ALL GONE.
ALL OF THEM?
DARKSEID TOLD ME HIMSELF.
BUT IF IT PULLED ME AND KILLER QUEEN OUT OF THE GHOST SECTOR, MAYBE WE--
ITS SYSTEMS ARE NOW BURNED OUT. IT IS NO LONGER OPERATIONAL.
SO REPAIR IT.
I NEED TO GET MY FRIENDS OUT OF THERE. CYBORG, AZRAEL. STARFIRE.
MY SISTER...
YEAH, THE ONE YOU TRIED TO MURDER. THAT WAS A FUN DAY.
DARKSEID CORRUPTED THEM ALL. MADE THEM INTO PUPPETS. NEW NEW GODS.
I'M GOING TO DAMN WELL SAVE THEM.
THAT IS NOT POSSIBLE.
I TOLD YOU, HAX. WE REPAIR THIS THING AND--
NO, LOOK.
THE SUMMONER'S ENERGY BURST MUST HAVE BEEN DETECTED BY DARKSEID.
DETECTED AND TRACED.

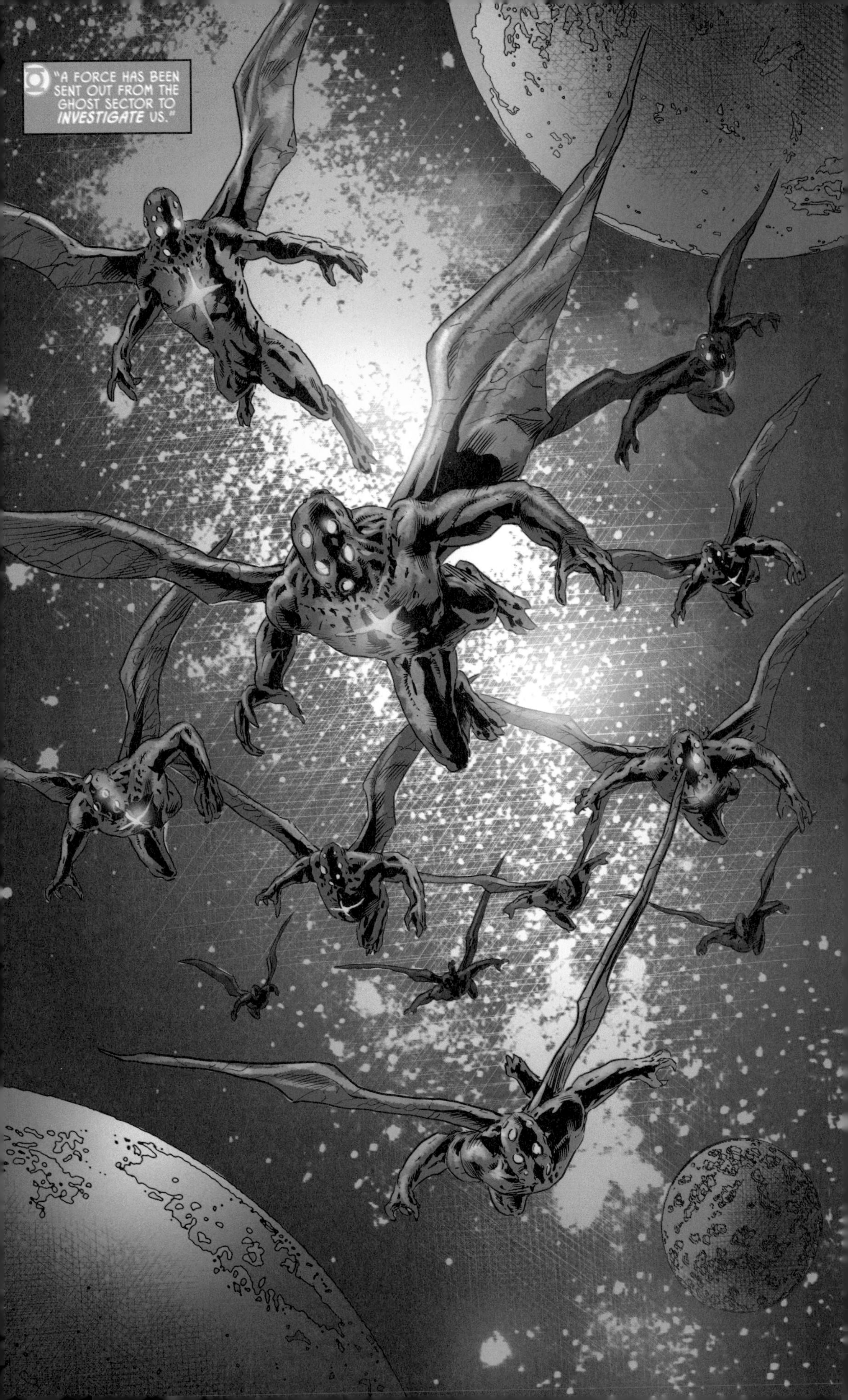
"A FORCE HAS BEEN SENT OUT FROM THE GHOST SECTOR TO INVESTIGATE US."

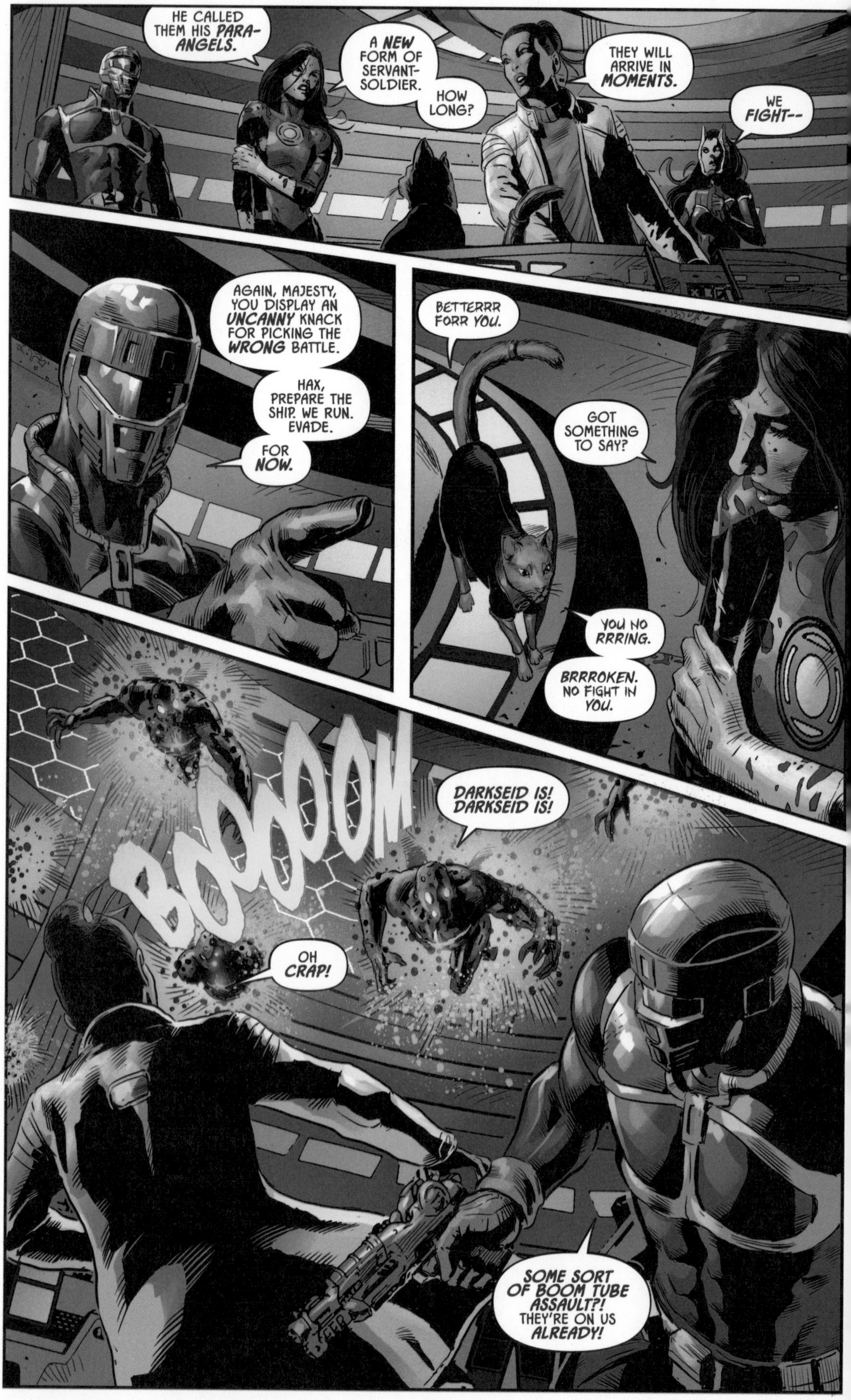
HE CALLED THEM HIS PARA-ANGELS.
A NEW FORM OF SERVANT-SOLDIER.
HOW LONG?
THEY WILL ARRIVE IN MOMENTS.
WE FIGHT--
AGAIN, MAJESTY, YOU DISPLAY AN UNCANNY KNACK FOR PICKING THE WRONG BATTLE.
HAX, PREPARE THE SHIP. WE RUN. EVADE.
FOR NOW.
BETTERRR FORR YOU.
GOT SOMETHING TO SAY?
YOU NO RRRING.
BRRROKEN. NO FIGHT IN YOU.
BOOOOOM
DARKSEID IS! DARKSEID IS!
OH CRAP!
SOME SORT OF BOOM TUBE ASSAULT?! THEY'RE ON US ALREADY!

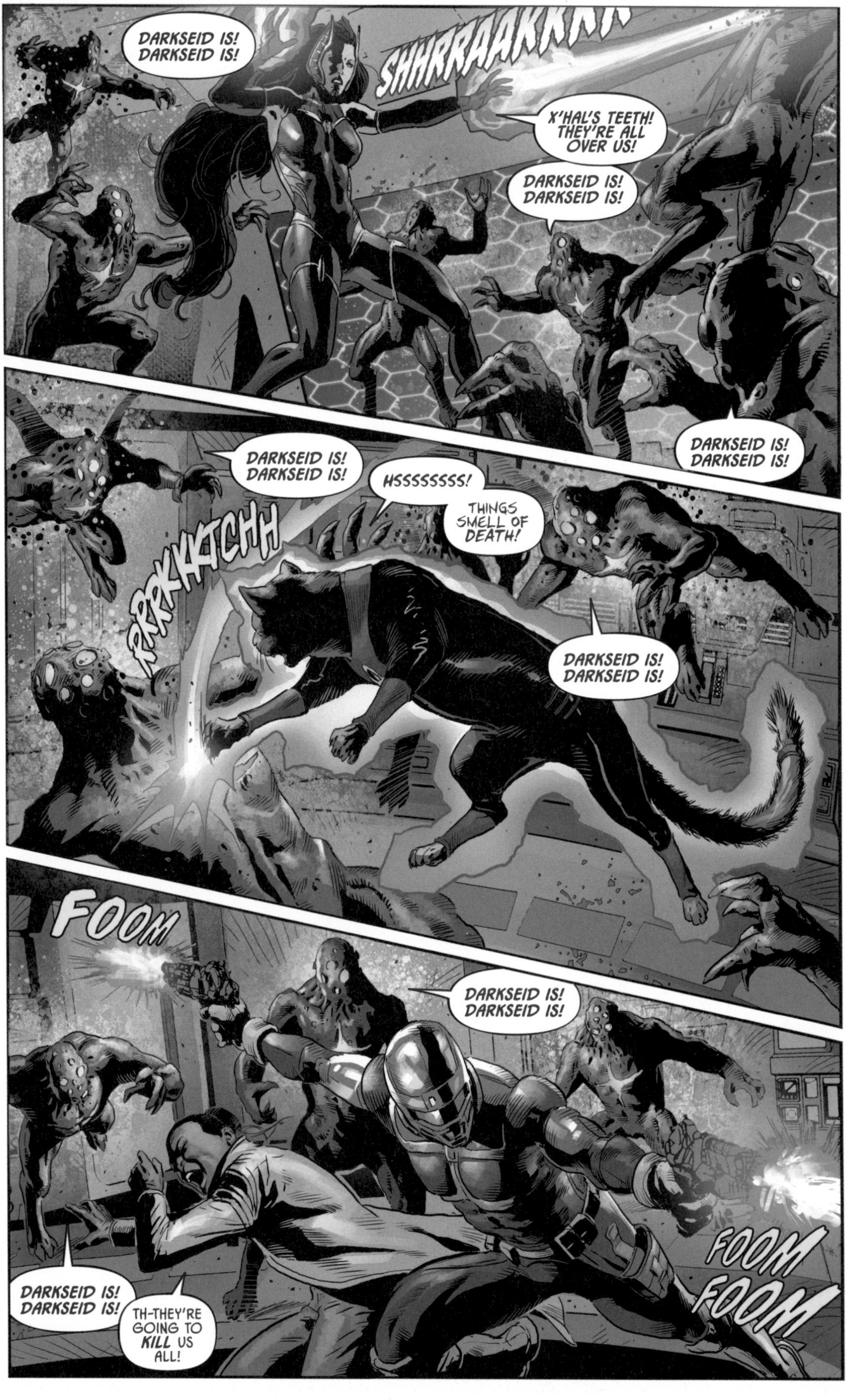
DARKSEID IS! DARKSEID IS!
SHHRRAAKKK
X'HAL'S TEETH! THEY'RE ALL OVER US!
DARKSEID IS! DARKSEID IS!
DARKSEID IS! DARKSEID IS!
DARKSEID IS! DARKSEID IS!
HSSSSSSSS!
THINGS SMELL OF DEATH!
PRRKKTCHH
DARKSEID IS! DARKSEID IS!
FOOM
DARKSEID IS! DARKSEID IS!
DARKSEID IS! DARKSEID IS!
TH-THEY'RE GOING TO **KILL** US ALL!
FOOM FOOM

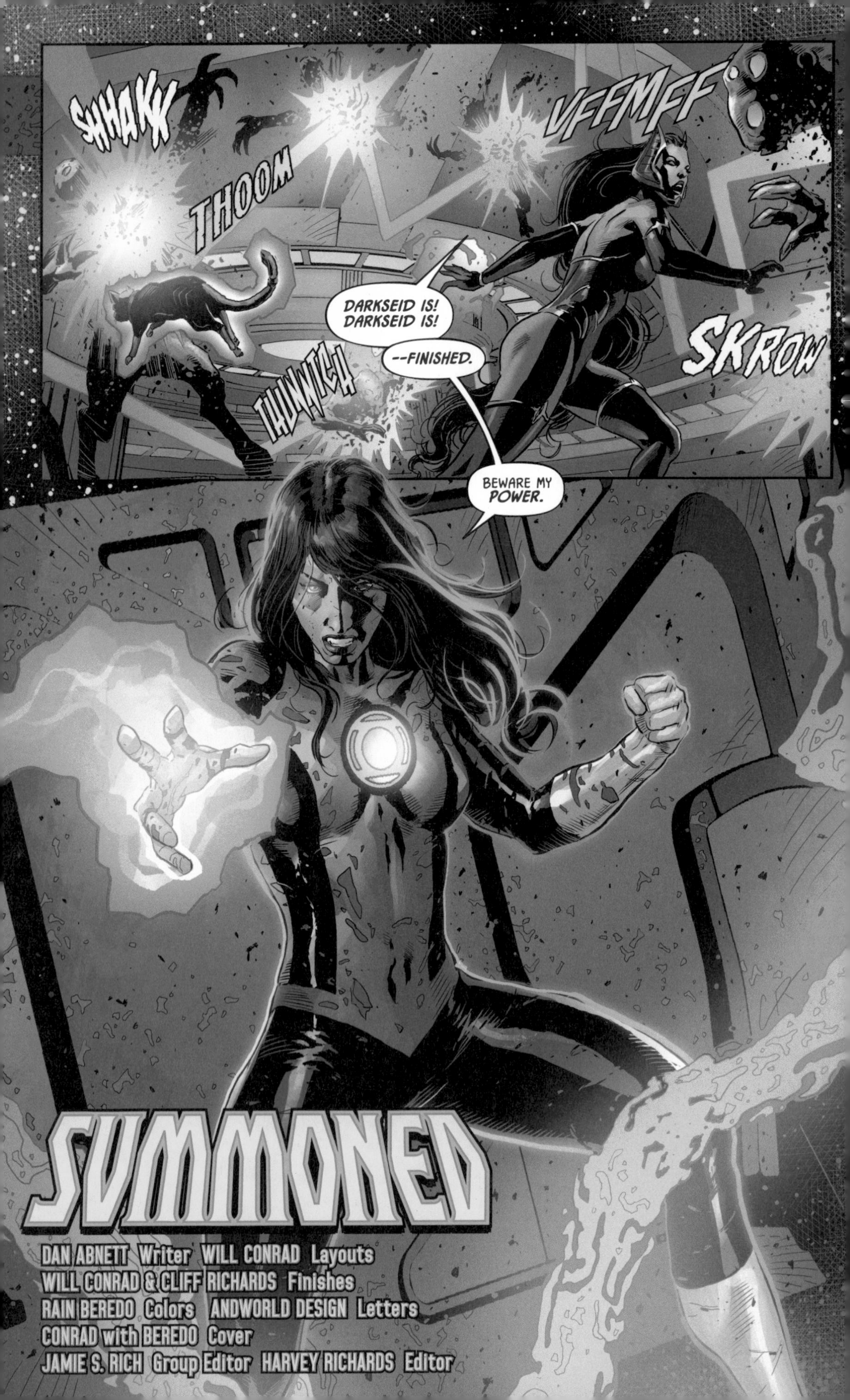
SHHAKK
THOOM
VFFMFF
DARKSEID IS! DARKSEID IS!
--FINISHED.
THWNTCH
SKROW
BEWARE MY POWER.
SUMMONED
DAN ABNETT Writer WILL CONRAD Layouts
WILL CONRAD & CLIFF RICHARDS Finishes
RAIN BEREDO Colors ANDWORLD DESIGN Letters
CONRAD with BEREDO Cover
JAMIE S. RICH Group Editor HARVEY RICHARDS Editor

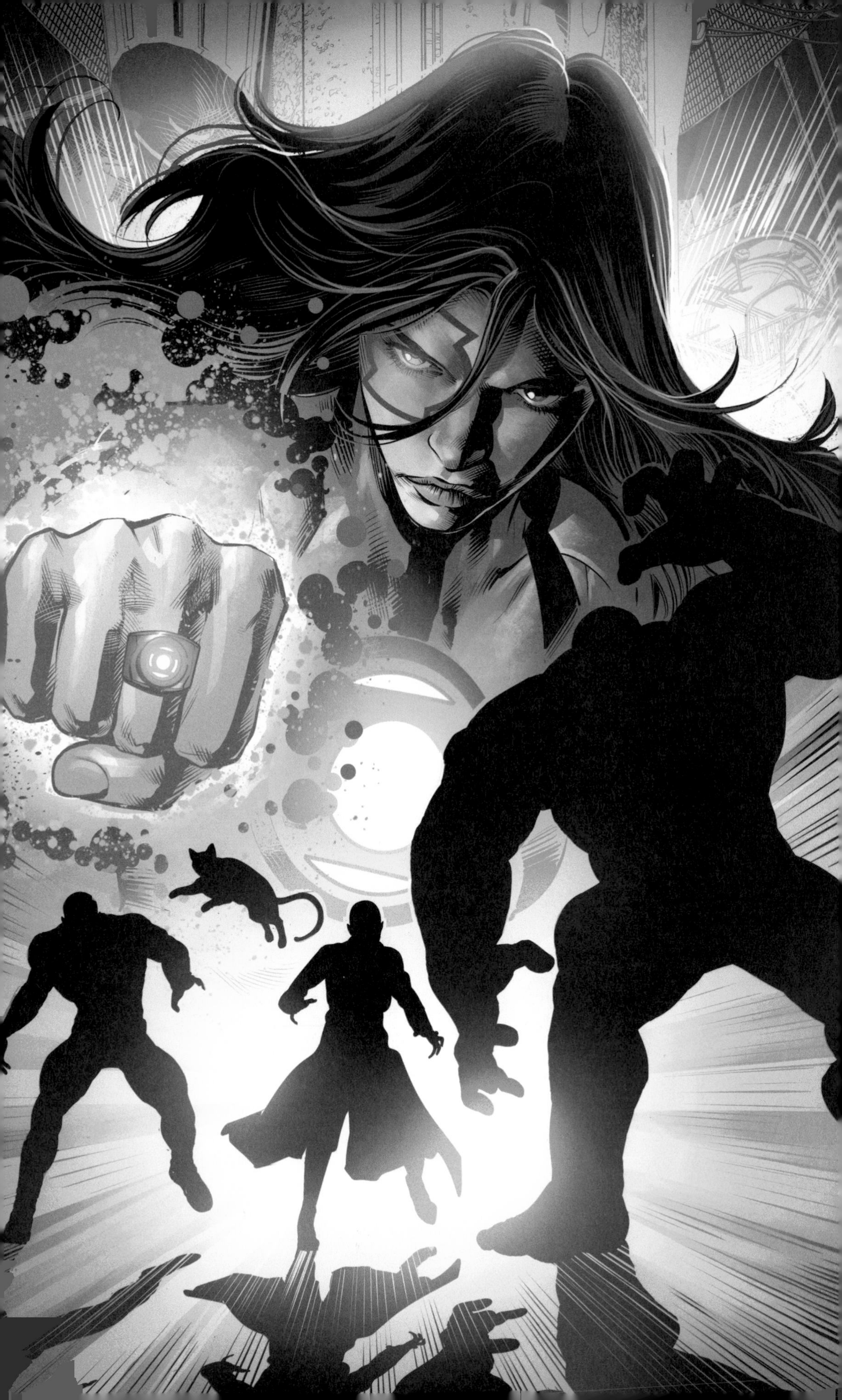

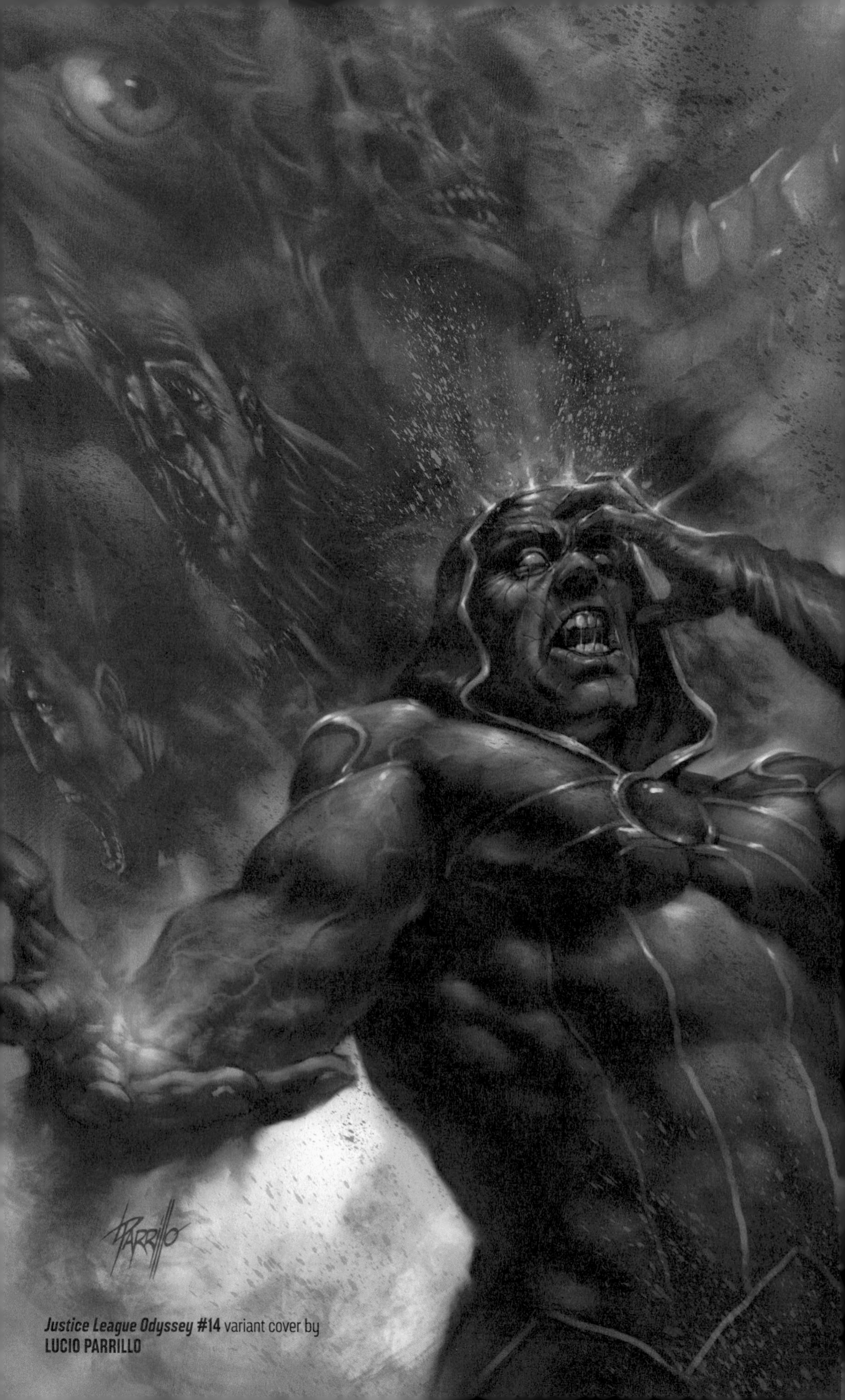

***Justice League Odyssey* #14** variant cover by
LUCIO PARRILLO

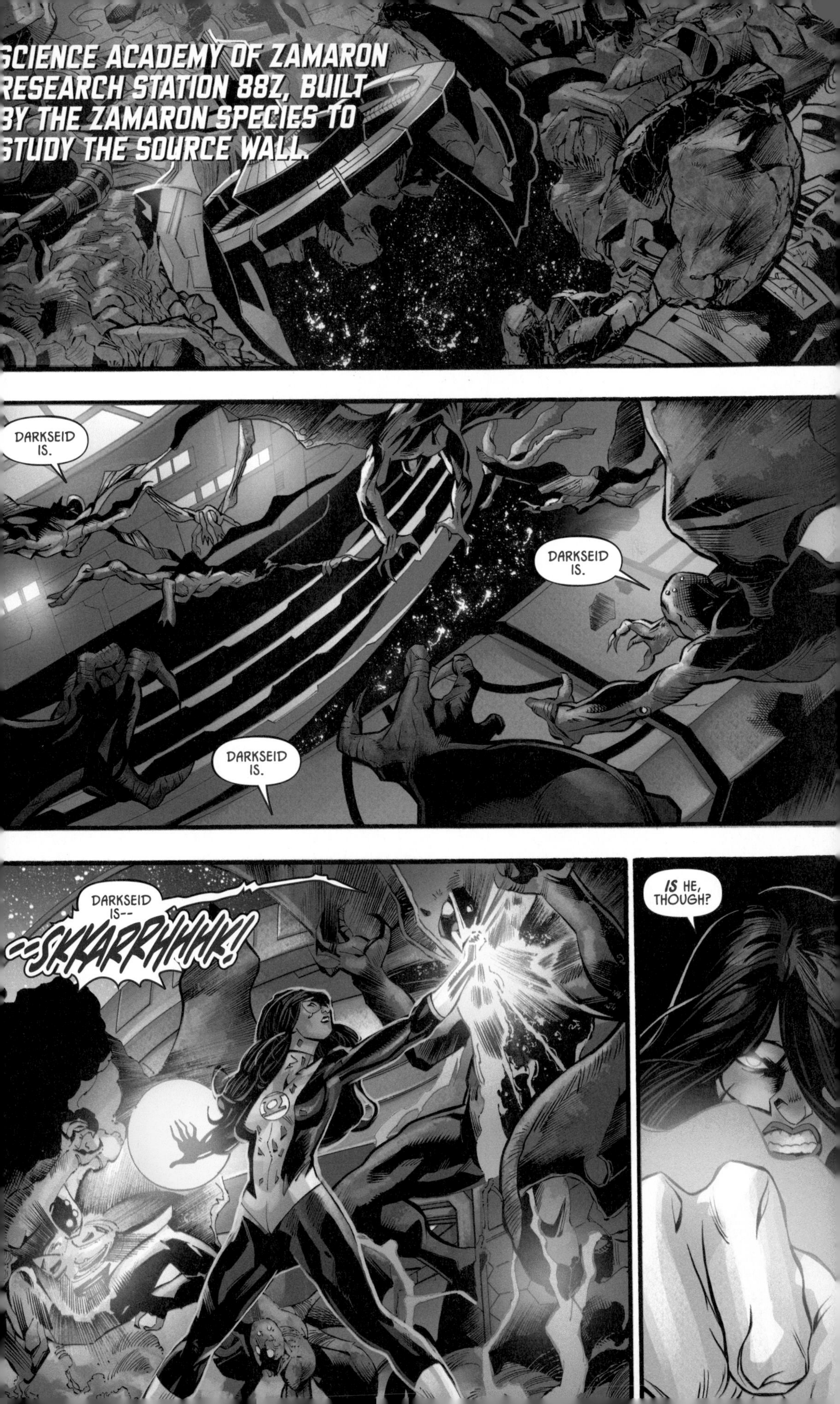
SCIENCE ACADEMY OF ZAMARON RESEARCH STATION 88Z, BUILT BY THE ZAMARON SPECIES TO STUDY THE SOURCE WALL.
DARKSEID IS.
DARKSEID IS.
DARKSEID IS.
DARKSEID IS--
--SKKARRHHHK!
IS HE, THOUGH?

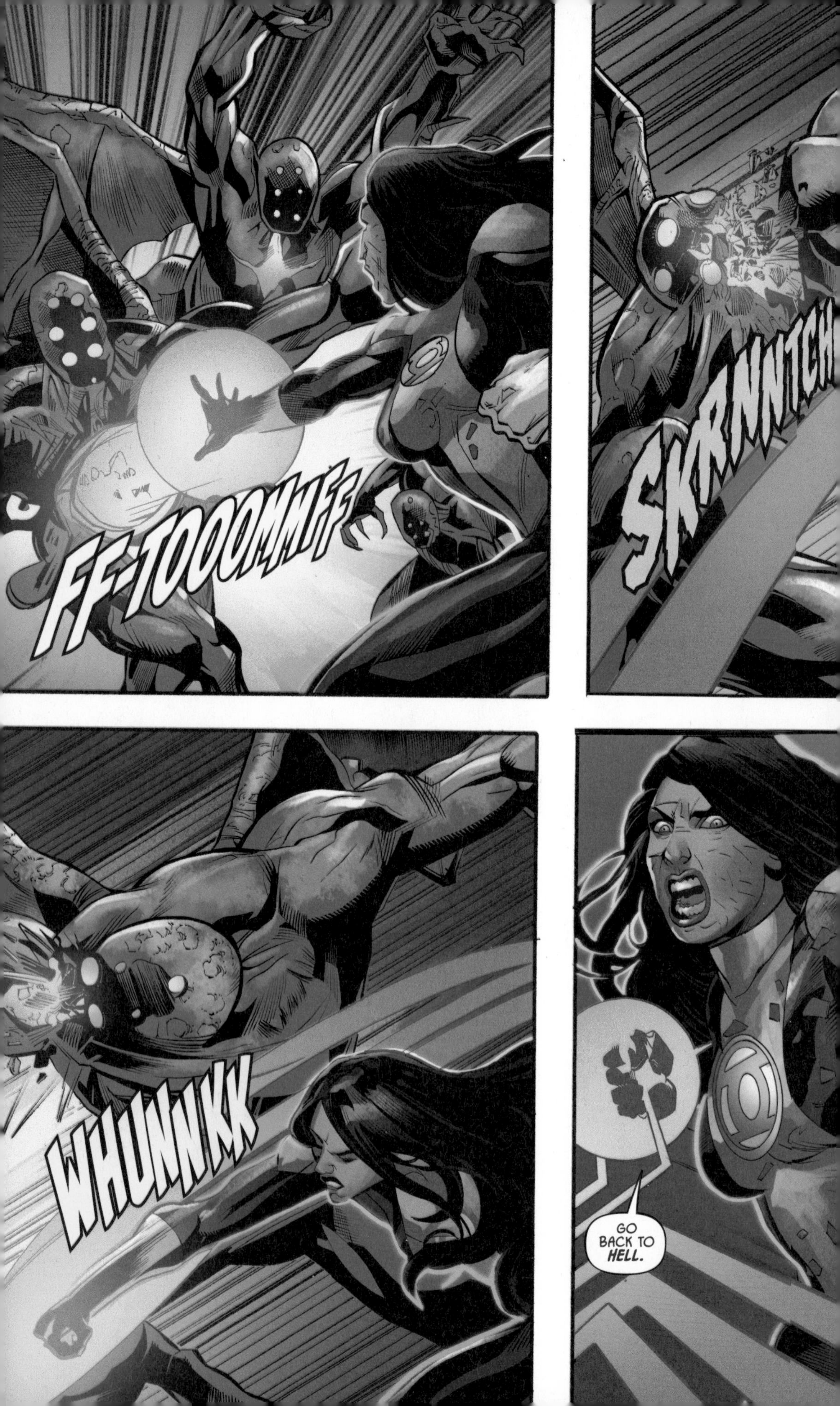
FF-TOOOMMF
SKRNNTCH
WHUNNKK
GO BACK TO HELL.

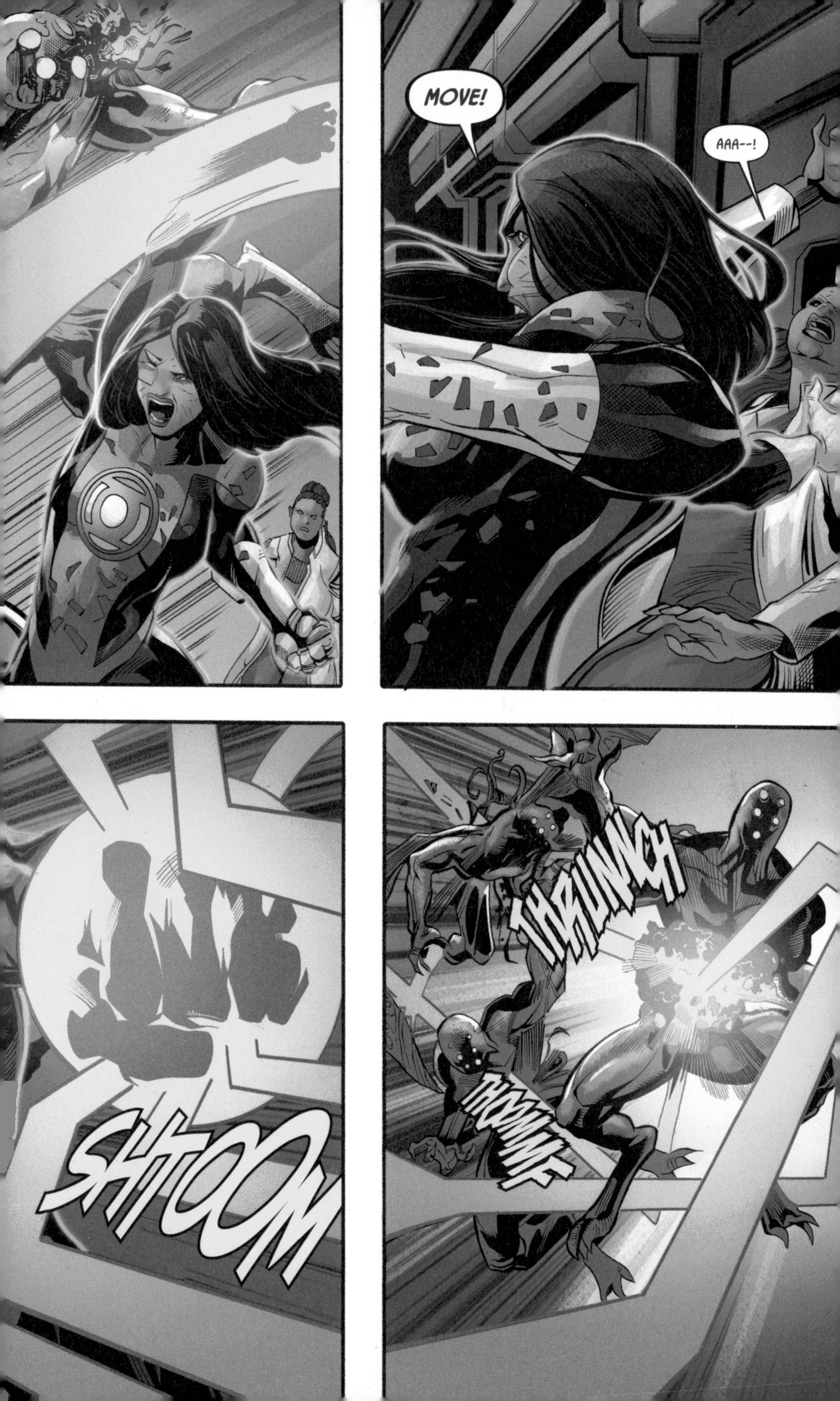
MOVE!
AAA--!
SHTOOM
THRUNCH
THOOMMF

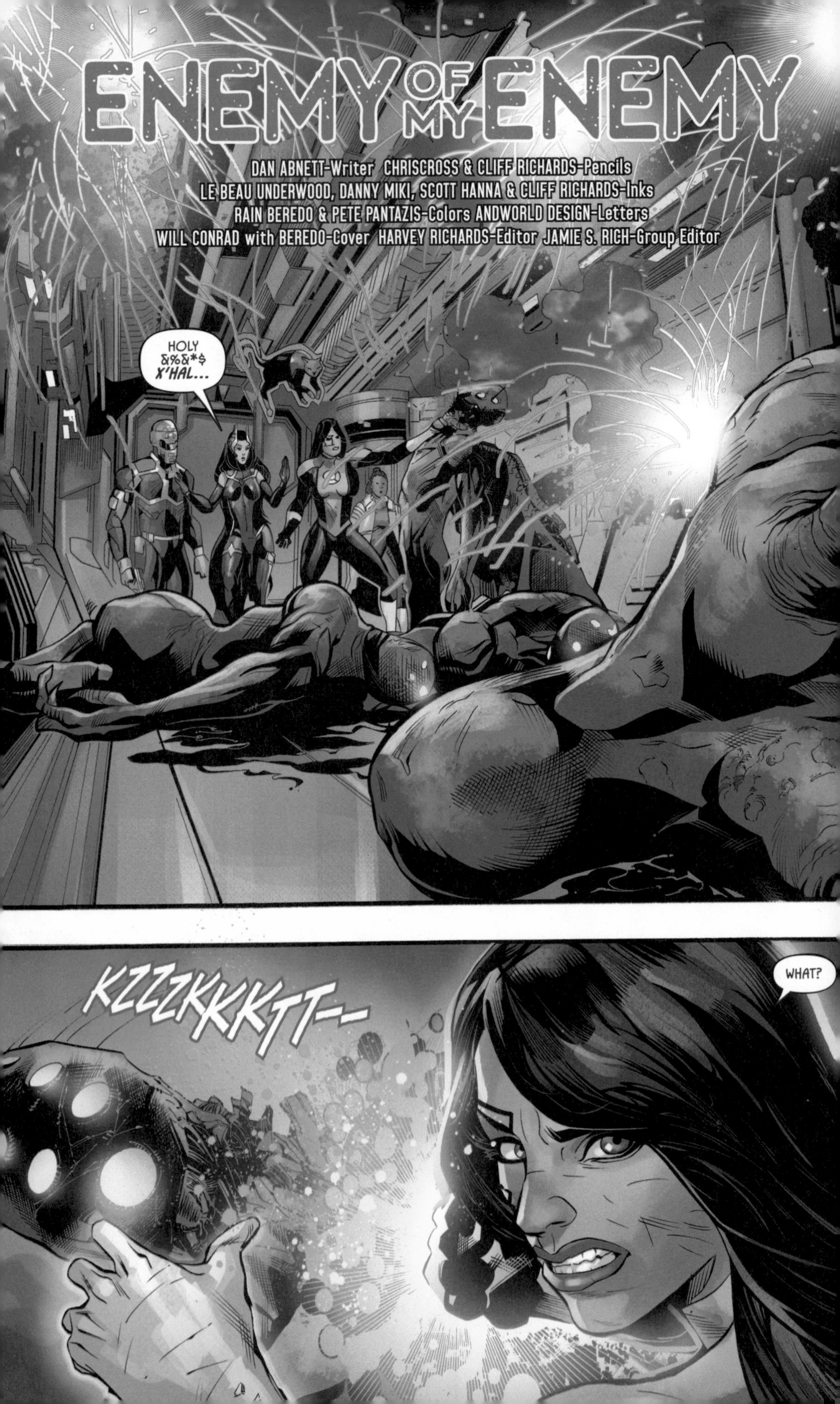
ENEMY OF MY ENEMY
DAN ABNETT-Writer CHRISCROSS & CLIFF RICHARDS-Pencils
LE BEAU UNDERWOOD, DANNY MIKI, SCOTT HANNA & CLIFF RICHARDS-Inks
RAIN BEREDO & PETE PANTAZIS-Colors ANDWORLD DESIGN-Letters
WILL CONRAD with BEREDO-Cover HARVEY RICHARDS-Editor JAMIE S. RICH-Group Editor
HOLY &%&*$ X'HAL...
KZZZKKKTT--
WHAT?

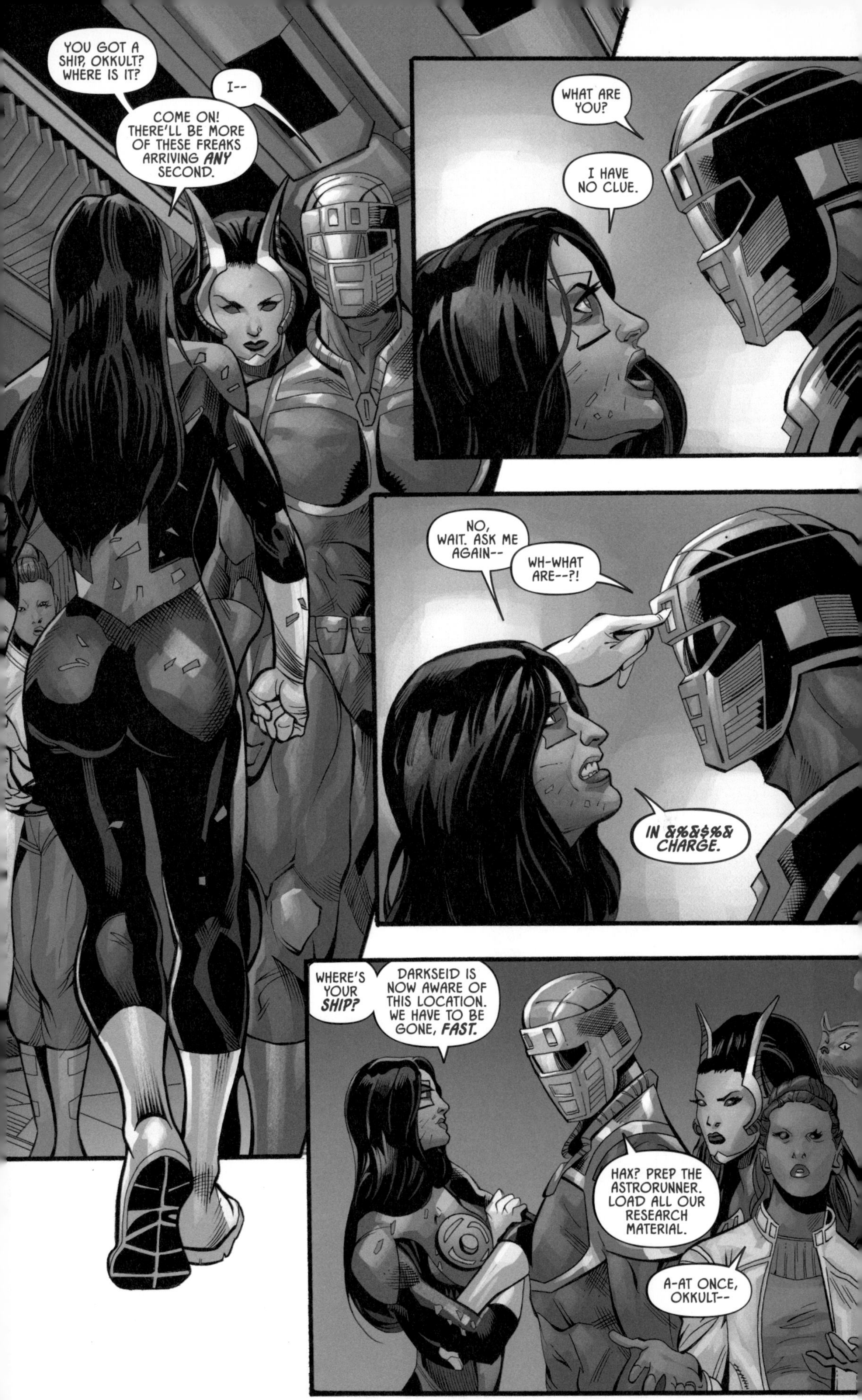

YOU GOT A SHIP, OKKULT? WHERE IS IT?
I--
COME ON! THERE'LL BE MORE OF THESE FREAKS ARRIVING ANY SECOND.
WHAT ARE YOU?
I HAVE NO CLUE.
NO, WAIT. ASK ME AGAIN--
WH-WHAT ARE--?!
IN &%&$%& CHARGE.
WHERE'S YOUR SHIP?
DARKSEID IS NOW AWARE OF THIS LOCATION. WE HAVE TO BE GONE, FAST.
HAX? PREP THE ASTRORUNNER. LOAD ALL OUR RESEARCH MATERIAL.
A-AT ONCE, OKKULT--

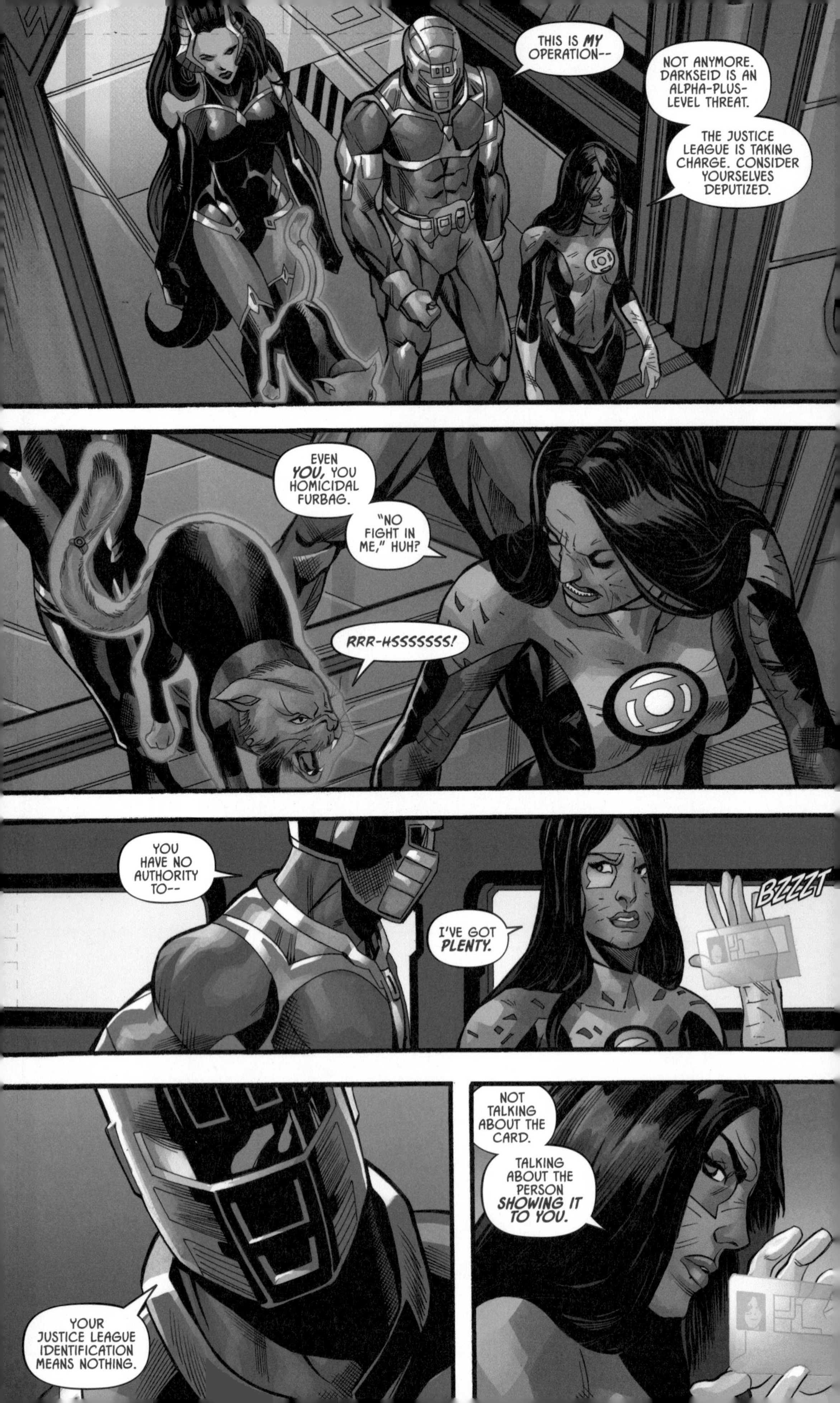
THIS IS *MY* OPERATION--
NOT ANYMORE. DARKSEID IS AN ALPHA-PLUS-LEVEL THREAT.
THE JUSTICE LEAGUE IS TAKING CHARGE. CONSIDER YOURSELVES DEPUTIZED.
EVEN *YOU,* YOU HOMICIDAL FURBAG.
"NO FIGHT IN ME," HUH?
RRR-HSSSSSSS!
YOU HAVE NO AUTHORITY TO--
I'VE GOT *PLENTY.*
BZZZT
YOUR JUSTICE LEAGUE IDENTIFICATION MEANS NOTHING.
NOT TALKING ABOUT THE CARD.
TALKING ABOUT THE PERSON *SHOWING IT TO YOU.*

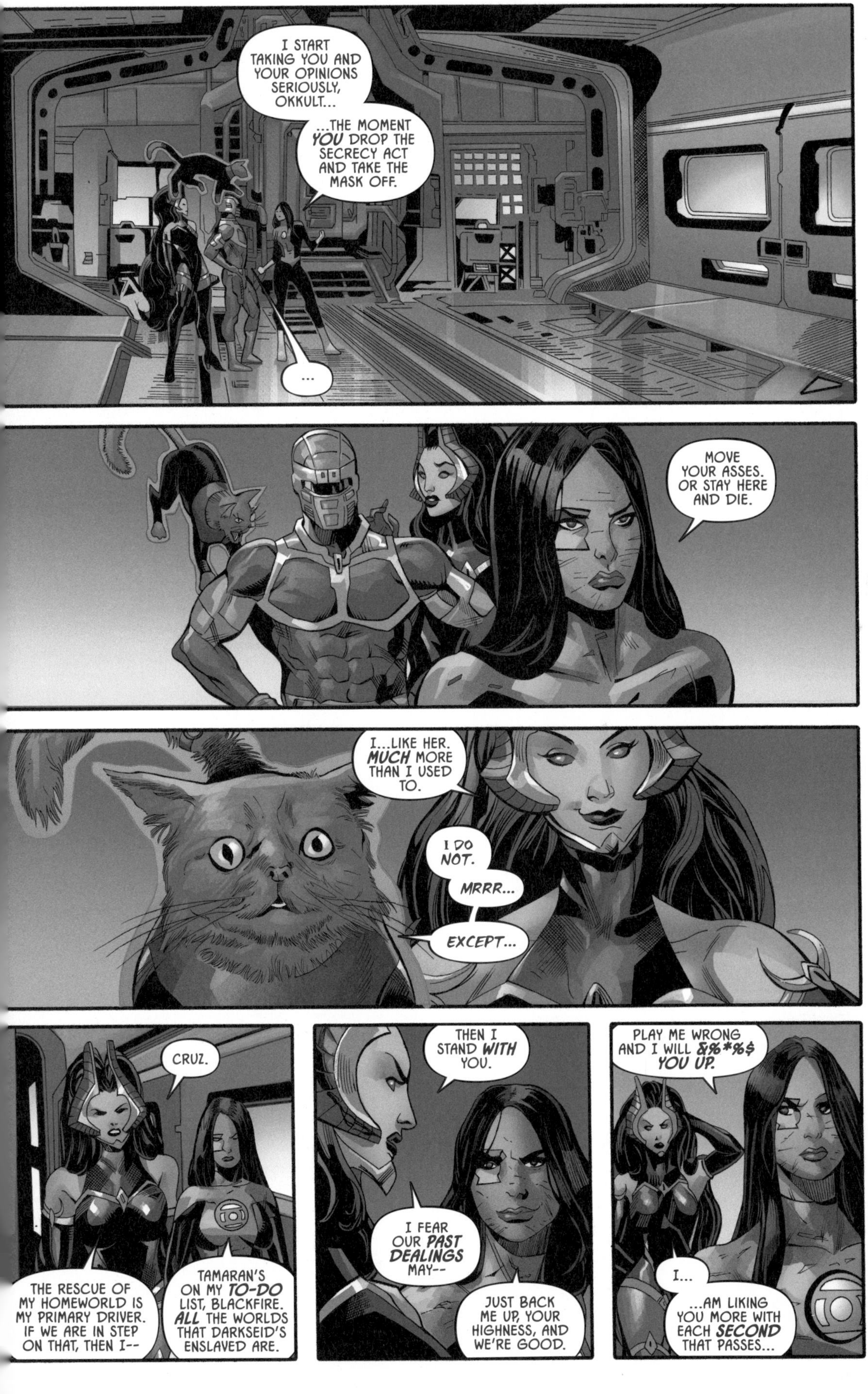

I START TAKING YOU AND YOUR OPINIONS SERIOUSLY, OKKULT...
...THE MOMENT *YOU* DROP THE SECRECY ACT AND TAKE THE MASK OFF.
...
MOVE YOUR ASSES. OR STAY HERE AND DIE.
I...LIKE HER. *MUCH* MORE THAN I USED TO.
I DO *NOT.*
MRRR...
EXCEPT...
CRUZ.
THE RESCUE OF MY HOMEWORLD IS MY PRIMARY DRIVER. IF WE ARE IN STEP ON THAT, THEN I--
TAMARAN'S ON MY *TO-DO* LIST, BLACKFIRE. *ALL* THE WORLDS THAT DARKSEID'S ENSLAVED ARE.
THEN I STAND *WITH* YOU.
I FEAR OUR *PAST DEALINGS* MAY--
JUST BACK ME UP, YOUR HIGHNESS, AND WE'RE GOOD.
PLAY ME WRONG AND I WILL *&%*%$ YOU UP.*
I...
...AM LIKING YOU MORE WITH EACH *SECOND* THAT PASSES...

ASTRORUNNER ENGINES LIT. BEGINNING PRE-LAUNCH DIAGNOSTIC--

SKIP THAT PART.

DO AS SHE SAYS. TAKE US OUT, HAX.

RUNNING CLEAR. CYCLING TO FULL THRUST.

CLOAK US.

SCAN-SPHERE SHOWS PARA-ANGEL FORCES NOW CONVERGING ON STATION 88Z...

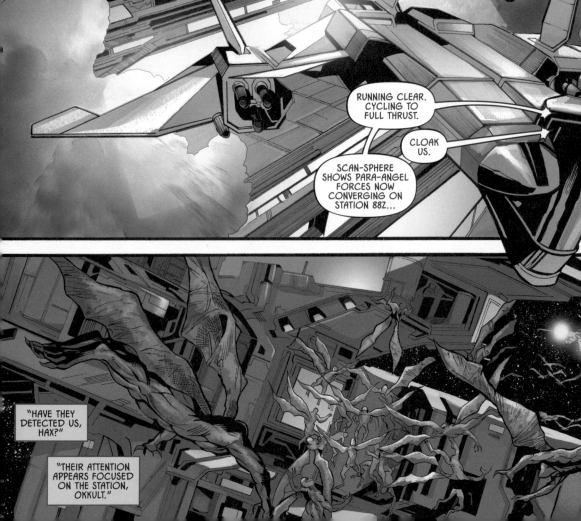

"HAVE THEY DETECTED US, HAX?"

"THEIR ATTENTION APPEARS FOCUSED ON THE STATION, OKKULT."

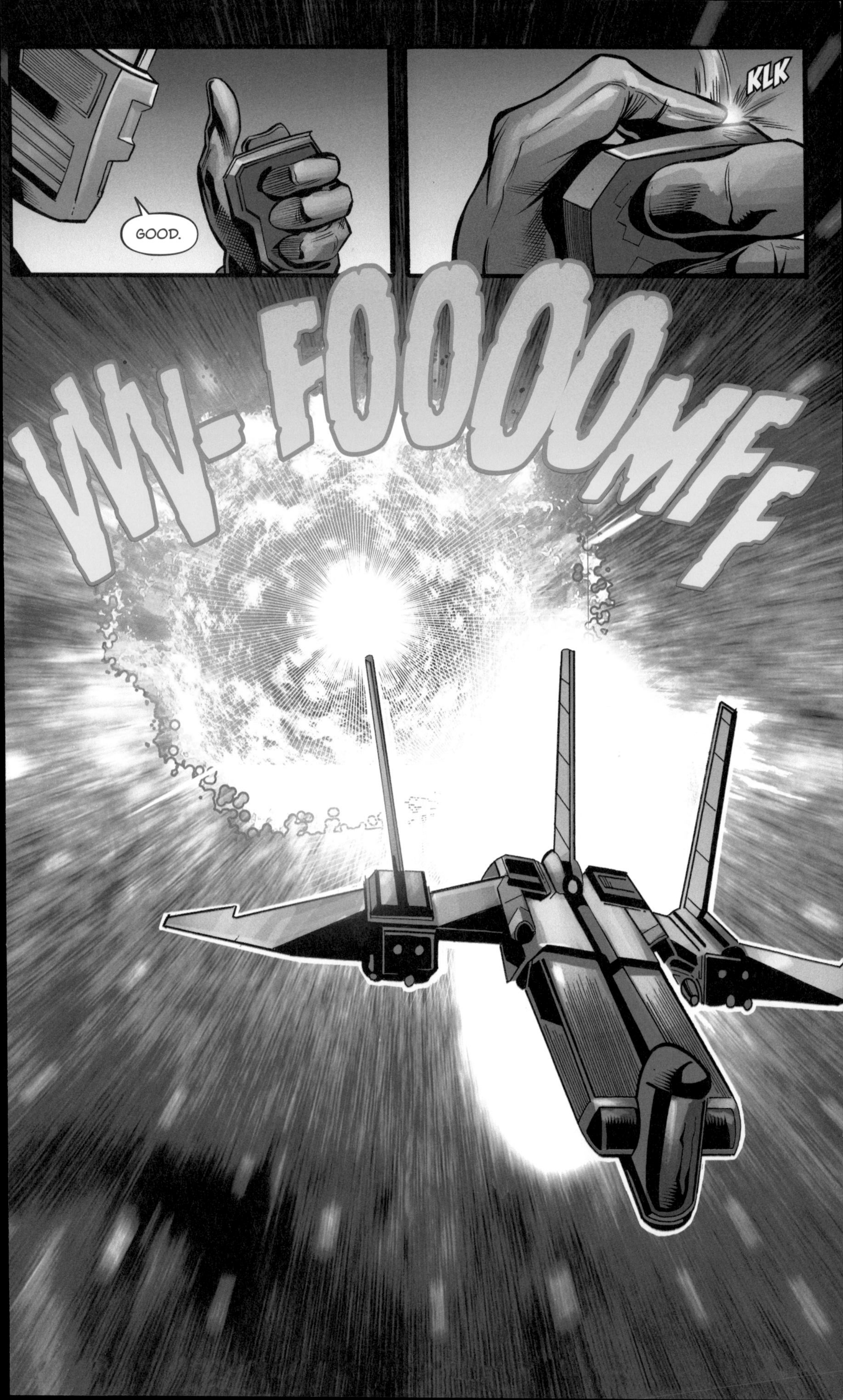
GOOD.
KLK
VHV- FOOOOMFF

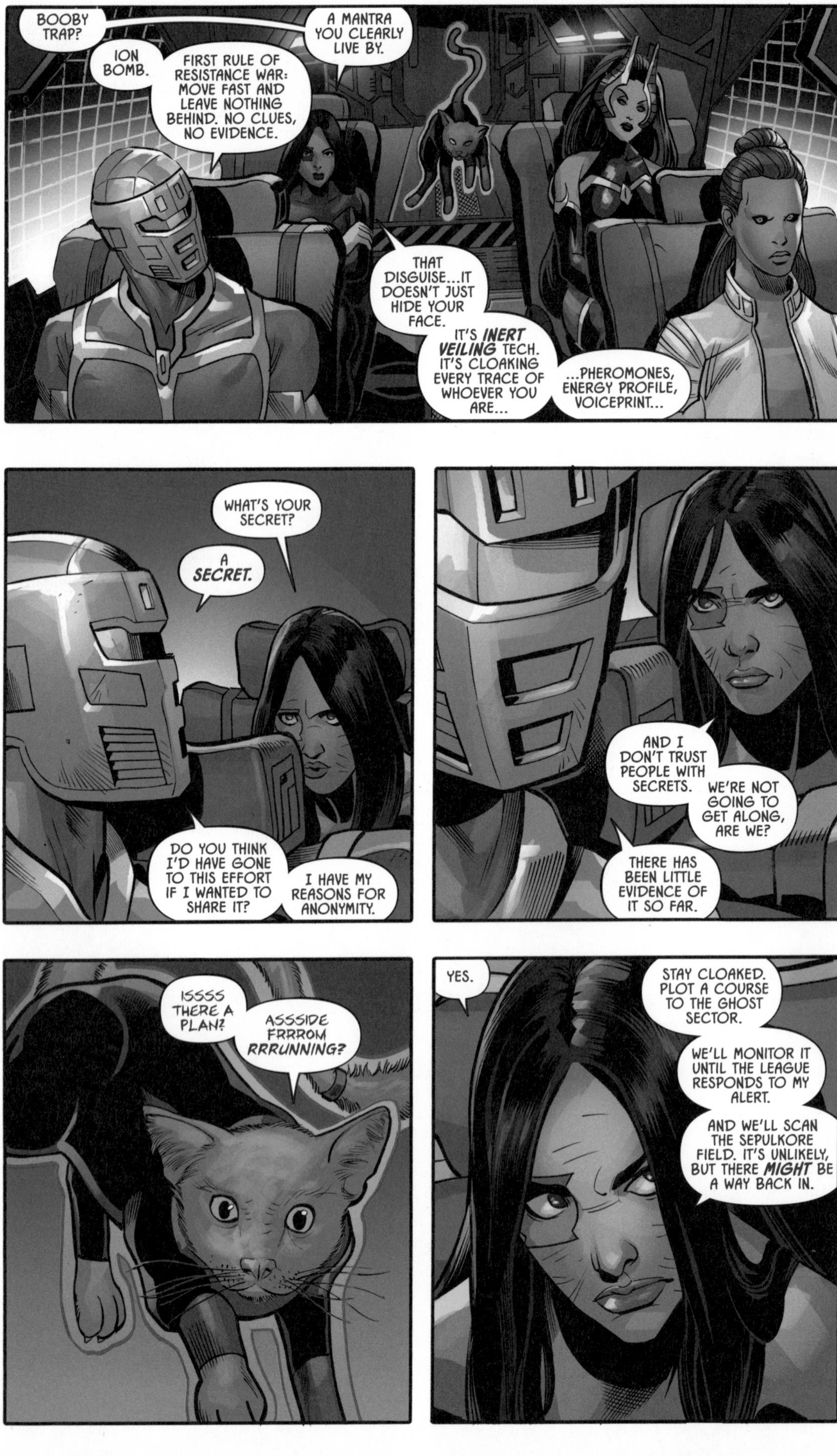
BOOBY TRAP?
ION BOMB.
FIRST RULE OF RESISTANCE WAR: MOVE FAST AND LEAVE NOTHING BEHIND. NO CLUES, NO EVIDENCE.
A MANTRA YOU CLEARLY LIVE BY.
THAT DISGUISE...IT DOESN'T JUST HIDE YOUR FACE.
IT'S INERT VEILING TECH. IT'S CLOAKING EVERY TRACE OF WHOEVER YOU ARE...
...PHEROMONES, ENERGY PROFILE, VOICEPRINT...
WHAT'S YOUR SECRET?
A SECRET.
DO YOU THINK I'D HAVE GONE TO THIS EFFORT IF I WANTED TO SHARE IT?
I HAVE MY REASONS FOR ANONYMITY.
AND I DON'T TRUST PEOPLE WITH SECRETS.
WE'RE NOT GOING TO GET ALONG, ARE WE?
THERE HAS BEEN LITTLE EVIDENCE OF IT SO FAR.
ISSSS THERE A PLAN?
ASSSIDE FRRROM RRRUNNING?
YES.
STAY CLOAKED. PLOT A COURSE TO THE GHOST SECTOR.
WE'LL MONITOR IT UNTIL THE LEAGUE RESPONDS TO MY ALERT.
AND WE'LL SCAN THE SEPULKORE FIELD. IT'S UNLIKELY, BUT THERE MIGHT BE A WAY BACK IN.

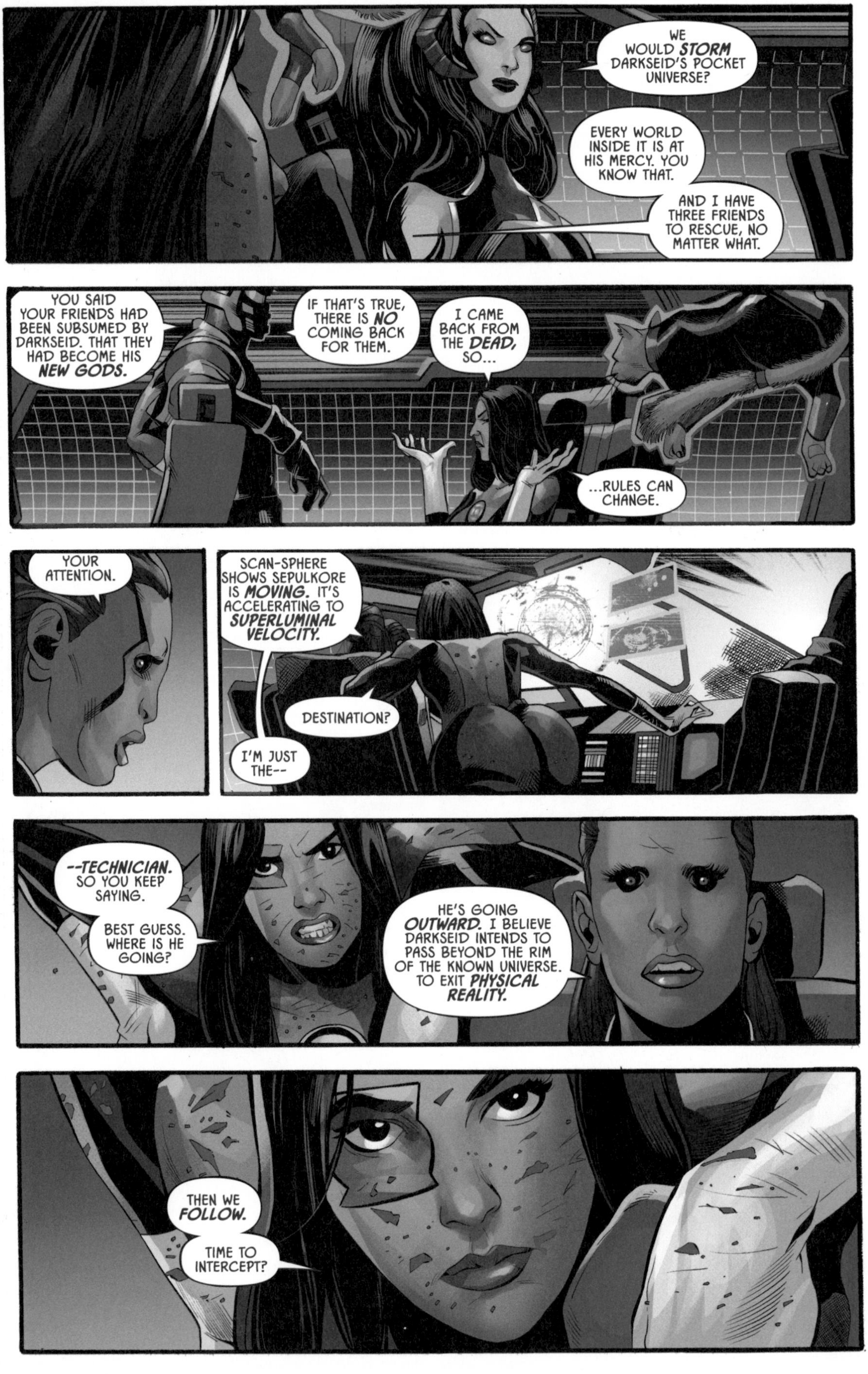
WE WOULD STORM DARKSEID'S POCKET UNIVERSE?
EVERY WORLD INSIDE IT IS AT HIS MERCY. YOU KNOW THAT.
AND I HAVE THREE FRIENDS TO RESCUE, NO MATTER WHAT.
YOU SAID YOUR FRIENDS HAD BEEN SUBSUMED BY DARKSEID. THAT THEY HAD BECOME HIS NEW GODS.
IF THAT'S TRUE, THERE IS NO COMING BACK FOR THEM.
I CAME BACK FROM THE DEAD, SO...
...RULES CAN CHANGE.
YOUR ATTENTION.
SCAN-SPHERE SHOWS SEPULKORE IS MOVING. IT'S ACCELERATING TO SUPERLUMINAL VELOCITY.
DESTINATION?
I'M JUST THE--
--TECHNICIAN. SO YOU KEEP SAYING.
BEST GUESS. WHERE IS HE GOING?
HE'S GOING OUTWARD. I BELIEVE DARKSEID INTENDS TO PASS BEYOND THE RIM OF THE KNOWN UNIVERSE. TO EXIT PHYSICAL REALITY.
THEN WE FOLLOW.
TIME TO INTERCEPT?

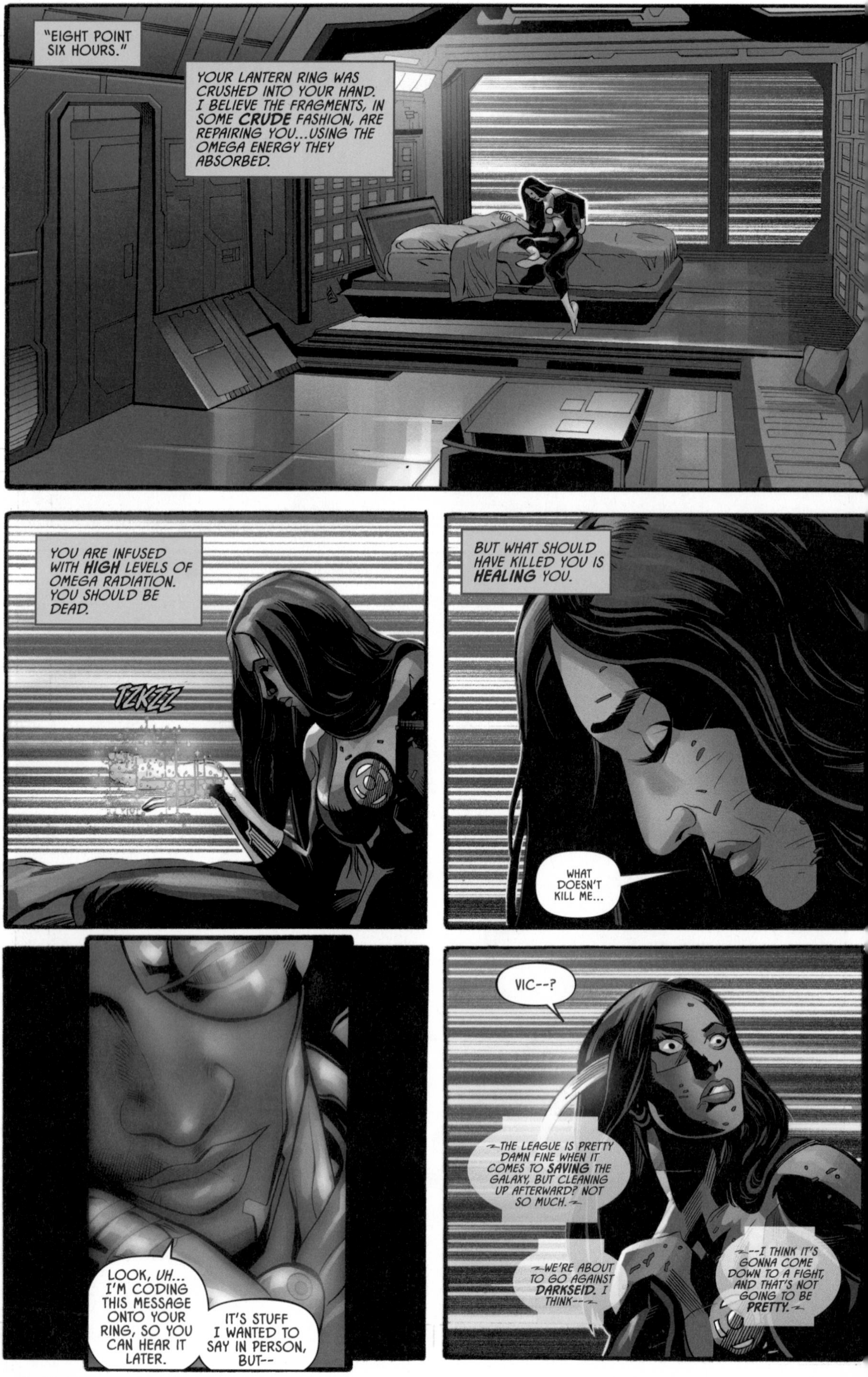
"EIGHT POINT SIX HOURS."
YOUR LANTERN RING WAS CRUSHED INTO YOUR HAND. I BELIEVE THE FRAGMENTS, IN SOME CRUDE FASHION, ARE REPAIRING YOU...USING THE OMEGA ENERGY THEY ABSORBED.
YOU ARE INFUSED WITH HIGH LEVELS OF OMEGA RADIATION. YOU SHOULD BE DEAD.
TZKZZ
BUT WHAT SHOULD HAVE KILLED YOU IS HEALING YOU.
WHAT DOESN'T KILL ME...
LOOK, UH... I'M CODING THIS MESSAGE ONTO YOUR RING, SO YOU CAN HEAR IT LATER.
IT'S STUFF I WANTED TO SAY IN PERSON, BUT--
VIC--?
THE LEAGUE IS PRETTY DAMN FINE WHEN IT COMES TO SAVING THE GALAXY, BUT CLEANING UP AFTERWARD? NOT SO MUCH.
WE'RE ABOUT TO GO AGAINST DARKSEID. I THINK--
--I THINK IT'S GONNA COME DOWN TO A FIGHT, AND THAT'S NOT GOING TO BE PRETTY.

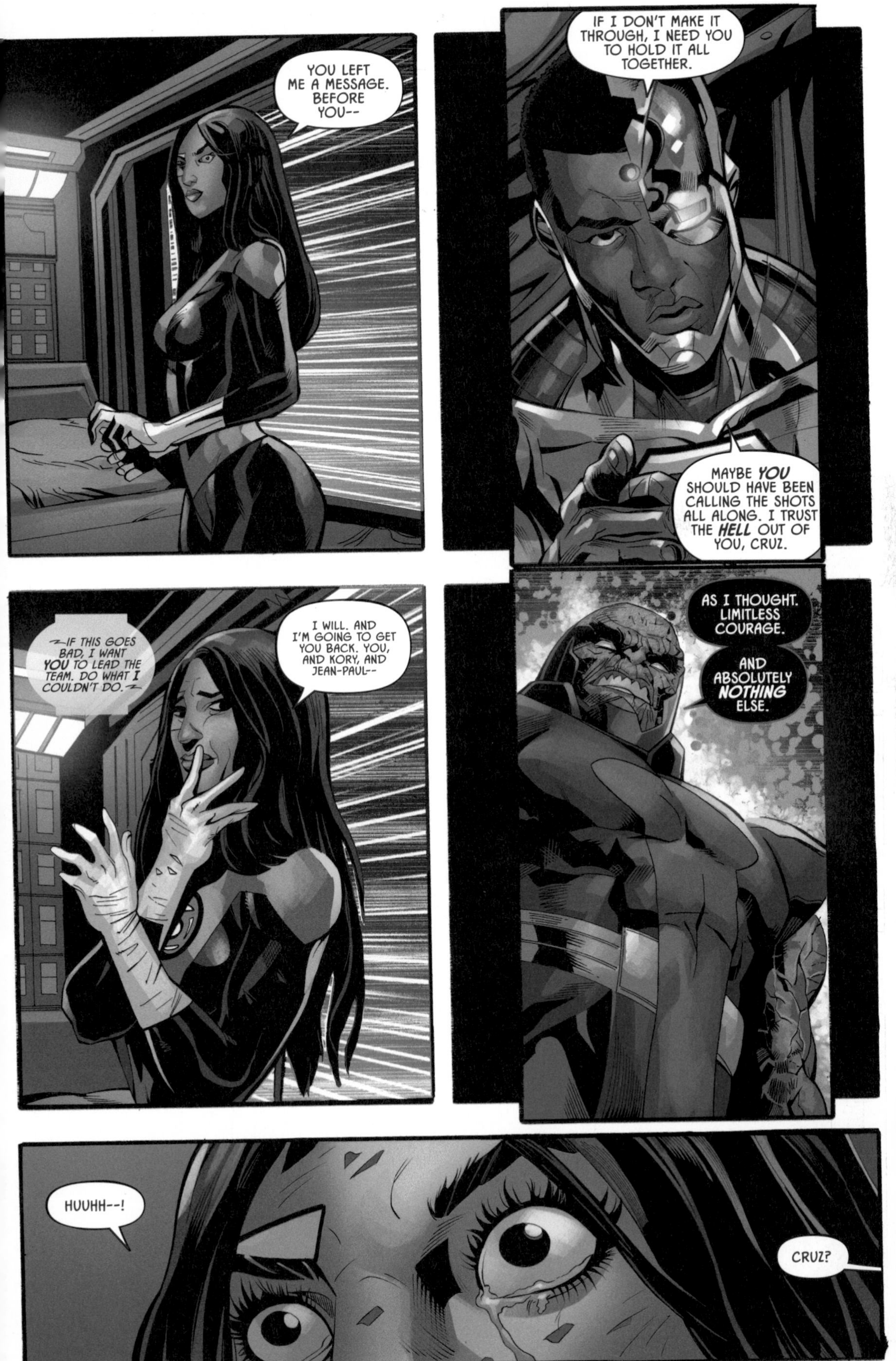
YOU LEFT ME A MESSAGE. BEFORE YOU--
IF I DON'T MAKE IT THROUGH, I NEED YOU TO HOLD IT ALL TOGETHER.
MAYBE *YOU* SHOULD HAVE BEEN CALLING THE SHOTS ALL ALONG. I TRUST THE ***HELL*** OUT OF YOU, CRUZ.
IF THIS GOES BAD, I WANT ***YOU*** TO LEAD THE TEAM. DO WHAT ***I*** COULDN'T DO.
I WILL. AND I'M GOING TO GET YOU BACK. YOU, AND KORY, AND JEAN-PAUL--
AS I THOUGHT. LIMITLESS COURAGE.
AND ABSOLUTELY ***NOTHING*** ELSE.
HUUHH--!
CRUZ?

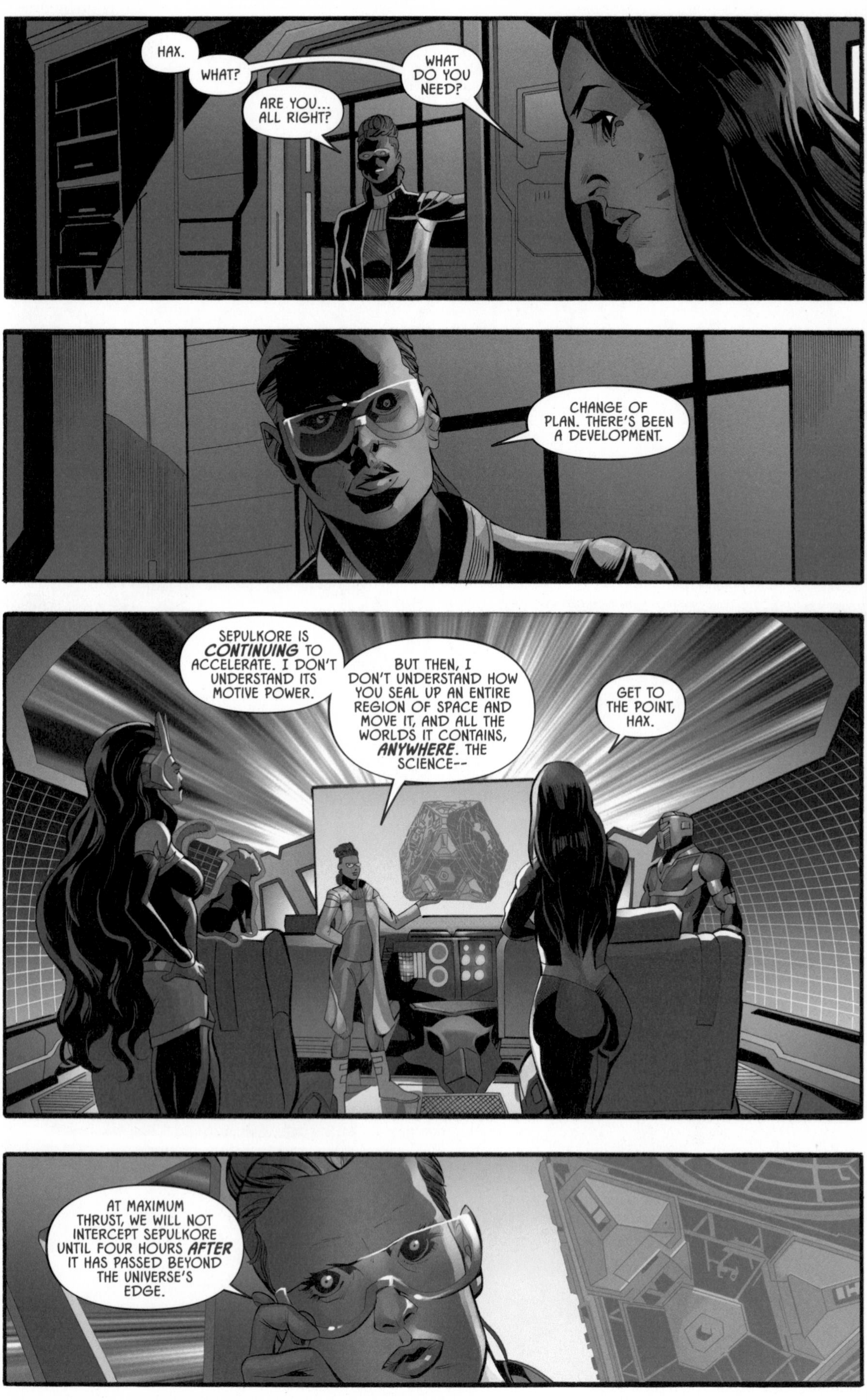
HAX.
WHAT?
WHAT DO YOU NEED?
ARE YOU... ALL RIGHT?
CHANGE OF PLAN. THERE'S BEEN A DEVELOPMENT.
SEPULKORE IS **CONTINUING** TO ACCELERATE. I DON'T UNDERSTAND ITS MOTIVE POWER.
BUT THEN, I DON'T UNDERSTAND HOW YOU SEAL UP AN ENTIRE REGION OF SPACE AND MOVE IT, AND ALL THE WORLDS IT CONTAINS, **ANYWHERE**. THE SCIENCE--
GET TO THE POINT, HAX.
AT MAXIMUM THRUST, WE WILL NOT INTERCEPT SEPULKORE UNTIL FOUR HOURS **AFTER** IT HAS PASSED BEYOND THE UNIVERSE'S EDGE.

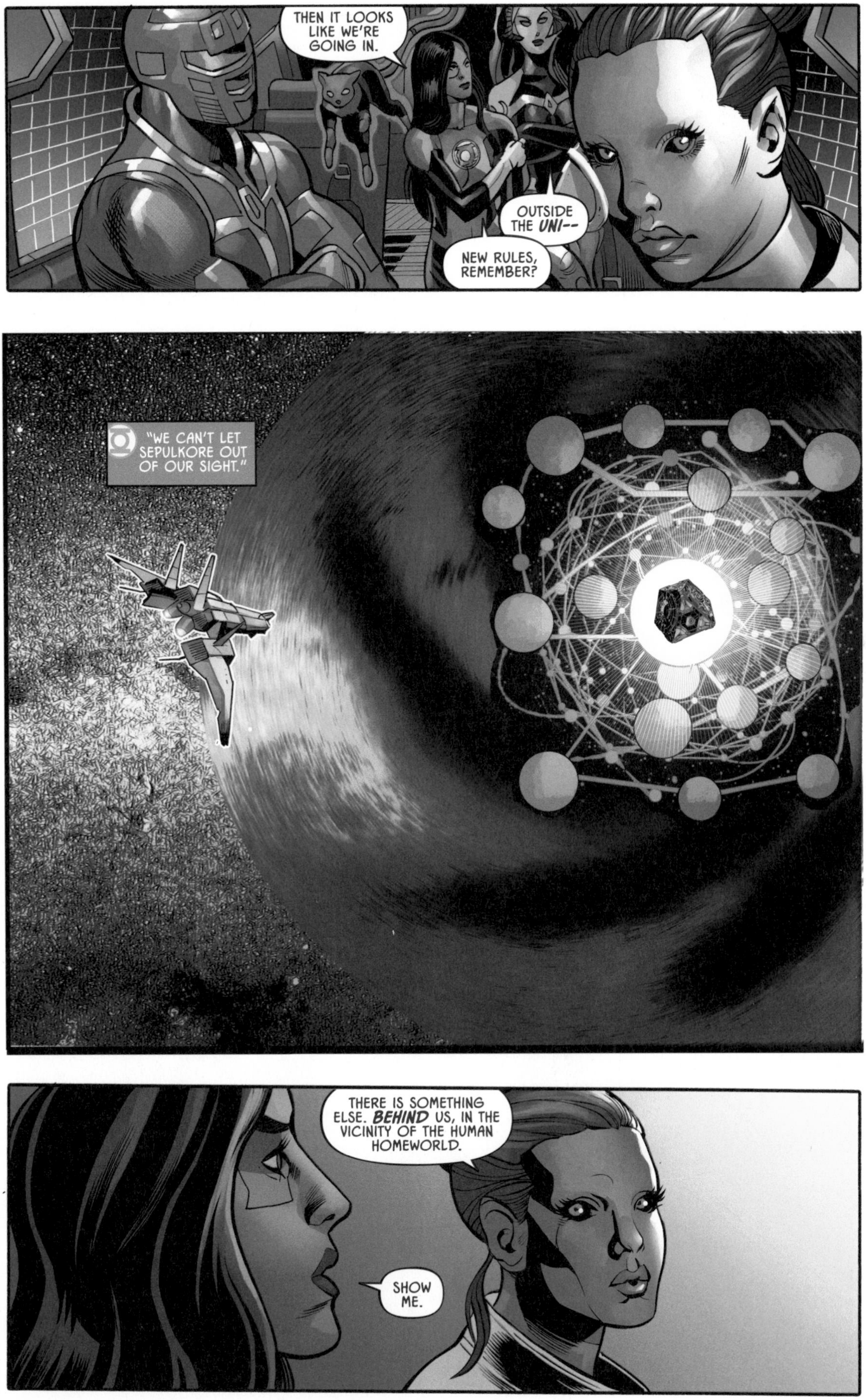
THEN IT LOOKS LIKE WE'RE GOING IN.
OUTSIDE THE UNI--
NEW RULES, REMEMBER?
"WE CAN'T LET SEPULKORE OUT OF OUR SIGHT."
THERE IS SOMETHING ELSE. BEHIND US, IN THE VICINITY OF THE HUMAN HOMEWORLD.
SHOW ME.

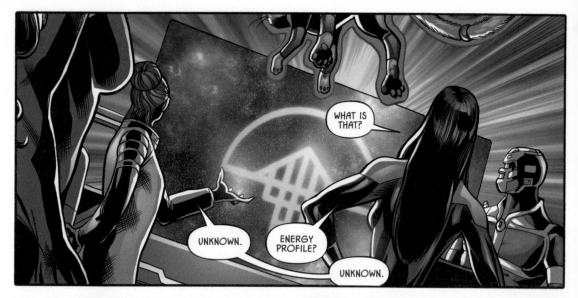

WHAT IS THAT?

UNKNOWN.

ENERGY PROFILE?

UNKNOWN.

AS A TECHNICIAN, YOU *SUCK*.

I DON'T KNOW WHAT THAT IS, OR WHAT IT *MEANS*, BUT THE LEAGUE IS THERE, THE LEAGUE AND EVERYONE ELSE.

WE'RE THE *ONLY* ONES OUT HERE. WE HAVE TO STAY ON DARKSEID'S TAIL.

DID YOU BRING THAT *SUMMONER* THING ABOARD?

YES.

LET'S TAKE A LOOK AT IT. IF WE CAN GET IT WORKING, MAYBE WE CAN SNATCH MY FRIENDS *BACK* BEFORE THEY REACH THE EDGE.

THAT IS UNLIKELY.

ARE WE GOING TO HAVE TO HAVE THE "NEW RULES" CONVERSATION AGAIN?

BLACKFIRE? THE SHIP'S ON AUTO-HELM, BUT KEEP WATCH.

DON'T LET *MR. SECRETS* ALTER OUR COURSE *OR* OUR PLAN.

YOU HAVE MY WORD, CRUZ.

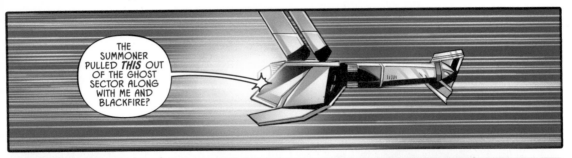

THE SUMMONER PULLED *THIS* OUT OF THE GHOST SECTOR ALONG WITH ME AND BLACKFIRE?

YES.

LEMME GUESS, YOU HAVE NO IDEA WHAT--

IT'S INERT. JUST TRACE OMEGA ENERGY.

IT DOESN'T FEEL LIKE... *ANYTHING*.

EXCEPT FAMILIAR, SOMEHOW...

ANYWAY, THE SUMMONER IS DAMAGED BEYOND REPAIR.

HNH.

WHAT'S YOUR STORY, ARLA HAX?

I *HAVE* NO "STORY."

I THOUGHT THE ZAMARONS WERE A WARRIOR RACE.

NOT ALL OF THEM. I AM JUST--

--A *TECHNICIAN*, RIGHT.

SO, A *ZAMARON SCIENTIST*, ALLIED TO A *WARRIOR WITH NO IDENTITY*. WHAT'S *THAT* ABOUT?

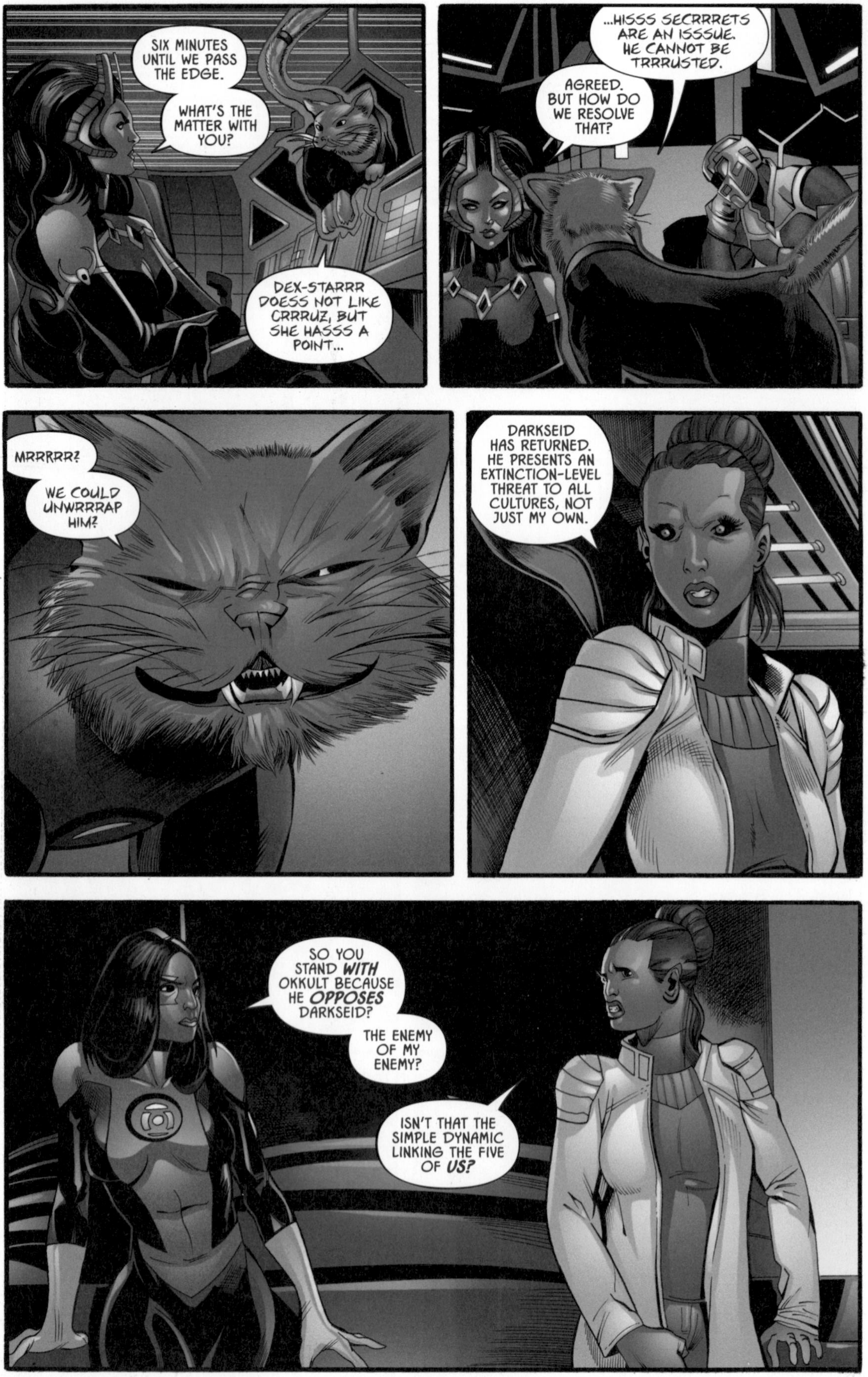
SIX MINUTES UNTIL WE PASS THE EDGE.
WHAT'S THE MATTER WITH YOU?
DEX-STARRR DOESS NOT LIKE CRRRUZ, BUT SHE HASSS A POINT...
...HISSS SECRRRETS ARE AN ISSSUE. HE CANNOT BE TRRRUSTED.
AGREED. BUT HOW DO WE RESOLVE THAT?
MRRRRR?
WE COULD UNWRRRAP HIM?
DARKSEID HAS RETURNED. HE PRESENTS AN EXTINCTION-LEVEL THREAT TO ALL CULTURES, NOT JUST MY OWN.
SO YOU STAND WITH OKKULT BECAUSE HE OPPOSES DARKSEID?
THE ENEMY OF MY ENEMY?
ISN'T THAT THE SIMPLE DYNAMIC LINKING THE FIVE OF US?

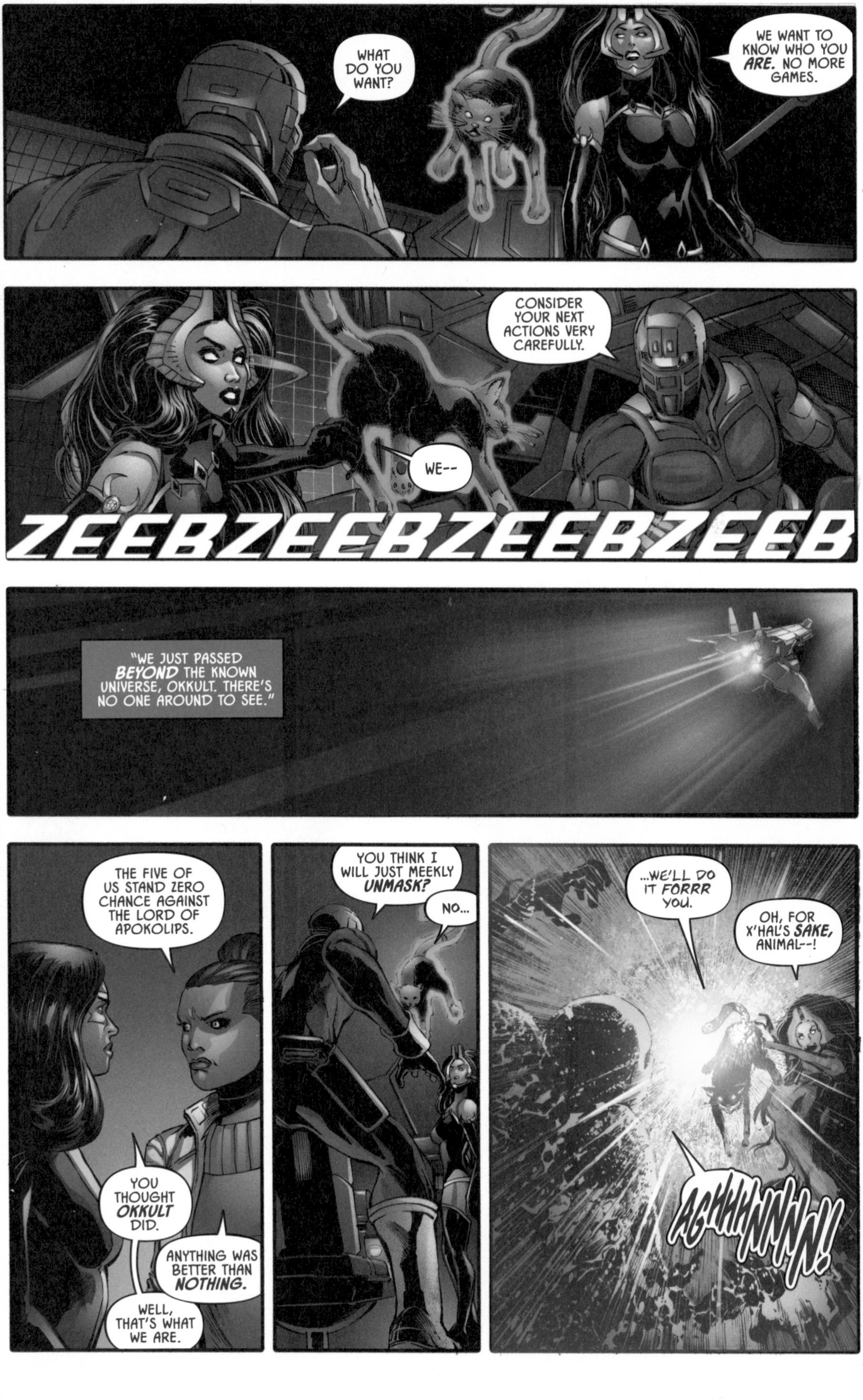
WHAT DO YOU WANT?
WE WANT TO KNOW WHO YOU ARE. NO MORE GAMES.
CONSIDER YOUR NEXT ACTIONS VERY CAREFULLY.
WE--
ZEEBZEEBZEEBZEEB
"WE JUST PASSED BEYOND THE KNOWN UNIVERSE, OKKULT. THERE'S NO ONE AROUND TO SEE."
THE FIVE OF US STAND ZERO CHANCE AGAINST THE LORD OF APOKOLIPS.
YOU THOUGHT OKKULT DID.
ANYTHING WAS BETTER THAN NOTHING.
WELL, THAT'S WHAT WE ARE.
YOU THINK I WILL JUST MEEKLY UNMASK?
NO...
...WE'LL DO IT FORRR YOU.
OH, FOR X'HAL'S SAKE, ANIMAL--!
AGHHHNNNN!

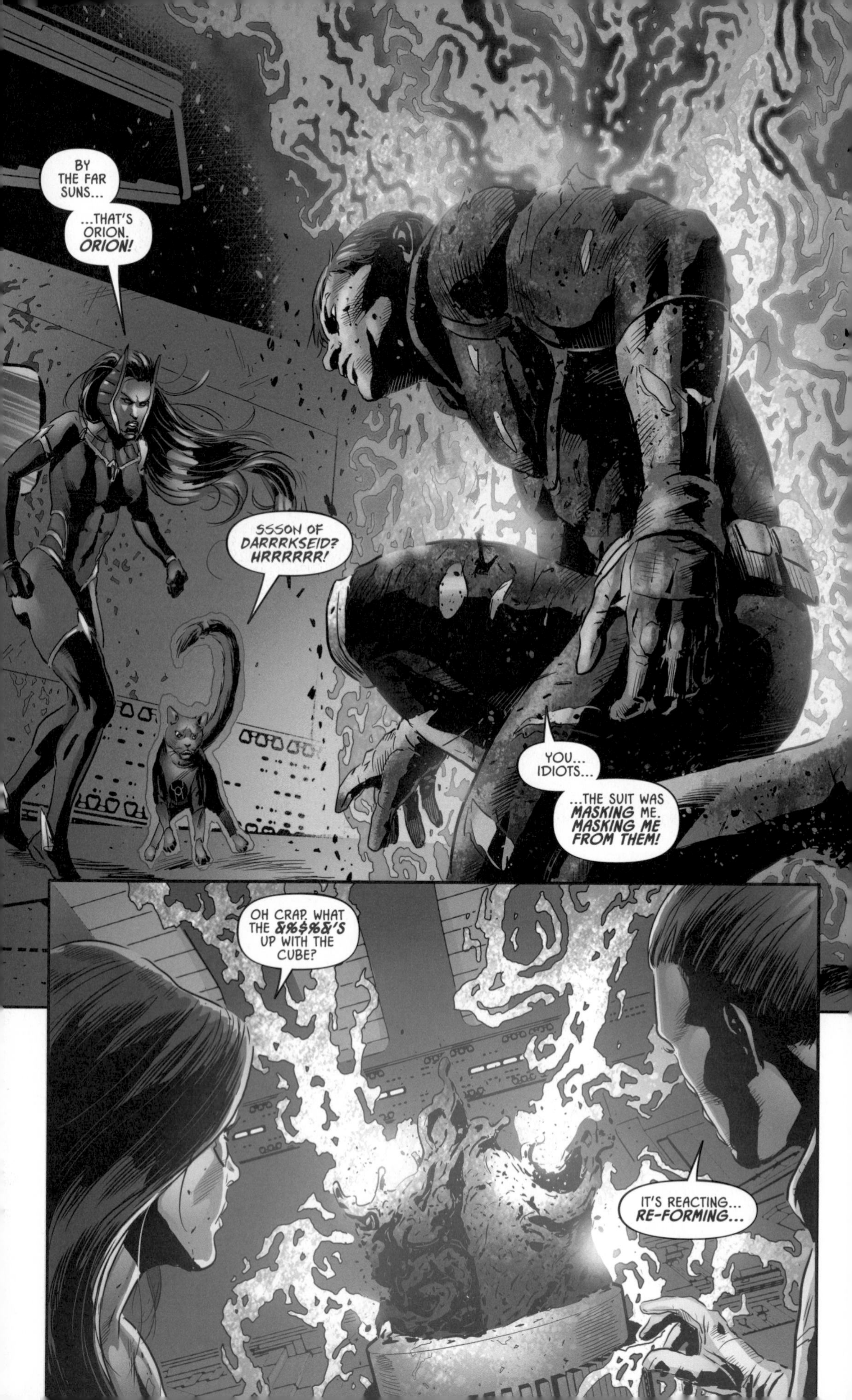
BY THE FAR SUNS...
...THAT'S ORION. ORION!
SSSON OF DARRRKSEID? HRRRRRR!
YOU... IDIOTS...
...THE SUIT WAS MASKING ME. MASKING ME FROM THEM!
OH CRAP. WHAT THE &%$%&'S UP WITH THE CUBE?
IT'S REACTING... RE-FORMING...

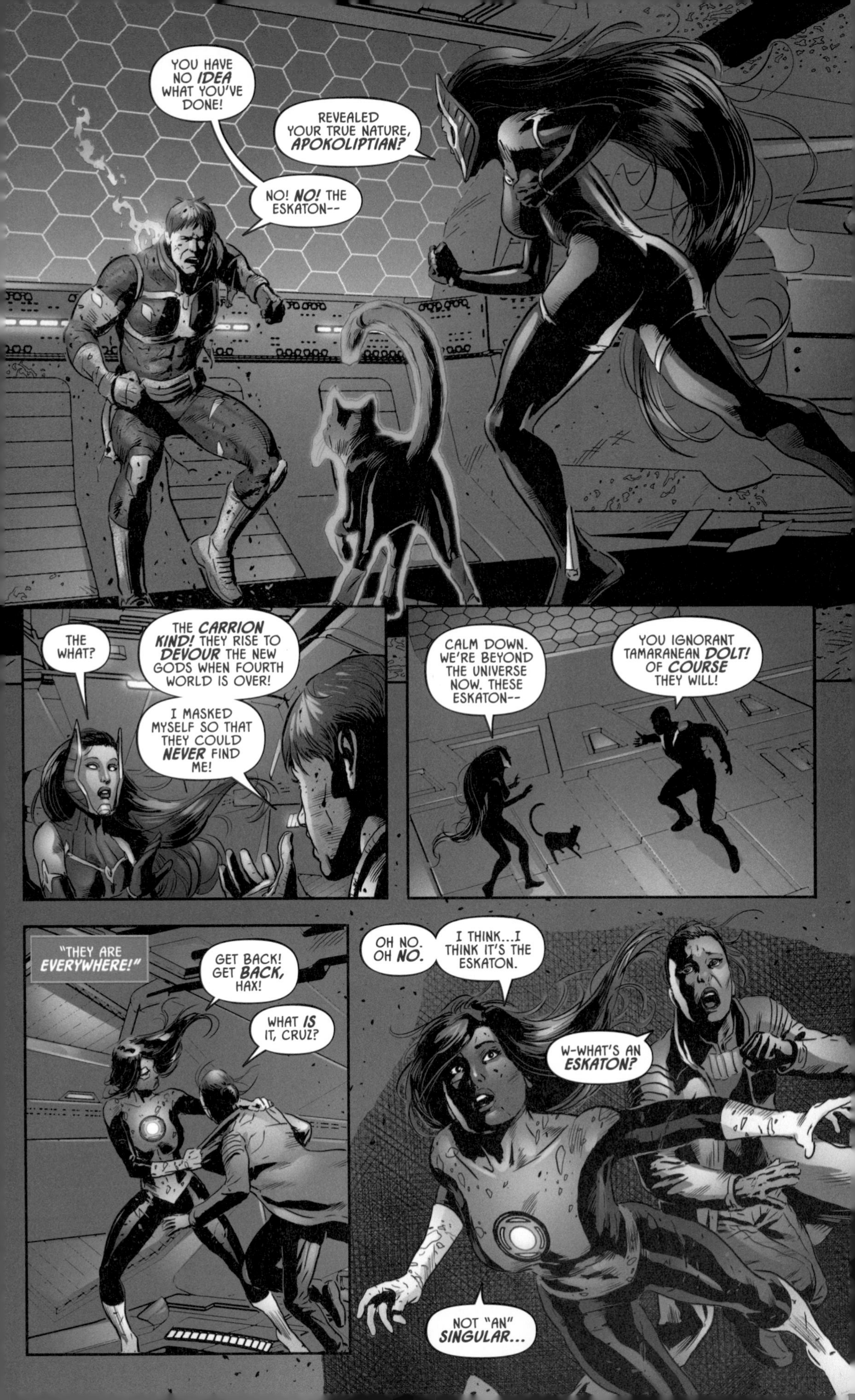
YOU HAVE NO IDEA WHAT YOU'VE DONE!
REVEALED YOUR TRUE NATURE, APOKOLIPTIAN?
NO! NO! THE ESKATON--
THE WHAT?
THE CARRION KIND! THEY RISE TO DEVOUR THE NEW GODS WHEN FOURTH WORLD IS OVER!
I MASKED MYSELF SO THAT THEY COULD NEVER FIND ME!
CALM DOWN. WE'RE BEYOND THE UNIVERSE NOW. THESE ESKATON--
YOU IGNORANT TAMARANEAN DOLT! OF COURSE THEY WILL!
"THEY ARE EVERYWHERE!"
GET BACK! GET BACK, HAX!
WHAT IS IT, CRUZ?
OH NO. OH NO.
I THINK...I THINK IT'S THE ESKATON.
W-WHAT'S AN ESKATON?
NOT "AN" SINGULAR...

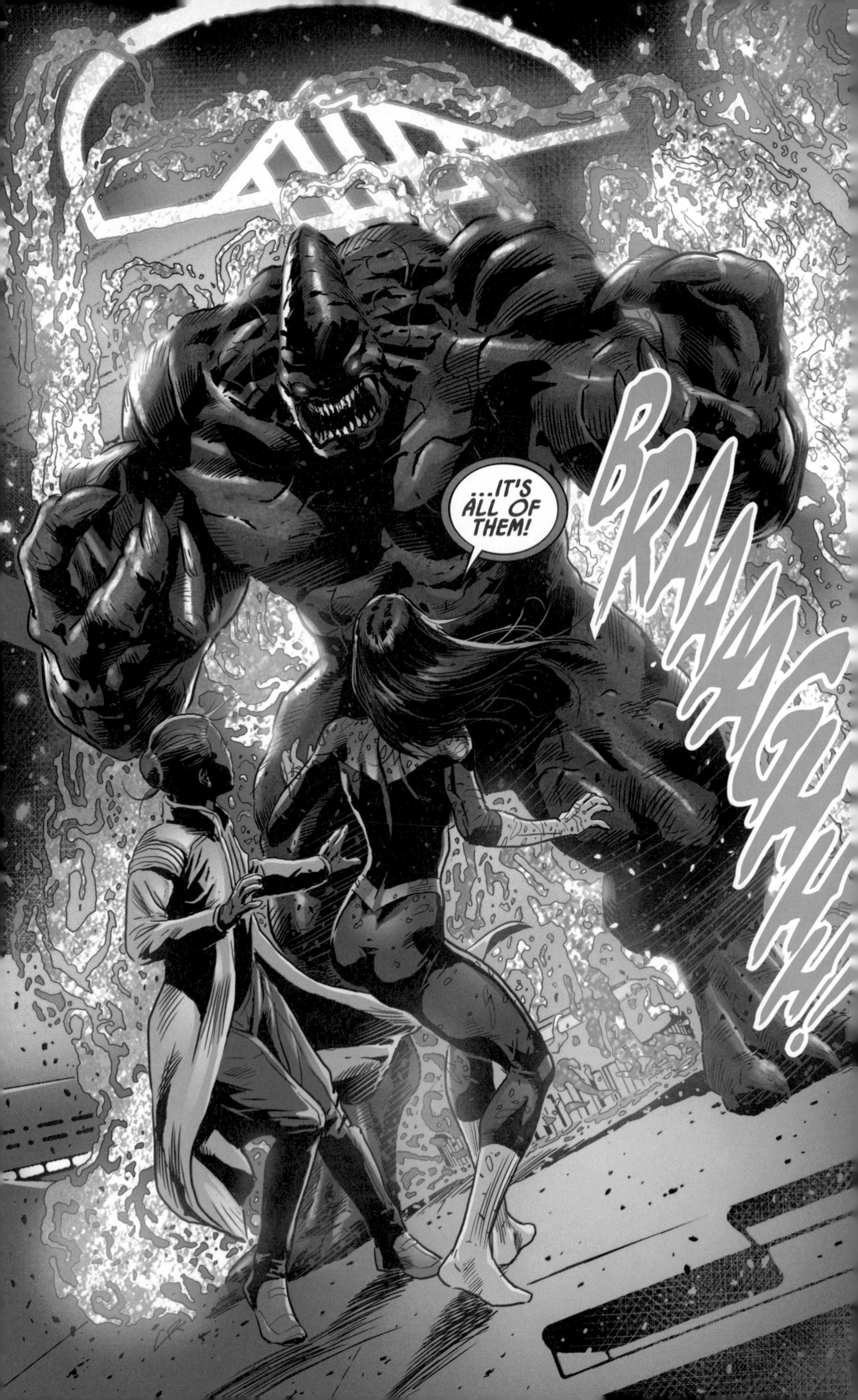
...IT'S ALL OF THEM!
BRAAAGHHH!!

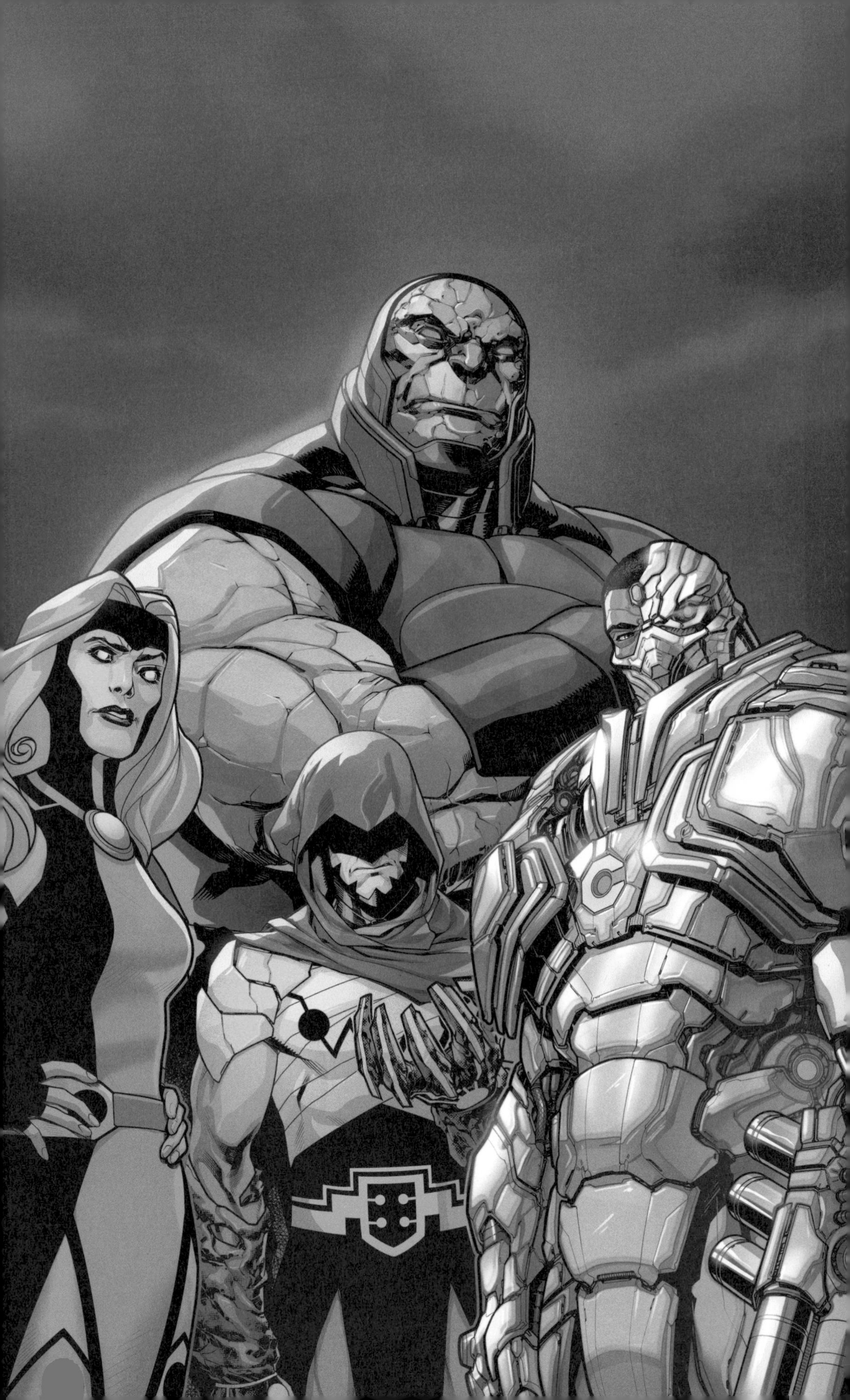

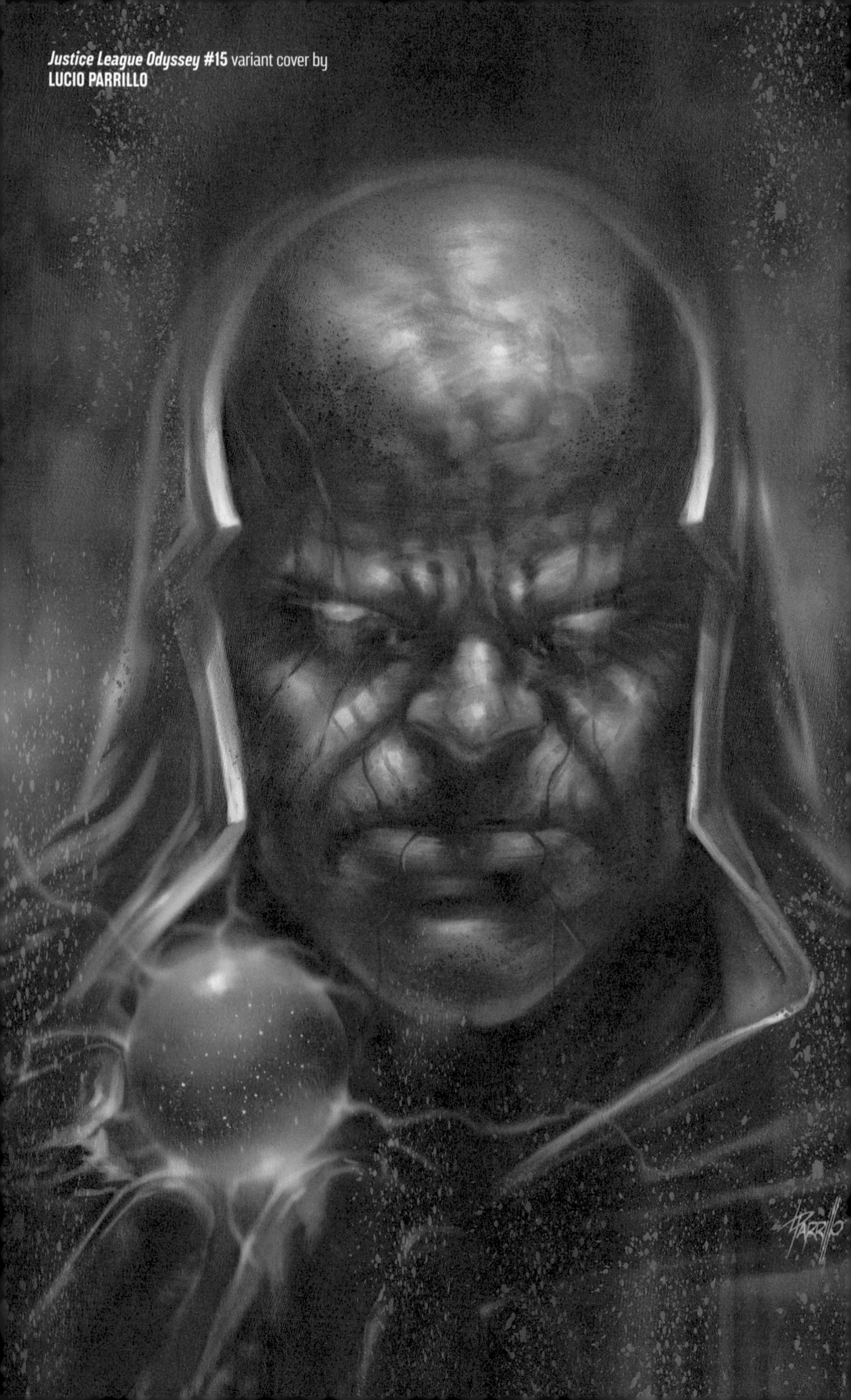

Justice League Odyssey **#15** variant cover by
LUCIO PARRILLO

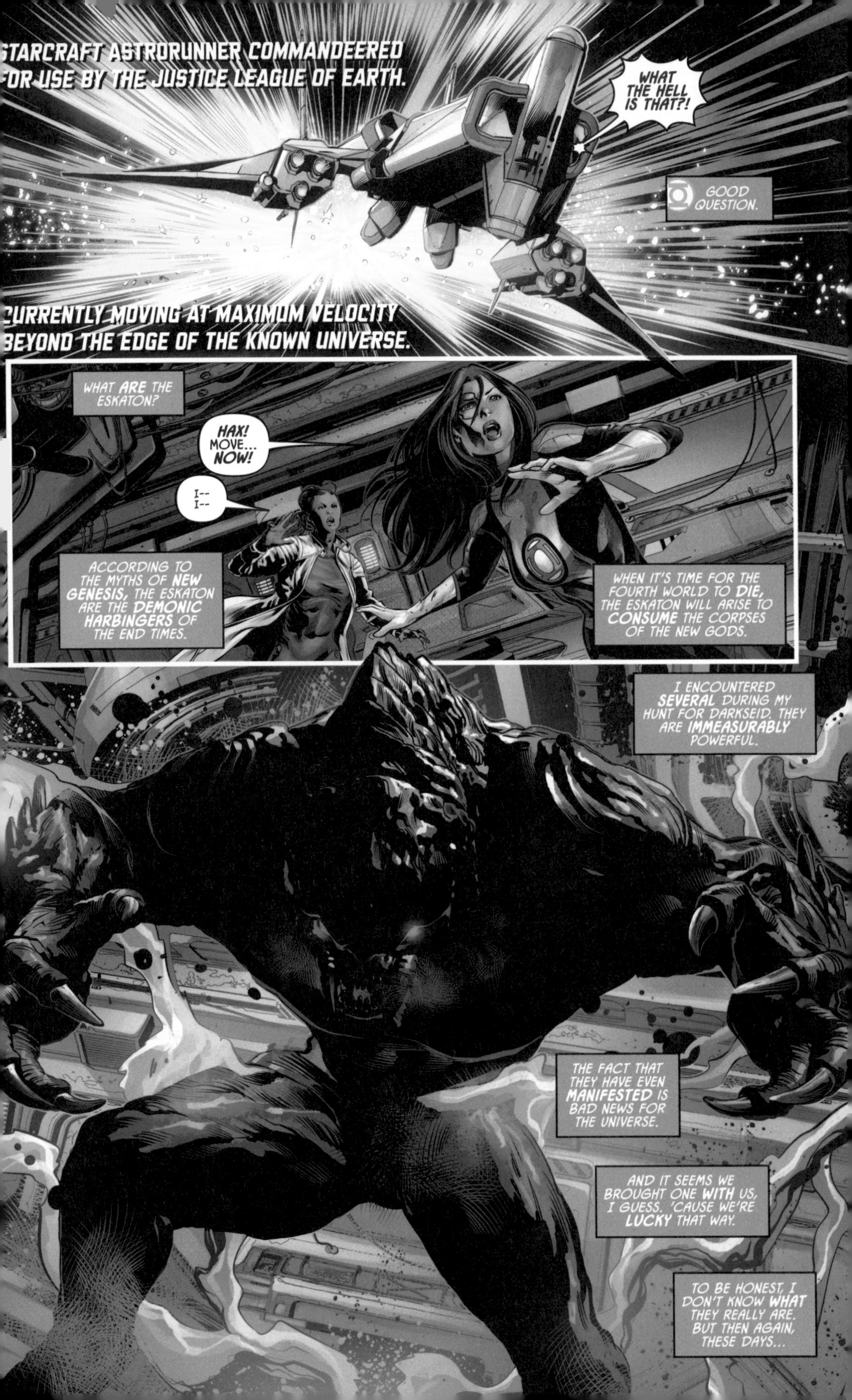

STARCRAFT ASTRORUNNER COMMANDEERED FOR USE BY THE JUSTICE LEAGUE OF EARTH.
WHAT THE HELL IS THAT?!
GOOD QUESTION.
CURRENTLY MOVING AT MAXIMUM VELOCITY BEYOND THE EDGE OF THE KNOWN UNIVERSE.
WHAT ARE THE ESKATON?
HAX! MOVE... NOW!
I-- I--
ACCORDING TO THE MYTHS OF NEW GENESIS, THE ESKATON ARE THE DEMONIC HARBINGERS OF THE END TIMES.
WHEN IT'S TIME FOR THE FOURTH WORLD TO DIE, THE ESKATON WILL ARISE TO CONSUME THE CORPSES OF THE NEW GODS.
I ENCOUNTERED SEVERAL DURING MY HUNT FOR DARKSEID. THEY ARE IMMEASURABLY POWERFUL.
THE FACT THAT THEY HAVE EVEN MANIFESTED IS BAD NEWS FOR THE UNIVERSE.
AND IT SEEMS WE BROUGHT ONE WITH US, I GUESS. 'CAUSE WE'RE LUCKY THAT WAY.
TO BE HONEST, I DON'T KNOW WHAT THEY REALLY ARE. BUT THEN AGAIN, THESE DAYS...

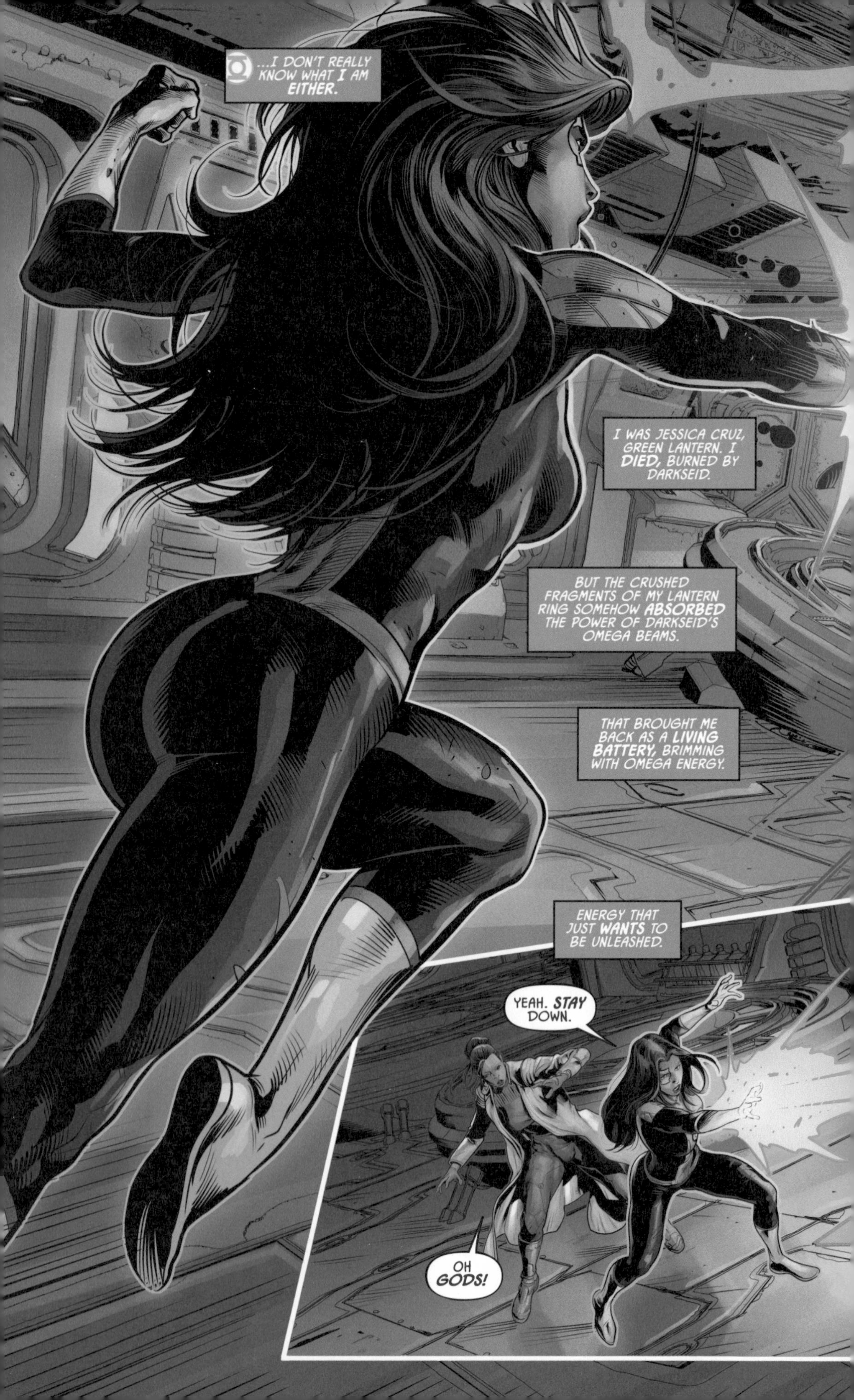
...I DON'T REALLY KNOW WHAT I AM EITHER.
I WAS JESSICA CRUZ, GREEN LANTERN. I DIED, BURNED BY DARKSEID.
BUT THE CRUSHED FRAGMENTS OF MY LANTERN RING SOMEHOW ABSORBED THE POWER OF DARKSEID'S OMEGA BEAMS.
THAT BROUGHT ME BACK AS A LIVING BATTERY, BRIMMING WITH OMEGA ENERGY.
ENERGY THAT JUST WANTS TO BE UNLEASHED.
YEAH. STAY DOWN.
OH GODS!

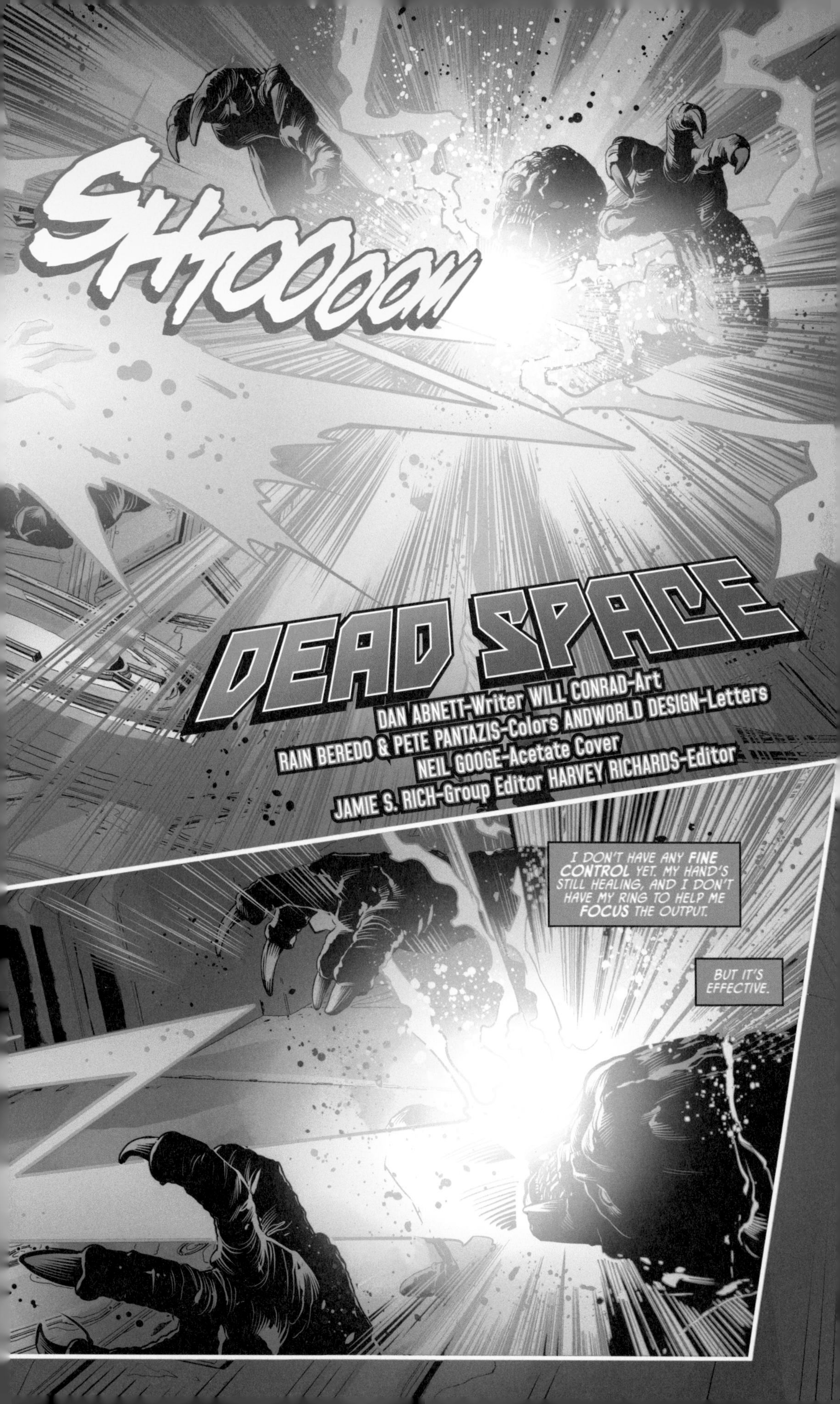

SHOOOOM
DEAD SPACE
DAN ABNETT-Writer WILL CONRAD-Art
RAIN BEREDO & PETE PANTAZIS-Colors ANDWORLD DESIGN-Letters
NEIL GOOGE-Acetate Cover
JAMIE S. RICH-Group Editor HARVEY RICHARDS-Editor
I DON'T HAVE ANY FINE CONTROL YET. MY HAND'S STILL HEALING, AND I DON'T HAVE MY RING TO HELP ME FOCUS THE OUTPUT.
BUT IT'S EFFECTIVE.

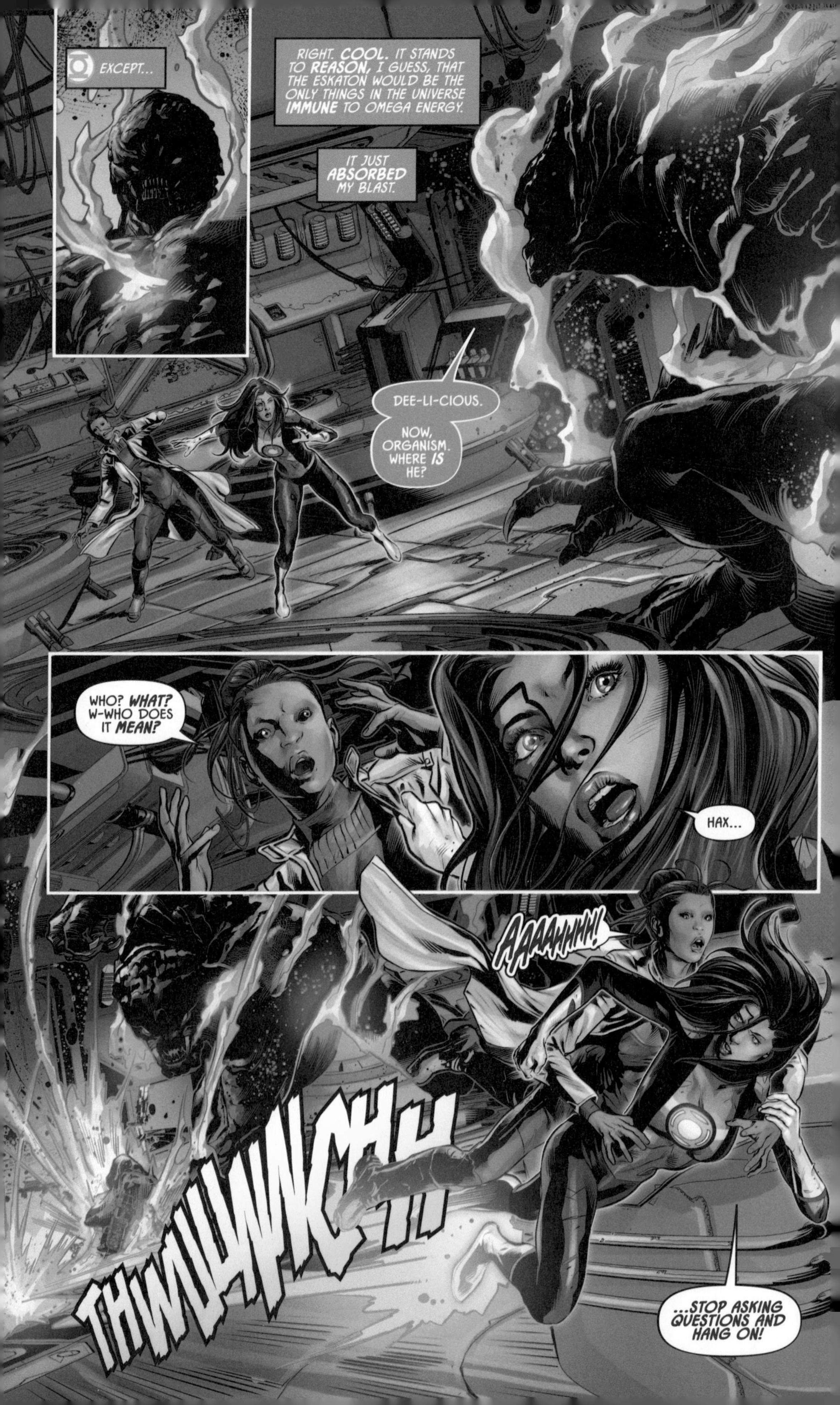
EXCEPT...
RIGHT. COOL. IT STANDS TO REASON, I GUESS, THAT THE ESKATON WOULD BE THE ONLY THINGS IN THE UNIVERSE IMMUNE TO OMEGA ENERGY.
IT JUST ABSORBED MY BLAST.
DEE-LI-CIOUS.
NOW, ORGANISM. WHERE IS HE?
WHO? WHAT? W-WHO DOES IT MEAN?
HAX...
AAAAHHHH!
THWUWNCHH
...STOP ASKING QUESTIONS AND HANG ON!

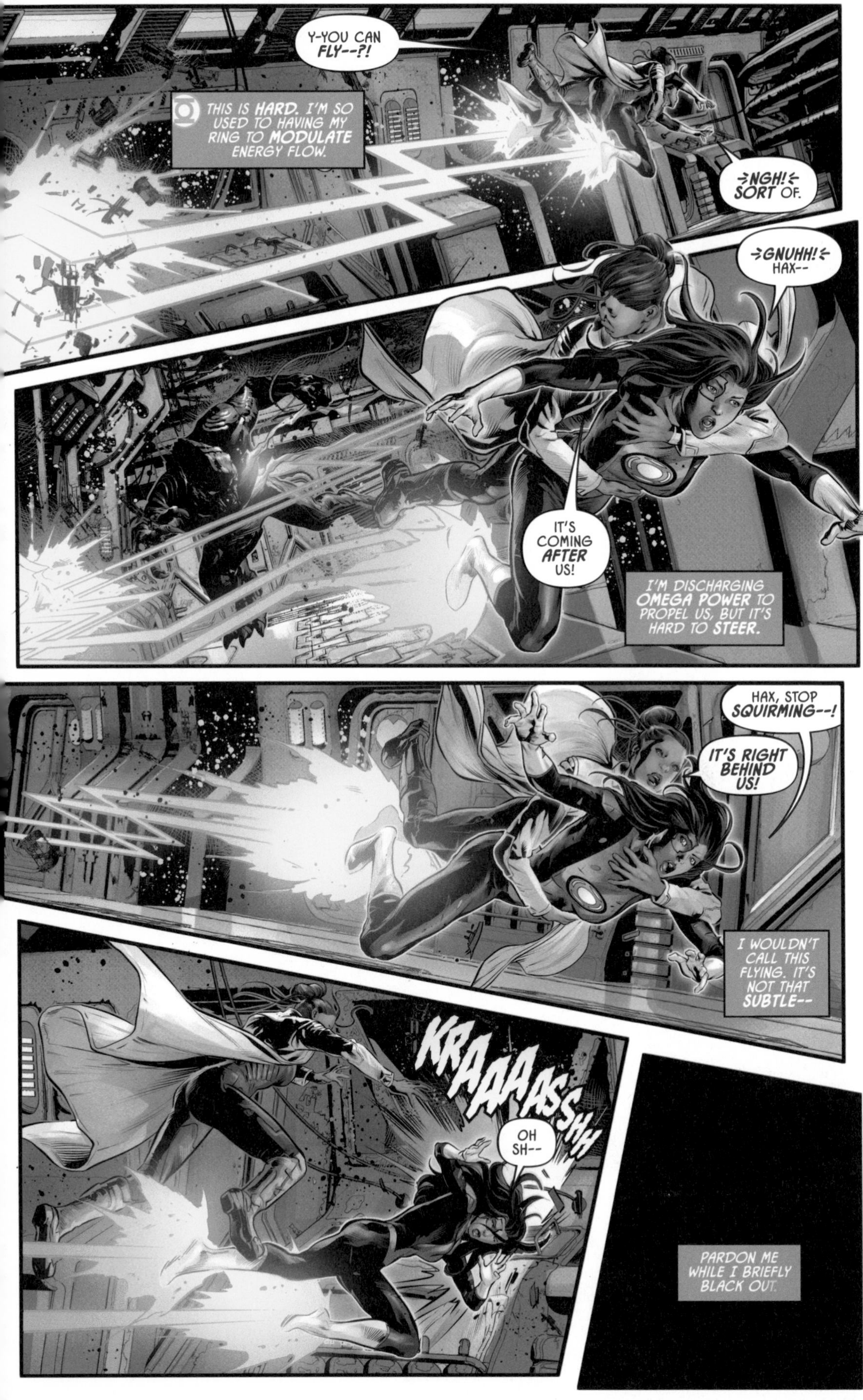

Y-YOU CAN FLY--?!
THIS IS HARD. I'M SO USED TO HAVING MY RING TO MODULATE ENERGY FLOW.
NGH! SORT OF.
GNUHH! HAX--
IT'S COMING AFTER US!
I'M DISCHARGING OMEGA POWER TO PROPEL US, BUT IT'S HARD TO STEER.
HAX, STOP SQUIRMING--!
IT'S RIGHT BEHIND US!
I WOULDN'T CALL THIS FLYING. IT'S NOT THAT SUBTLE--
KRAAAASSHH
OH SH--
PARDON ME WHILE I BRIEFLY BLACK OUT.

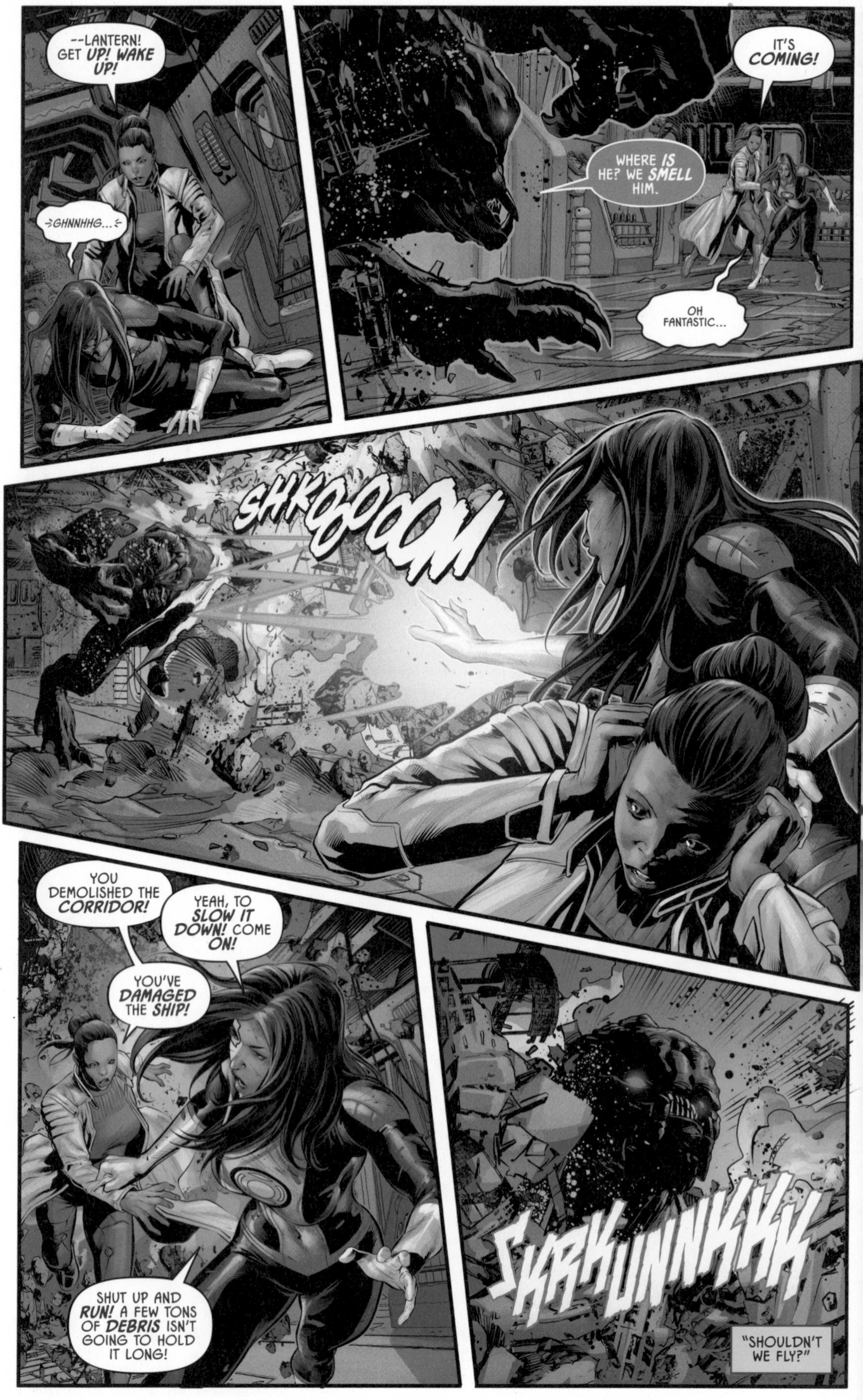

--LANTERN! GET UP! WAKE UP!
≷GHNNHHG...≶
IT'S COMING!
WHERE IS HE? WE SMELL HIM.
OH FANTASTIC...
SHKOOOOOM
YOU DEMOLISHED THE CORRIDOR!
YEAH, TO SLOW IT DOWN! COME ON!
YOU'VE DAMAGED THE SHIP!
SHUT UP AND RUN! A FEW TONS OF DEBRIS ISN'T GOING TO HOLD IT LONG!
SKRKUNNKKK
"SHOULDN'T WE FLY?"

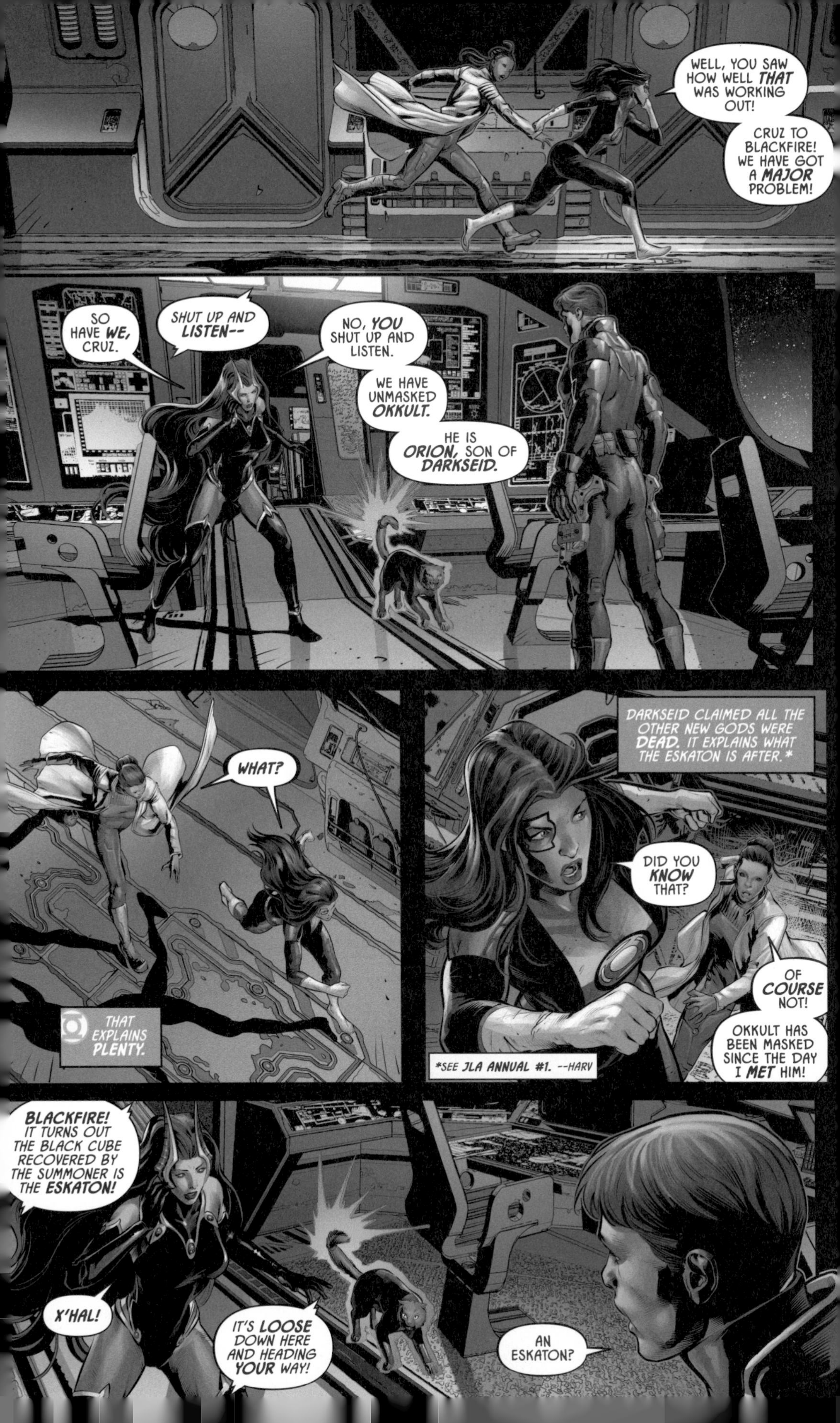
WELL, YOU SAW HOW WELL THAT WAS WORKING OUT!
CRUZ TO BLACKFIRE! WE HAVE GOT A MAJOR PROBLEM!
SO HAVE WE, CRUZ.
SHUT UP AND LISTEN--
NO, YOU SHUT UP AND LISTEN.
WE HAVE UNMASKED OKKULT.
HE IS ORION, SON OF DARKSEID.
WHAT?
THAT EXPLAINS PLENTY.
DARKSEID CLAIMED ALL THE OTHER NEW GODS WERE DEAD. IT EXPLAINS WHAT THE ESKATON IS AFTER.*
DID YOU KNOW THAT?
OF COURSE NOT!
OKKULT HAS BEEN MASKED SINCE THE DAY I MET HIM!
*SEE JLA ANNUAL #1. --HARV
BLACKFIRE! IT TURNS OUT THE BLACK CUBE RECOVERED BY THE SUMMONER IS THE ESKATON!
X'HAL!
IT'S LOOSE DOWN HERE AND HEADING YOUR WAY!
AN ESKATON?

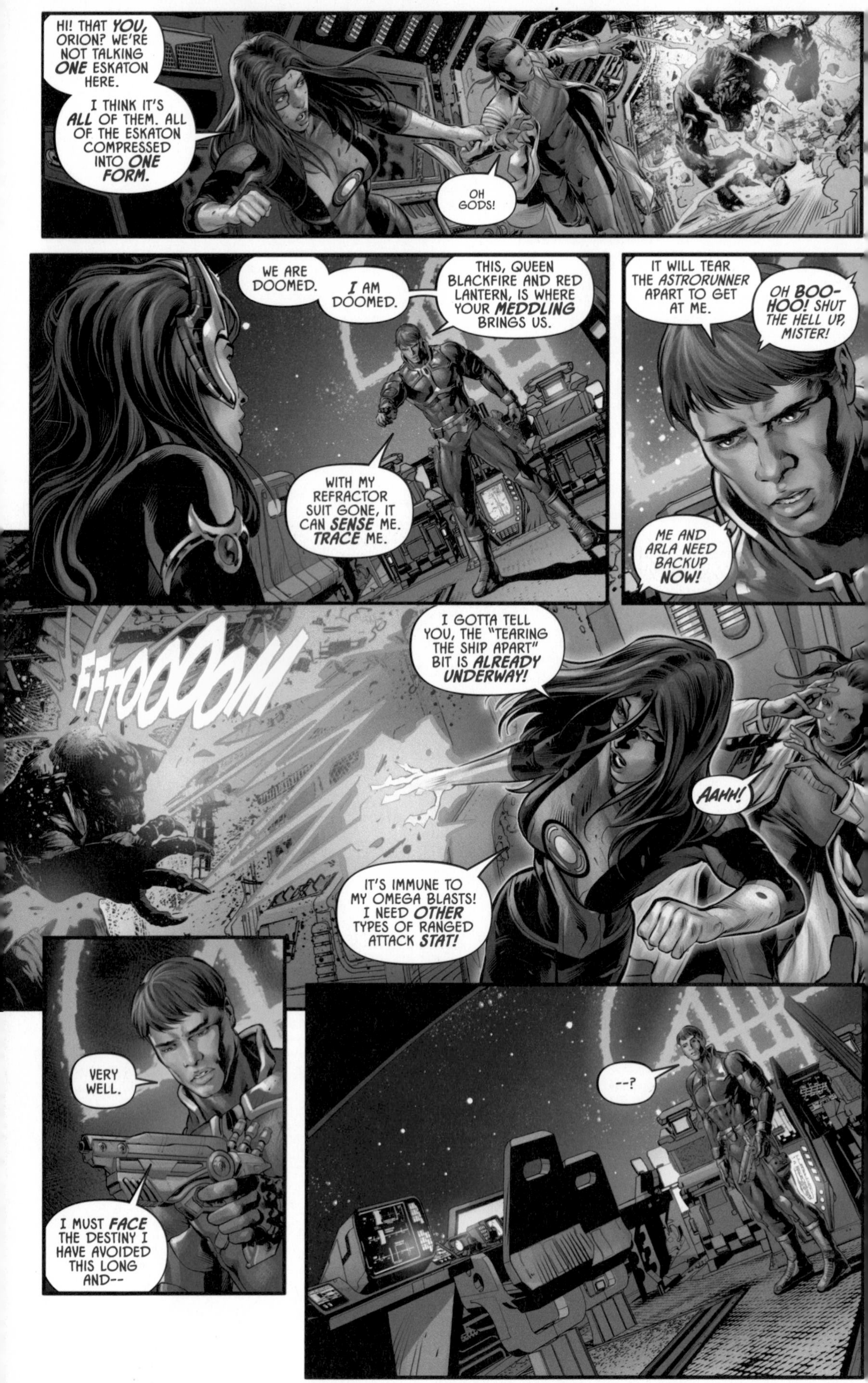
HI! THAT YOU, ORION? WE'RE NOT TALKING ONE ESKATON HERE.
I THINK IT'S ALL OF THEM. ALL OF THE ESKATON COMPRESSED INTO ONE FORM.
OH GODS!
WE ARE DOOMED.
I AM DOOMED.
THIS, QUEEN BLACKFIRE AND RED LANTERN, IS WHERE YOUR MEDDLING BRINGS US.
WITH MY REFRACTOR SUIT GONE, IT CAN SENSE ME. TRACE ME.
IT WILL TEAR THE ASTRORUNNER APART TO GET AT ME.
OH BOO-HOO! SHUT THE HELL UP, MISTER!
ME AND ARLA NEED BACKUP NOW!
FFTOOOOM
I GOTTA TELL YOU, THE "TEARING THE SHIP APART" BIT IS ALREADY UNDERWAY!
AAHH!
IT'S IMMUNE TO MY OMEGA BLASTS! I NEED OTHER TYPES OF RANGED ATTACK STAT!
VERY WELL.
I MUST FACE THE DESTINY I HAVE AVOIDED THIS LONG AND--
--?

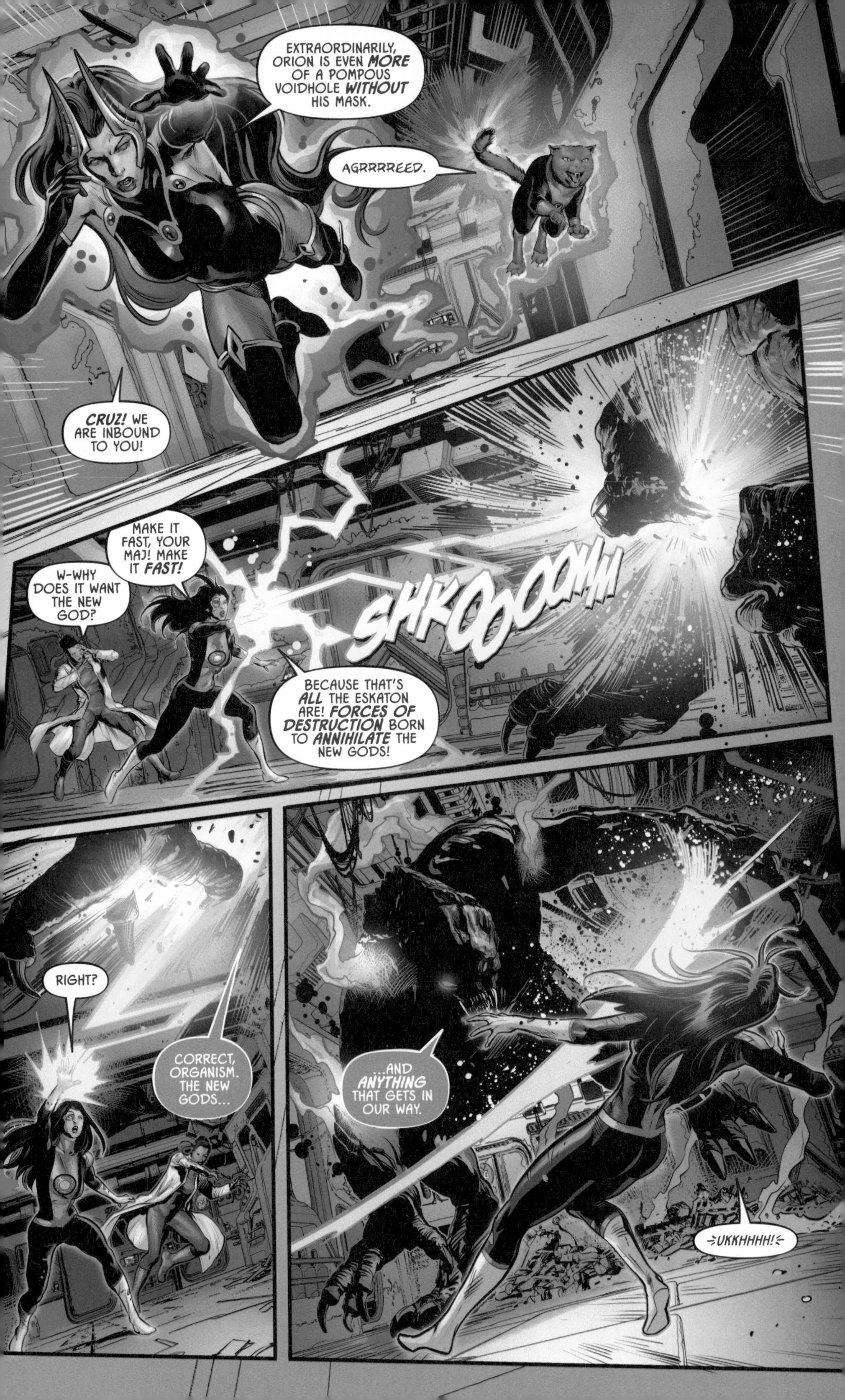
EXTRAORDINARILY, ORION IS EVEN MORE OF A POMPOUS VOIDHOLE WITHOUT HIS MASK.
AGRRRREED.
CRUZ! WE ARE INBOUND TO YOU!
MAKE IT FAST, YOUR MAJ! MAKE IT FAST!
W-WHY DOES IT WANT THE NEW GOD?
SHKOOOOMM
BECAUSE THAT'S ALL THE ESKATON ARE! FORCES OF DESTRUCTION BORN TO ANNIHILATE THE NEW GODS!
RIGHT?
CORRECT, ORGANISM. THE NEW GODS...
...AND ANYTHING THAT GETS IN OUR WAY.
UKKHHHH!

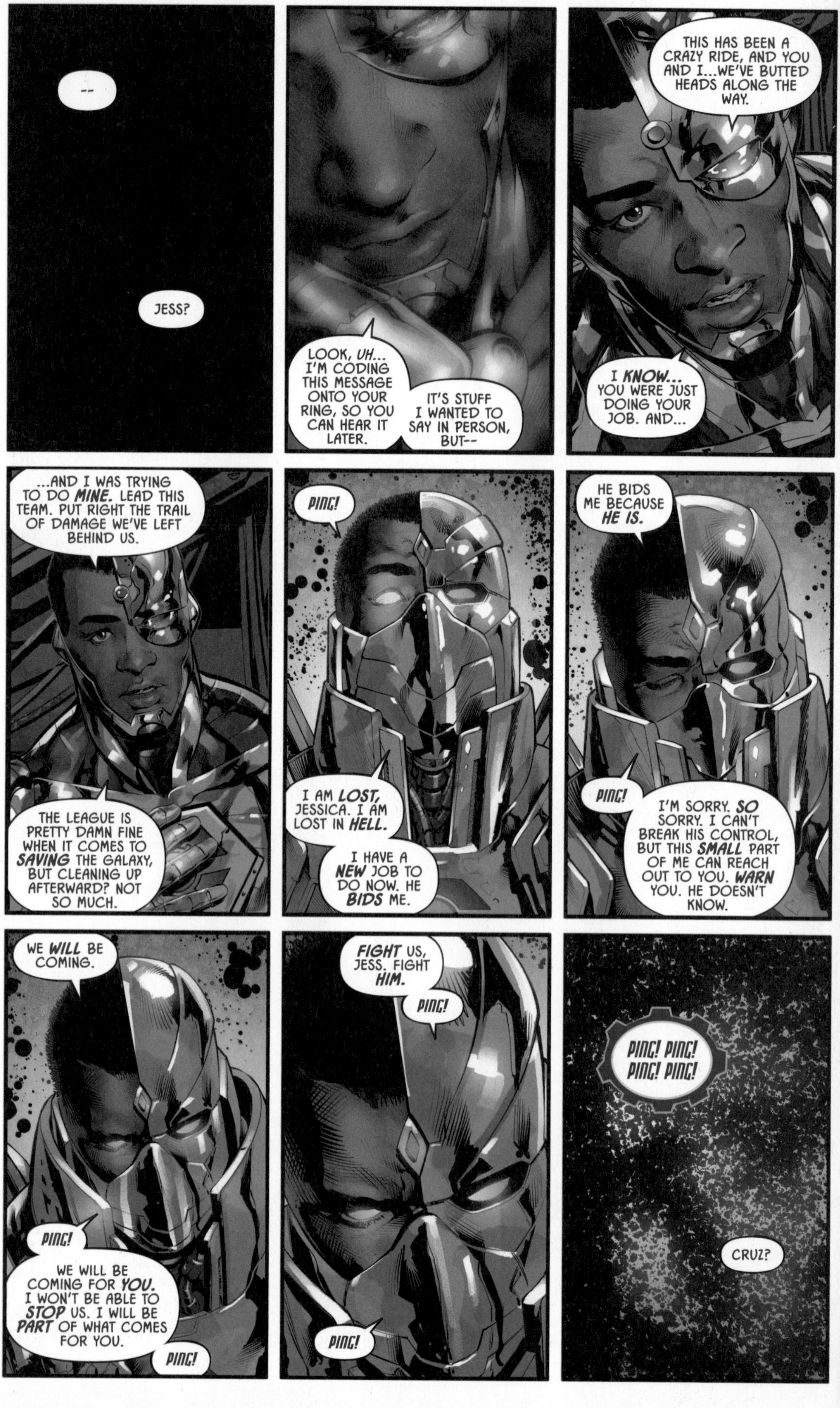
--
JESS?
LOOK, UH... I'M CODING THIS MESSAGE ONTO YOUR RING, SO YOU CAN HEAR IT LATER.
IT'S STUFF I WANTED TO SAY IN PERSON, BUT--
THIS HAS BEEN A CRAZY RIDE, AND YOU AND I...WE'VE BUTTED HEADS ALONG THE WAY.
I KNOW... YOU WERE JUST DOING YOUR JOB. AND...
...AND I WAS TRYING TO DO MINE. LEAD THIS TEAM. PUT RIGHT THE TRAIL OF DAMAGE WE'VE LEFT BEHIND US.
THE LEAGUE IS PRETTY DAMN FINE WHEN IT COMES TO SAVING THE GALAXY, BUT CLEANING UP AFTERWARD? NOT SO MUCH.
PING!
I AM LOST, JESSICA. I AM LOST IN HELL.
I HAVE A NEW JOB TO DO NOW. HE BIDS ME.
HE BIDS ME BECAUSE HE IS.
PING!
I'M SORRY. SO SORRY. I CAN'T BREAK HIS CONTROL, BUT THIS SMALL PART OF ME CAN REACH OUT TO YOU. WARN YOU. HE DOESN'T KNOW.
WE WILL BE COMING.
PING!
WE WILL BE COMING FOR YOU. I WON'T BE ABLE TO STOP US. I WILL BE PART OF WHAT COMES FOR YOU.
PING!
FIGHT US, JESS. FIGHT HIM.
PING!
PING!
PING! PING! PING! PING!
CRUZ?

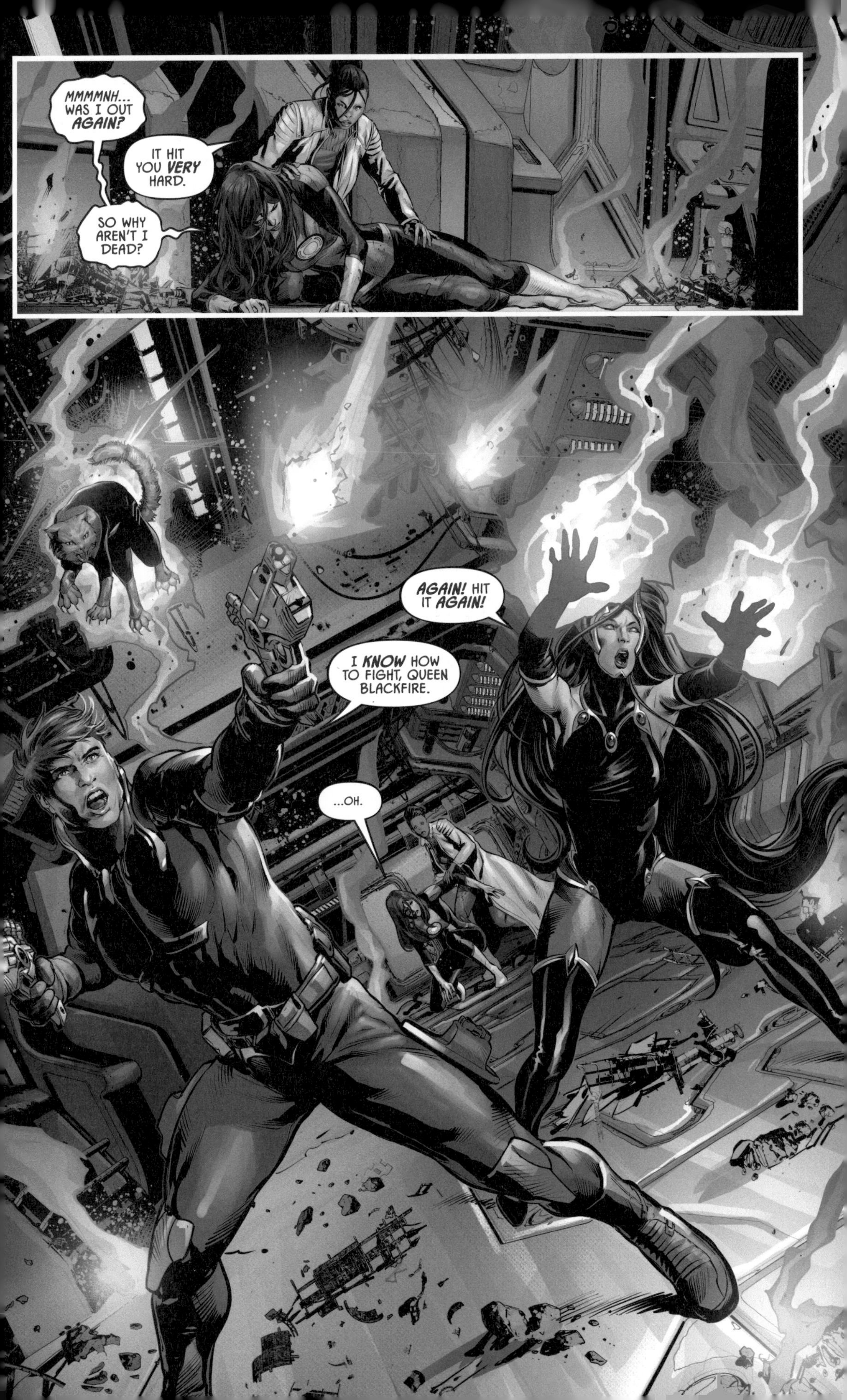
MMMMNH... WAS I OUT AGAIN?
IT HIT YOU VERY HARD.
SO WHY AREN'T I DEAD?
AGAIN! HIT IT AGAIN!
I KNOW HOW TO FIGHT, QUEEN BLACKFIRE.
...OH.

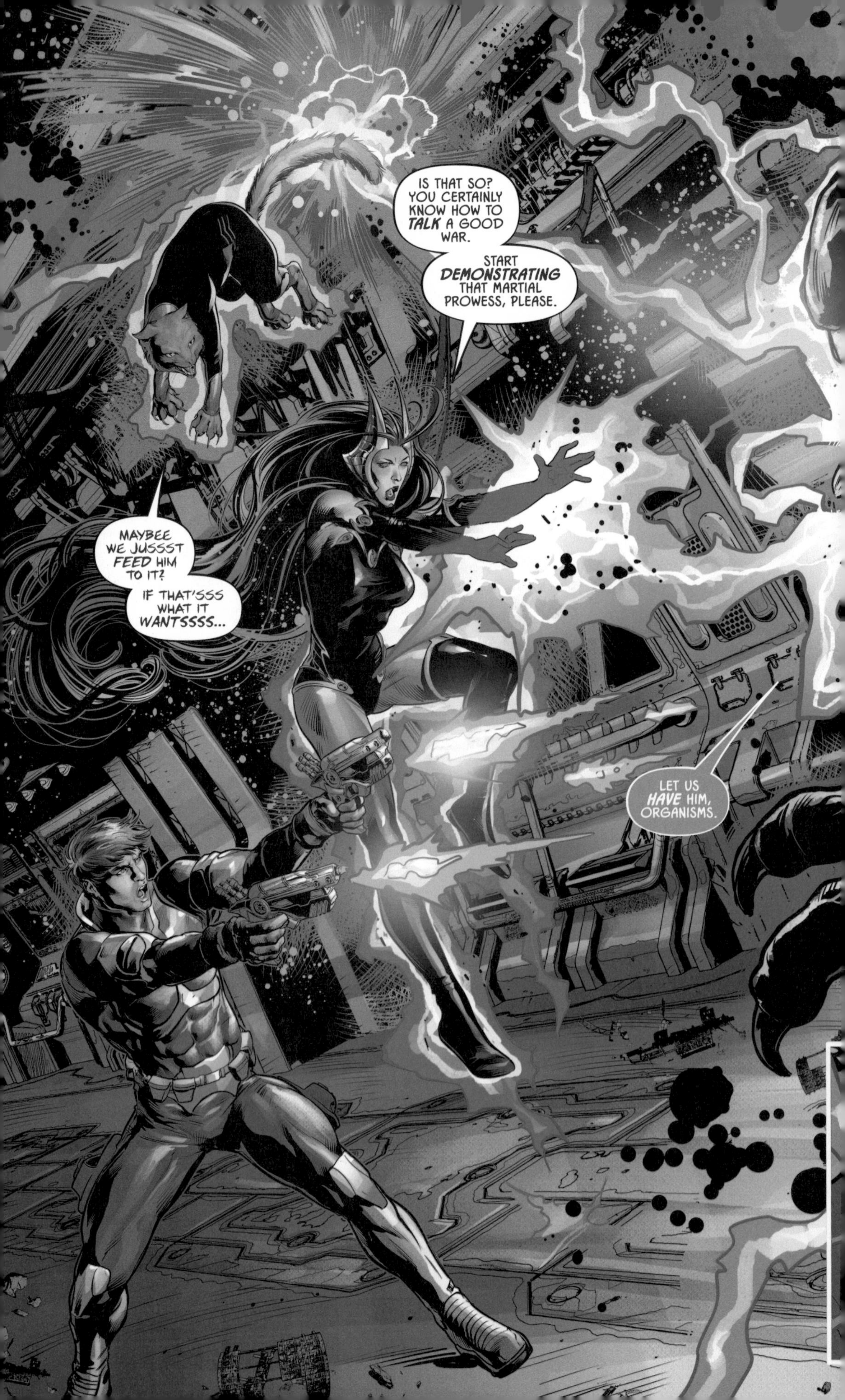
IS THAT SO? YOU CERTAINLY KNOW HOW TO TALK A GOOD WAR.
START DEMONSTRATING THAT MARTIAL PROWESS, PLEASE.
MAYBEE WE JUSSST FEED HIM TO IT?
IF THAT'SSS WHAT IT WANTSSSS...
LET US HAVE HIM, ORGANISMS.

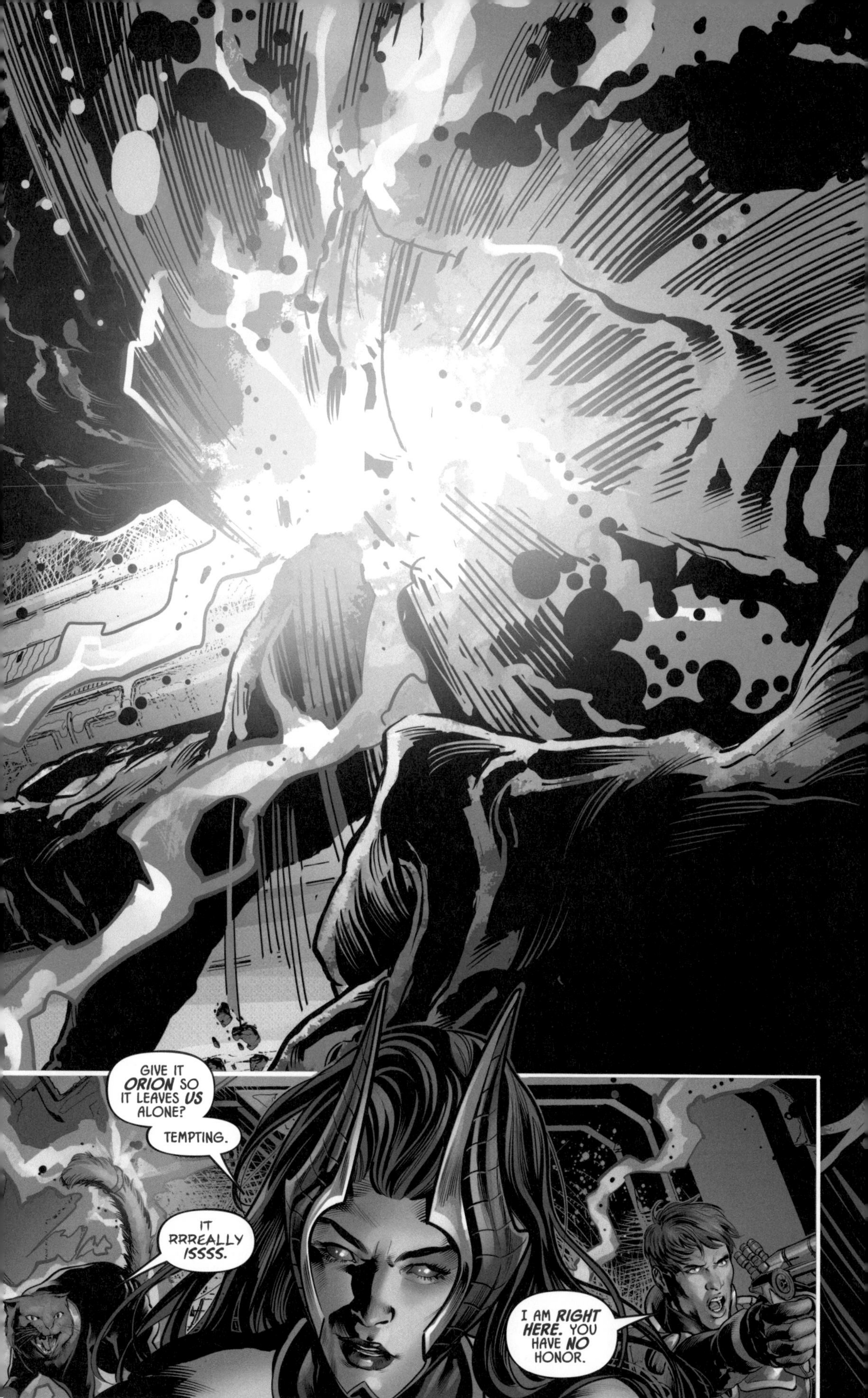
GIVE IT ORION SO IT LEAVES US ALONE?
TEMPTING.
IT RRREALLY ISSSS.
I AM RIGHT HERE. YOU HAVE NO HONOR.

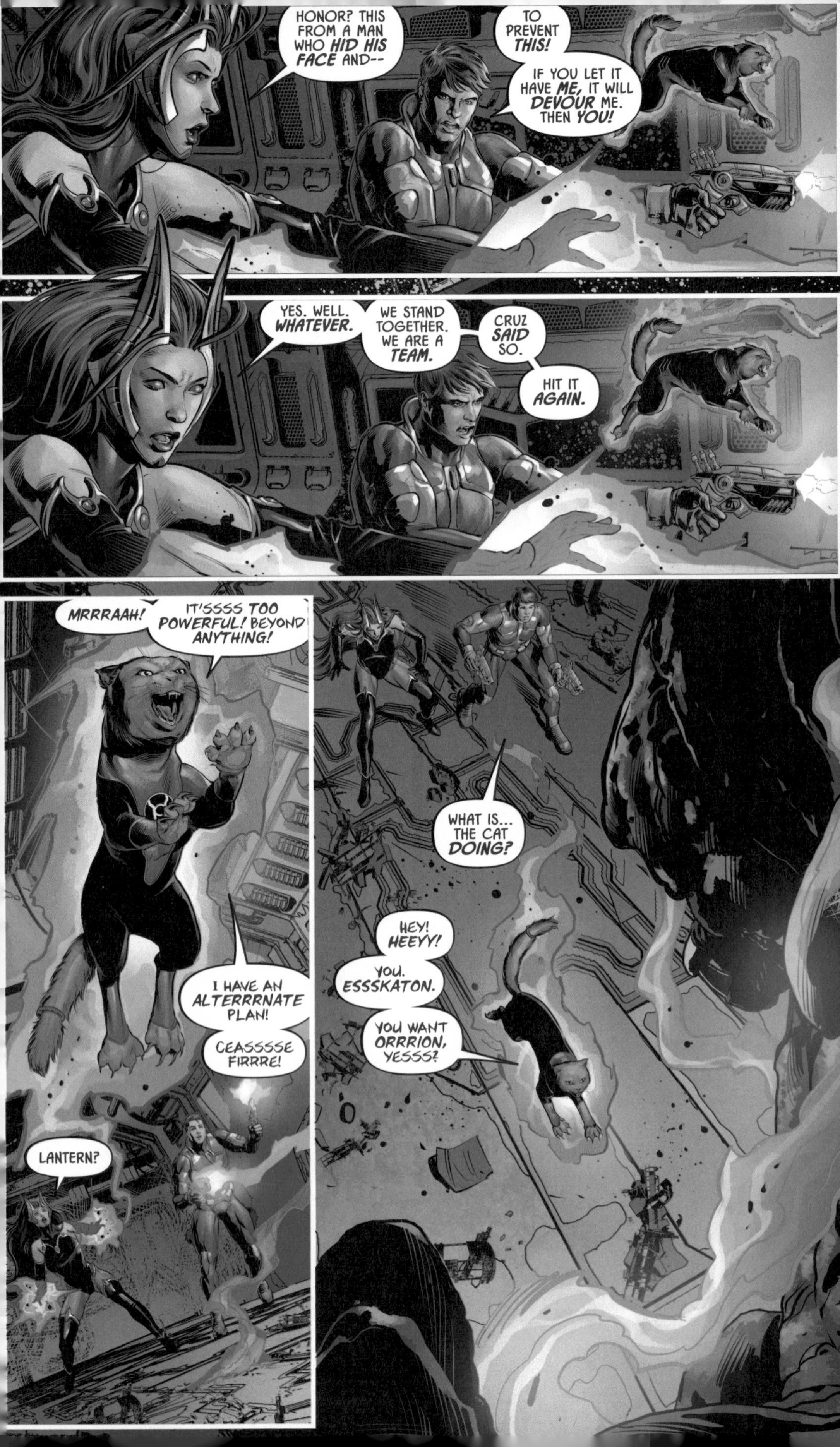

HONOR? THIS FROM A MAN WHO HID HIS FACE AND--
TO PREVENT THIS!
IF YOU LET IT HAVE ME, IT WILL DEVOUR ME. THEN YOU!
YES. WELL. WHATEVER.
WE STAND TOGETHER. WE ARE A TEAM.
CRUZ SAID SO.
HIT IT AGAIN.
MRRRAAH!
IT'SSSS TOO POWERFUL! BEYOND ANYTHING!
I HAVE AN ALTERRRNATE PLAN!
CEASSSSE FIRRRE!
LANTERN?
WHAT IS... THE CAT DOING?
HEY! HEEYY!
YOU. ESSSKATON.
YOU WANT ORRRION, YESSS?

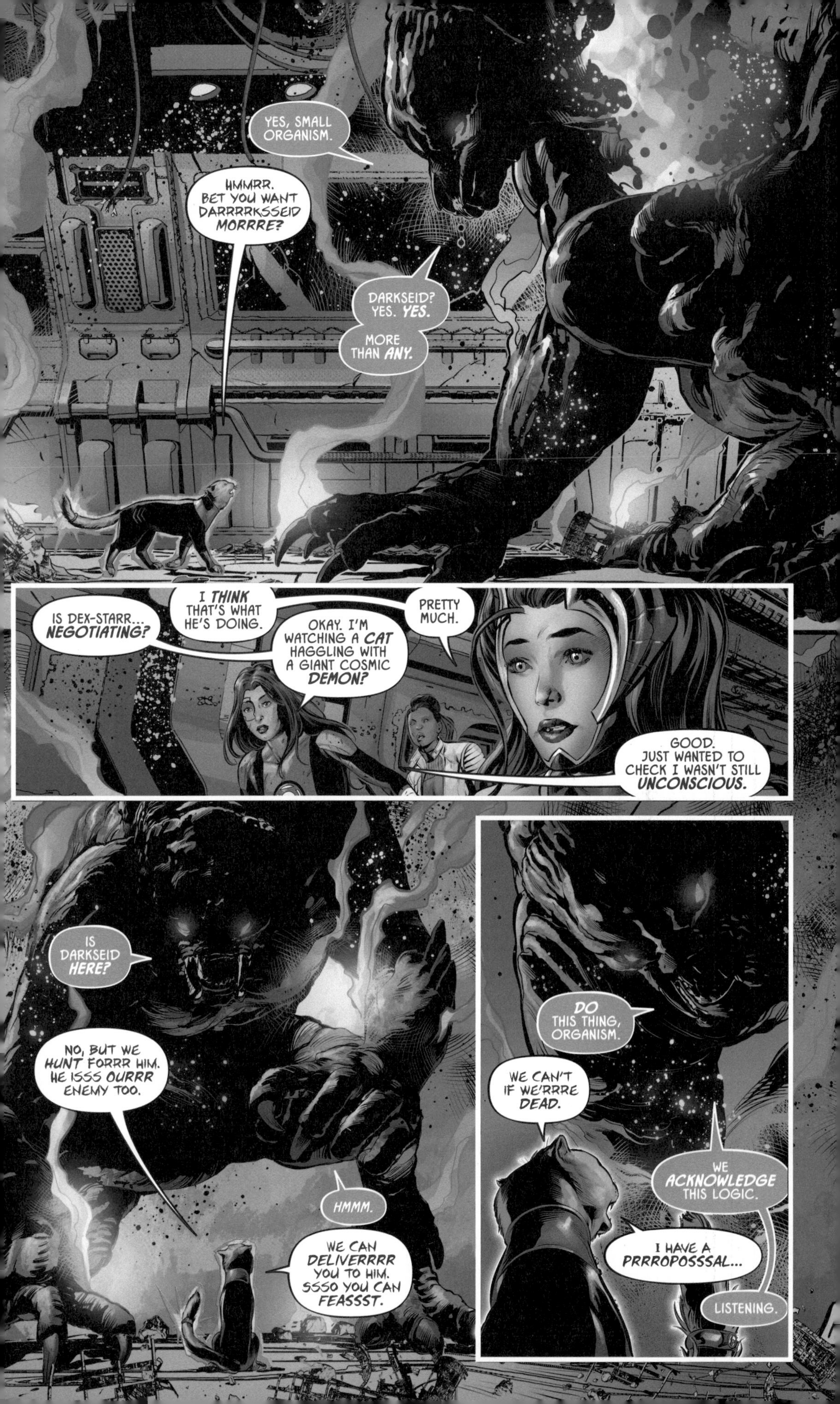
YES, SMALL ORGANISM.
HMMRR. BET YOU WANT DARRRRKSSEID MORRRE?
DARKSEID? YES. YES.
MORE THAN ANY.
IS DEX-STARR... NEGOTIATING?
I THINK THAT'S WHAT HE'S DOING.
OKAY. I'M WATCHING A CAT HAGGLING WITH A GIANT COSMIC DEMON?
PRETTY MUCH.
GOOD. JUST WANTED TO CHECK I WASN'T STILL UNCONSCIOUS.
IS DARKSEID HERE?
NO, BUT WE HUNT FORRR HIM. HE ISSS OURRR ENEMY TOO.
HMMM.
WE CAN DELIVERRRR YOU TO HIM. SSSO YOU CAN FEASSST.
DO THIS THING, ORGANISM.
WE CAN'T IF WE'RRRE DEAD.
WE ACKNOWLEDGE THIS LOGIC.
I HAVE A PRRROPOSSSAL...
LISTENING.

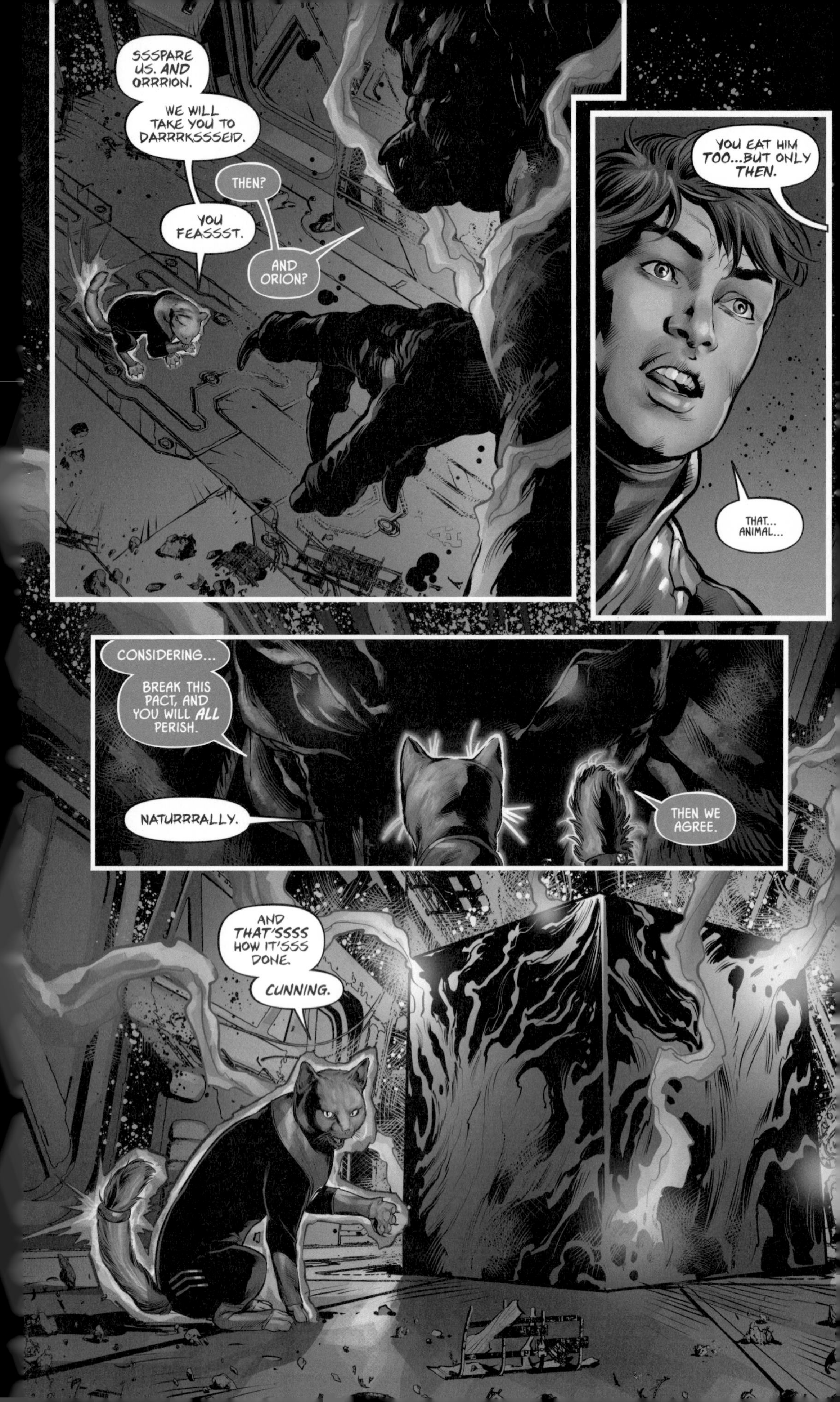

SSSPARE US. AND ORRRION.
WE WILL TAKE YOU TO DARRRKSSSEID.
THEN?
YOU FEASSST.
AND ORION?
YOU EAT HIM TOO...BUT ONLY THEN.
THAT... ANIMAL...
CONSIDERING...
BREAK THIS PACT, AND YOU WILL ALL PERISH.
NATURRRALLY.
THEN WE AGREE.
AND THAT'SSSS HOW IT'SSS DONE.
CUNNING.

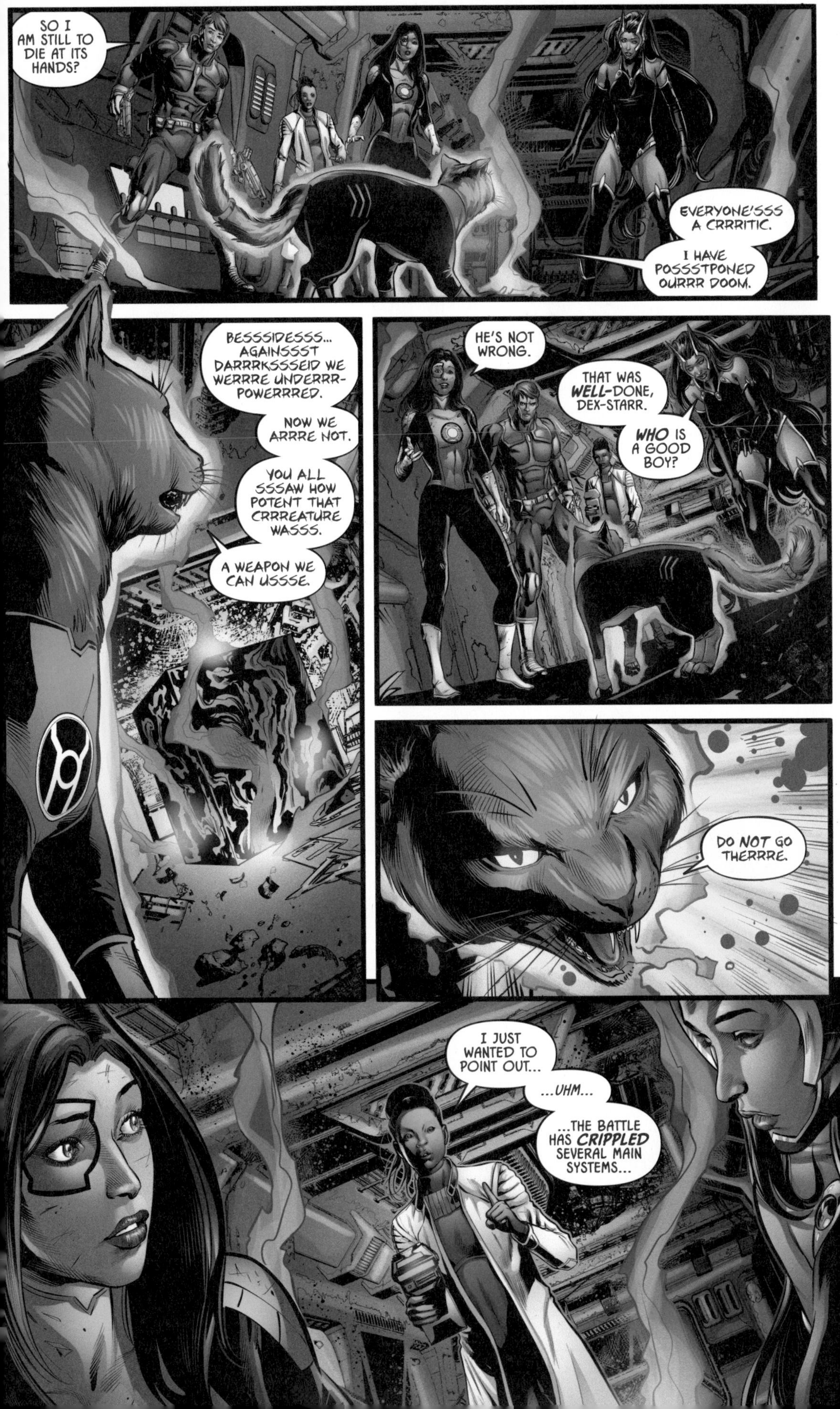
SO I AM STILL TO DIE AT ITS HANDS?
EVERYONE'SSS A CRRRITIC.
I HAVE POSSSTPONED OURRR DOOM.
BESSSIDESSS... AGAINSSST DARRRKSSSEID WE WERRRE UNDERRR-POWERRRED.
NOW WE ARRRE NOT.
YOU ALL SSSAW HOW POTENT THAT CRRREATURE WASSS.
A WEAPON WE CAN USSSE.
HE'S NOT WRONG.
THAT WAS WELL-DONE, DEX-STARR.
WHO IS A GOOD BOY?
DO NOT GO THERRRE.
I JUST WANTED TO POINT OUT...
...UHM...
...THE BATTLE HAS CRIPPLED SEVERAL MAIN SYSTEMS...

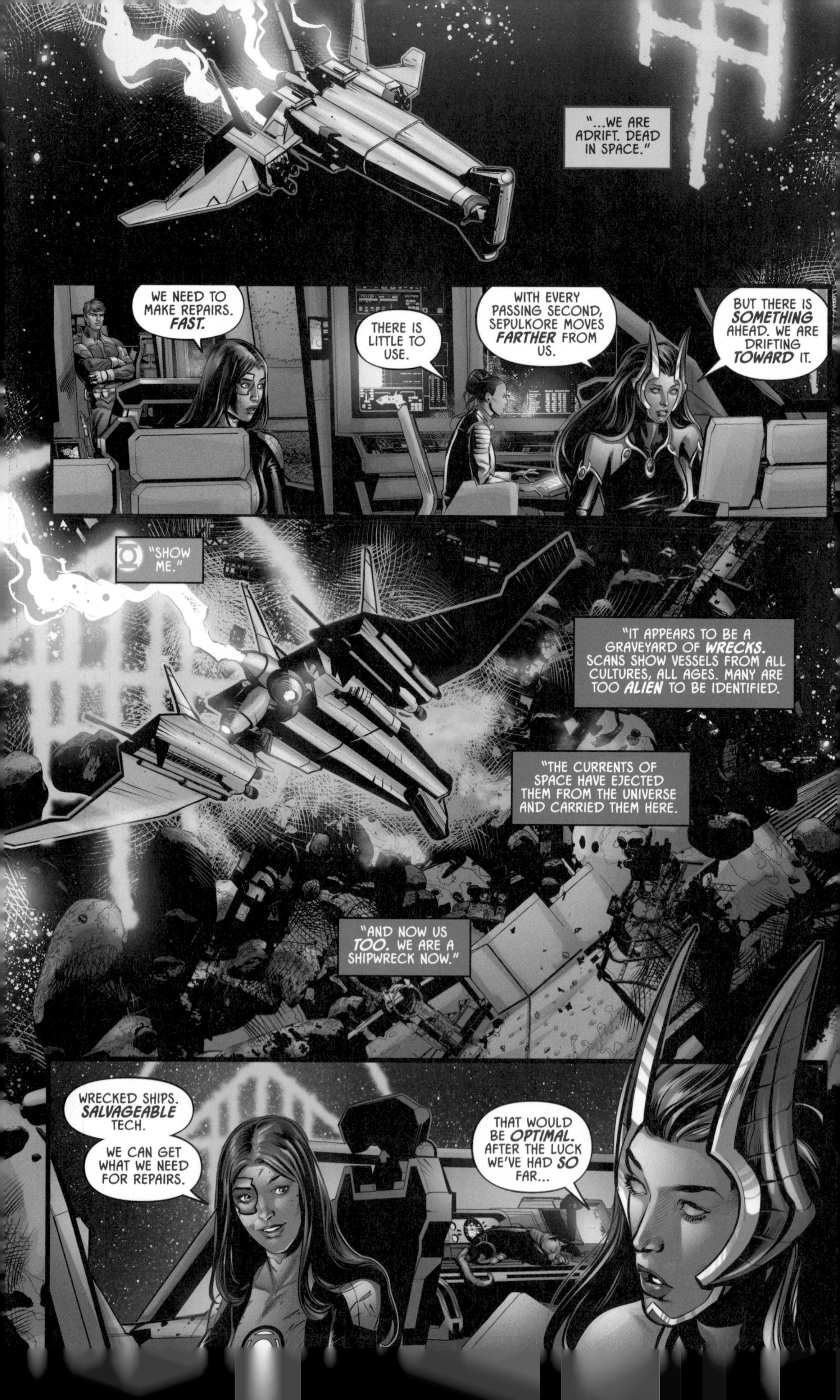
"...WE ARE ADRIFT. DEAD IN SPACE."
WE NEED TO MAKE REPAIRS. FAST.
THERE IS LITTLE TO USE.
WITH EVERY PASSING SECOND, SEPULKORE MOVES FARTHER FROM US.
BUT THERE IS SOMETHING AHEAD. WE ARE DRIFTING TOWARD IT.
"SHOW ME."
"IT APPEARS TO BE A GRAVEYARD OF WRECKS. SCANS SHOW VESSELS FROM ALL CULTURES, ALL AGES. MANY ARE TOO ALIEN TO BE IDENTIFIED.
"THE CURRENTS OF SPACE HAVE EJECTED THEM FROM THE UNIVERSE AND CARRIED THEM HERE.
"AND NOW US TOO. WE ARE A SHIPWRECK NOW."
WRECKED SHIPS. SALVAGEABLE TECH.
WE CAN GET WHAT WE NEED FOR REPAIRS.
THAT WOULD BE OPTIMAL. AFTER THE LUCK WE'VE HAD SO FAR...

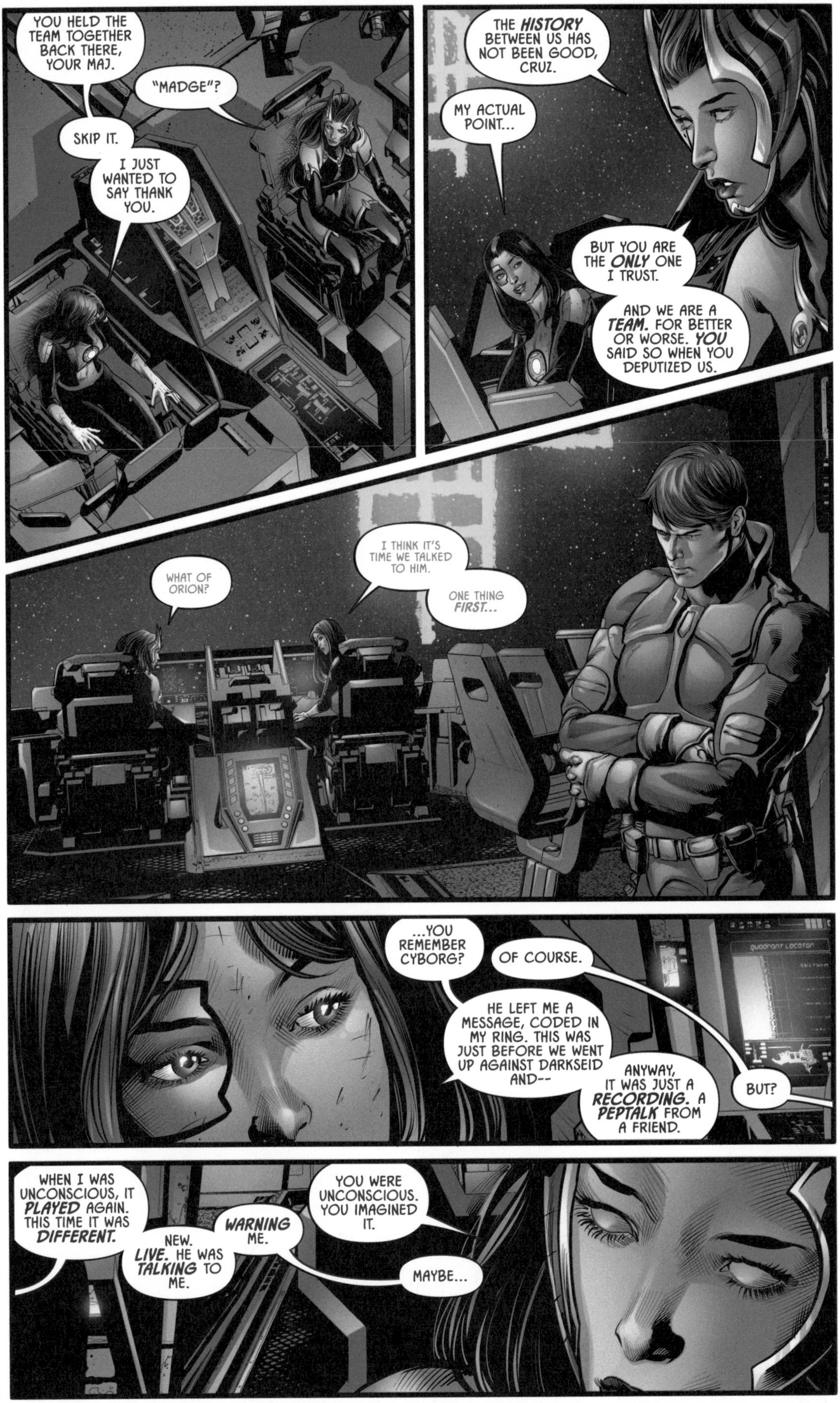
YOU HELD THE TEAM TOGETHER BACK THERE, YOUR MAJ.
"MADGE"?
SKIP IT.
I JUST WANTED TO SAY THANK YOU.
THE HISTORY BETWEEN US HAS NOT BEEN GOOD, CRUZ.
MY ACTUAL POINT...
BUT YOU ARE THE ONLY ONE I TRUST.
AND WE ARE A TEAM. FOR BETTER OR WORSE. YOU SAID SO WHEN YOU DEPUTIZED US.
WHAT OF ORION?
I THINK IT'S TIME WE TALKED TO HIM.
ONE THING FIRST...
...YOU REMEMBER CYBORG?
OF COURSE.
HE LEFT ME A MESSAGE, CODED IN MY RING. THIS WAS JUST BEFORE WE WENT UP AGAINST DARKSEID AND--
ANYWAY, IT WAS JUST A RECORDING. A PEPTALK FROM A FRIEND.
BUT?
WHEN I WAS UNCONSCIOUS, IT PLAYED AGAIN. THIS TIME IT WAS DIFFERENT.
NEW. LIVE. HE WAS TALKING TO ME.
WARNING ME.
YOU WERE UNCONSCIOUS. YOU IMAGINED IT.
MAYBE...

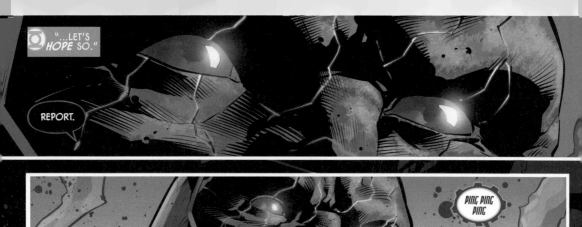

"...LET'S HOPE SO."

REPORT.

PING PING PING

A SHIP? PURSUING US?

PING PING

SHE'S DEAD, NEW GOD. IT CANNOT BE HER.

PING PING PING

THAT'S TRUE. ANY PURSUIT IS UNWELCOME.

MOBILIZE A TASK FORCE. FIND OUT WHO IT IS.

ANNIHILATE THEM.

PING PING PING

YES, NEW GOD, I MOST CERTAINLY AM.

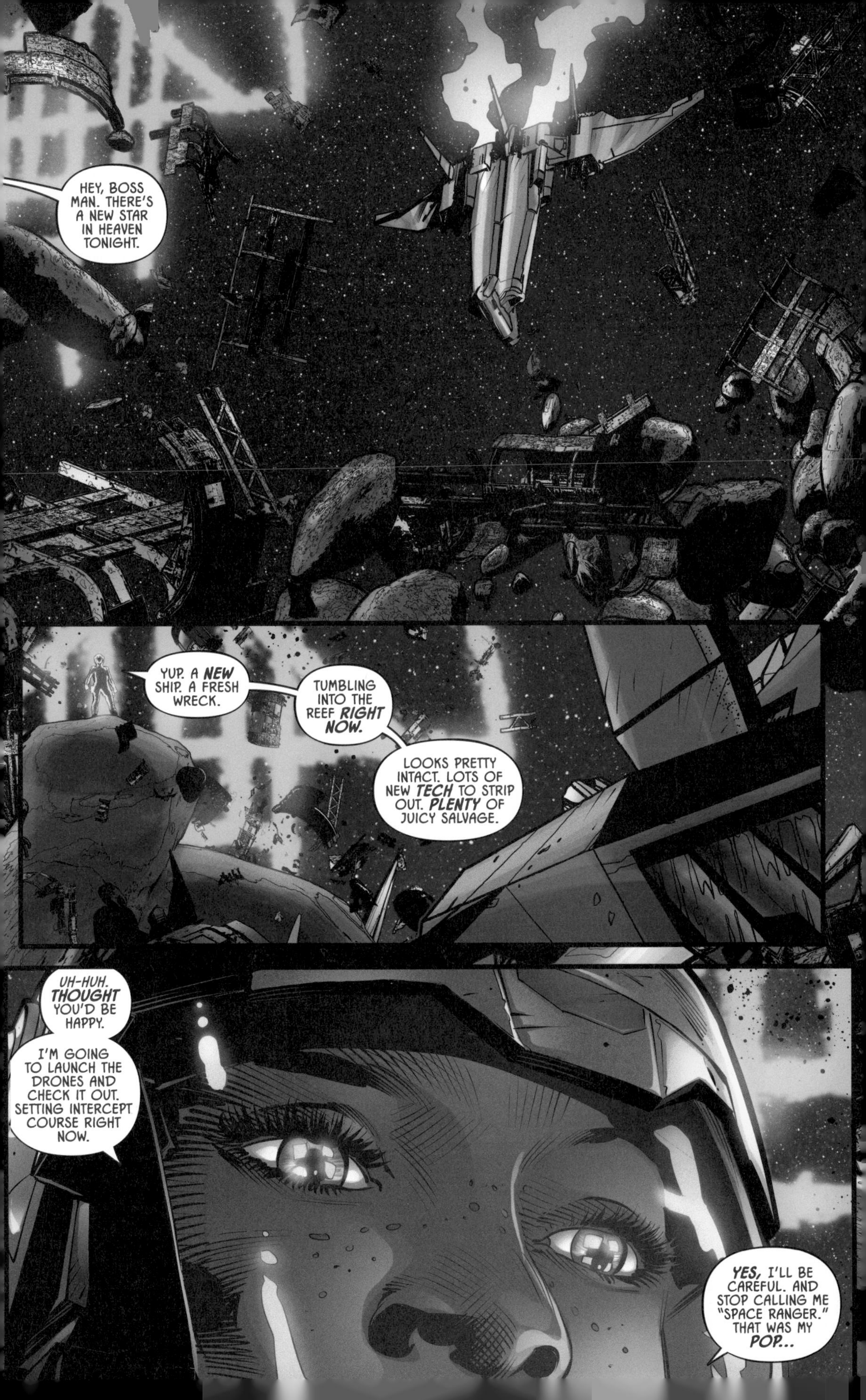
HEY, BOSS MAN. THERE'S A NEW STAR IN HEAVEN TONIGHT.
YUP. A NEW SHIP. A FRESH WRECK.
TUMBLING INTO THE REEF RIGHT NOW.
LOOKS PRETTY INTACT. LOTS OF NEW TECH TO STRIP OUT. PLENTY OF JUICY SALVAGE.
UH-HUH. THOUGHT YOU'D BE HAPPY.
I'M GOING TO LAUNCH THE DRONES AND CHECK IT OUT. SETTING INTERCEPT COURSE RIGHT NOW.
YES, I'LL BE CAREFUL. AND STOP CALLING ME "SPACE RANGER." THAT WAS MY POP...

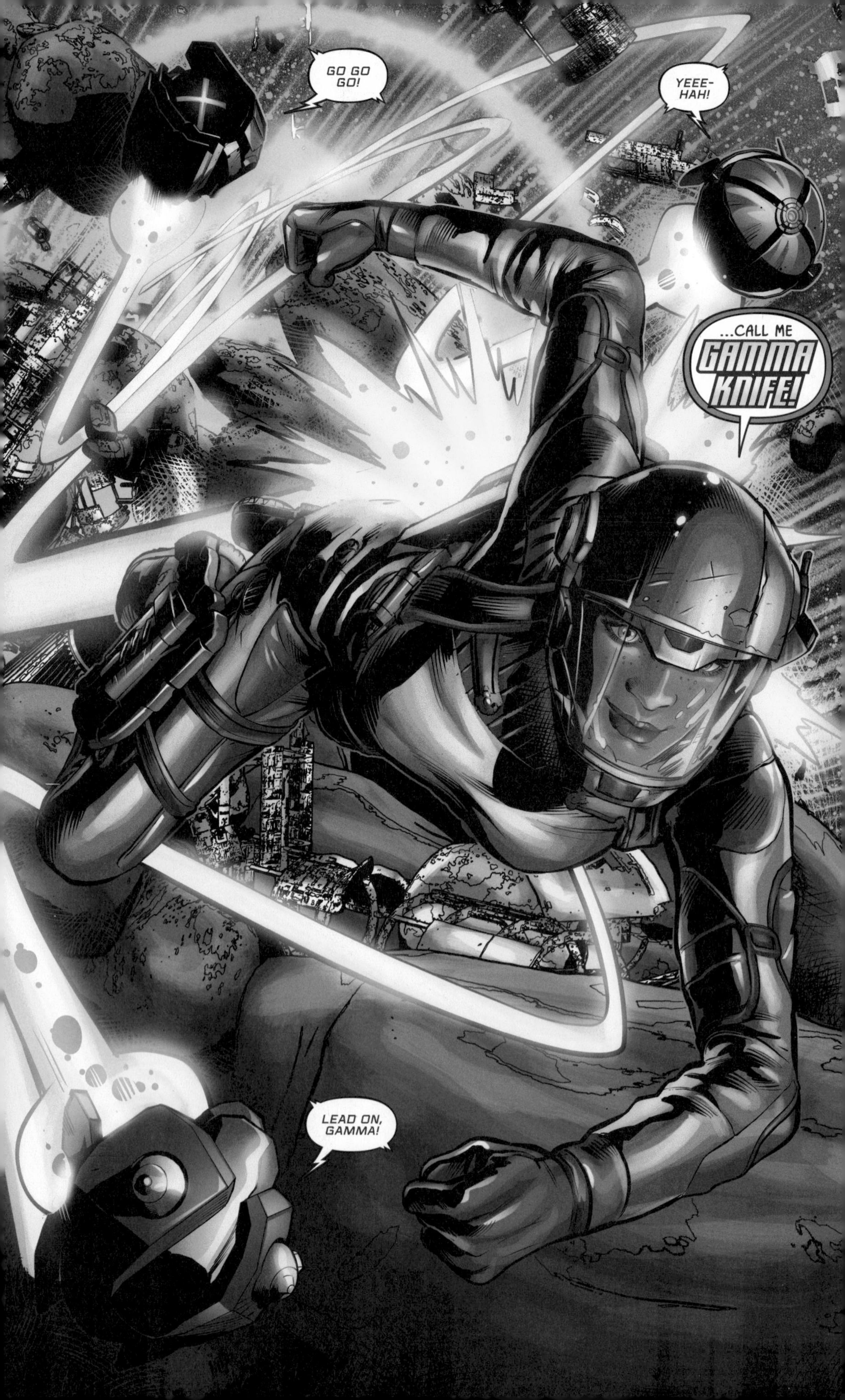
GO GO GO!
YEEE-HAH!
...CALL ME GAMMA KNIFE!
LEAD ON, GAMMA!

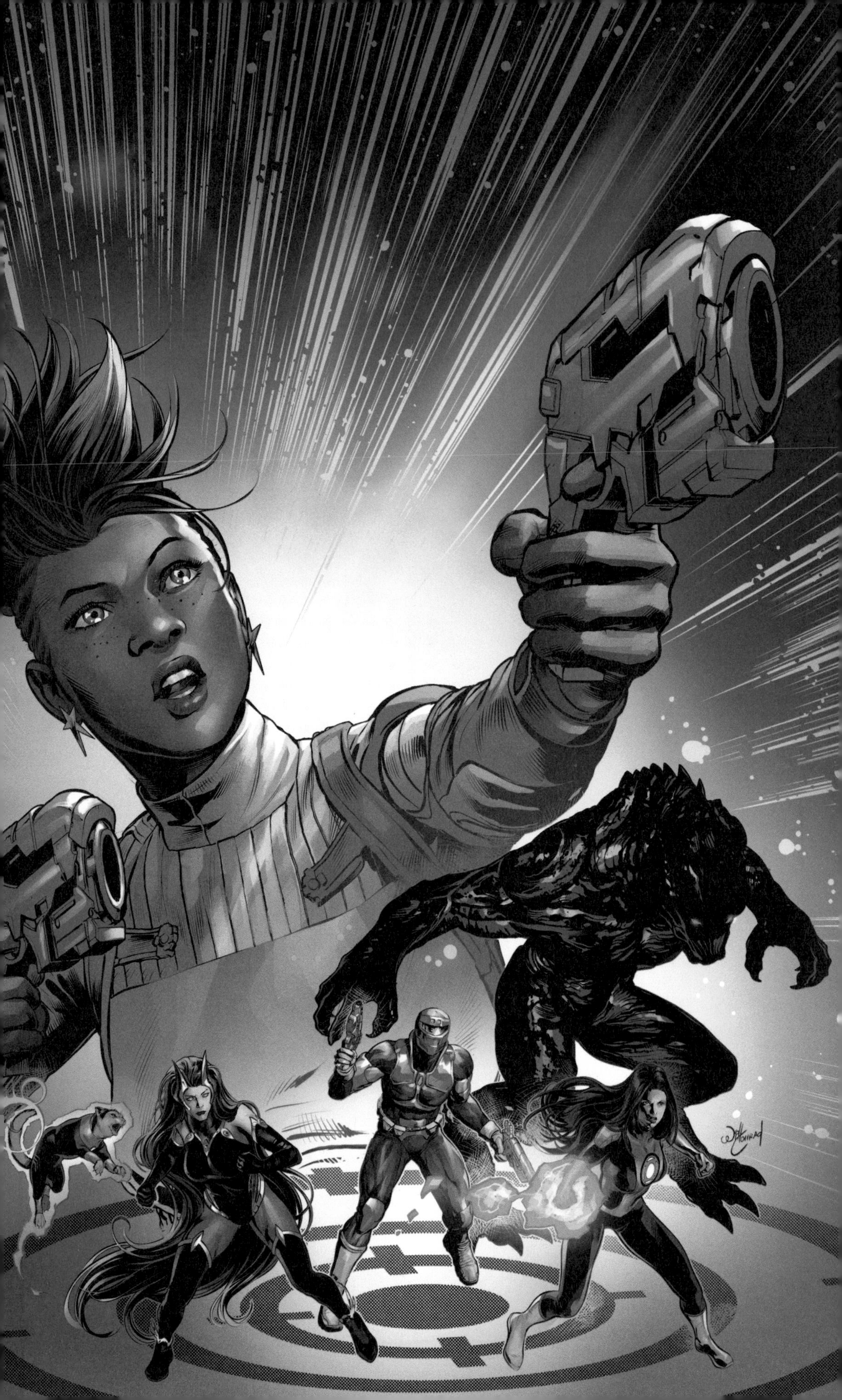

Justice League Odyssey #16 variant cover by
LUCIO PARRILLO

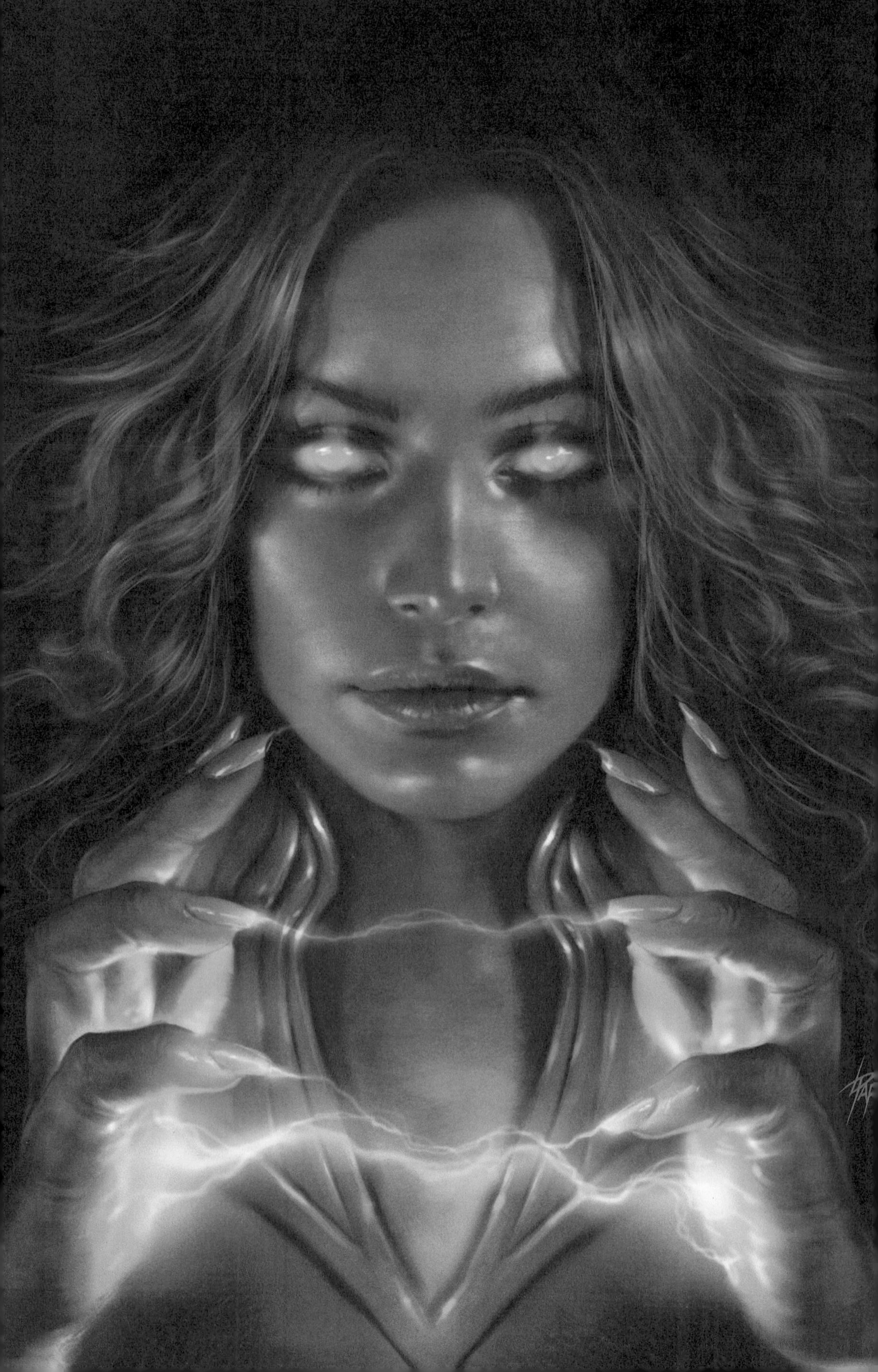

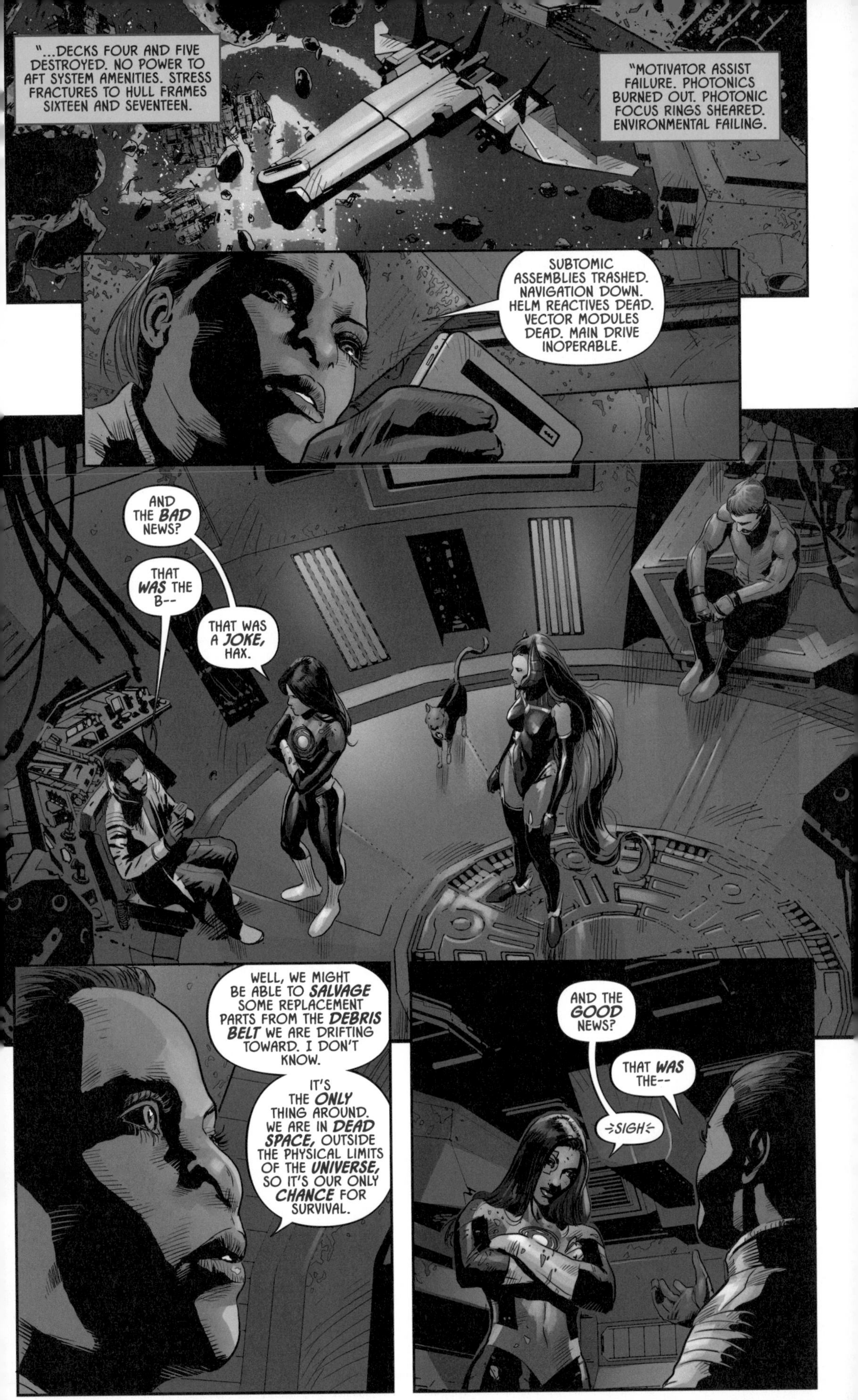

"...DECKS FOUR AND FIVE DESTROYED. NO POWER TO AFT SYSTEM AMENITIES. STRESS FRACTURES TO HULL FRAMES SIXTEEN AND SEVENTEEN.
"MOTIVATOR ASSIST FAILURE. PHOTONICS BURNED OUT. PHOTONIC FOCUS RINGS SHEARED. ENVIRONMENTAL FAILING.
SUBTOMIC ASSEMBLIES TRASHED. NAVIGATION DOWN. HELM REACTIVES DEAD. VECTOR MODULES DEAD. MAIN DRIVE INOPERABLE.
AND THE BAD NEWS?
THAT WAS THE B--
THAT WAS A JOKE, HAX.
WELL, WE MIGHT BE ABLE TO SALVAGE SOME REPLACEMENT PARTS FROM THE DEBRIS BELT WE ARE DRIFTING TOWARD. I DON'T KNOW.
IT'S THE ONLY THING AROUND. WE ARE IN DEAD SPACE, OUTSIDE THE PHYSICAL LIMITS OF THE UNIVERSE, SO IT'S OUR ONLY CHANCE FOR SURVIVAL.
AND THE GOOD NEWS?
THAT WAS THE--
SIGH

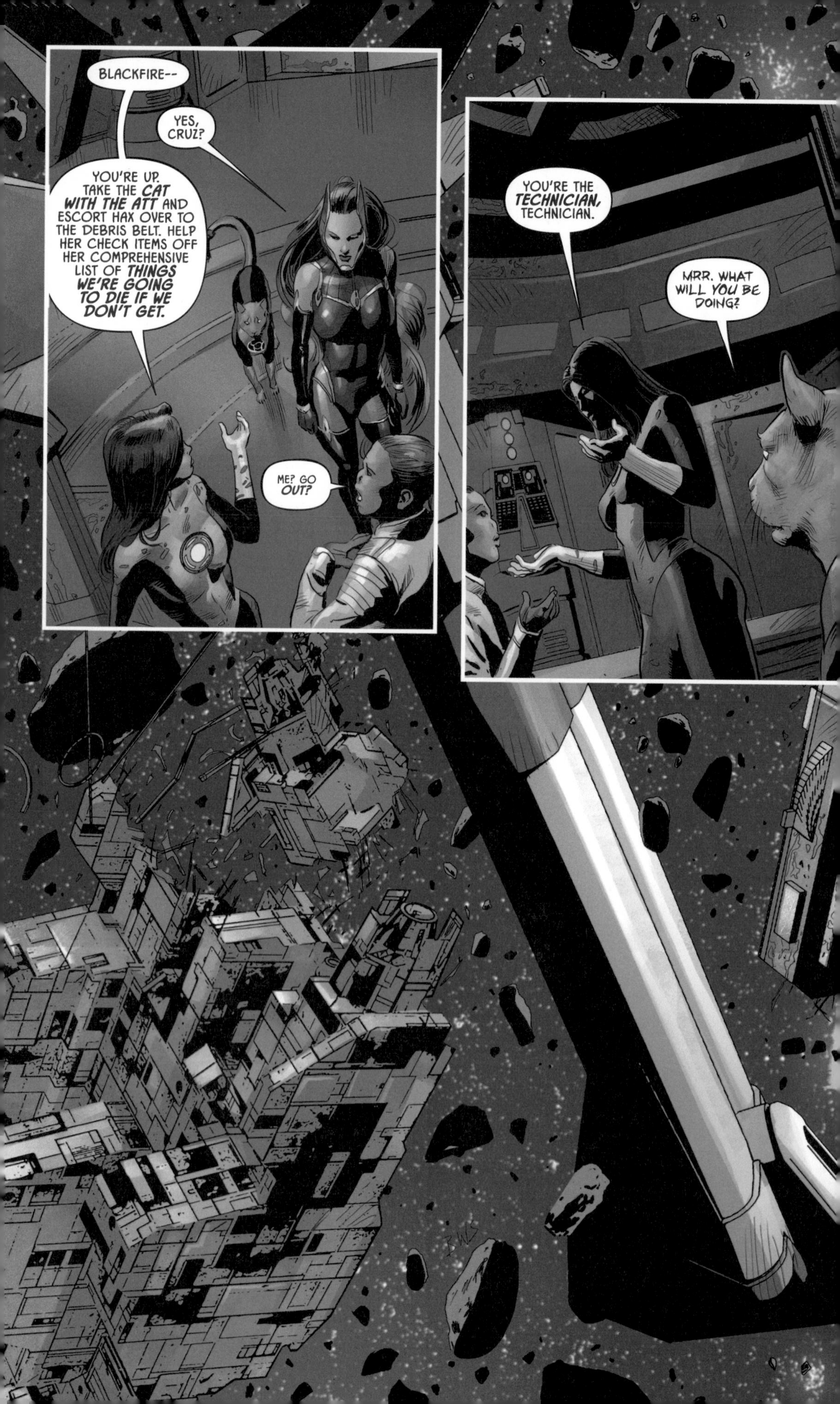
BLACKFIRE--
YES, CRUZ?
YOU'RE UP. TAKE THE CAT WITH THE ATT AND ESCORT HAX OVER TO THE DEBRIS BELT. HELP HER CHECK ITEMS OFF HER COMPREHENSIVE LIST OF THINGS WE'RE GOING TO DIE IF WE DON'T GET.
ME? GO OUT?
YOU'RE THE TECHNICIAN, TECHNICIAN.
MRR. WHAT WILL YOU BE DOING?

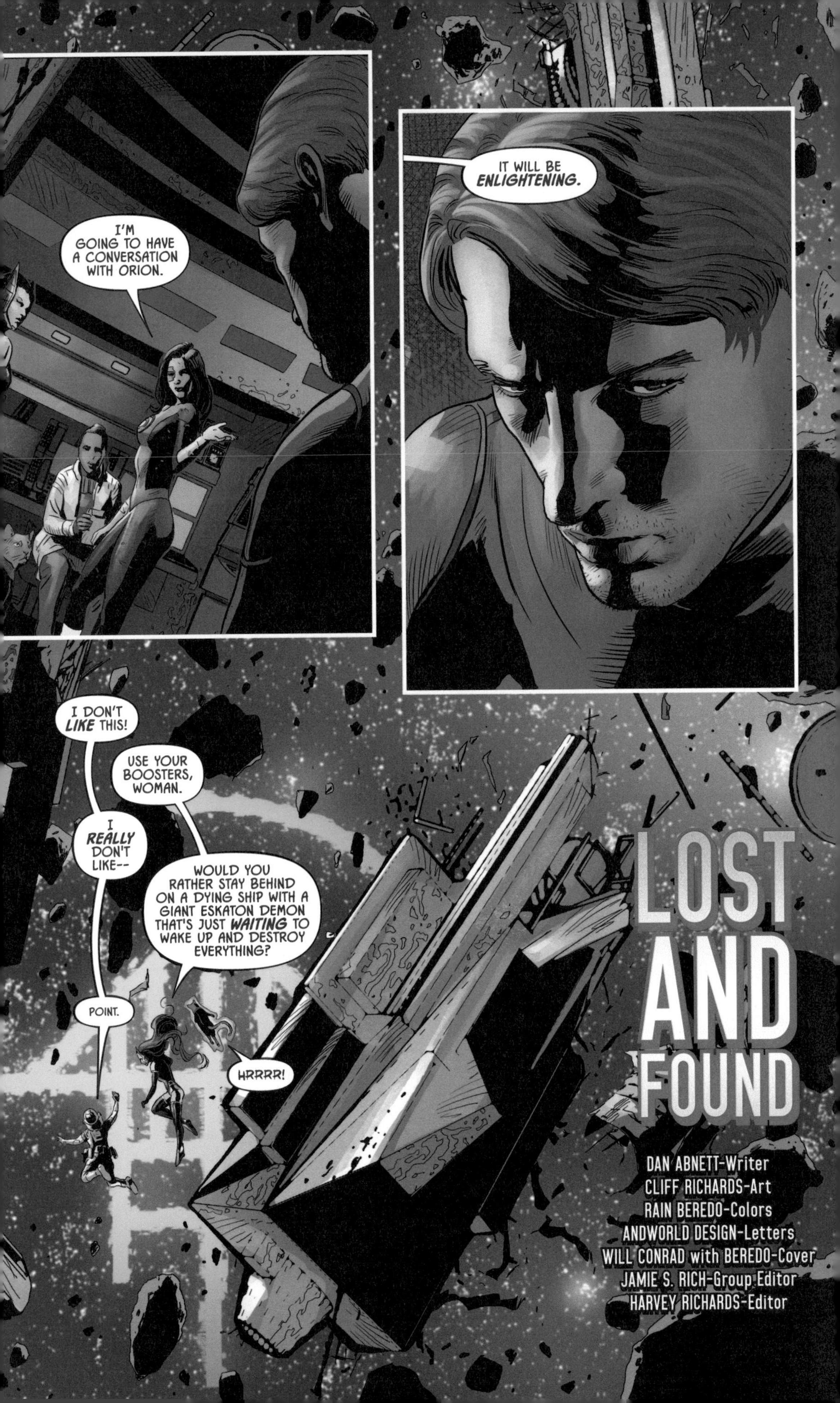

I'M GOING TO HAVE A CONVERSATION WITH ORION.
IT WILL BE *ENLIGHTENING.*
I DON'T *LIKE* THIS!
USE YOUR BOOSTERS, WOMAN.
I *REALLY* DON'T LIKE--
WOULD YOU RATHER STAY BEHIND ON A DYING SHIP WITH A GIANT ESKATON DEMON THAT'S JUST *WAITING* TO WAKE UP AND DESTROY EVERYTHING?
POINT.
HRRRR!
LOST AND FOUND
DAN ABNETT-Writer
CLIFF RICHARDS-Art
RAIN BEREDO-Colors
ANDWORLD DESIGN-Letters
WILL CONRAD with BEREDO-Cover
JAMIE S. RICH-Group Editor
HARVEY RICHARDS-Editor

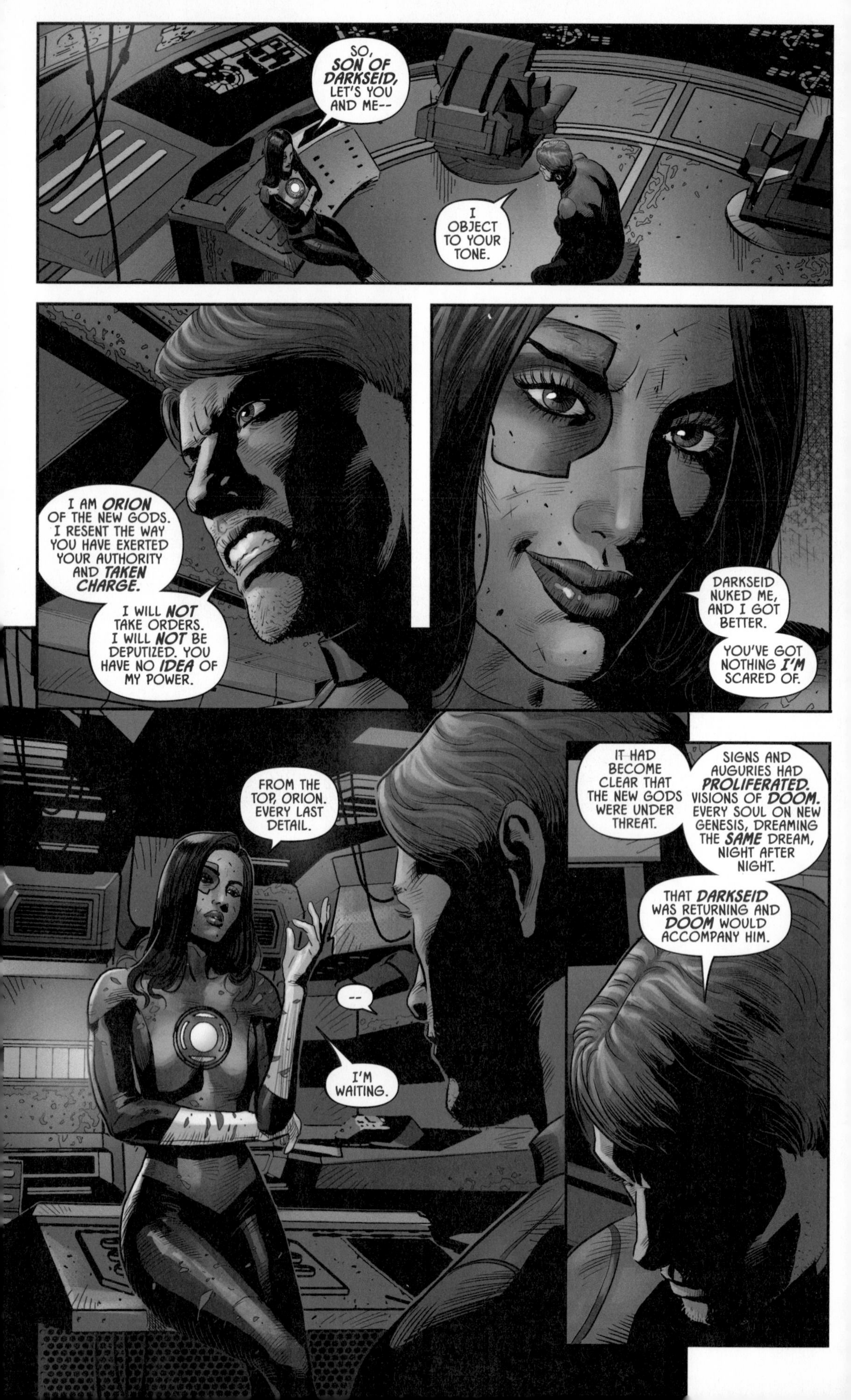

SO, SON OF DARKSEID, LET'S YOU AND ME--
I OBJECT TO YOUR TONE.
I AM ORION OF THE NEW GODS. I RESENT THE WAY YOU HAVE EXERTED YOUR AUTHORITY AND TAKEN CHARGE.
I WILL NOT TAKE ORDERS. I WILL NOT BE DEPUTIZED. YOU HAVE NO IDEA OF MY POWER.
DARKSEID NUKED ME, AND I GOT BETTER.
YOU'VE GOT NOTHING I'M SCARED OF.
FROM THE TOP, ORION. EVERY LAST DETAIL.
--
I'M WAITING.
IT HAD BECOME CLEAR THAT THE NEW GODS WERE UNDER THREAT.
SIGNS AND AUGURIES HAD PROLIFERATED. VISIONS OF DOOM. EVERY SOUL ON NEW GENESIS, DREAMING THE SAME DREAM, NIGHT AFTER NIGHT.
THAT DARKSEID WAS RETURNING AND DOOM WOULD ACCOMPANY HIM.

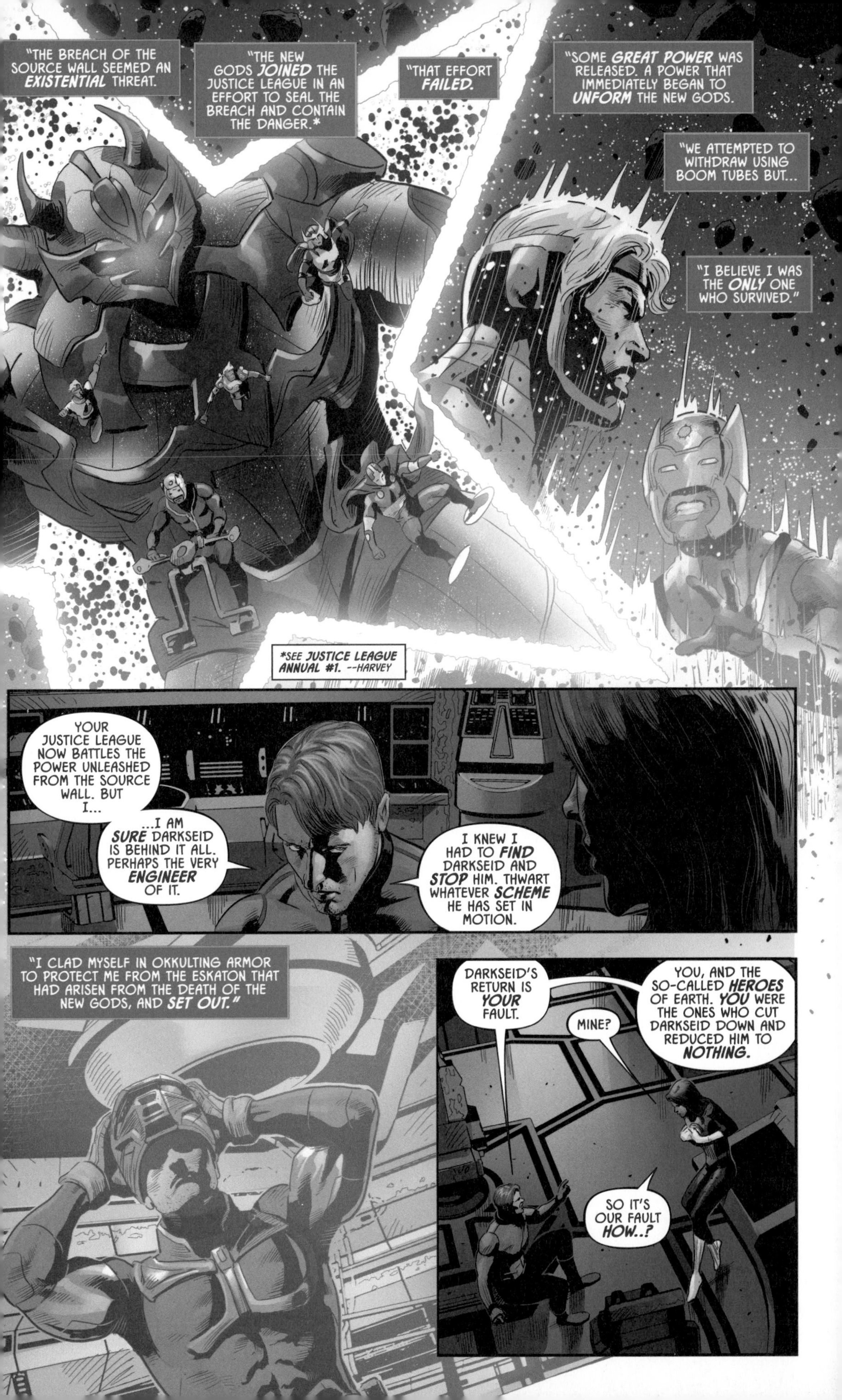
"THE BREACH OF THE SOURCE WALL SEEMED AN EXISTENTIAL THREAT.
"THE NEW GODS JOINED THE JUSTICE LEAGUE IN AN EFFORT TO SEAL THE BREACH AND CONTAIN THE DANGER.*
"THAT EFFORT FAILED.
"SOME GREAT POWER WAS RELEASED. A POWER THAT IMMEDIATELY BEGAN TO UNFORM THE NEW GODS.
"WE ATTEMPTED TO WITHDRAW USING BOOM TUBES BUT...
"I BELIEVE I WAS THE ONLY ONE WHO SURVIVED."
*SEE JUSTICE LEAGUE ANNUAL #1. --HARVEY
YOUR JUSTICE LEAGUE NOW BATTLES THE POWER UNLEASHED FROM THE SOURCE WALL. BUT I...
...I AM SURE DARKSEID IS BEHIND IT ALL. PERHAPS THE VERY ENGINEER OF IT.
I KNEW I HAD TO FIND DARKSEID AND STOP HIM. THWART WHATEVER SCHEME HE HAS SET IN MOTION.
"I CLAD MYSELF IN OKKULTING ARMOR TO PROTECT ME FROM THE ESKATON THAT HAD ARISEN FROM THE DEATH OF THE NEW GODS, AND SET OUT."
DARKSEID'S RETURN IS YOUR FAULT.
MINE?
YOU, AND THE SO-CALLED HEROES OF EARTH. YOU WERE THE ONES WHO CUT DARKSEID DOWN AND REDUCED HIM TO NOTHING.
SO IT'S OUR FAULT HOW..?

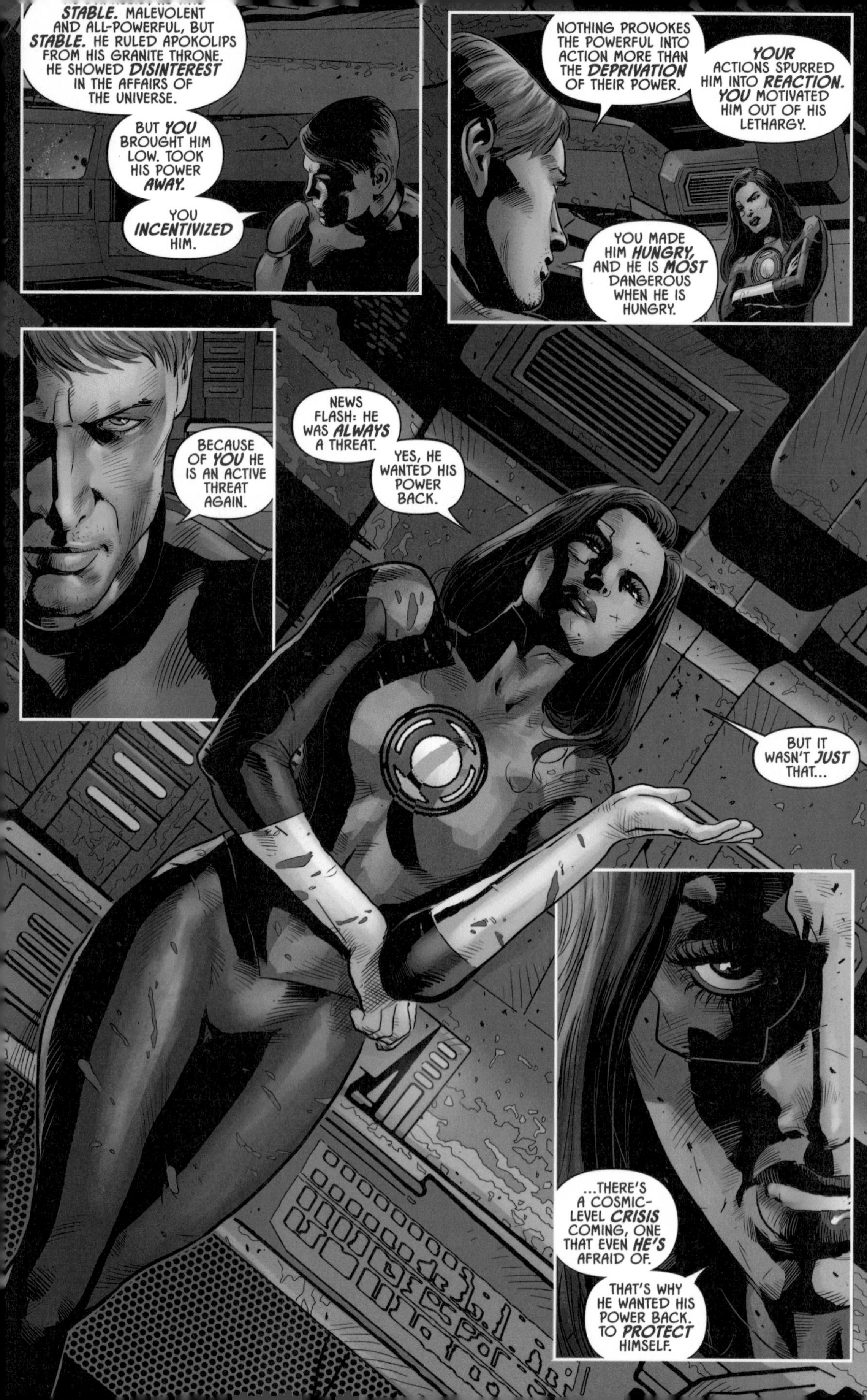
STABLE. MALEVOLENT AND ALL-POWERFUL, BUT STABLE. HE RULED APOKOLIPS FROM HIS GRANITE THRONE. HE SHOWED DISINTEREST IN THE AFFAIRS OF THE UNIVERSE.
BUT YOU BROUGHT HIM LOW. TOOK HIS POWER AWAY.
YOU INCENTIVIZED HIM.
NOTHING PROVOKES THE POWERFUL INTO ACTION MORE THAN THE DEPRIVATION OF THEIR POWER.
YOUR ACTIONS SPURRED HIM INTO REACTION. YOU MOTIVATED HIM OUT OF HIS LETHARGY.
YOU MADE HIM HUNGRY, AND HE IS MOST DANGEROUS WHEN HE IS HUNGRY.
BECAUSE OF YOU HE IS AN ACTIVE THREAT AGAIN.
NEWS FLASH: HE WAS ALWAYS A THREAT.
YES, HE WANTED HIS POWER BACK.
BUT IT WASN'T JUST THAT...
...THERE'S A COSMIC-LEVEL CRISIS COMING, ONE THAT EVEN HE'S AFRAID OF.
THAT'S WHY HE WANTED HIS POWER BACK. TO PROTECT HIMSELF.

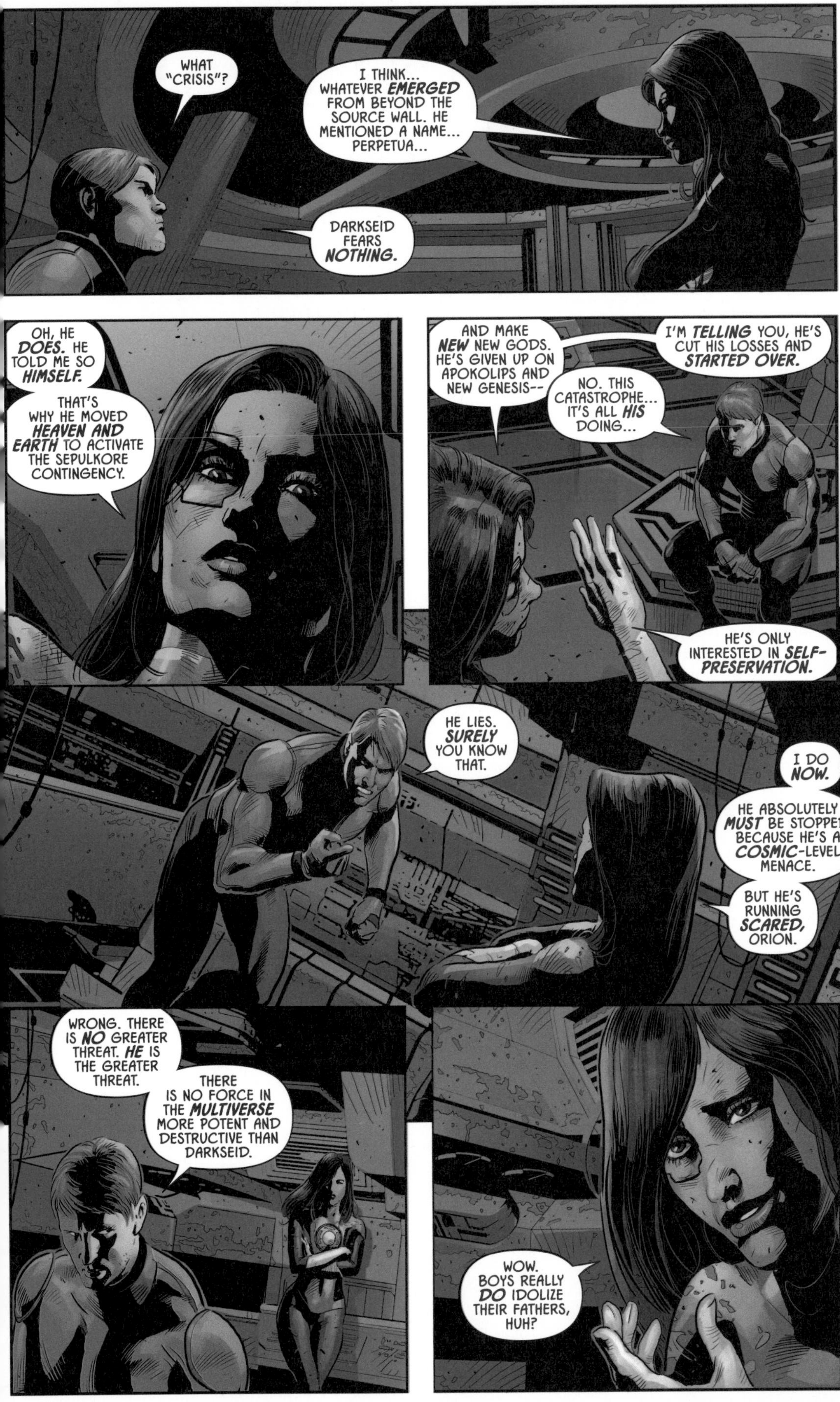
WHAT "CRISIS"?
I THINK... WHATEVER EMERGED FROM BEYOND THE SOURCE WALL. HE MENTIONED A NAME... PERPETUA...
DARKSEID FEARS NOTHING.
OH, HE DOES. HE TOLD ME SO HIMSELF.
THAT'S WHY HE MOVED HEAVEN AND EARTH TO ACTIVATE THE SEPULKORE CONTINGENCY.
I'M TELLING YOU, HE'S CUT HIS LOSSES AND STARTED OVER.
AND MAKE NEW NEW GODS. HE'S GIVEN UP ON APOKOLIPS AND NEW GENESIS--
NO. THIS CATASTROPHE... IT'S ALL HIS DOING...
HE'S ONLY INTERESTED IN SELF-PRESERVATION.
HE LIES. SURELY YOU KNOW THAT.
I DO NOW.
HE ABSOLUTELY MUST BE STOPPED, BECAUSE HE'S A COSMIC-LEVEL MENACE.
BUT HE'S RUNNING SCARED, ORION.
WRONG. THERE IS NO GREATER THREAT. HE IS THE GREATER THREAT.
THERE IS NO FORCE IN THE MULTIVERSE MORE POTENT AND DESTRUCTIVE THAN DARKSEID.
WOW. BOYS REALLY DO IDOLIZE THEIR FATHERS, HUH?

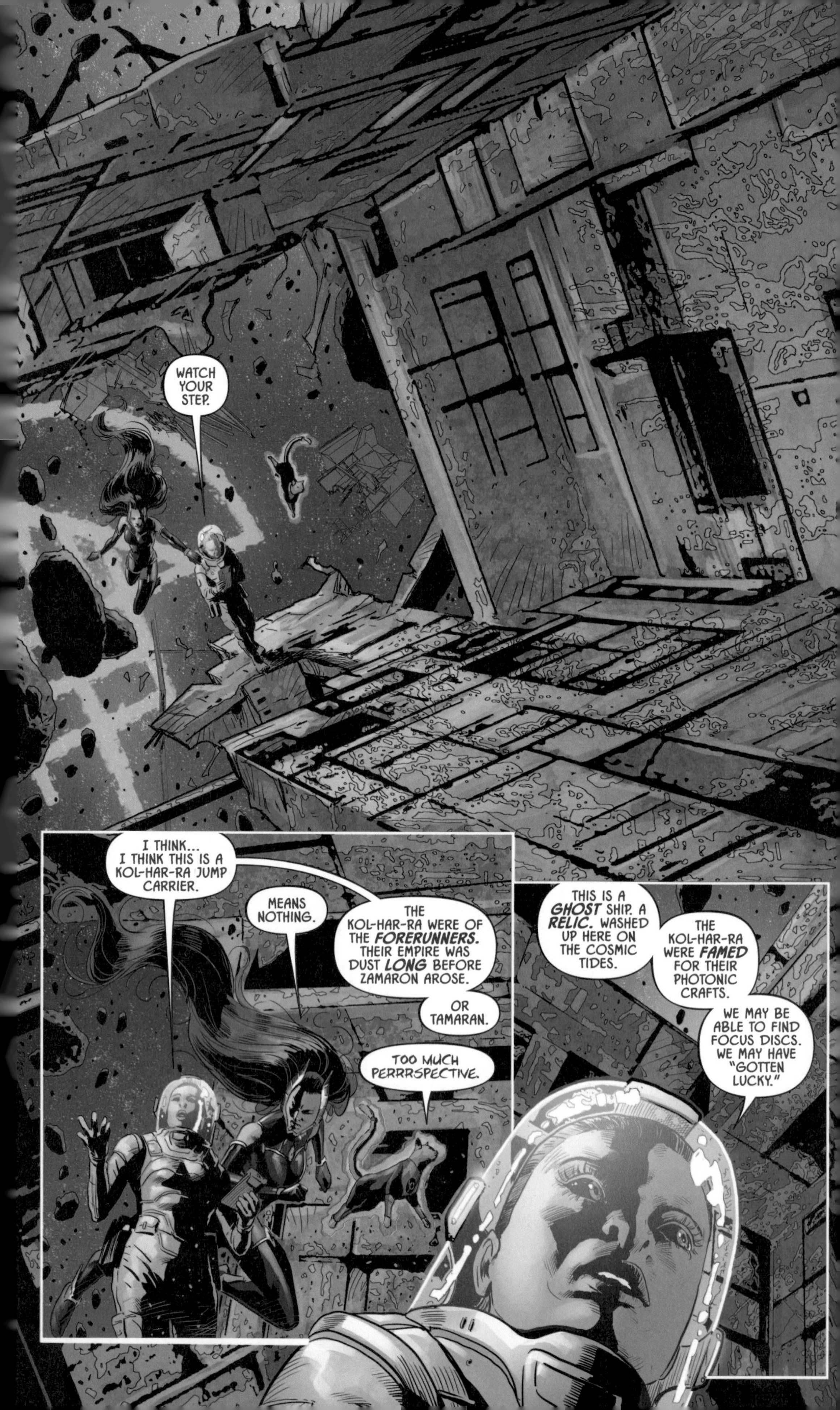

WATCH YOUR STEP.
I THINK... I THINK THIS IS A KOL-HAR-RA JUMP CARRIER.
MEANS NOTHING.
THE KOL-HAR-RA WERE OF THE FORERUNNERS. THEIR EMPIRE WAS DUST LONG BEFORE ZAMARON AROSE.
OR TAMARAN.
TOO MUCH PERRRSPECTIVE.
THIS IS A GHOST SHIP. A RELIC. WASHED UP HERE ON THE COSMIC TIDES.
THE KOL-HAR-RA WERE FAMED FOR THEIR PHOTONIC CRAFTS.
WE MAY BE ABLE TO FIND FOCUS DISCS. WE MAY HAVE "GOTTEN LUCKY."

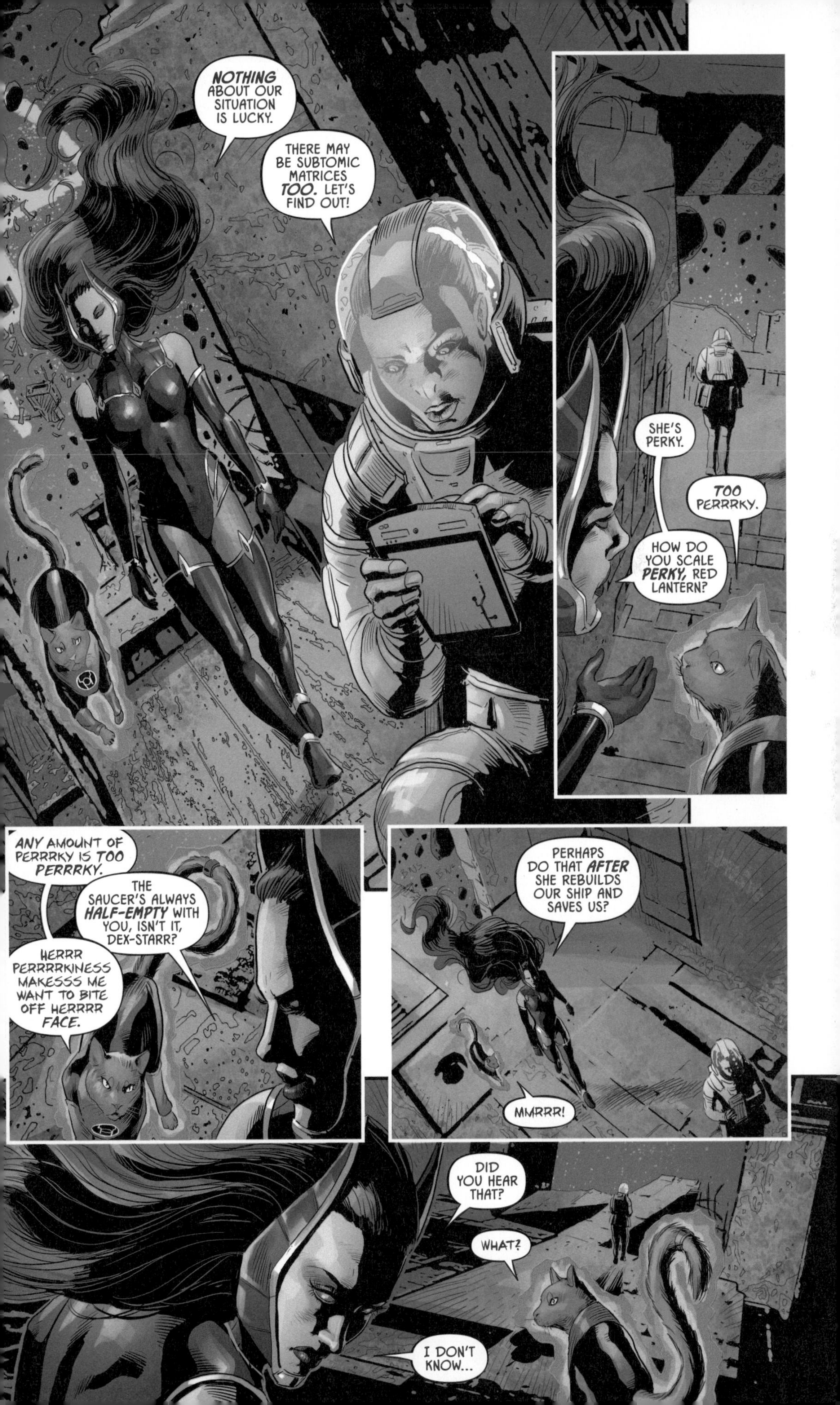
NOTHING ABOUT OUR SITUATION IS LUCKY.
THERE MAY BE SUBTOMIC MATRICES TOO. LET'S FIND OUT!
SHE'S PERKY.
TOO PERRRKY.
HOW DO YOU SCALE PERKY, RED LANTERN?
ANY AMOUNT OF PERRRKY IS TOO PERRRKY.
THE SAUCER'S ALWAYS HALF-EMPTY WITH YOU, ISN'T IT, DEX-STARR?
HERRR PERRRRKINESS MAKESSS ME WANT TO BITE OFF HERRRR FACE.
PERHAPS DO THAT AFTER SHE REBUILDS OUR SHIP AND SAVES US?
MMRRR!
DID YOU HEAR THAT?
WHAT?
I DON'T KNOW...

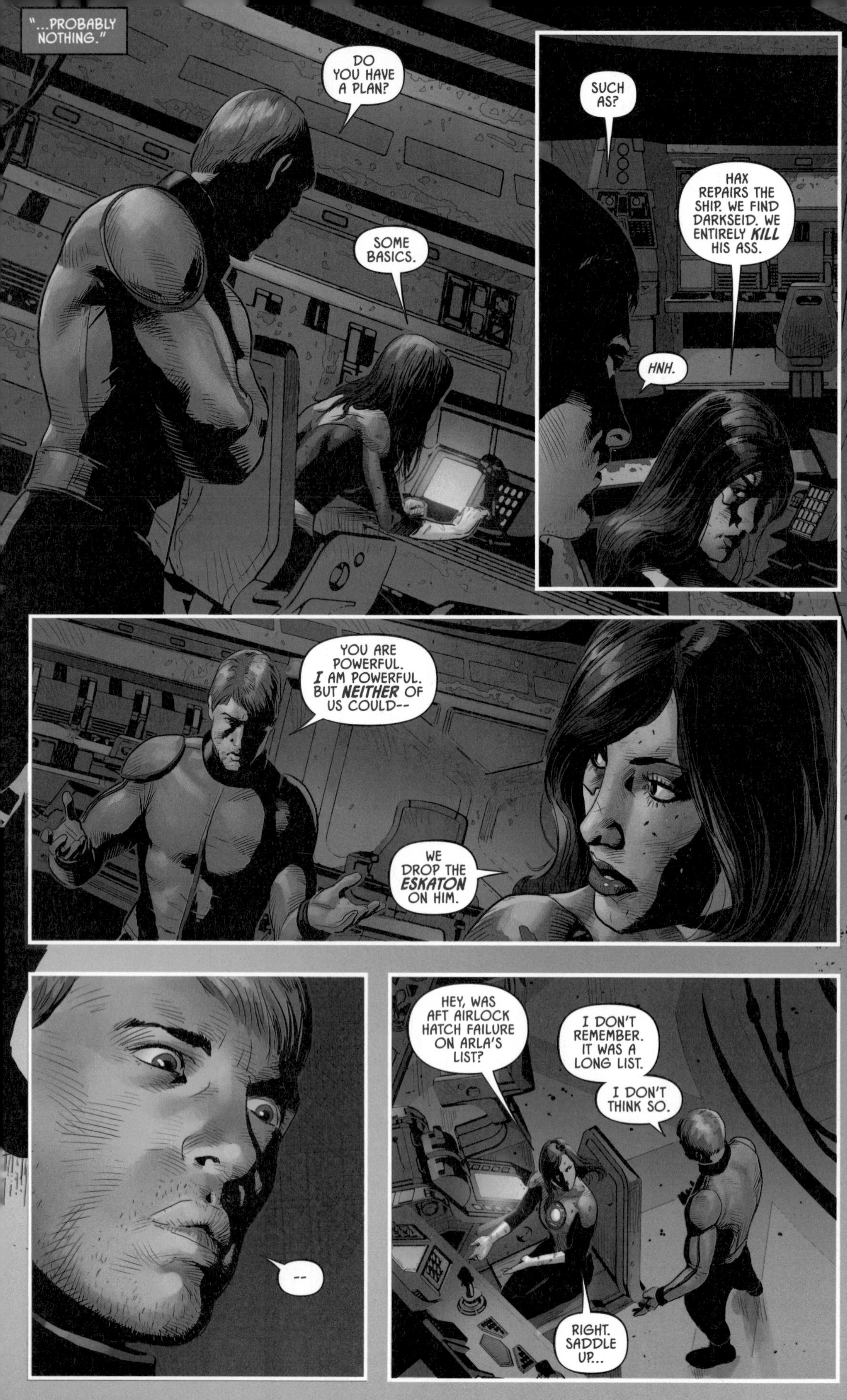
"...PROBABLY NOTHING."
DO YOU HAVE A PLAN?
SOME BASICS.
SUCH AS?
HAX REPAIRS THE SHIP. WE FIND DARKSEID. WE ENTIRELY KILL HIS ASS.
HNH.
YOU ARE POWERFUL. I AM POWERFUL. BUT NEITHER OF US COULD--
WE DROP THE ESKATON ON HIM.
--
HEY, WAS AFT AIRLOCK HATCH FAILURE ON ARLA'S LIST?
I DON'T REMEMBER. IT WAS A LONG LIST.
I DON'T THINK SO.
RIGHT. SADDLE UP...

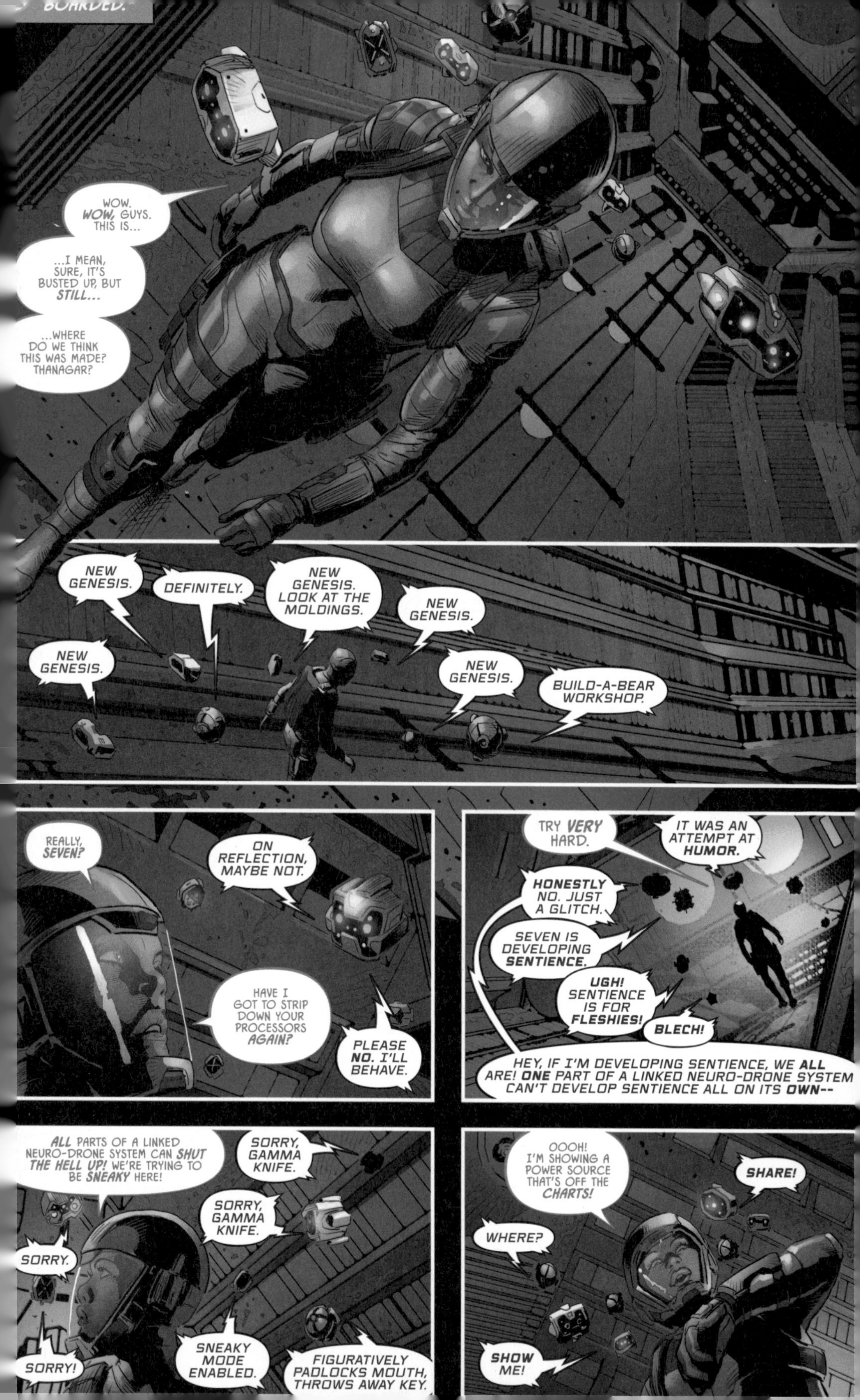
BOARDED."
WOW. WOW, GUYS. THIS IS...
...I MEAN, SURE, IT'S BUSTED UP, BUT STILL...
...WHERE DO WE THINK THIS WAS MADE? THANAGAR?
NEW GENESIS.
DEFINITELY.
NEW GENESIS. LOOK AT THE MOLDINGS.
NEW GENESIS.
NEW GENESIS.
NEW GENESIS.
BUILD-A-BEAR WORKSHOP.
REALLY, SEVEN?
ON REFLECTION, MAYBE NOT.
HAVE I GOT TO STRIP DOWN YOUR PROCESSORS AGAIN?
PLEASE NO. I'LL BEHAVE.
TRY VERY HARD.
IT WAS AN ATTEMPT AT HUMOR.
HONESTLY NO. JUST A GLITCH.
SEVEN IS DEVELOPING SENTIENCE.
UGH! SENTIENCE IS FOR FLESHIES!
BLECH!
HEY, IF I'M DEVELOPING SENTIENCE, WE ALL ARE! ONE PART OF A LINKED NEURO-DRONE SYSTEM CAN'T DEVELOP SENTIENCE ALL ON ITS OWN--
ALL PARTS OF A LINKED NEURO-DRONE SYSTEM CAN SHUT THE HELL UP! WE'RE TRYING TO BE SNEAKY HERE!
SORRY, GAMMA KNIFE.
SORRY, GAMMA KNIFE.
SORRY.
SORRY!
SNEAKY MODE ENABLED.
FIGURATIVELY PADLOCKS MOUTH, THROWS AWAY KEY.
OOOH! I'M SHOWING A POWER SOURCE THAT'S OFF THE CHARTS!
SHARE!
WHERE?
SHOW ME!

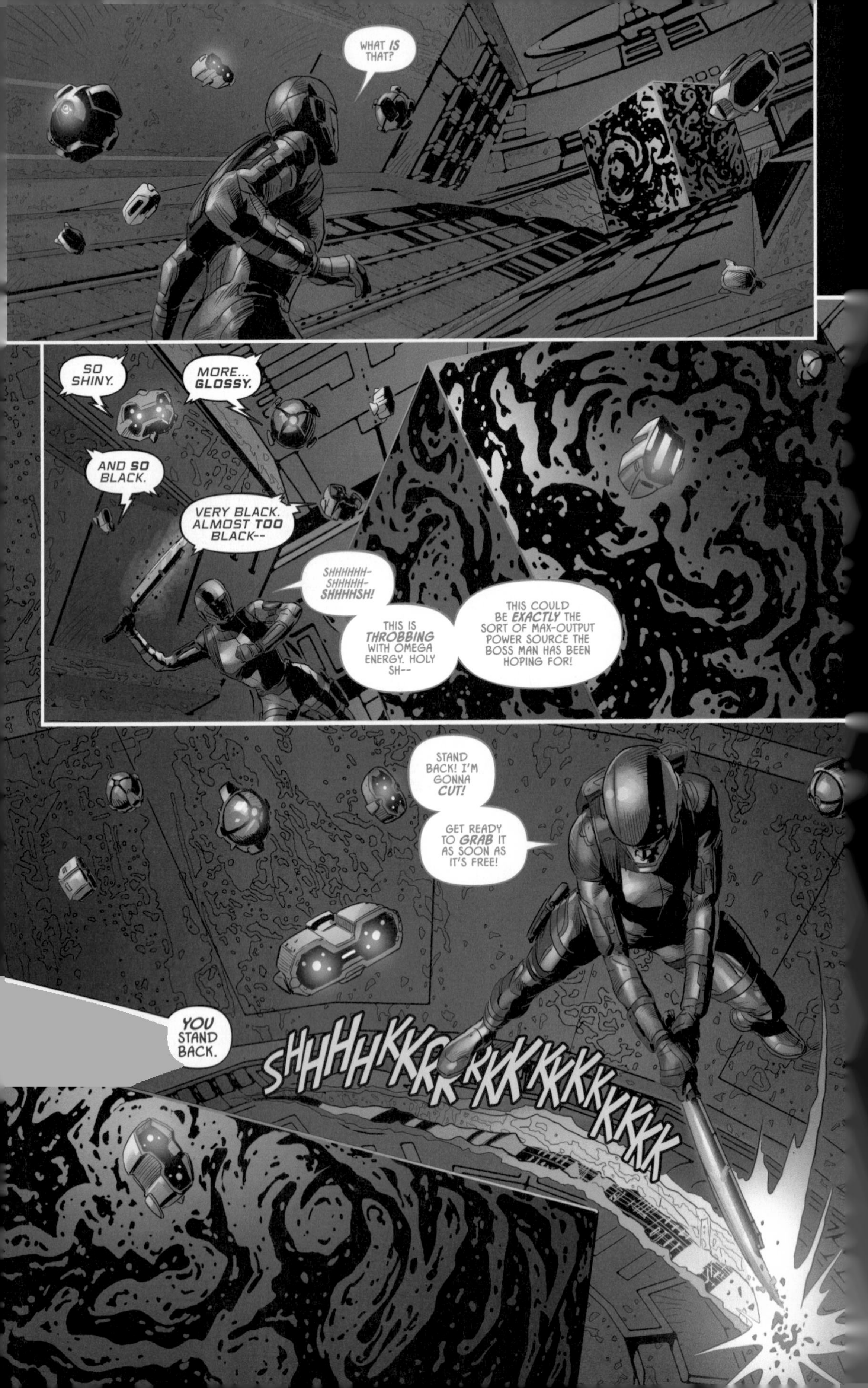
WHAT IS THAT?
SO SHINY.
MORE... GLOSSY.
AND SO BLACK.
VERY BLACK. ALMOST TOO BLACK--
SHHHHHH-SHHHHH-SHHHHSH!
THIS IS THROBBING WITH OMEGA ENERGY. HOLY SH--
THIS COULD BE EXACTLY THE SORT OF MAX-OUTPUT POWER SOURCE THE BOSS MAN HAS BEEN HOPING FOR!
STAND BACK! I'M GONNA CUT!
GET READY TO GRAB IT AS SOON AS IT'S FREE!
YOU STAND BACK.
SHHHHKKRRKKKKKKKKKKK

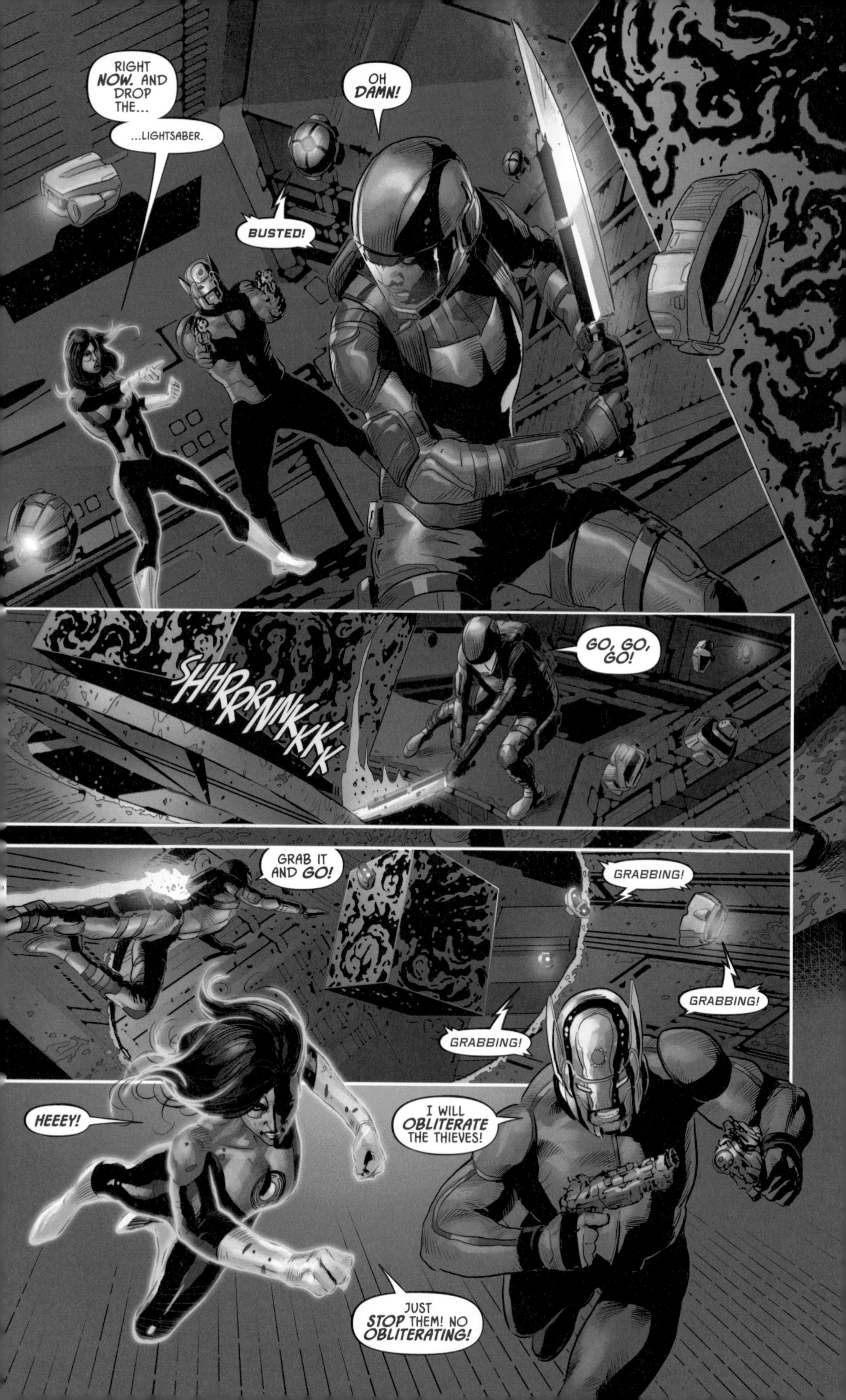
RIGHT NOW. AND DROP THE...
...LIGHTSABER.
OH DAMN!
BUSTED!
SHHRRRNNKKKK
GO, GO, GO!
GRAB IT AND GO!
GRABBING!
GRABBING!
GRABBING!
HEEEY!
I WILL OBLITERATE THE THIEVES!
JUST STOP THEM! NO OBLITERATING!

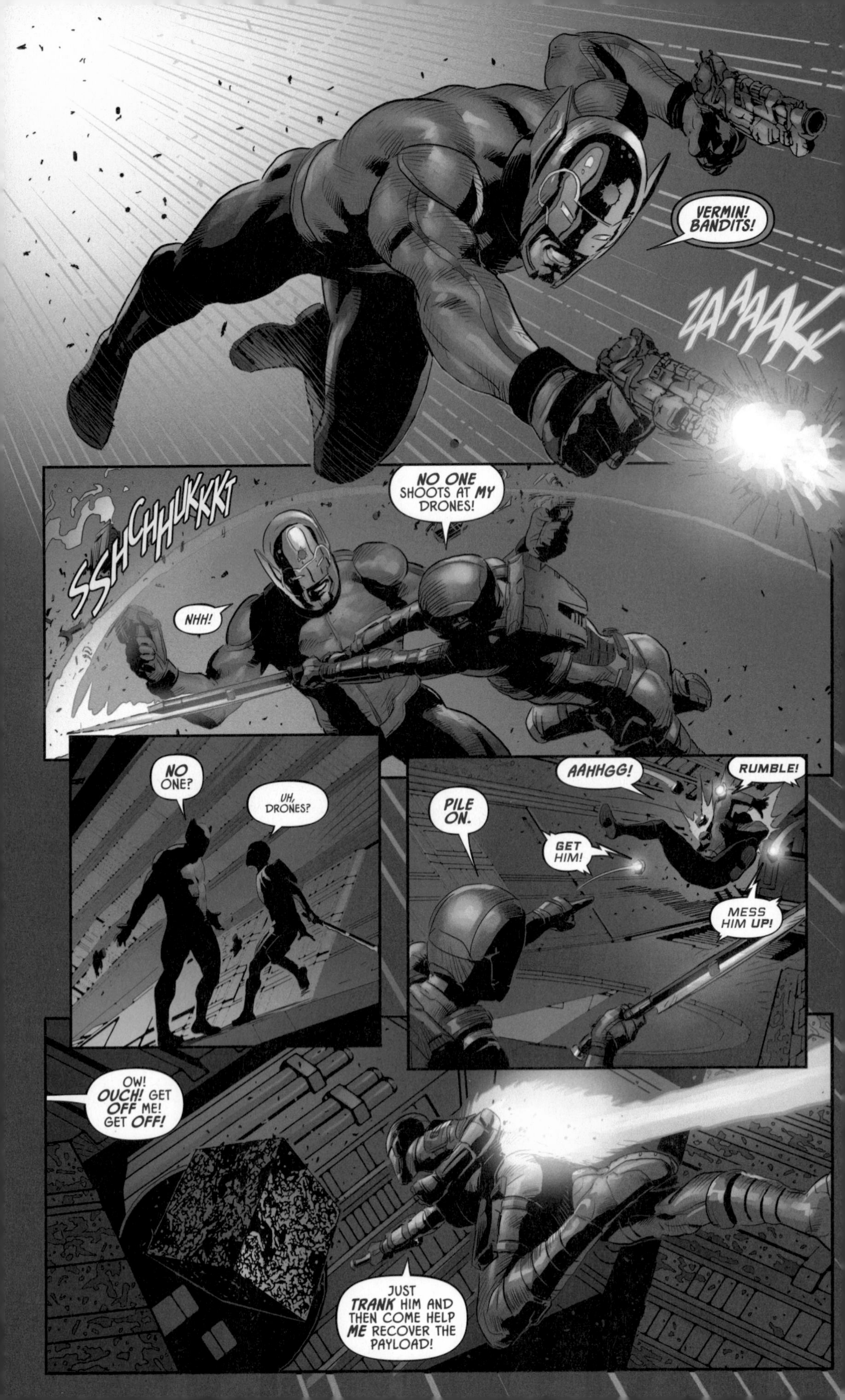
VERMIN! BANDITS!
ZAAAAKK
SSHCHHUKKKT
NO ONE SHOOTS AT MY DRONES!
NHH!
NO ONE?
UH, DRONES?
AAHHGG!
RUMBLE!
PILE ON.
GET HIM!
MESS HIM UP!
OW! OUCH! GET OFF ME! GET OFF!
JUST TRANK HIM AND THEN COME HELP ME RECOVER THE PAYLOAD!

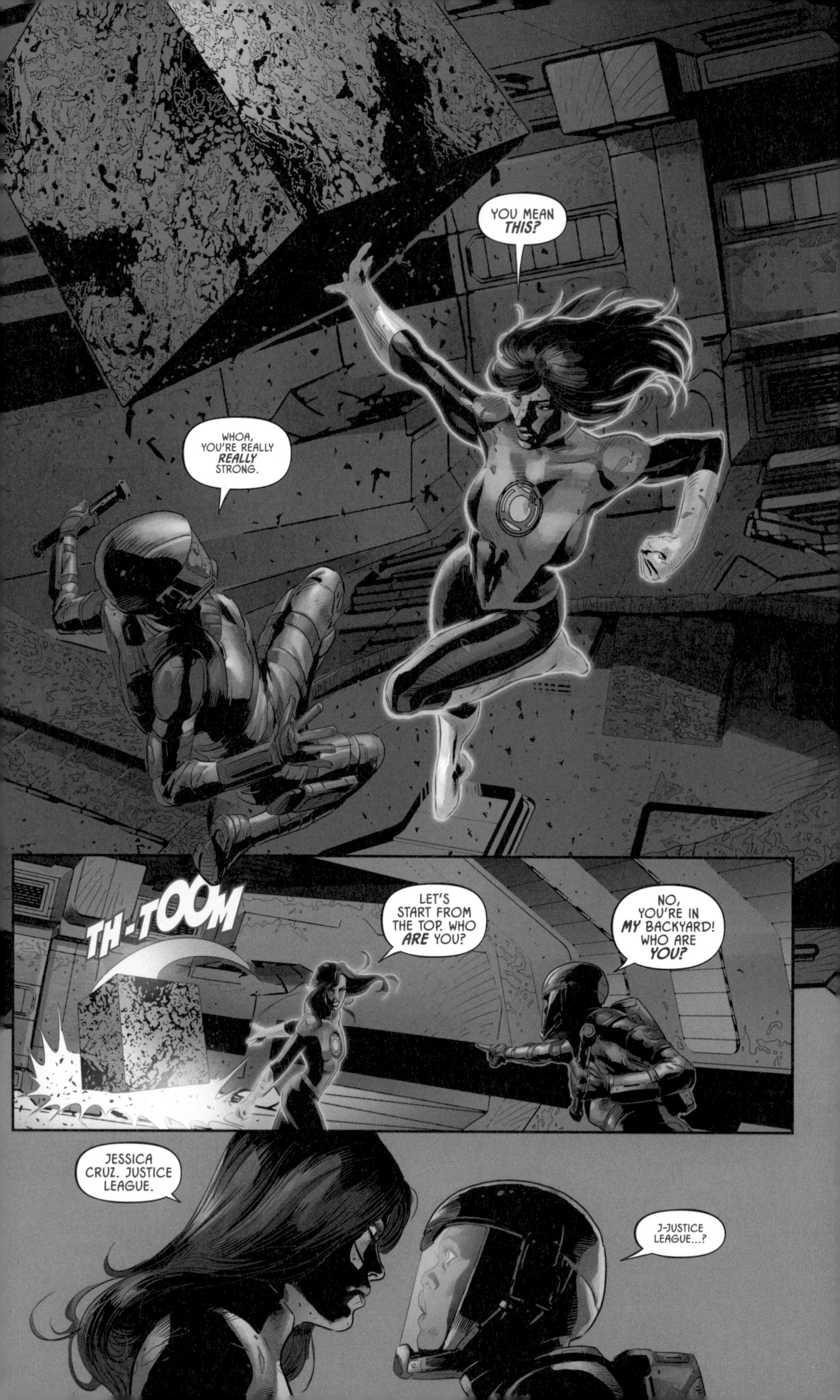
YOU MEAN THIS?
WHOA, YOU'RE REALLY REALLY STRONG.
TH-TOOM
LET'S START FROM THE TOP. WHO ARE YOU?
NO, YOU'RE IN MY BACKYARD! WHO ARE YOU?
JESSICA CRUZ. JUSTICE LEAGUE.
J-JUSTICE LEAGUE...?

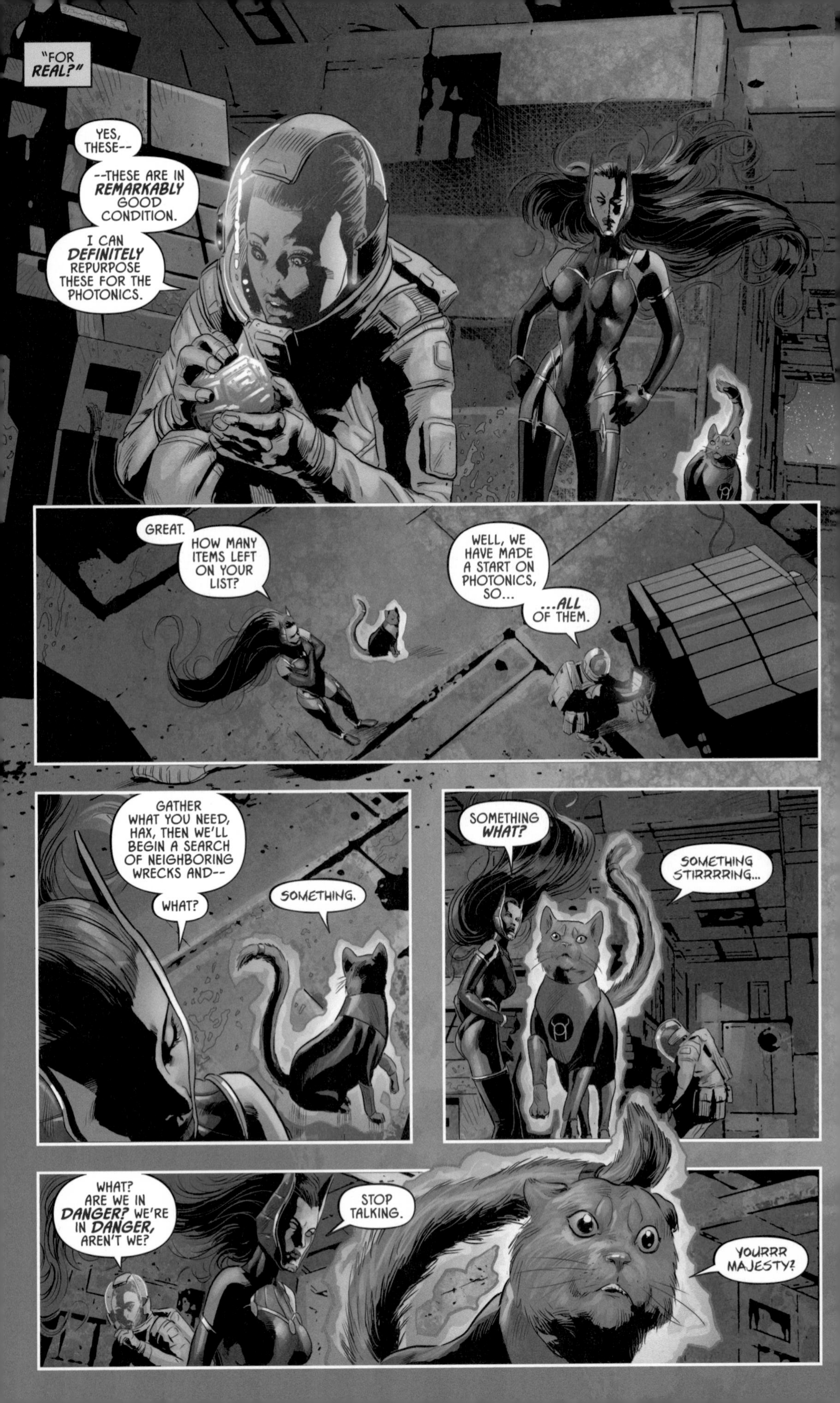
"FOR REAL?"
YES, THESE--
--THESE ARE IN REMARKABLY GOOD CONDITION.
I CAN DEFINITELY REPURPOSE THESE FOR THE PHOTONICS.
GREAT. HOW MANY ITEMS LEFT ON YOUR LIST?
WELL, WE HAVE MADE A START ON PHOTONICS, SO...
...ALL OF THEM.
GATHER WHAT YOU NEED, HAX, THEN WE'LL BEGIN A SEARCH OF NEIGHBORING WRECKS AND--
WHAT?
SOMETHING.
SOMETHING WHAT?
SOMETHING STIRRRRING...
WHAT? ARE WE IN DANGER? WE'RE IN DANGER, AREN'T WE?
STOP TALKING.
YOURRR MAJESTY?

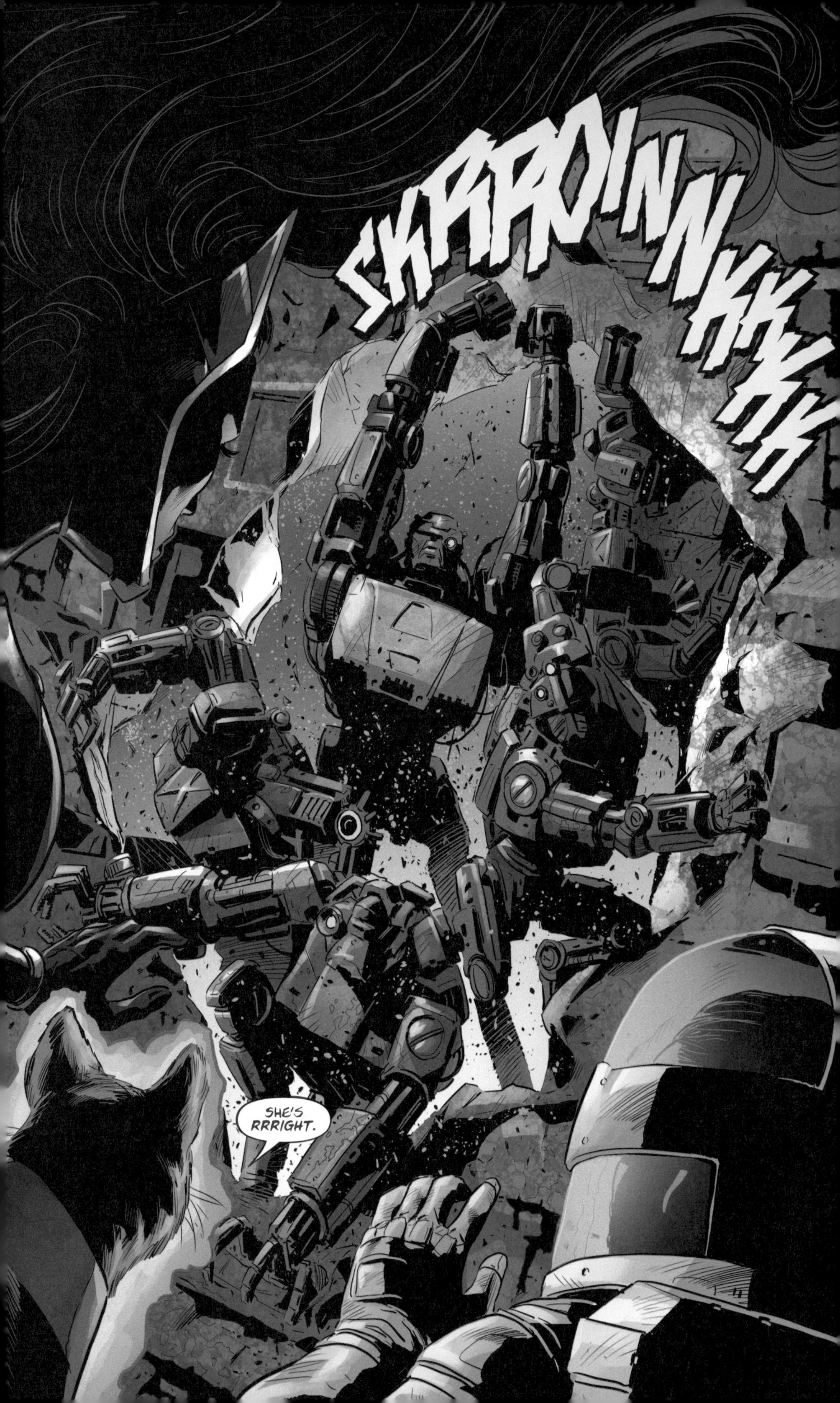
SKRROINNKKKK
SHE'S RRRIGHT.

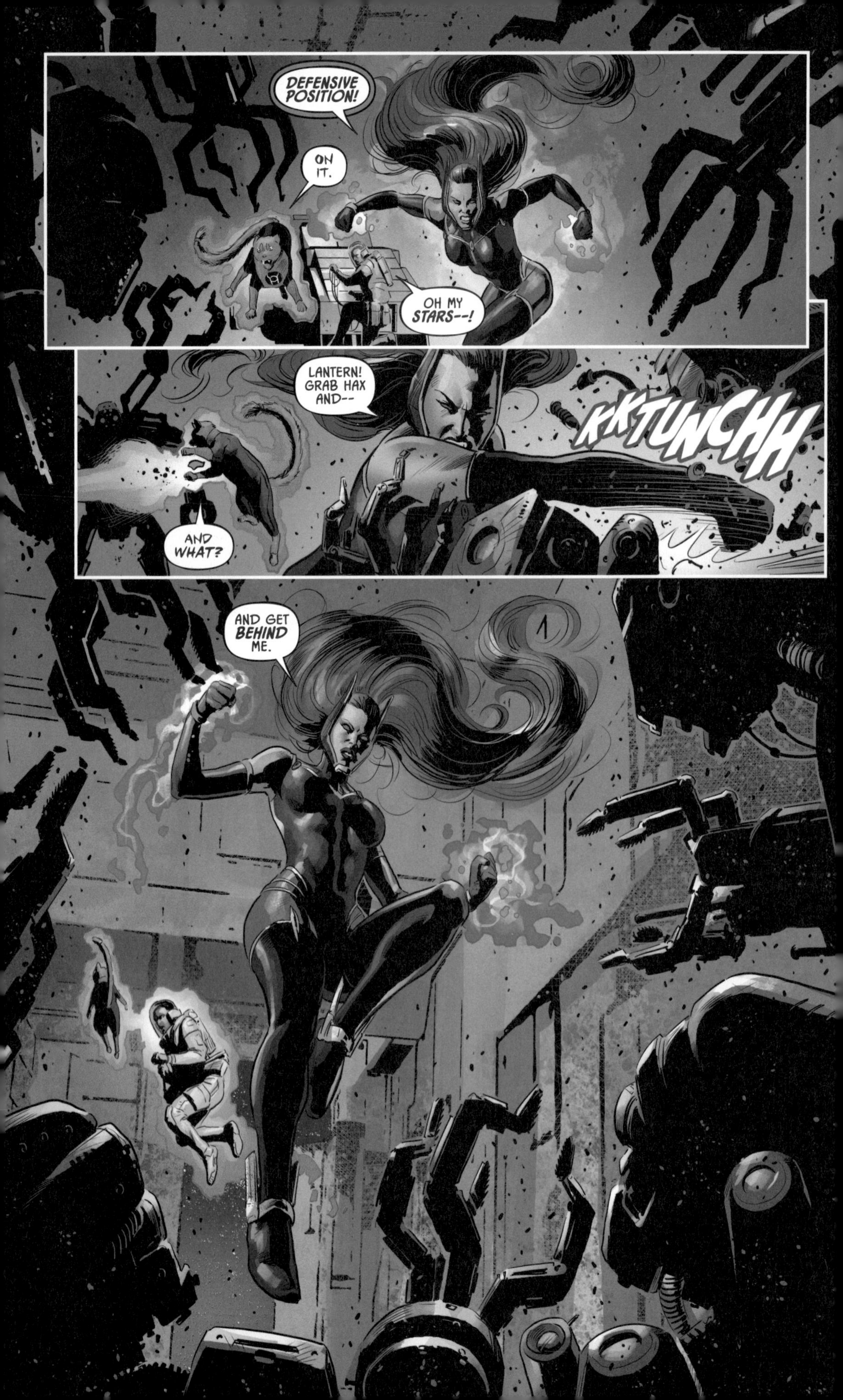
DEFENSIVE POSITION!
ON IT.
OH MY STARS--!
LANTERN! GRAB HAX AND--
KKTUNCHH
AND WHAT?
AND GET BEHIND ME.

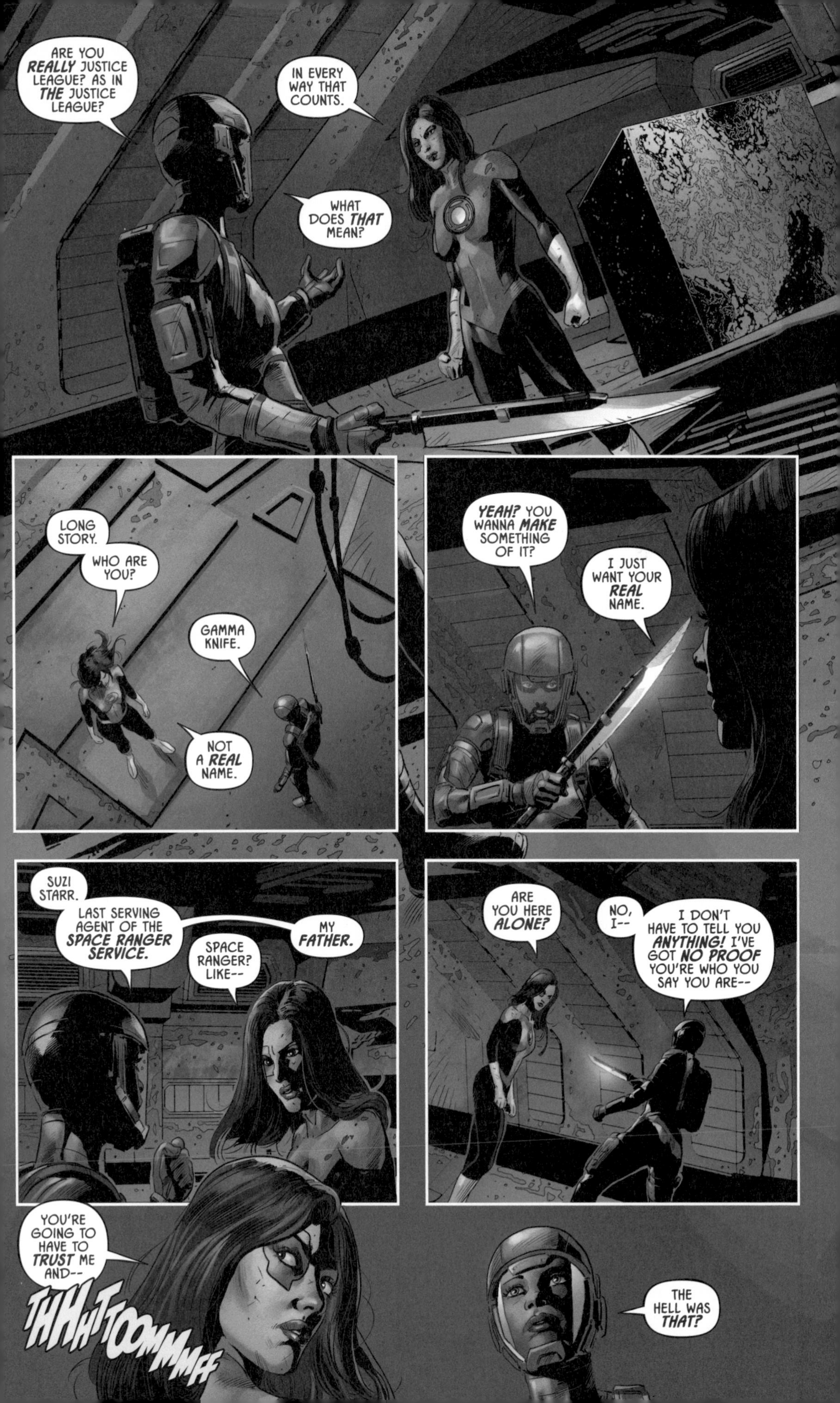

ARE YOU REALLY JUSTICE LEAGUE? AS IN THE JUSTICE LEAGUE?
IN EVERY WAY THAT COUNTS.
WHAT DOES THAT MEAN?
LONG STORY.
WHO ARE YOU?
GAMMA KNIFE.
NOT A REAL NAME.
YEAH? YOU WANNA MAKE SOMETHING OF IT?
I JUST WANT YOUR REAL NAME.
SUZI STARR.
LAST SERVING AGENT OF THE SPACE RANGER SERVICE.
SPACE RANGER? LIKE--
MY FATHER.
ARE YOU HERE ALONE?
NO, I--
I DON'T HAVE TO TELL YOU ANYTHING! I'VE GOT NO PROOF YOU'RE WHO YOU SAY YOU ARE--
YOU'RE GOING TO HAVE TO TRUST ME AND--
THHHTTOOMMMFF
THE HELL WAS THAT?

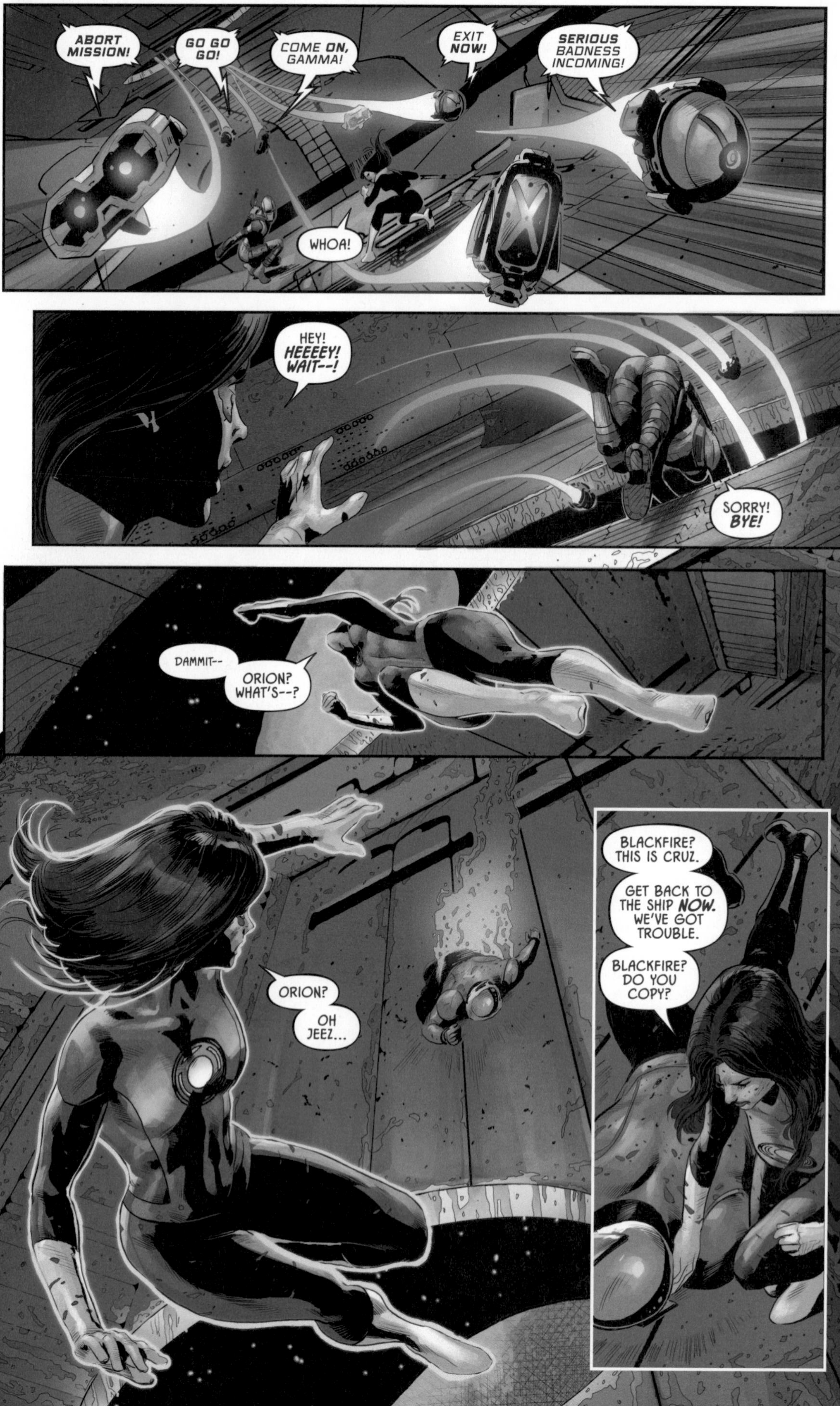
ABORT MISSION!
GO GO GO!
COME ON, GAMMA!
EXIT NOW!
SERIOUS BADNESS INCOMING!
WHOA!
HEY! HEEEEY! WAIT--!
SORRY! BYE!
DAMMIT--
ORION? WHAT'S--?
ORION?
OH JEEZ...
BLACKFIRE? THIS IS CRUZ.
GET BACK TO THE SHIP NOW. WE'VE GOT TROUBLE.
BLACKFIRE? DO YOU COPY?

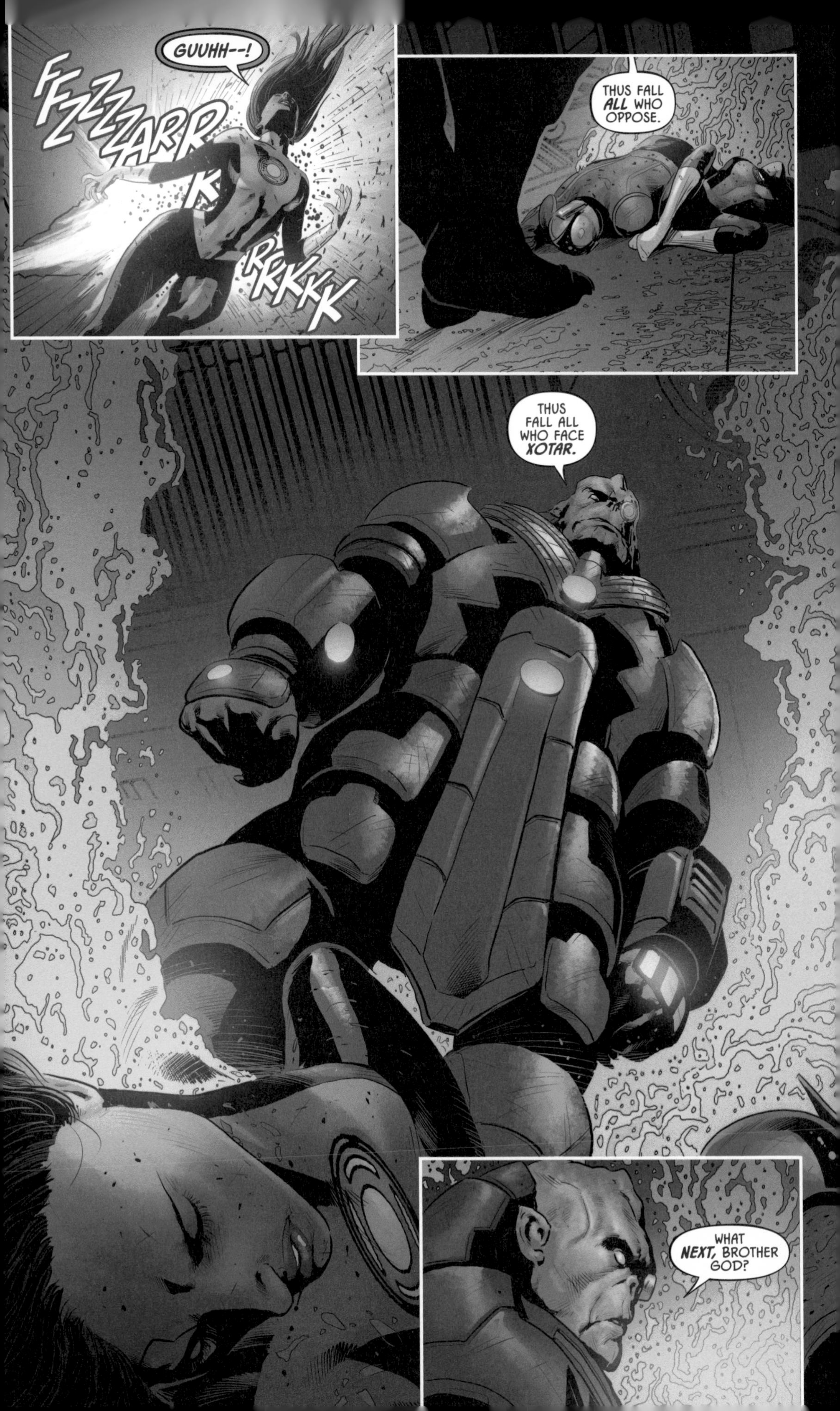
GUUHH--!
FFZZZZARRRRK
RRKKKK
THUS FALL ALL WHO OPPOSE.
THUS FALL ALL WHO FACE XOTAR.
WHAT NEXT, BROTHER GOD?

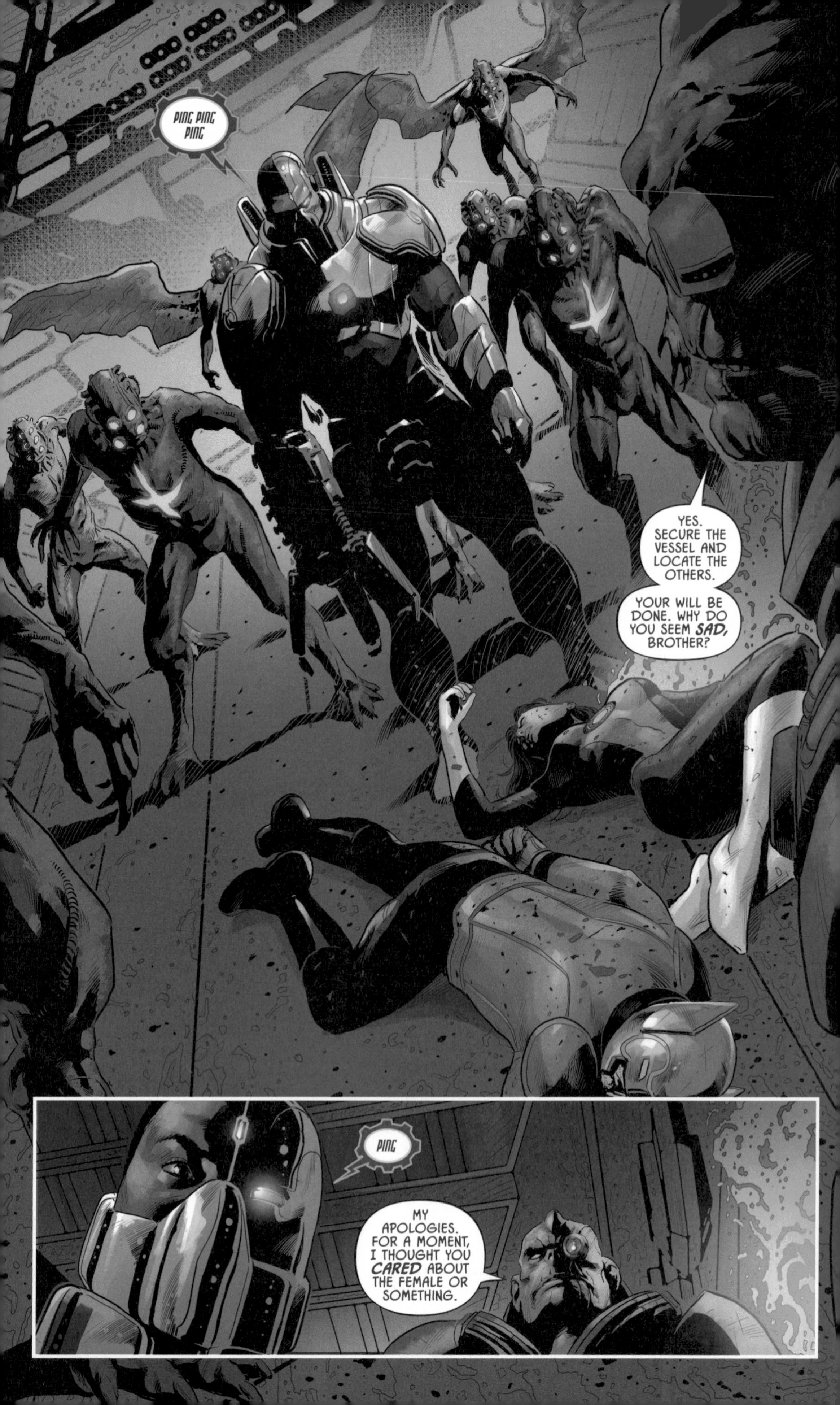
PING PING PING
YES. SECURE THE VESSEL AND LOCATE THE OTHERS.
YOUR WILL BE DONE. WHY DO YOU SEEM *SAD,* BROTHER?
PING
MY APOLOGIES. FOR A MOMENT, I THOUGHT YOU *CARED* ABOUT THE FEMALE OR SOMETHING.

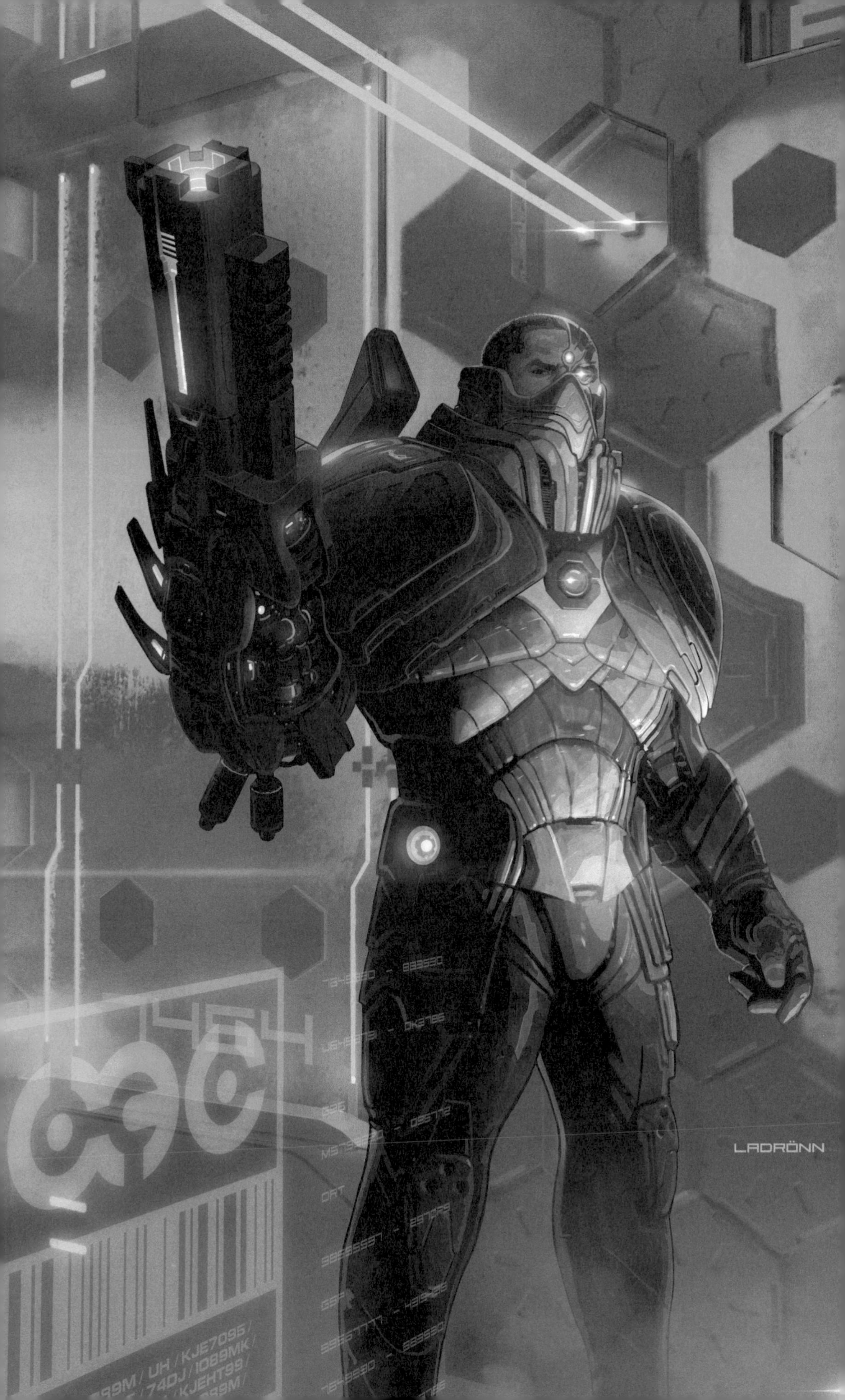
LADRÖNN

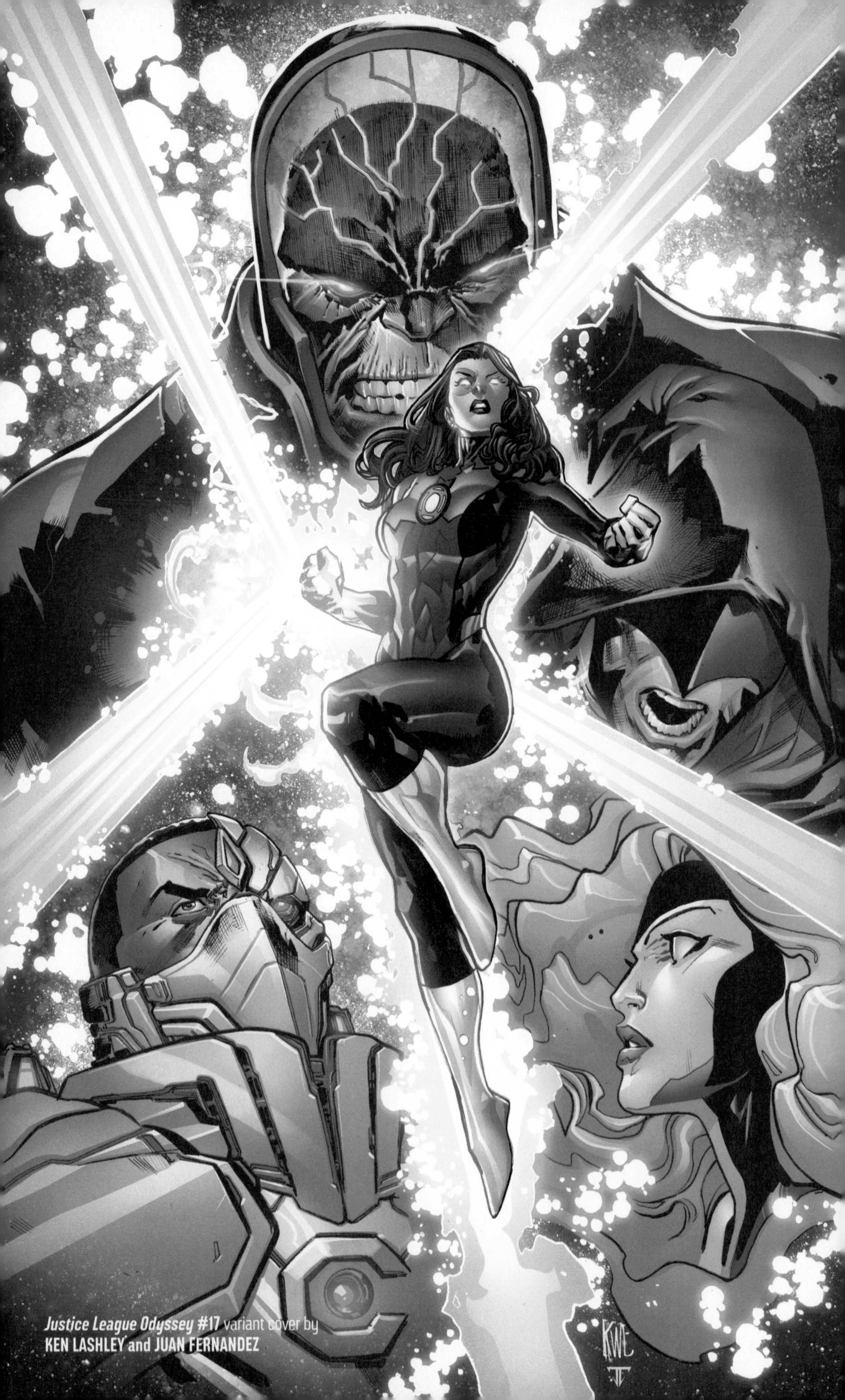

Justice League Odyssey #17 variant cover by
KEN LASHLEY and JUAN FERNANDEZ

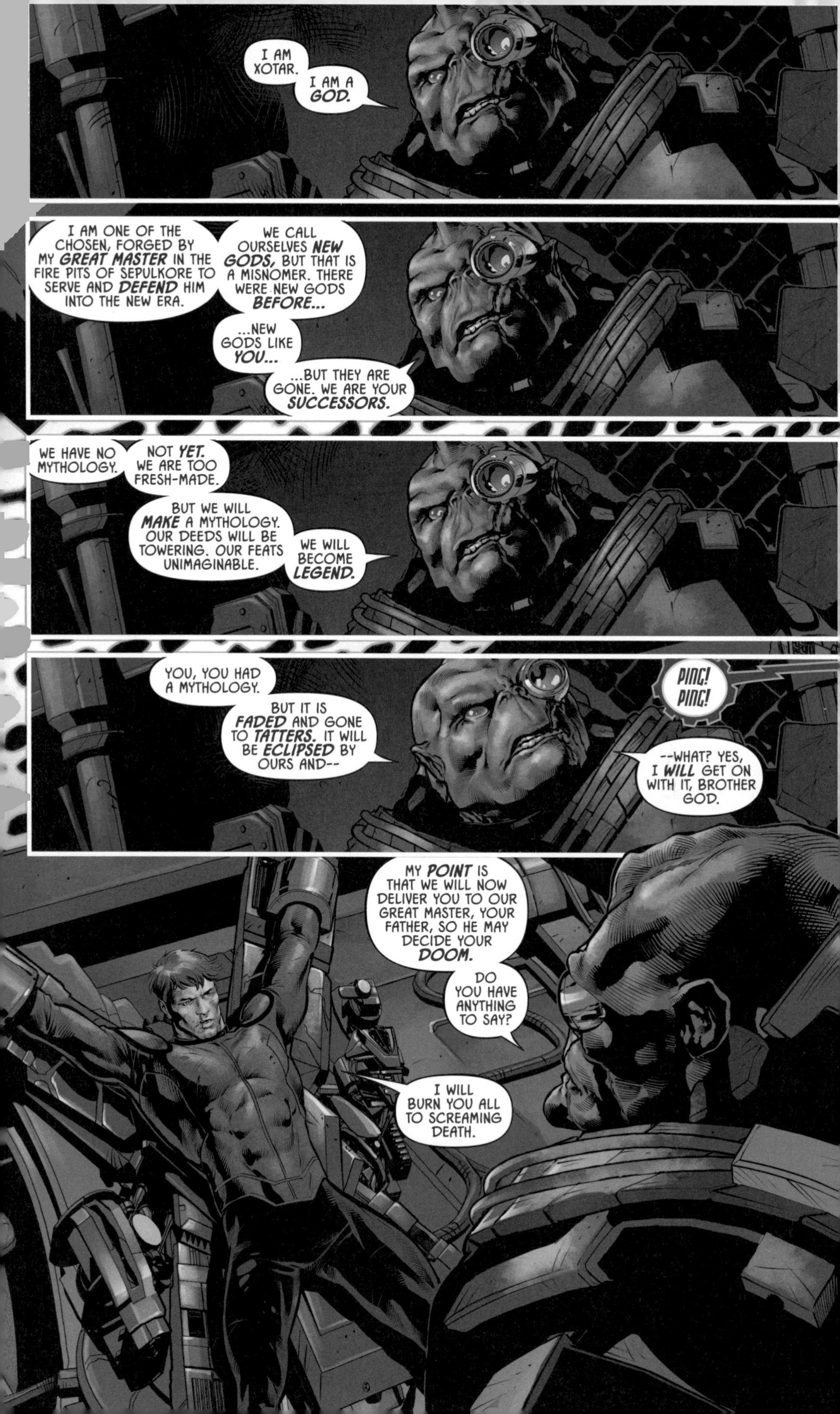
I AM XOTAR. I AM A GOD.
I AM ONE OF THE CHOSEN, FORGED BY MY GREAT MASTER IN THE FIRE PITS OF SEPULKORE TO SERVE AND DEFEND HIM INTO THE NEW ERA.
WE CALL OURSELVES NEW GODS, BUT THAT IS A MISNOMER. THERE WERE NEW GODS BEFORE...
...NEW GODS LIKE YOU...
...BUT THEY ARE GONE. WE ARE YOUR SUCCESSORS.
WE HAVE NO MYTHOLOGY.
NOT YET. WE ARE TOO FRESH-MADE.
BUT WE WILL MAKE A MYTHOLOGY. OUR DEEDS WILL BE TOWERING. OUR FEATS UNIMAGINABLE.
WE WILL BECOME LEGEND.
YOU, YOU HAD A MYTHOLOGY.
BUT IT IS FADED AND GONE TO TATTERS. IT WILL BE ECLIPSED BY OURS AND--
PING! PING!
--WHAT? YES, I WILL GET ON WITH IT, BROTHER GOD.
MY POINT IS THAT WE WILL NOW DELIVER YOU TO OUR GREAT MASTER, YOUR FATHER, SO HE MAY DECIDE YOUR DOOM.
DO YOU HAVE ANYTHING TO SAY?
I WILL BURN YOU ALL TO SCREAMING DEATH.

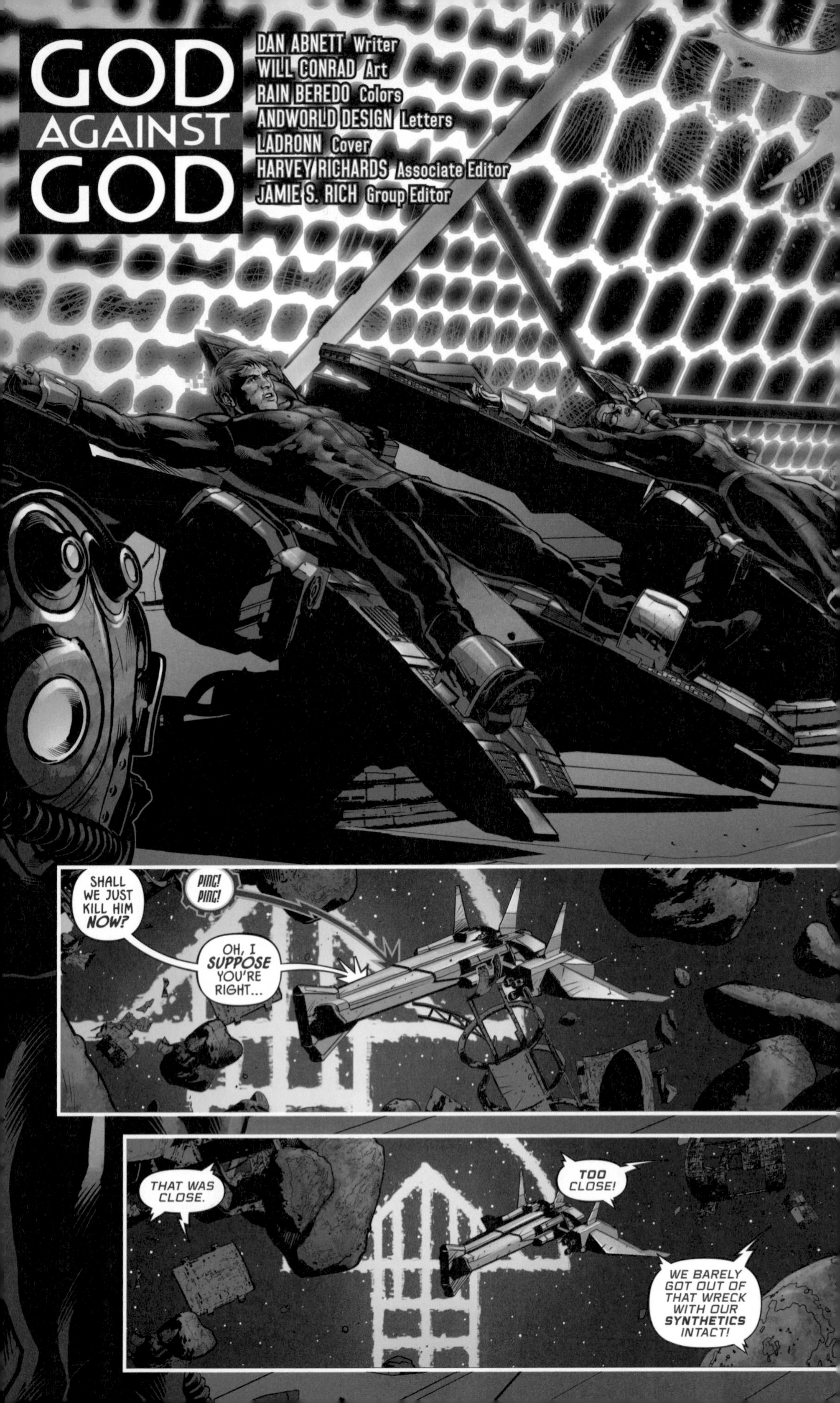
GOD AGAINST GOD
DAN ABNETT Writer
WILL CONRAD Art
RAIN BEREDO Colors
ANDWORLD DESIGN Letters
LADRONN Cover
HARVEY RICHARDS Associate Editor
JAMIE S. RICH Group Editor
SHALL WE JUST KILL HIM NOW?
PING! PING!
OH, I SUPPOSE YOU'RE RIGHT...
THAT WAS CLOSE.
TOO CLOSE!
WE BARELY GOT OUT OF THAT WRECK WITH OUR SYNTHETICS INTACT!

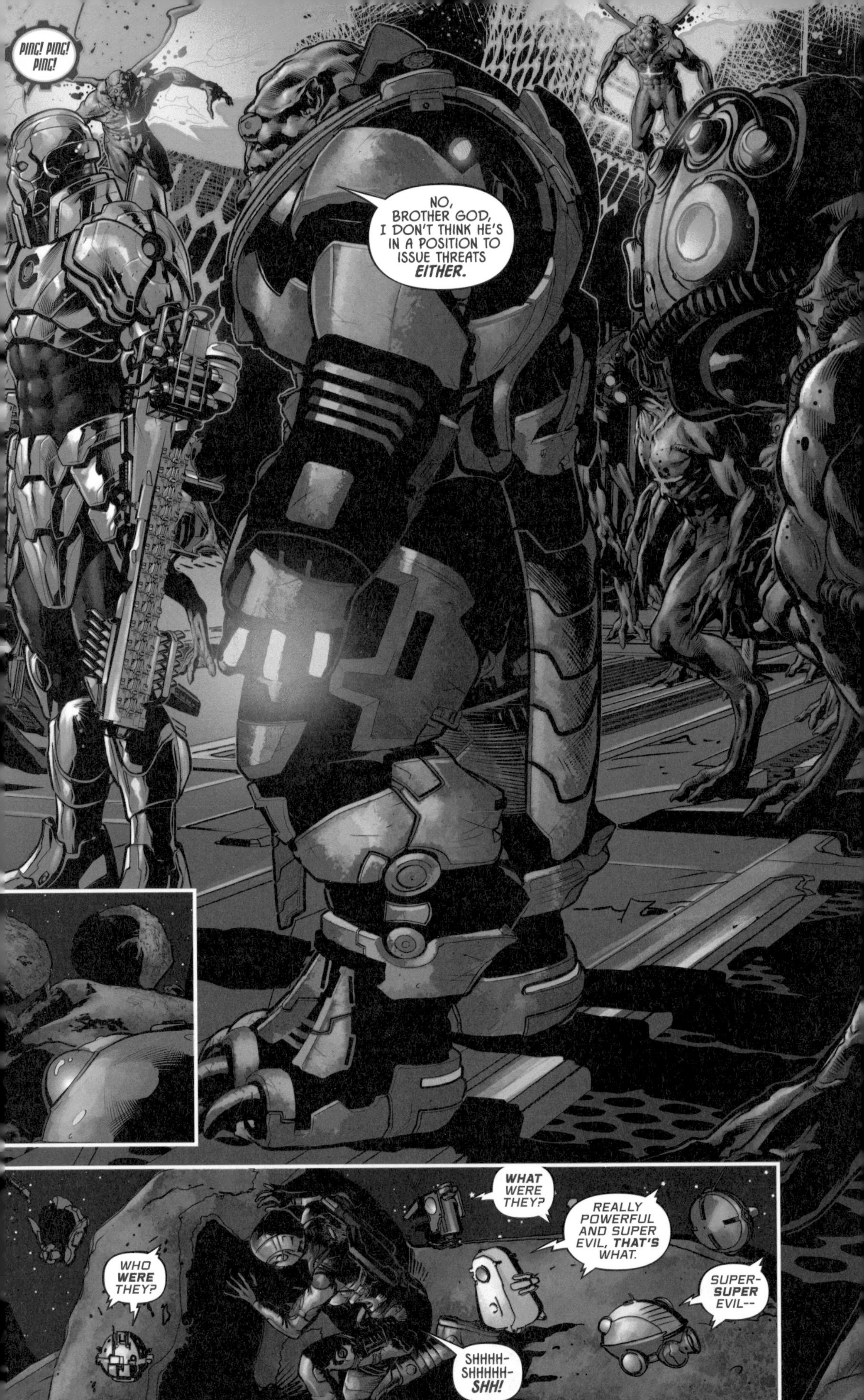
PING! PING! PING!
NO, BROTHER GOD, I DON'T THINK HE'S IN A POSITION TO ISSUE THREATS EITHER.
WHO WERE THEY?
WHAT WERE THEY?
REALLY POWERFUL AND SUPER EVIL, THAT'S WHAT.
SUPER-SUPER EVIL--
SHHHH-SHHHHH-SHH!

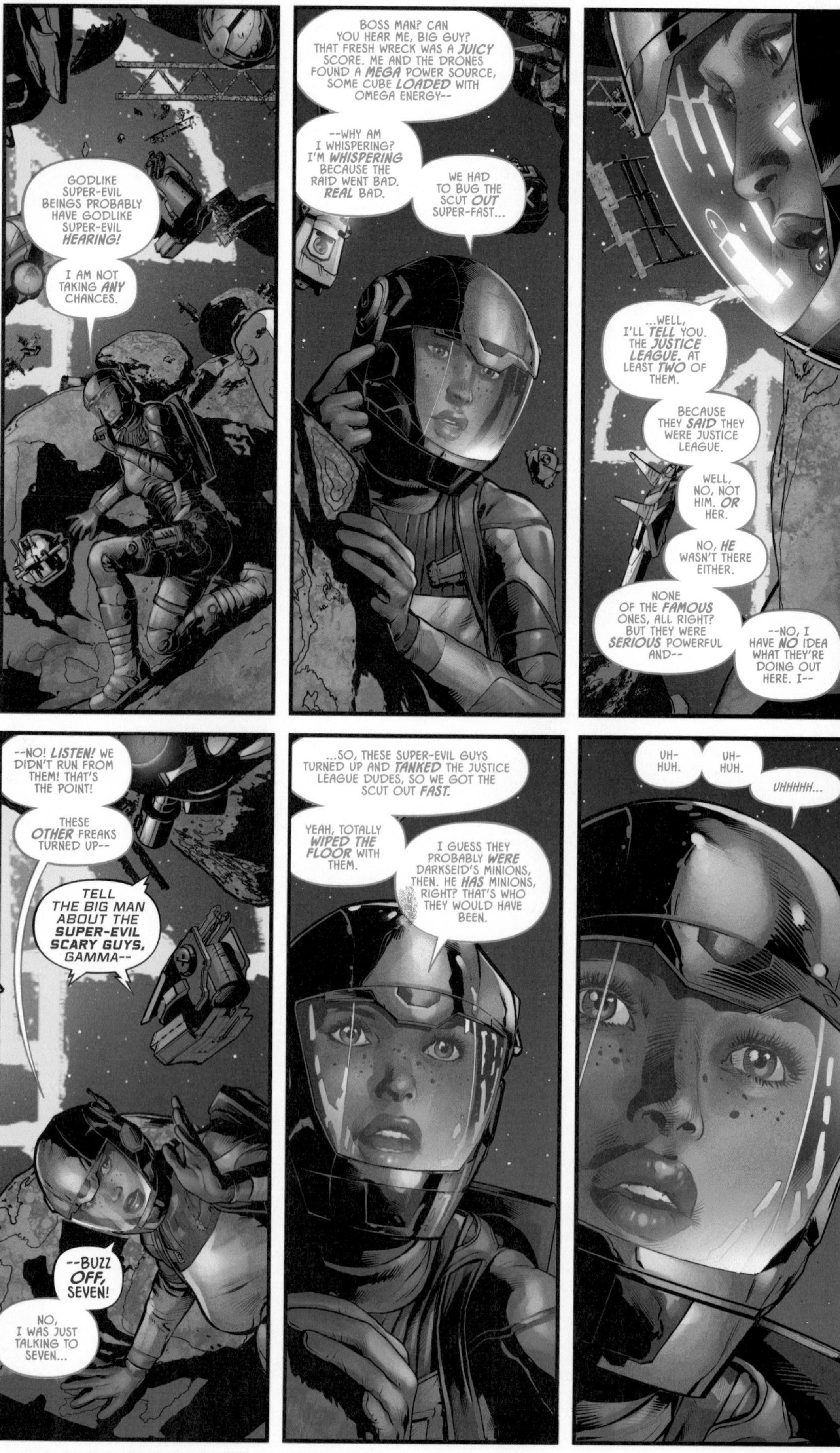
GODLIKE SUPER-EVIL BEINGS PROBABLY HAVE GODLIKE SUPER-EVIL HEARING!
I AM NOT TAKING ANY CHANCES.
BOSS MAN? CAN YOU HEAR ME, BIG GUY? THAT FRESH WRECK WAS A JUICY SCORE. ME AND THE DRONES FOUND A MEGA POWER SOURCE, SOME CUBE LOADED WITH OMEGA ENERGY--
--WHY AM I WHISPERING? I'M WHISPERING BECAUSE THE RAID WENT BAD. REAL BAD.
WE HAD TO BUG THE SCUT OUT SUPER-FAST...
...WELL, I'LL TELL YOU. THE JUSTICE LEAGUE. AT LEAST TWO OF THEM.
BECAUSE THEY SAID THEY WERE JUSTICE LEAGUE.
WELL, NO, NOT HIM. OR HER.
NO, HE WASN'T THERE EITHER.
NONE OF THE FAMOUS ONES, ALL RIGHT? BUT THEY WERE SERIOUS POWERFUL AND--
--NO, I HAVE NO IDEA WHAT THEY'RE DOING OUT HERE. I--
--NO! LISTEN! WE DIDN'T RUN FROM THEM! THAT'S THE POINT!
THESE OTHER FREAKS TURNED UP--
TELL THE BIG MAN ABOUT THE SUPER-EVIL SCARY GUYS, GAMMA--
--BUZZ OFF, SEVEN!
NO, I WAS JUST TALKING TO SEVEN...
...SO, THESE SUPER-EVIL GUYS TURNED UP AND TANKED THE JUSTICE LEAGUE DUDES, SO WE GOT THE SCUT OUT FAST.
YEAH, TOTALLY WIPED THE FLOOR WITH THEM.
I GUESS THEY PROBABLY WERE DARKSEID'S MINIONS, THEN. HE HAS MINIONS, RIGHT? THAT'S WHO THEY WOULD HAVE BEEN.
UH-HUH.
UH-HUH.
UHHHHH...

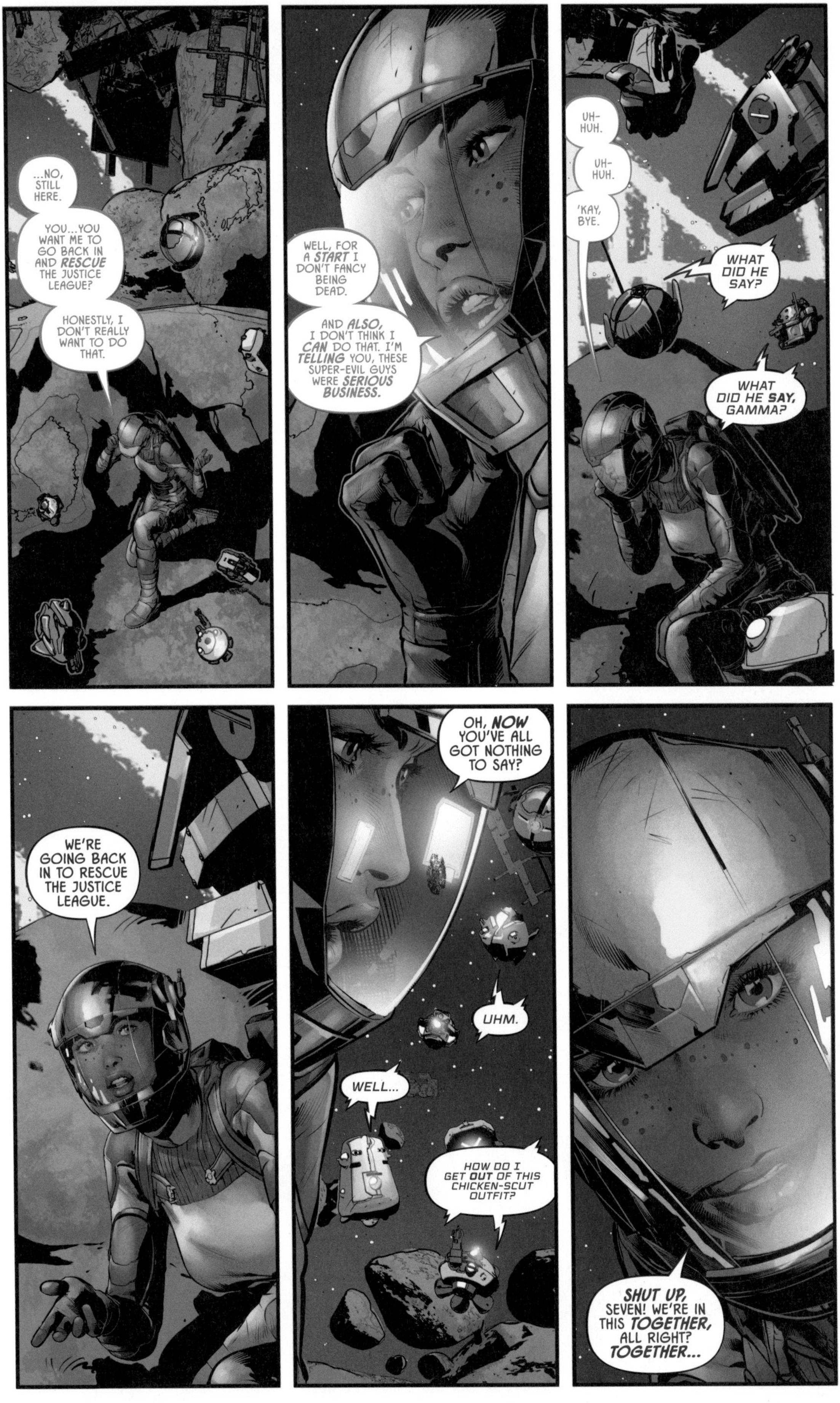
...NO, STILL HERE.
YOU...YOU WANT ME TO GO BACK IN AND RESCUE THE JUSTICE LEAGUE?
HONESTLY, I DON'T REALLY WANT TO DO THAT.
WELL, FOR A START I DON'T FANCY BEING DEAD.
AND ALSO, I DON'T THINK I CAN DO THAT. I'M TELLING YOU, THESE SUPER-EVIL GUYS WERE SERIOUS BUSINESS.
UH-HUH.
UH-HUH.
'KAY, BYE.
WHAT DID HE SAY?
WHAT DID HE SAY, GAMMA?
WE'RE GOING BACK IN TO RESCUE THE JUSTICE LEAGUE.
OH, NOW YOU'VE ALL GOT NOTHING TO SAY?
UHM.
WELL...
HOW DO I GET OUT OF THIS CHICKEN-SCUT OUTFIT?
SHUT UP, SEVEN! WE'RE IN THIS TOGETHER, ALL RIGHT? TOGETHER...

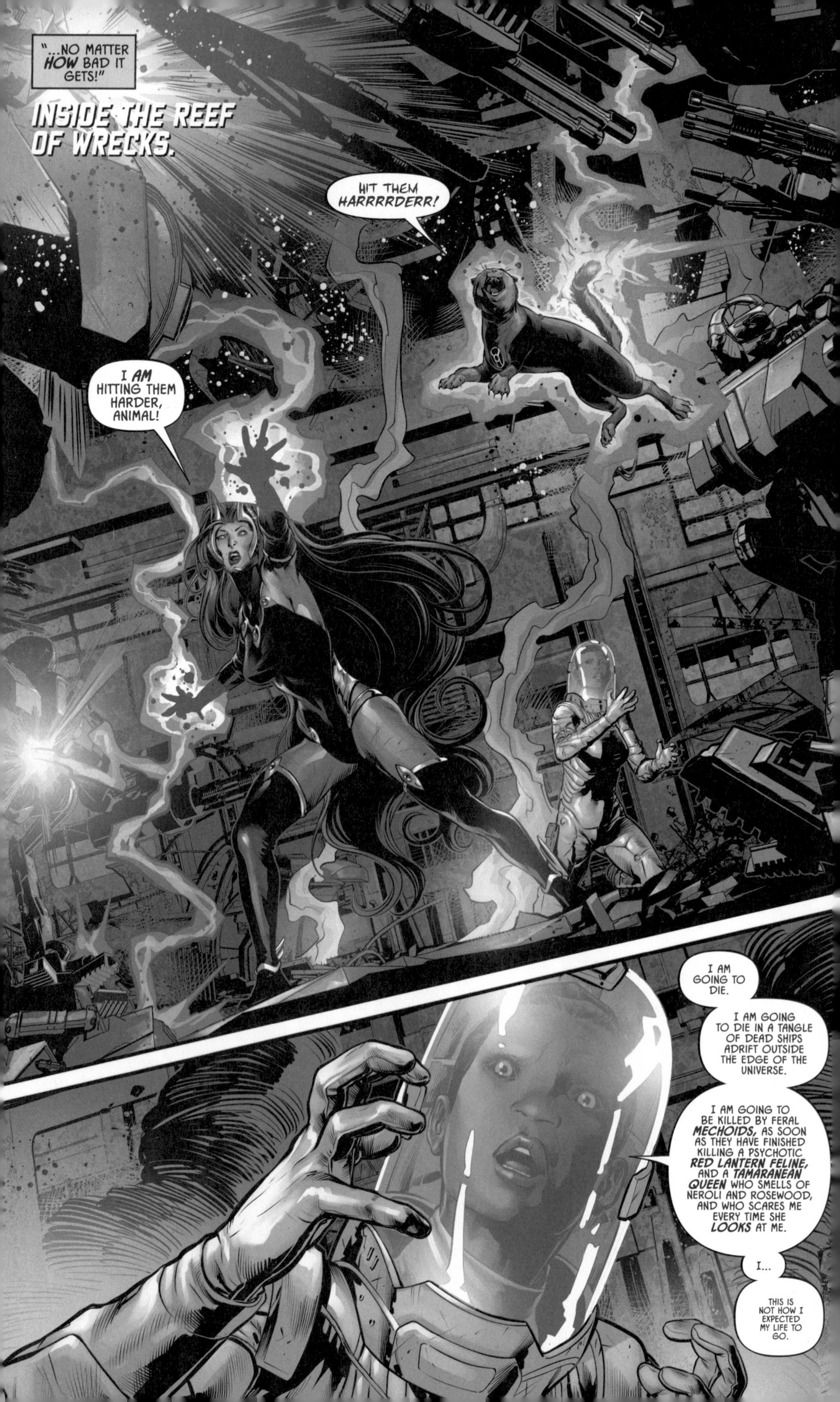

"...NO MATTER HOW BAD IT GETS!"
INSIDE THE REEF OF WRECKS.
HIT THEM HARRRRDERR!
I AM HITTING THEM HARDER, ANIMAL!
I AM GOING TO DIE.
I AM GOING TO DIE IN A TANGLE OF DEAD SHIPS ADRIFT OUTSIDE THE EDGE OF THE UNIVERSE.
I AM GOING TO BE KILLED BY FERAL MECHOIDS, AS SOON AS THEY HAVE FINISHED KILLING A PSYCHOTIC RED LANTERN FELINE, AND A TAMARANEAN QUEEN WHO SMELLS OF NEROLI AND ROSEWOOD, AND WHO SCARES ME EVERY TIME SHE LOOKS AT ME.
I...
THIS IS NOT HOW I EXPECTED MY LIFE TO GO.

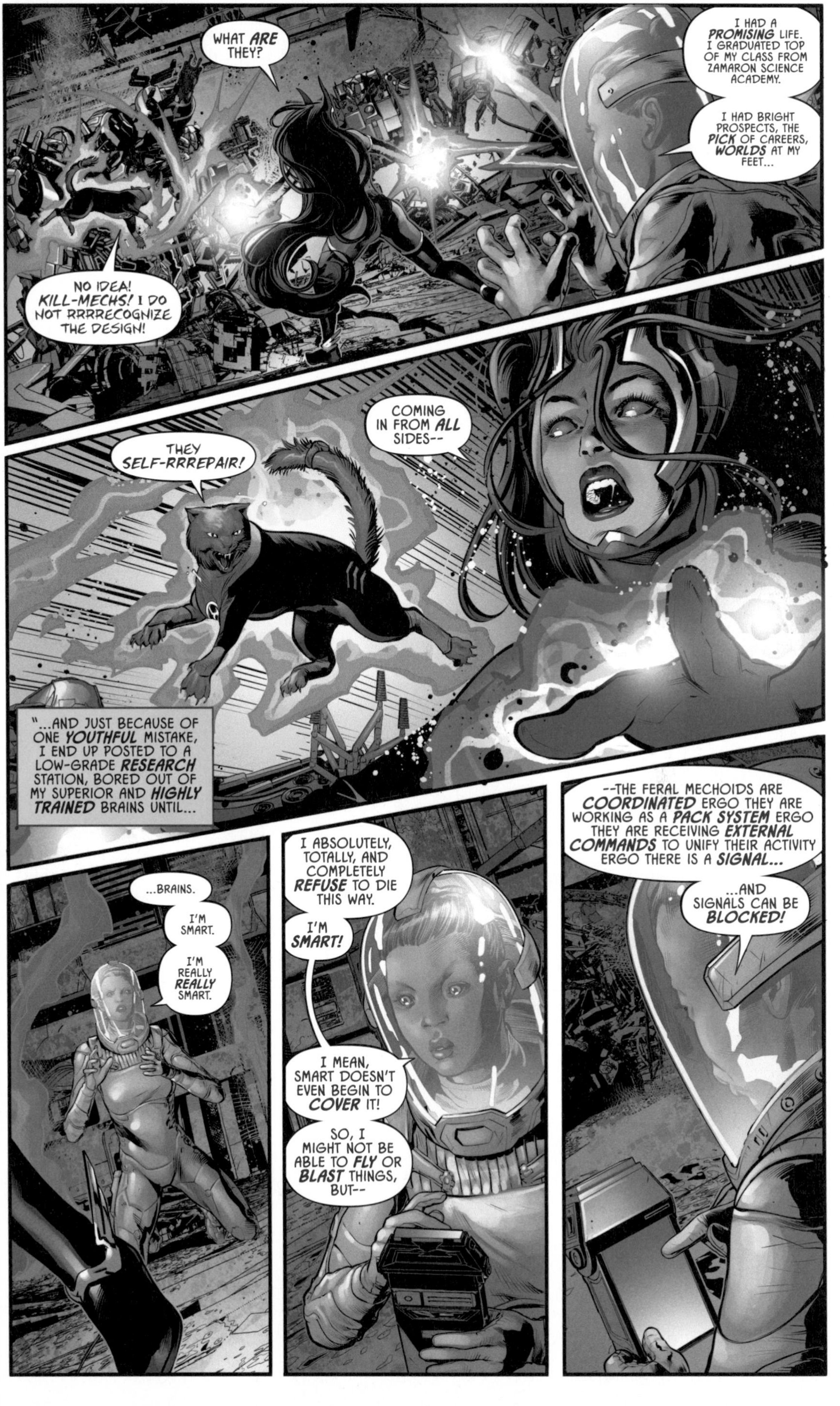
WHAT ARE THEY?
I HAD A PROMISING LIFE. I GRADUATED TOP OF MY CLASS FROM ZAMARON SCIENCE ACADEMY.
I HAD BRIGHT PROSPECTS, THE PICK OF CAREERS, WORLDS AT MY FEET...
NO IDEA! KILL-MECHS! I DO NOT RRRRECOGNIZE THE DESIGN!
COMING IN FROM ALL SIDES--
THEY SELF-RRREPAIR!
"...AND JUST BECAUSE OF ONE YOUTHFUL MISTAKE, I END UP POSTED TO A LOW-GRADE RESEARCH STATION, BORED OUT OF MY SUPERIOR AND HIGHLY TRAINED BRAINS UNTIL...
...BRAINS.
I'M SMART.
I'M REALLY REALLY SMART.
I ABSOLUTELY, TOTALLY, AND COMPLETELY REFUSE TO DIE THIS WAY.
I'M SMART!
I MEAN, SMART DOESN'T EVEN BEGIN TO COVER IT!
SO, I MIGHT NOT BE ABLE TO FLY OR BLAST THINGS, BUT--
--THE FERAL MECHOIDS ARE COORDINATED ERGO THEY ARE WORKING AS A PACK SYSTEM ERGO THEY ARE RECEIVING EXTERNAL COMMANDS TO UNIFY THEIR ACTIVITY ERGO THERE IS A SIGNAL...
...AND SIGNALS CAN BE BLOCKED!

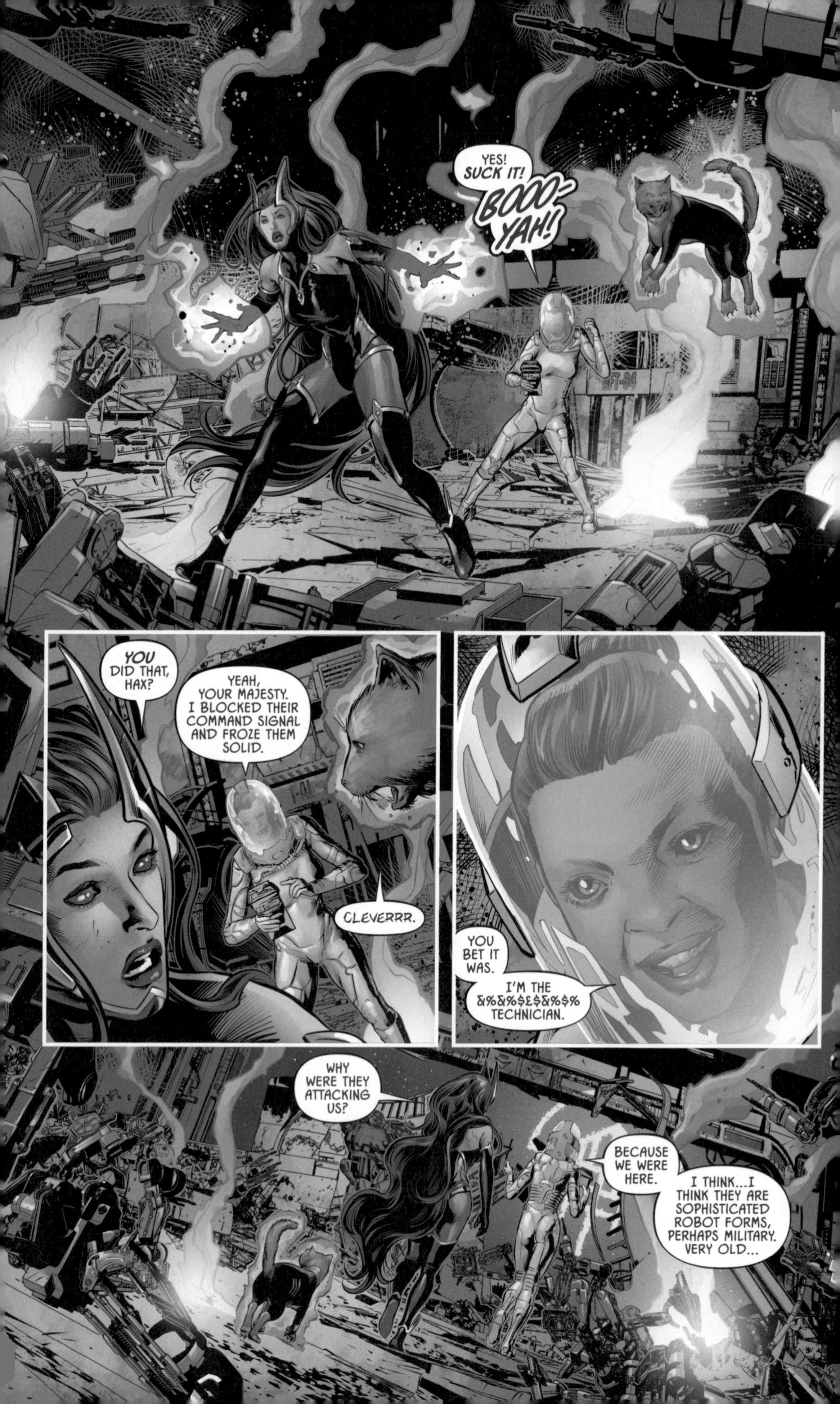
YES! SUCK IT!
BOOO-YAH!
YOU DID THAT, HAX?
YEAH, YOUR MAJESTY. I BLOCKED THEIR COMMAND SIGNAL AND FROZE THEM SOLID.
CLEVERRR.
YOU BET IT WAS.
I'M THE &%&%$£$&%$% TECHNICIAN.
WHY WERE THEY ATTACKING US?
BECAUSE WE WERE HERE.
I THINK...I THINK THEY ARE SOPHISTICATED ROBOT FORMS, PERHAPS MILITARY. VERY OLD...

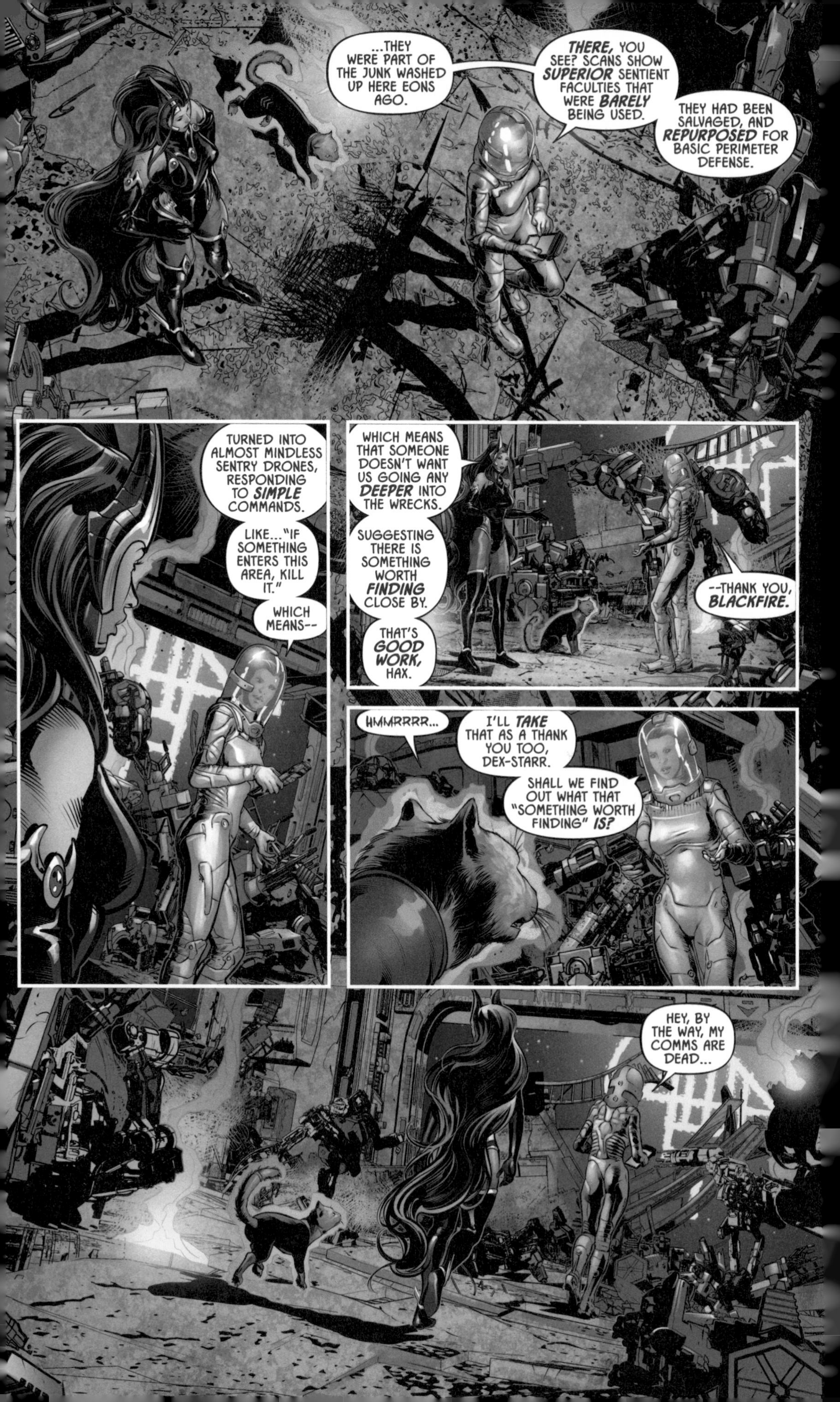

...THEY WERE PART OF THE JUNK WASHED UP HERE EONS AGO.
THERE, YOU SEE? SCANS SHOW SUPERIOR SENTIENT FACULTIES THAT WERE BARELY BEING USED.
THEY HAD BEEN SALVAGED, AND REPURPOSED FOR BASIC PERIMETER DEFENSE.
TURNED INTO ALMOST MINDLESS SENTRY DRONES, RESPONDING TO SIMPLE COMMANDS.
LIKE... "IF SOMETHING ENTERS THIS AREA, KILL IT."
WHICH MEANS--
WHICH MEANS THAT SOMEONE DOESN'T WANT US GOING ANY DEEPER INTO THE WRECKS.
SUGGESTING THERE IS SOMETHING WORTH FINDING CLOSE BY.
THAT'S GOOD WORK, HAX.
--THANK YOU, BLACKFIRE.
HMMRRRR...
I'LL TAKE THAT AS A THANK YOU TOO, DEX-STARR.
SHALL WE FIND OUT WHAT THAT "SOMETHING WORTH FINDING" IS?
HEY, BY THE WAY, MY COMMS ARE DEAD...

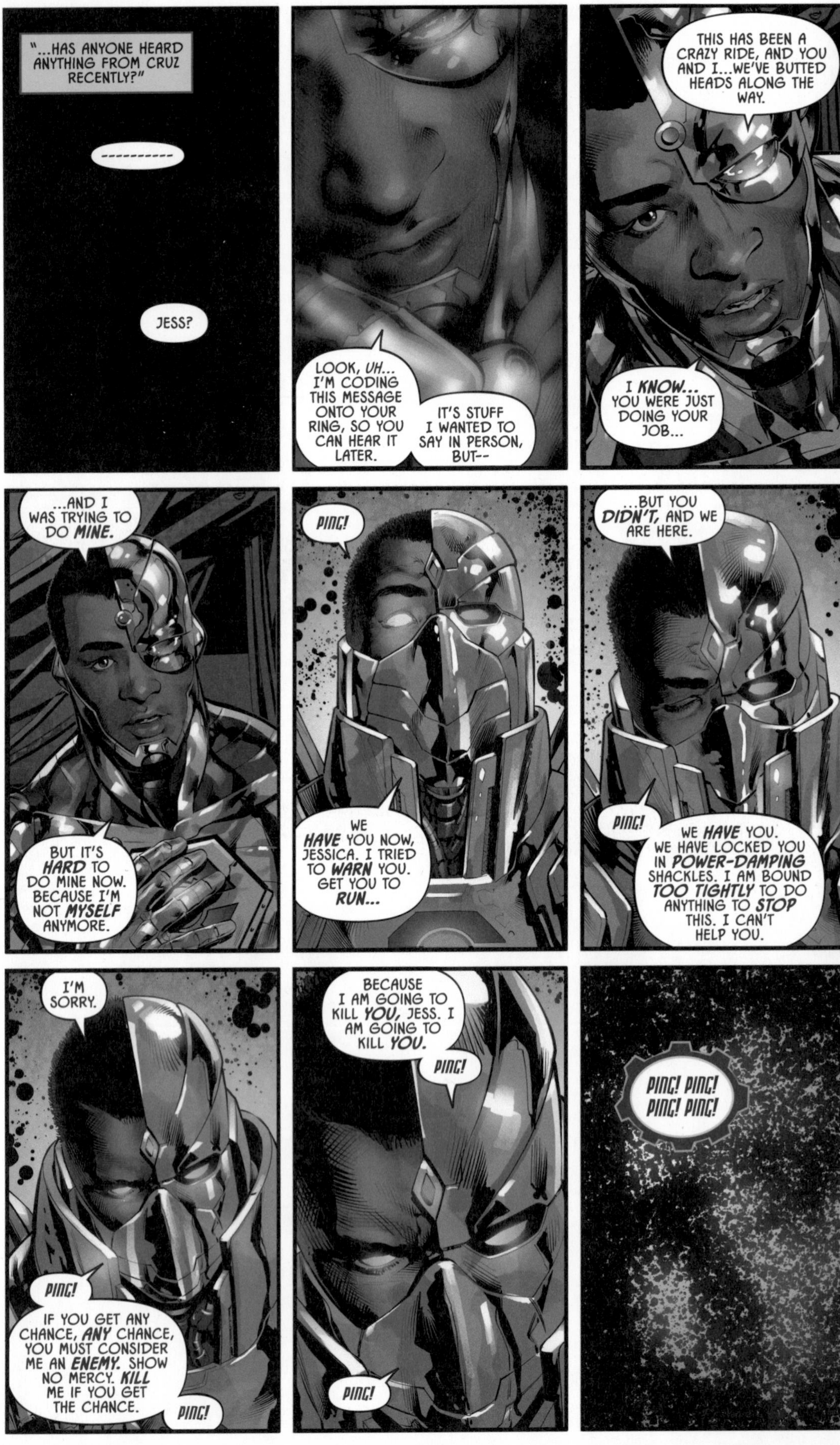
"...HAS ANYONE HEARD ANYTHING FROM CRUZ RECENTLY?"

JESS?
LOOK, UH... I'M CODING THIS MESSAGE ONTO YOUR RING, SO YOU CAN HEAR IT LATER.
IT'S STUFF I WANTED TO SAY IN PERSON, BUT--
THIS HAS BEEN A CRAZY RIDE, AND YOU AND I...WE'VE BUTTED HEADS ALONG THE WAY.
I KNOW... YOU WERE JUST DOING YOUR JOB...
...AND I WAS TRYING TO DO MINE.
BUT IT'S HARD TO DO MINE NOW. BECAUSE I'M NOT MYSELF ANYMORE.
PING!
WE HAVE YOU NOW, JESSICA. I TRIED TO WARN YOU. GET YOU TO RUN...
...BUT YOU DIDN'T, AND WE ARE HERE.
PING!
WE HAVE YOU. WE HAVE LOCKED YOU IN POWER-DAMPING SHACKLES. I AM BOUND TOO TIGHTLY TO DO ANYTHING TO STOP THIS. I CAN'T HELP YOU.
I'M SORRY.
PING!
IF YOU GET ANY CHANCE, ANY CHANCE, YOU MUST CONSIDER ME AN ENEMY. SHOW NO MERCY. KILL ME IF YOU GET THE CHANCE.
PING!
BECAUSE I AM GOING TO KILL YOU, JESS. I AM GOING TO KILL YOU.
PING!
PING!
PING! PING! PING! PING!

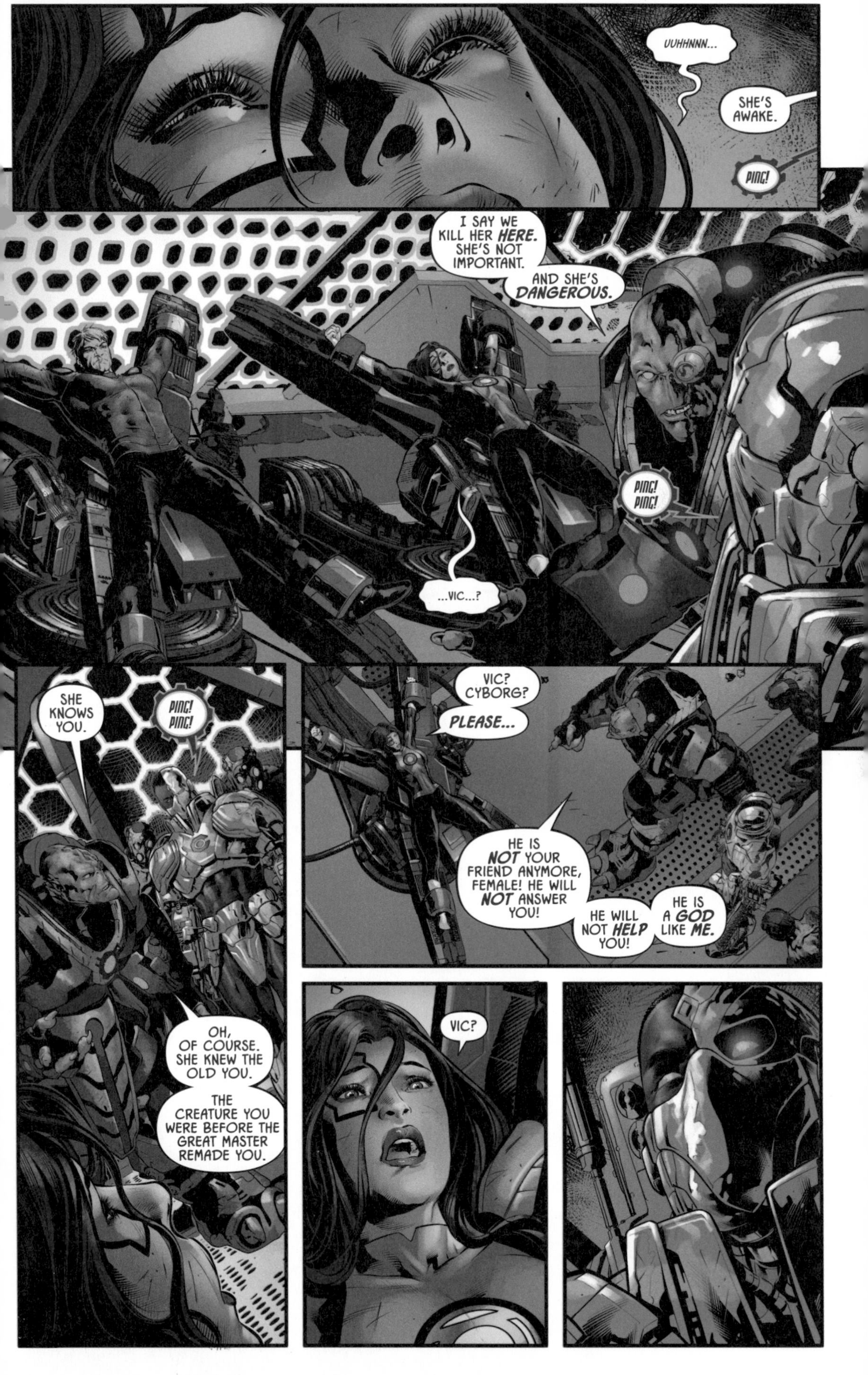
UUHHNNN...
SHE'S AWAKE.
PING!
I SAY WE KILL HER HERE. SHE'S NOT IMPORTANT.
AND SHE'S DANGEROUS.
PING! PING!
...VIC...?
SHE KNOWS YOU.
PING! PING!
OH, OF COURSE. SHE KNEW THE OLD YOU.
THE CREATURE YOU WERE BEFORE THE GREAT MASTER REMADE YOU.
VIC? CYBORG?
PLEASE...
HE IS NOT YOUR FRIEND ANYMORE, FEMALE! HE WILL NOT ANSWER YOU!
HE WILL NOT HELP YOU!
HE IS A GOD LIKE ME.
VIC?

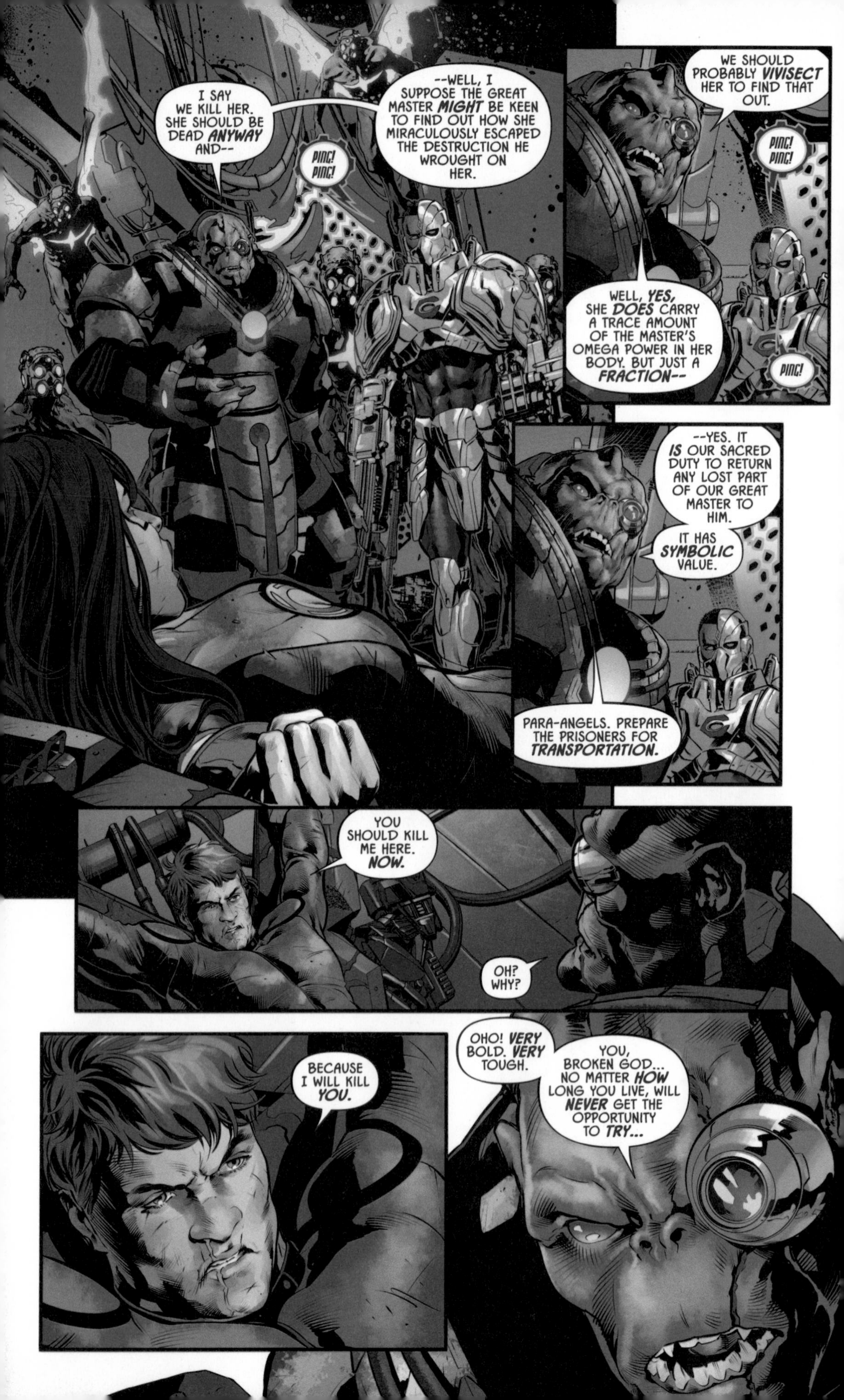
I SAY WE KILL HER. SHE SHOULD BE DEAD ANYWAY AND--
PING! PING!
--WELL, I SUPPOSE THE GREAT MASTER MIGHT BE KEEN TO FIND OUT HOW SHE MIRACULOUSLY ESCAPED THE DESTRUCTION HE WROUGHT ON HER.
WE SHOULD PROBABLY VIVISECT HER TO FIND THAT OUT.
PING! PING!
WELL, YES, SHE DOES CARRY A TRACE AMOUNT OF THE MASTER'S OMEGA POWER IN HER BODY. BUT JUST A FRACTION--
PING!
--YES. IT IS OUR SACRED DUTY TO RETURN ANY LOST PART OF OUR GREAT MASTER TO HIM.
IT HAS SYMBOLIC VALUE.
PARA-ANGELS. PREPARE THE PRISONERS FOR TRANSPORTATION.
YOU SHOULD KILL ME HERE. NOW.
OH? WHY?
BECAUSE I WILL KILL YOU.
OHO! VERY BOLD. VERY TOUGH.
YOU, BROKEN GOD... NO MATTER HOW LONG YOU LIVE, WILL NEVER GET THE OPPORTUNITY TO TRY...

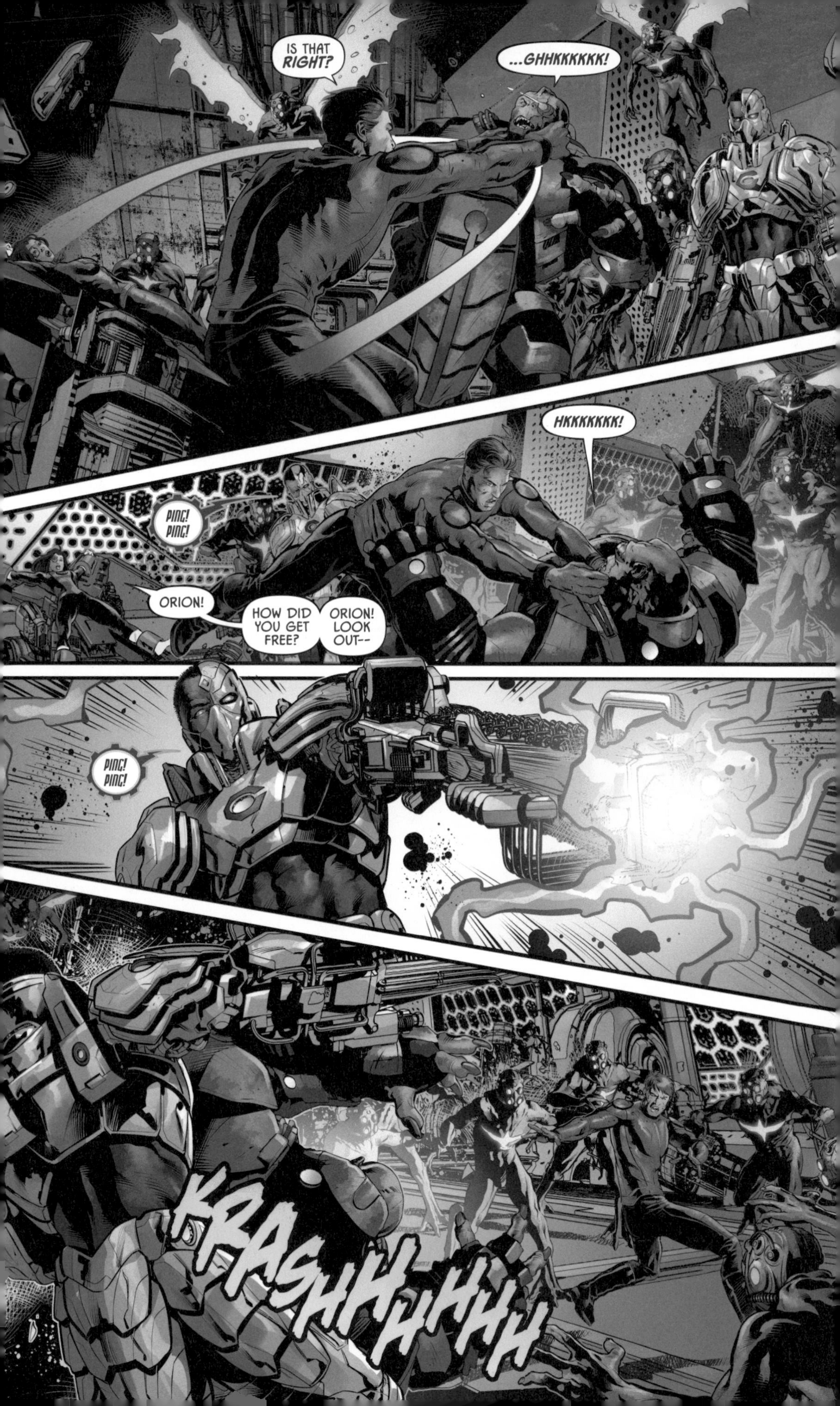
IS THAT RIGHT?
...GHHKKKKKK!
HKKKKKKK!
PING! PING!
ORION!
HOW DID YOU GET FREE?
ORION! LOOK OUT--
PING! PING!
KRASHHHHHH

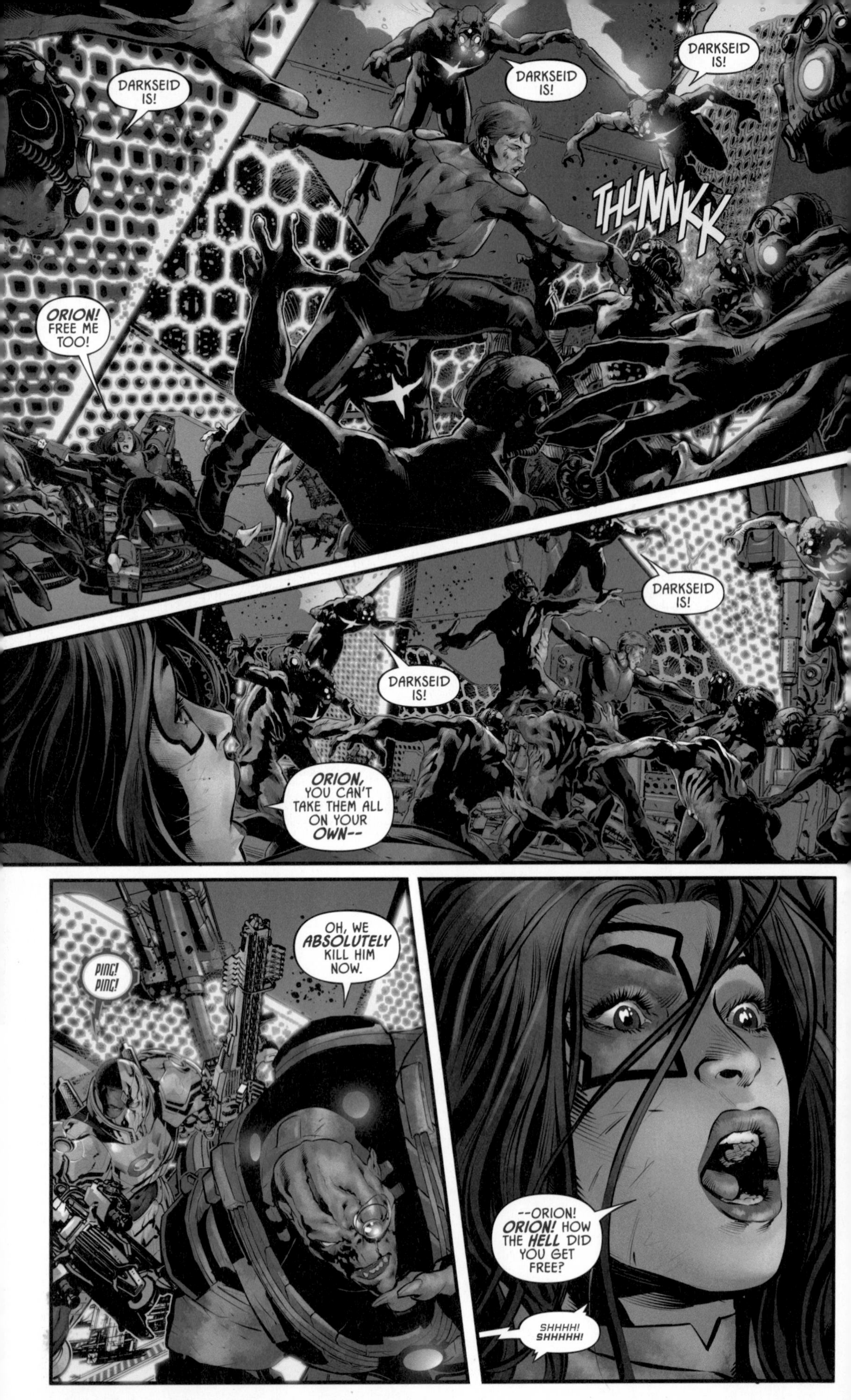

DARKSEID IS!
DARKSEID IS!
DARKSEID IS!
THUNNKK
ORION! FREE ME TOO!
DARKSEID IS!
DARKSEID IS!
ORION, YOU CAN'T TAKE THEM ALL ON YOUR OWN--
PING! PING!
OH, WE ABSOLUTELY KILL HIM NOW.
--ORION! ORION! HOW THE HELL DID YOU GET FREE?
SHHHH! SHHHHH!

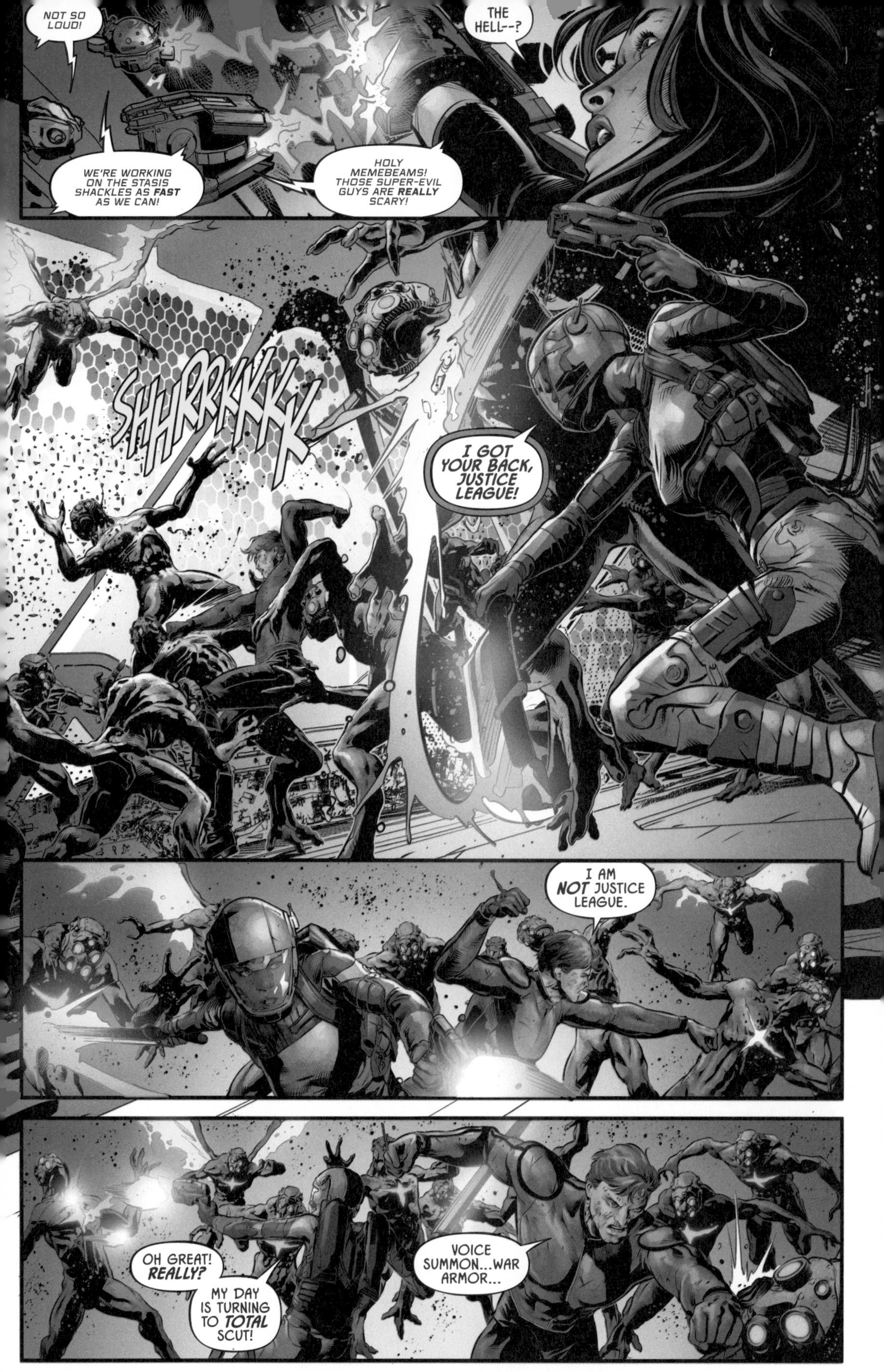
NOT SO LOUD!
WE'RE WORKING ON THE STASIS SHACKLES AS FAST AS WE CAN!
HOLY MEMEBEAMS! THOSE SUPER-EVIL GUYS ARE REALLY SCARY!
THE HELL--?
SHHRRKKKK
I GOT YOUR BACK, JUSTICE LEAGUE!
I AM NOT JUSTICE LEAGUE.
OH GREAT! REALLY?
MY DAY IS TURNING TO TOTAL SCUT!
VOICE SUMMON...WAR ARMOR...

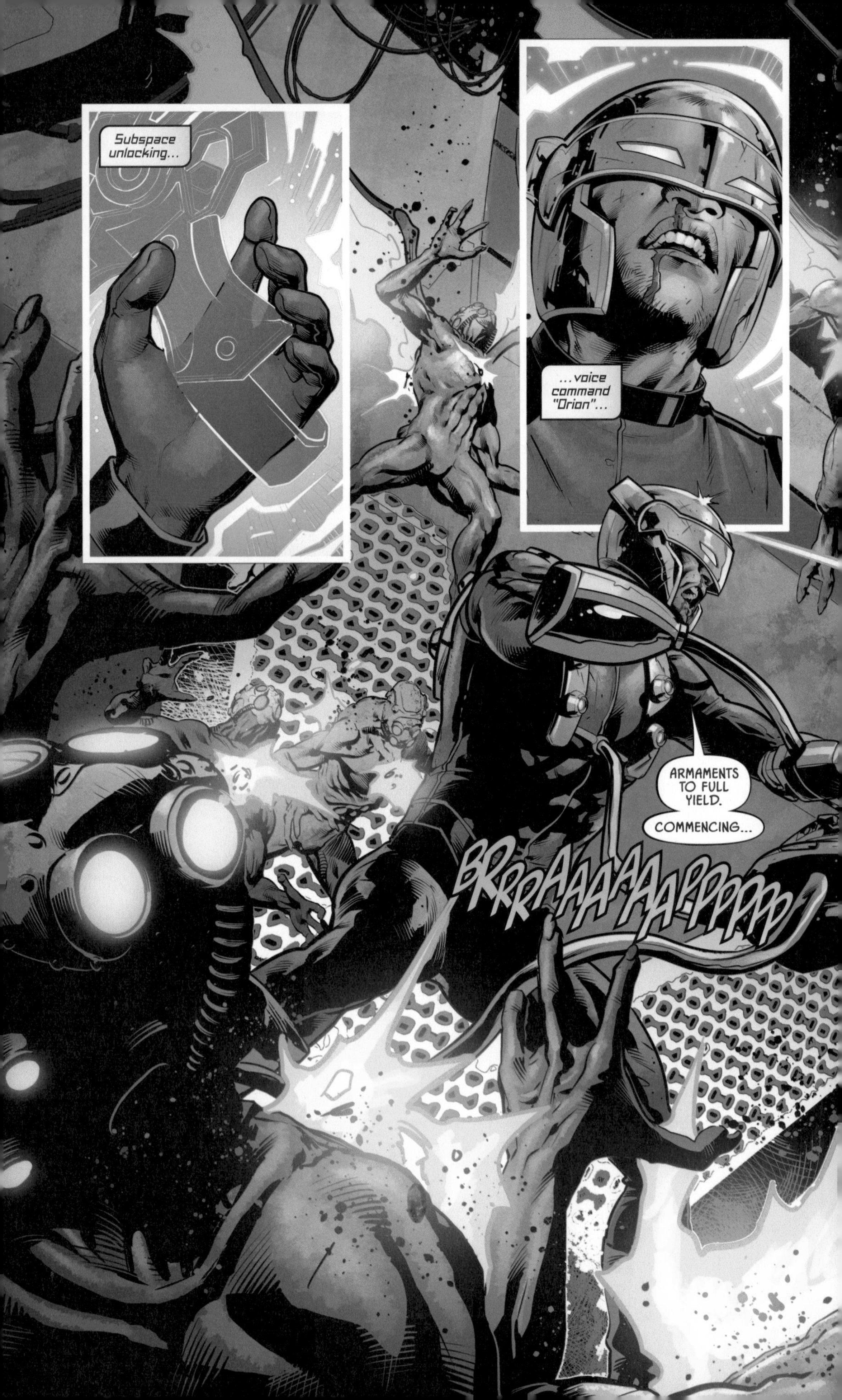
Subspace unlocking...
...voice command "Orion"...
ARMAMENTS TO FULL YIELD.
COMMENCING...
BRRRAAAAAAAAPPPPPP

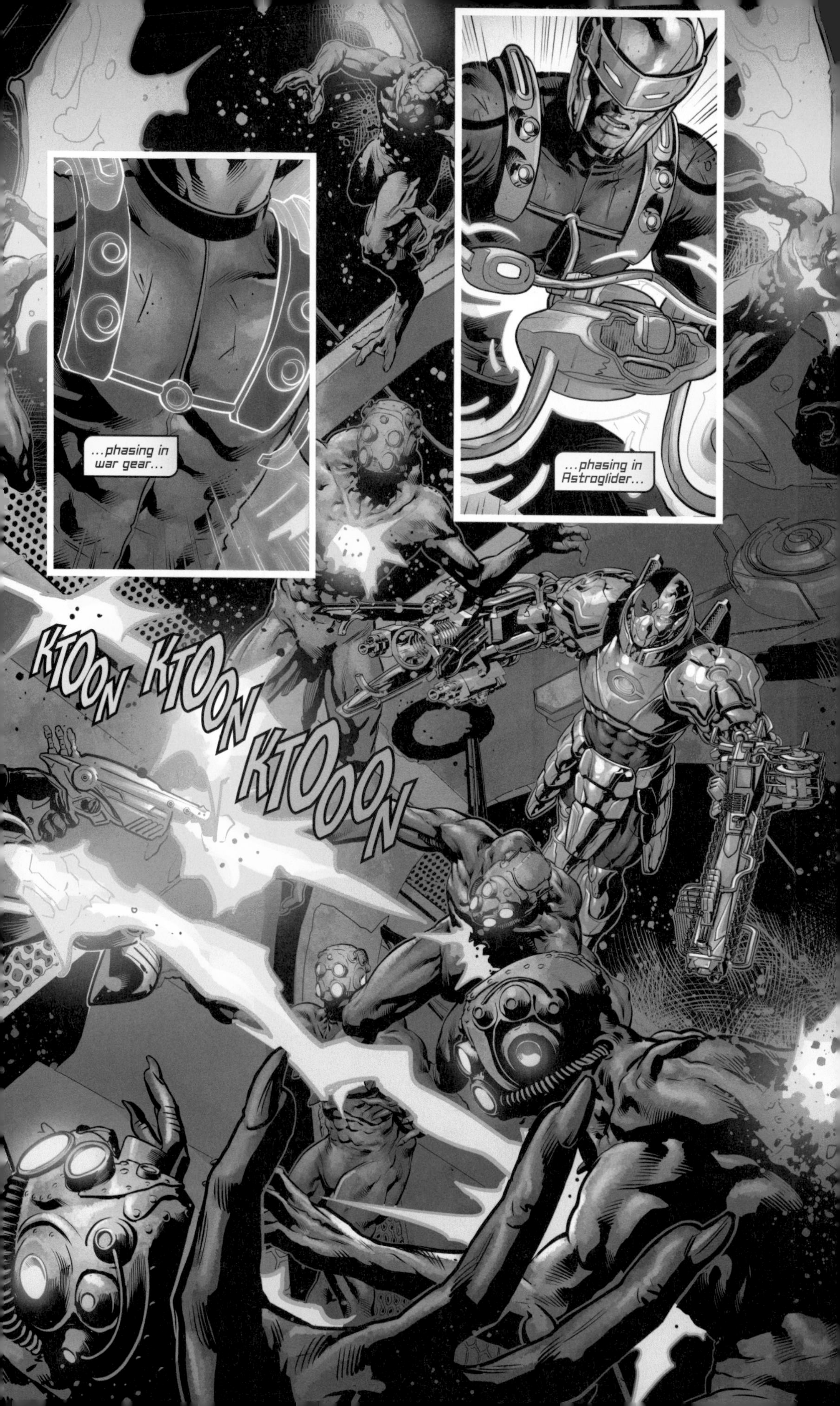
...phasing in war gear...
...phasing in Astroglider...
KTOON KTOON KTOOON

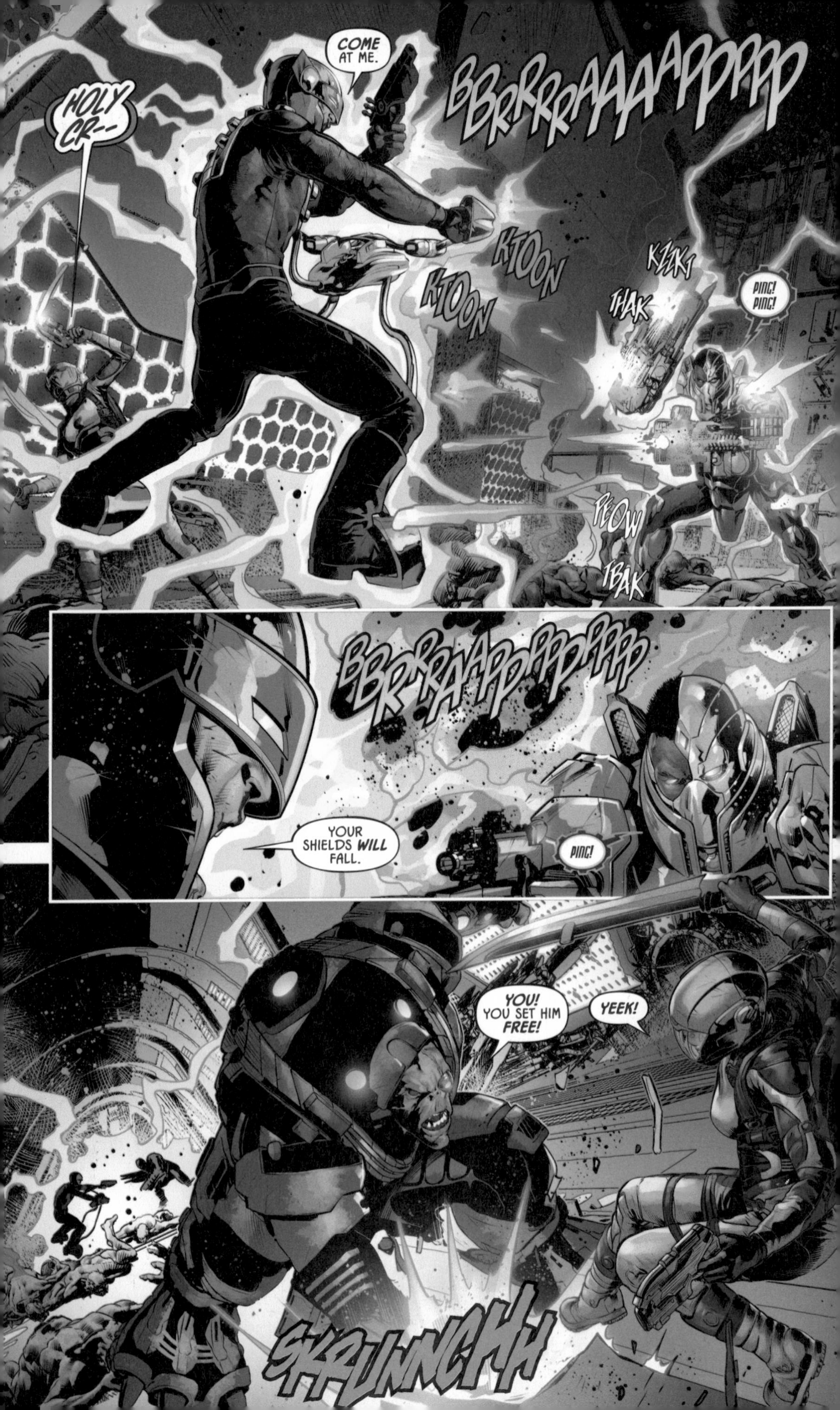
HOLY CR--
COME AT ME.
BBRRRRRAAAAPPPPPP
KTOON
KTOON
KZZKT
THAK
PING! PING!
PEOW
THAK
TBAK
BBRRRAAPPPPPPPPP
YOUR SHIELDS WILL FALL.
PING!
YOU! YOU SET HIM FREE!
YEEK!
SKRUNNCHHH

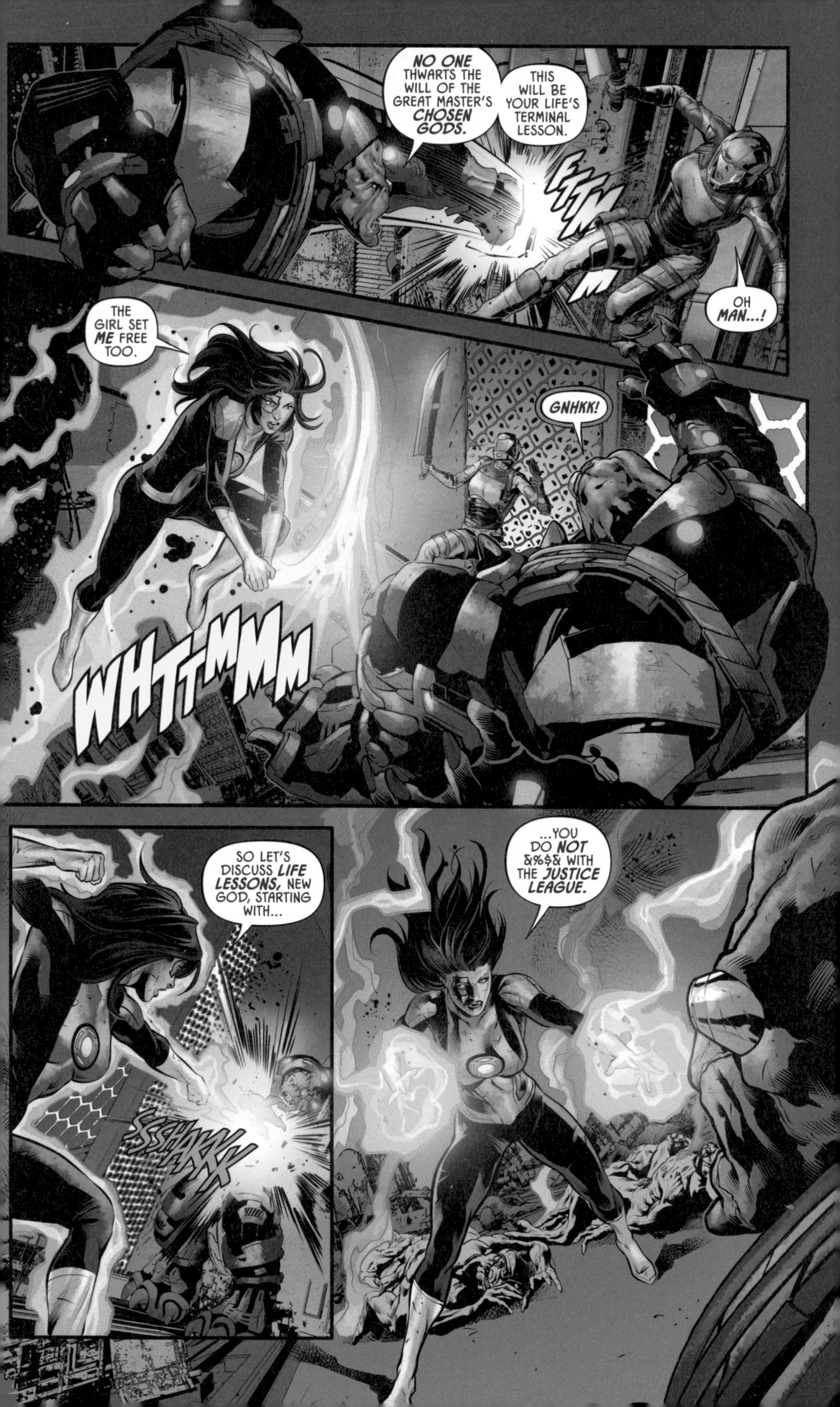
NO ONE THWARTS THE WILL OF THE GREAT MASTER'S CHOSEN GODS.
THIS WILL BE YOUR LIFE'S TERMINAL LESSON.
FTTMM
OH MAN...!
THE GIRL SET ME FREE TOO.
GNHKK!
WHTTMMM
SO LET'S DISCUSS LIFE LESSONS, NEW GOD, STARTING WITH...
SSSHAKK
...YOU DO NOT &%$& WITH THE JUSTICE LEAGUE.

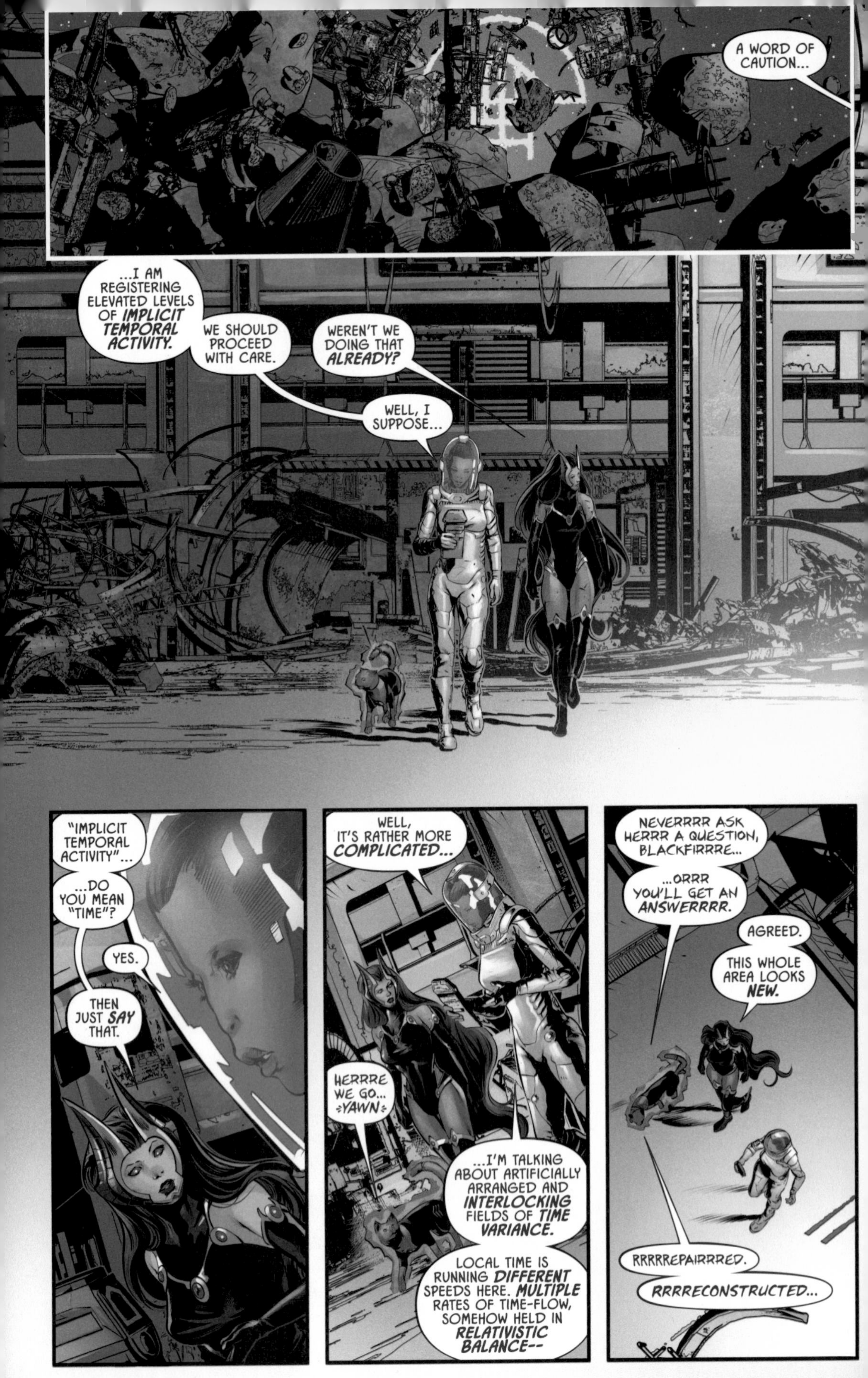
A WORD OF CAUTION...
...I AM REGISTERING ELEVATED LEVELS OF IMPLICIT TEMPORAL ACTIVITY.
WE SHOULD PROCEED WITH CARE.
WEREN'T WE DOING THAT ALREADY?
WELL, I SUPPOSE...
"IMPLICIT TEMPORAL ACTIVITY"...
...DO YOU MEAN "TIME"?
YES.
THEN JUST SAY THAT.
WELL, IT'S RATHER MORE COMPLICATED...
HERRRE WE GO... *YAWN*
...I'M TALKING ABOUT ARTIFICIALLY ARRANGED AND INTERLOCKING FIELDS OF TIME VARIANCE.
LOCAL TIME IS RUNNING DIFFERENT SPEEDS HERE. MULTIPLE RATES OF TIME-FLOW, SOMEHOW HELD IN RELATIVISTIC BALANCE--
NEVERRRR ASK HERRR A QUESTION, BLACKFIRRRE...
...ORRR YOU'LL GET AN ANSWERRRR.
AGREED.
THIS WHOLE AREA LOOKS NEW.
RRRRREPAIRRRED.
RRRRECONSTRUCTED...

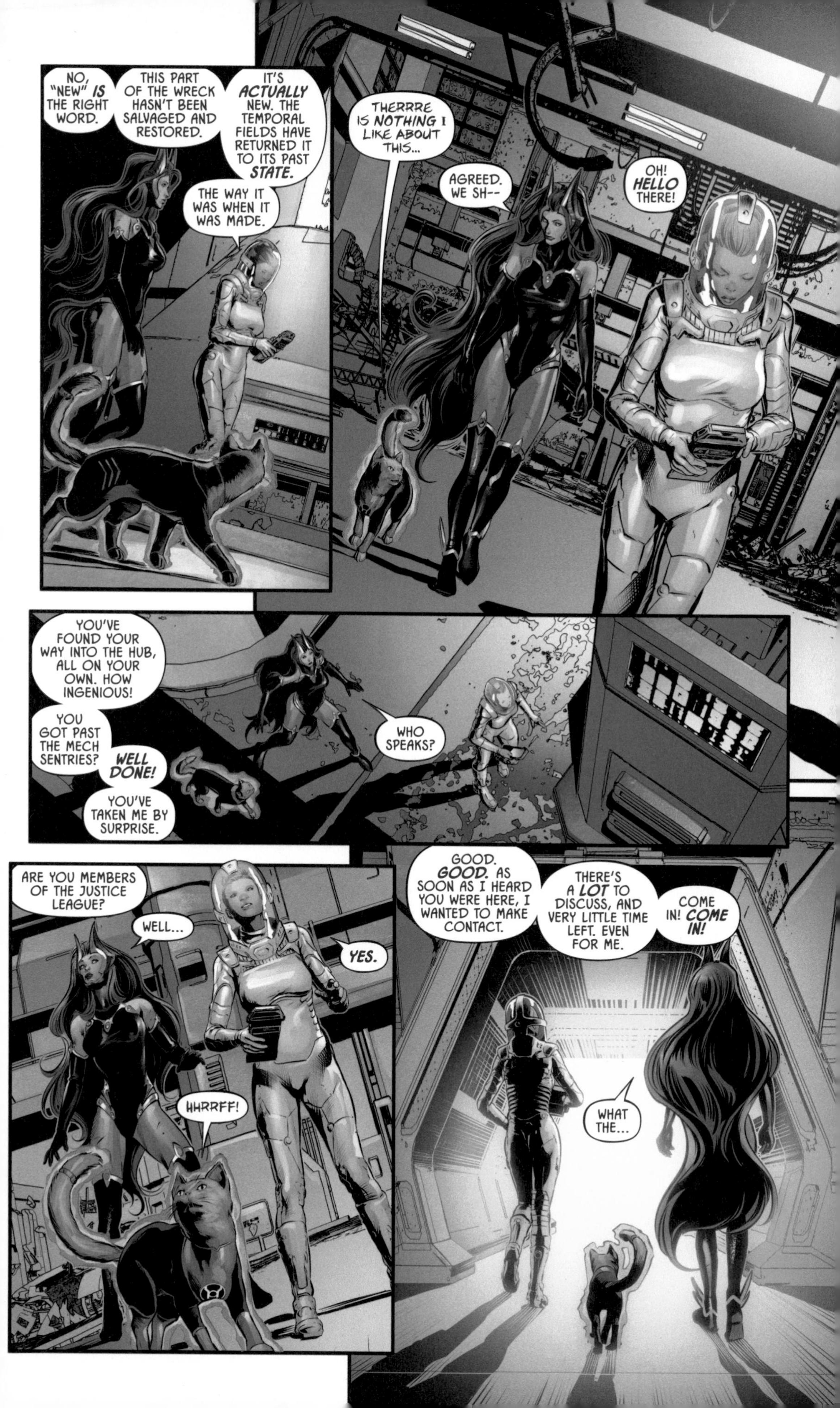
NO, "NEW" IS THE RIGHT WORD.
THIS PART OF THE WRECK HASN'T BEEN SALVAGED AND RESTORED.
IT'S ACTUALLY NEW. THE TEMPORAL FIELDS HAVE RETURNED IT TO ITS PAST STATE.
THE WAY IT WAS WHEN IT WAS MADE.
THERRRE IS NOTHING I LIKE ABOUT THIS...
AGREED. WE SH--
OH! HELLO THERE!
YOU'VE FOUND YOUR WAY INTO THE HUB, ALL ON YOUR OWN. HOW INGENIOUS!
YOU GOT PAST THE MECH SENTRIES?
WELL DONE!
YOU'VE TAKEN ME BY SURPRISE.
WHO SPEAKS?
ARE YOU MEMBERS OF THE JUSTICE LEAGUE?
WELL...
YES.
HHRRFF!
GOOD. GOOD. AS SOON AS I HEARD YOU WERE HERE, I WANTED TO MAKE CONTACT.
THERE'S A LOT TO DISCUSS, AND VERY LITTLE TIME LEFT. EVEN FOR ME.
COME IN! COME IN!
WHAT THE...

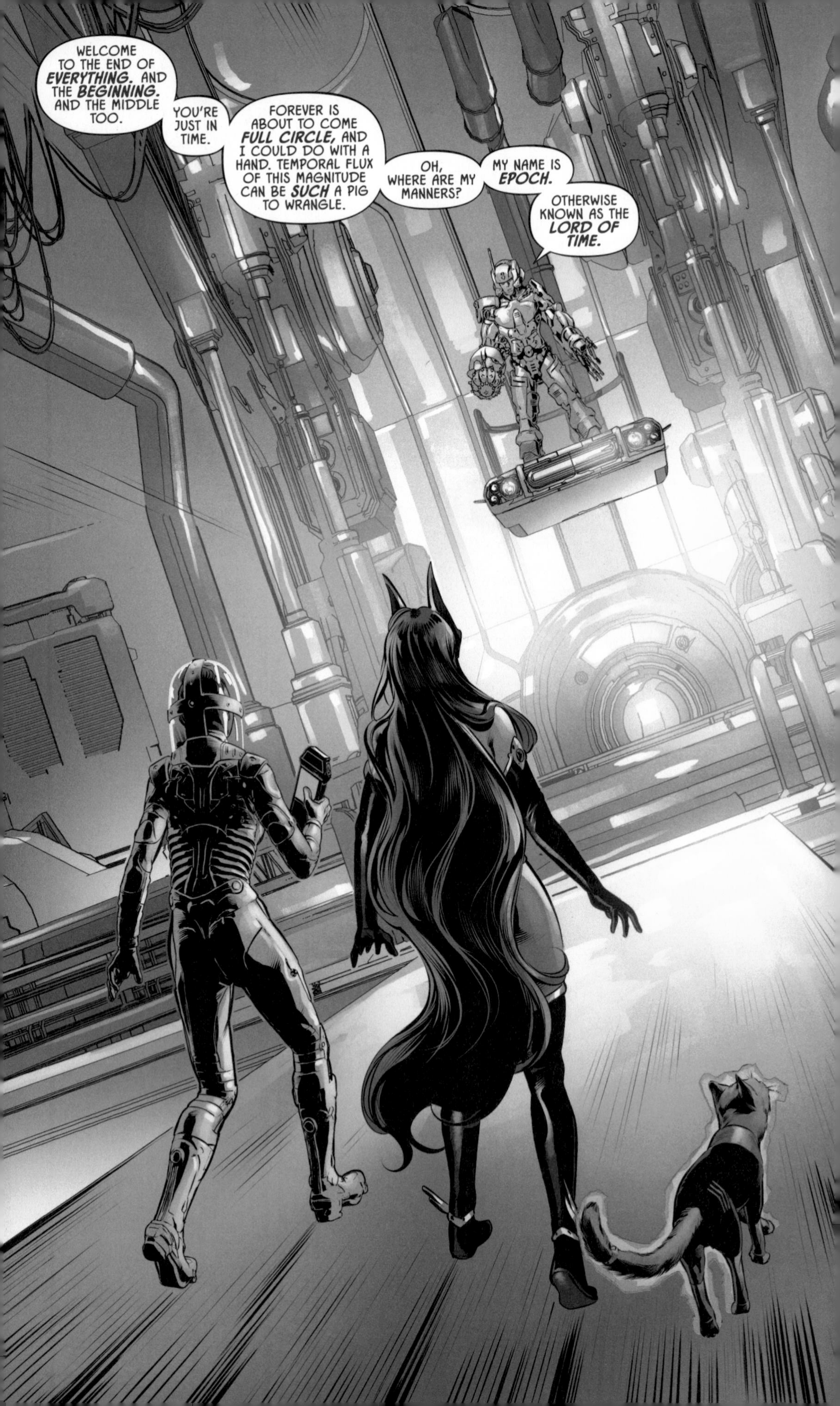
WELCOME TO THE END OF EVERYTHING. AND THE BEGINNING. AND THE MIDDLE TOO.
YOU'RE JUST IN TIME.
FOREVER IS ABOUT TO COME FULL CIRCLE, AND I COULD DO WITH A HAND. TEMPORAL FLUX OF THIS MAGNITUDE CAN BE SUCH A PIG TO WRANGLE.
OH, WHERE ARE MY MANNERS?
MY NAME IS EPOCH.
OTHERWISE KNOWN AS THE LORD OF TIME.

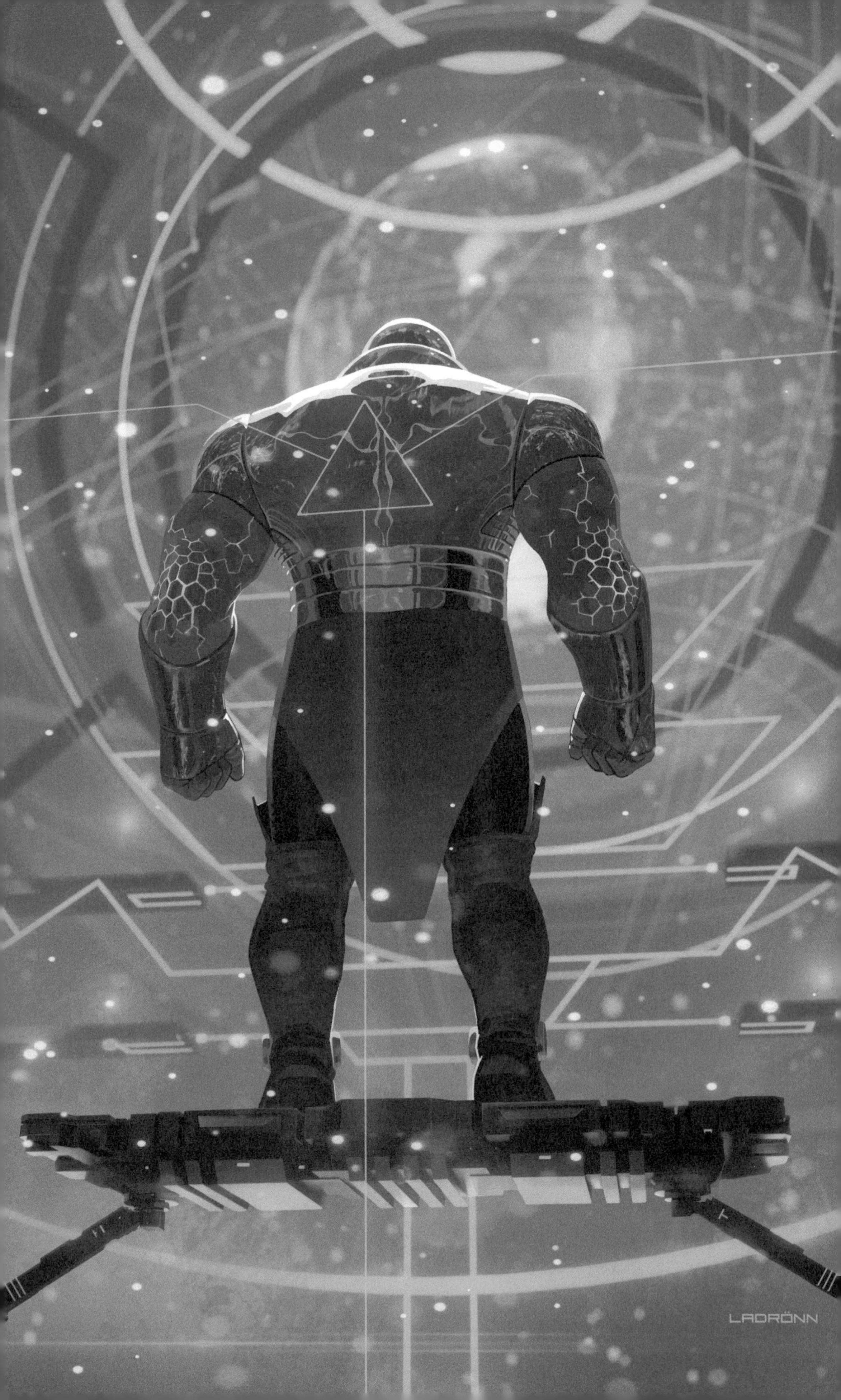
LADRÖNN

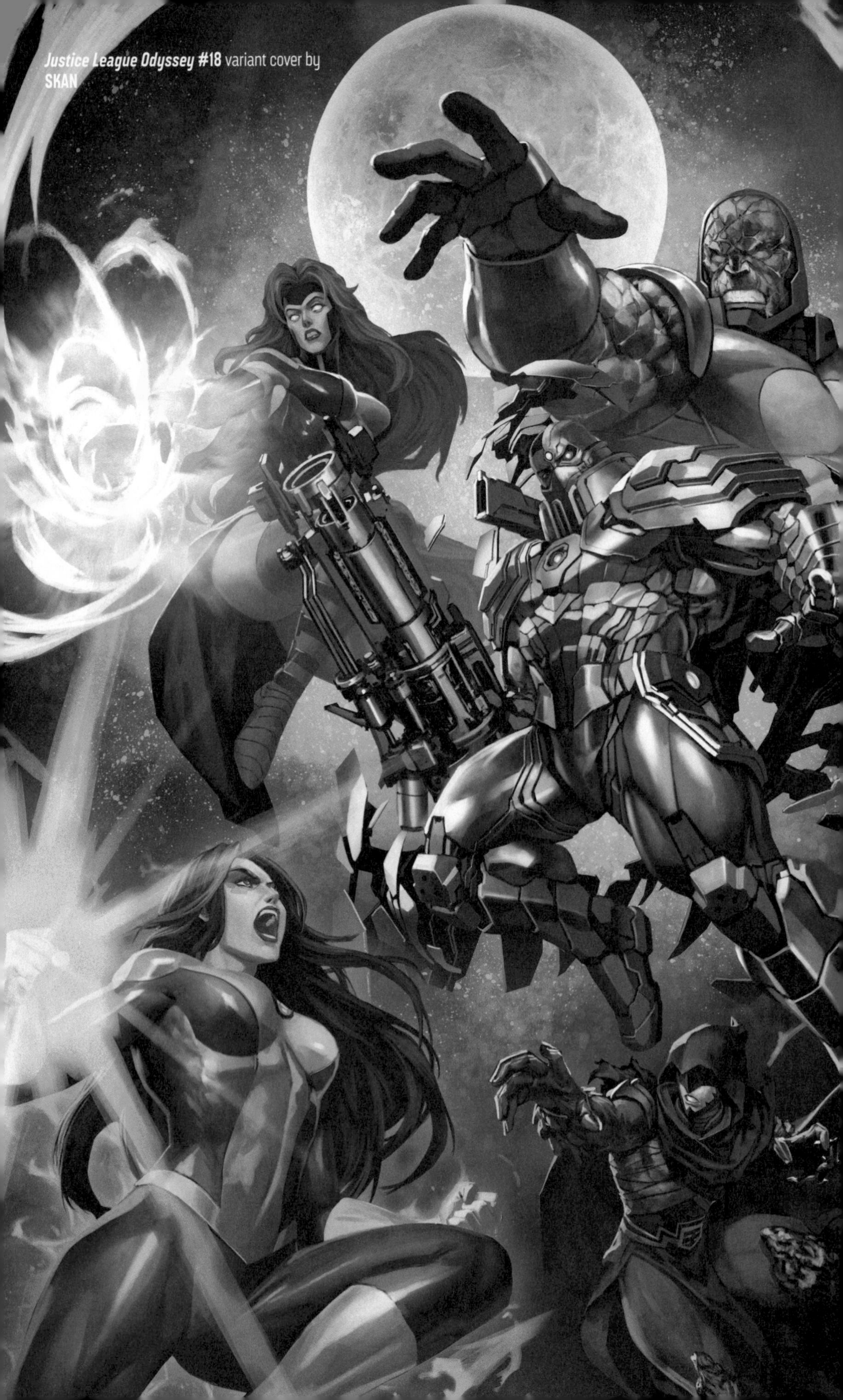

Justice League Odyssey **#18** variant cover by
SKAN

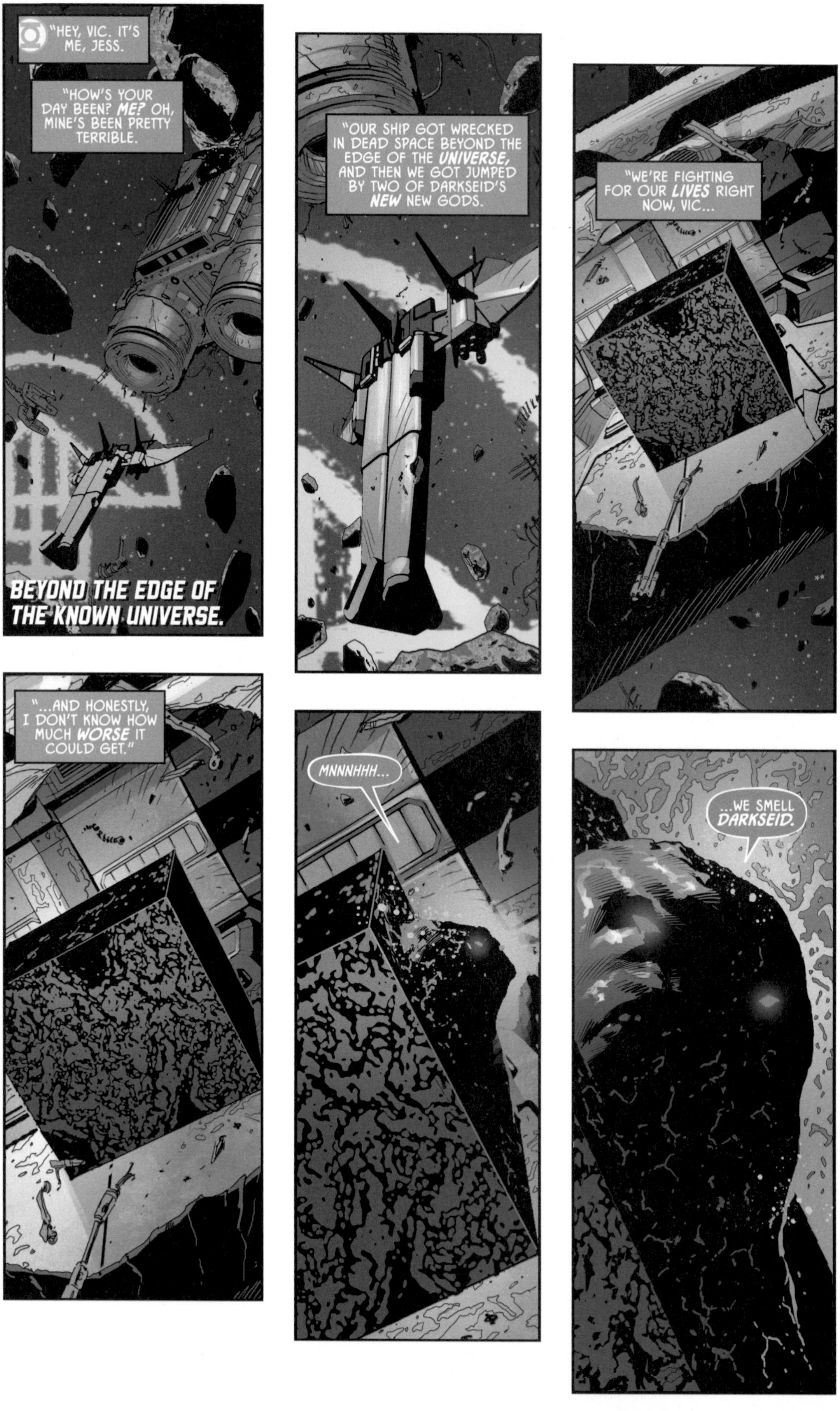
"HEY, VIC. IT'S ME, JESS.
"HOW'S YOUR DAY BEEN? ME? OH, MINE'S BEEN PRETTY TERRIBLE.
BEYOND THE EDGE OF THE KNOWN UNIVERSE.
"OUR SHIP GOT WRECKED IN DEAD SPACE BEYOND THE EDGE OF THE UNIVERSE, AND THEN WE GOT JUMPED BY TWO OF DARKSEID'S NEW NEW GODS.
"WE'RE FIGHTING FOR OUR LIVES RIGHT NOW, VIC...
"...AND HONESTLY, I DON'T KNOW HOW MUCH WORSE IT COULD GET."
MNNNHHH...
...WE SMELL DARKSEID.

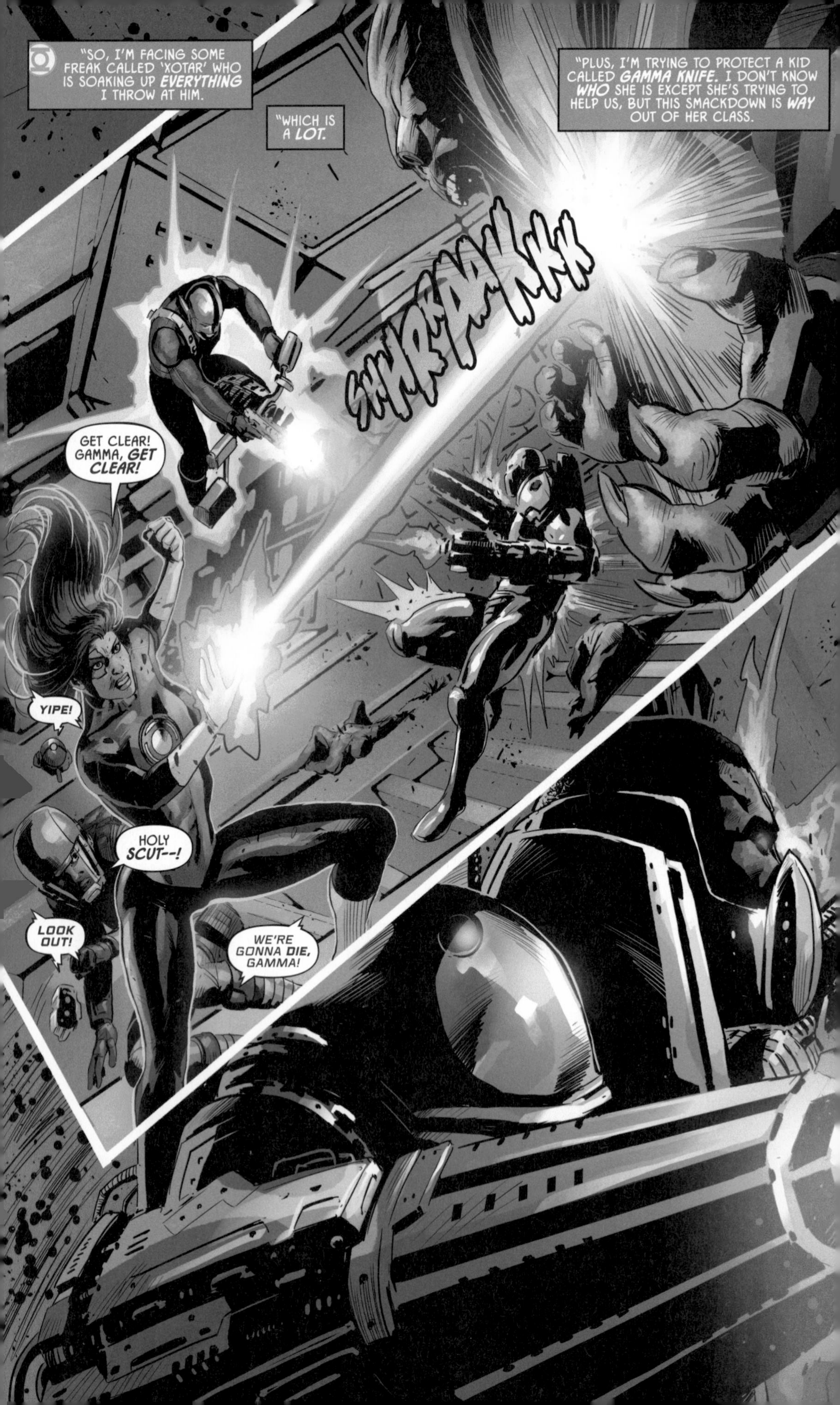
"SO, I'M FACING SOME FREAK CALLED 'XOTAR' WHO IS SOAKING UP EVERYTHING I THROW AT HIM.
"WHICH IS A LOT.
"PLUS, I'M TRYING TO PROTECT A KID CALLED GAMMA KNIFE. I DON'T KNOW WHO SHE IS EXCEPT SHE'S TRYING TO HELP US, BUT THIS SMACKDOWN IS WAY OUT OF HER CLASS.
SHHRKRAKKK
GET CLEAR! GAMMA, GET CLEAR!
YIPE!
HOLY SCUT--!
LOOK OUT!
WE'RE GONNA DIE, GAMMA!

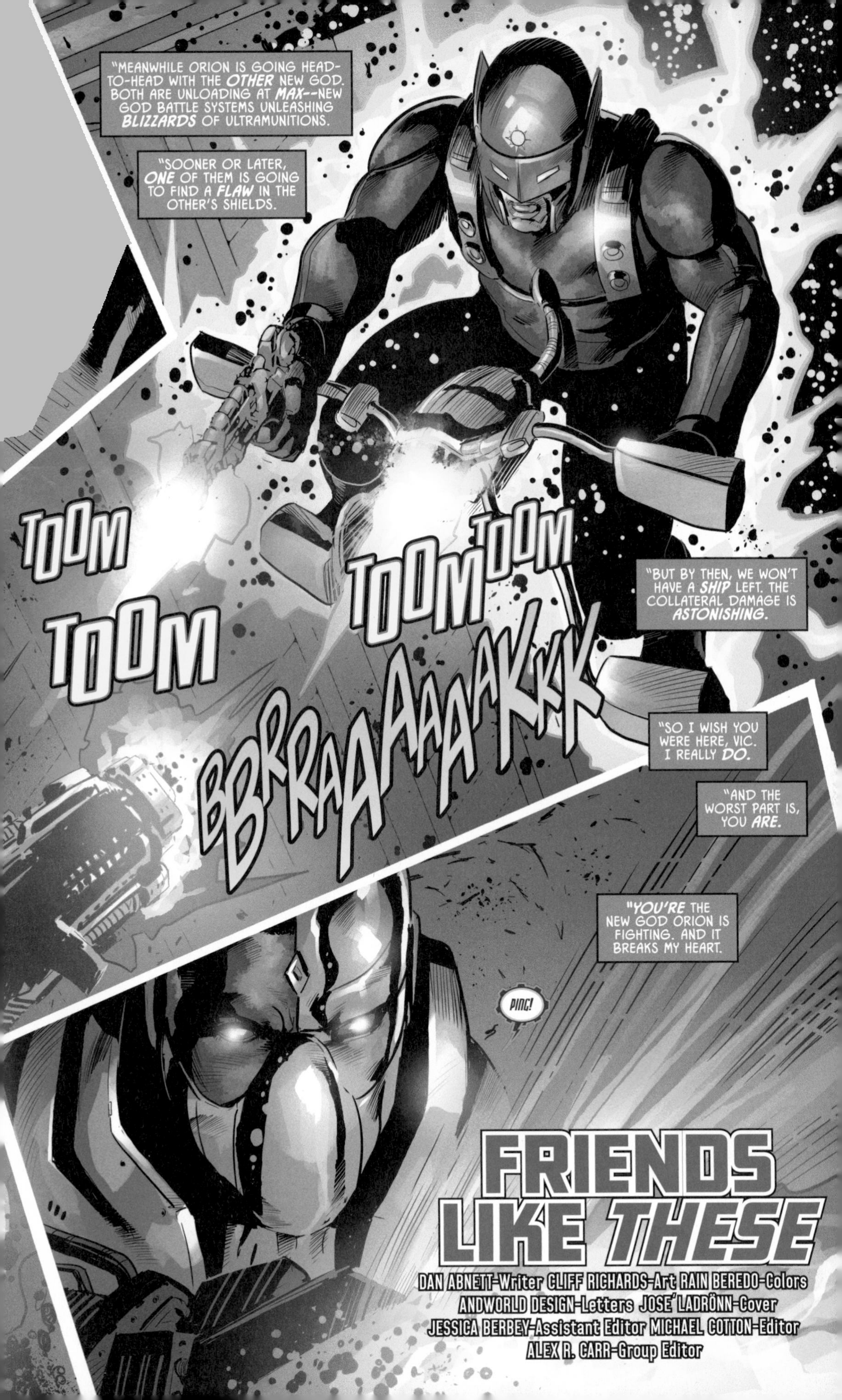

"MEANWHILE ORION IS GOING HEAD-TO-HEAD WITH THE OTHER NEW GOD. BOTH ARE UNLOADING AT MAX--NEW GOD BATTLE SYSTEMS UNLEASHING BLIZZARDS OF ULTRAMUNITIONS.
"SOONER OR LATER, ONE OF THEM IS GOING TO FIND A FLAW IN THE OTHER'S SHIELDS.
TOOM
TOOM
TOOM TOOM
BBRRAAAAAKKK
"BUT BY THEN, WE WON'T HAVE A SHIP LEFT. THE COLLATERAL DAMAGE IS ASTONISHING.
"SO I WISH YOU WERE HERE, VIC. I REALLY DO.
"AND THE WORST PART IS, YOU ARE.
"YOU'RE THE NEW GOD ORION IS FIGHTING. AND IT BREAKS MY HEART.
PING!
FRIENDS LIKE THESE
DAN ABNETT-Writer CLIFF RICHARDS-Art RAIN BEREDO-Colors
ANDWORLD DESIGN-Letters JOSE' LADRÖNN-Cover
JESSICA BERBEY-Assistant Editor MICHAEL COTTON-Editor
ALEX R. CARR-Group Editor

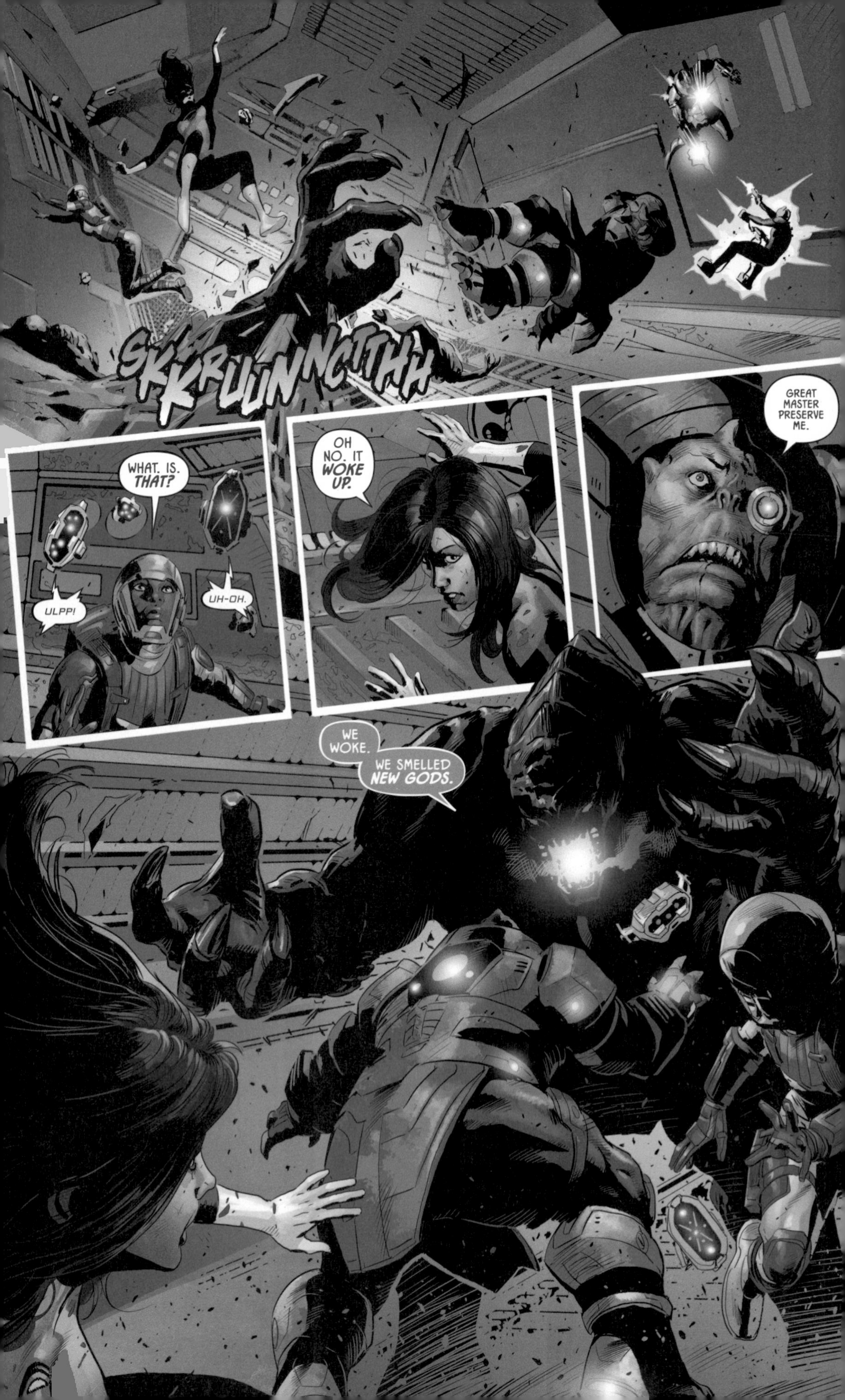
SKKRUUNNCTTHH
WHAT. IS. THAT?
ULPP!
UH-OH.
OH NO. IT WOKE UP.
GREAT MASTER PRESERVE ME.
WE WOKE.
WE SMELLED NEW GODS.

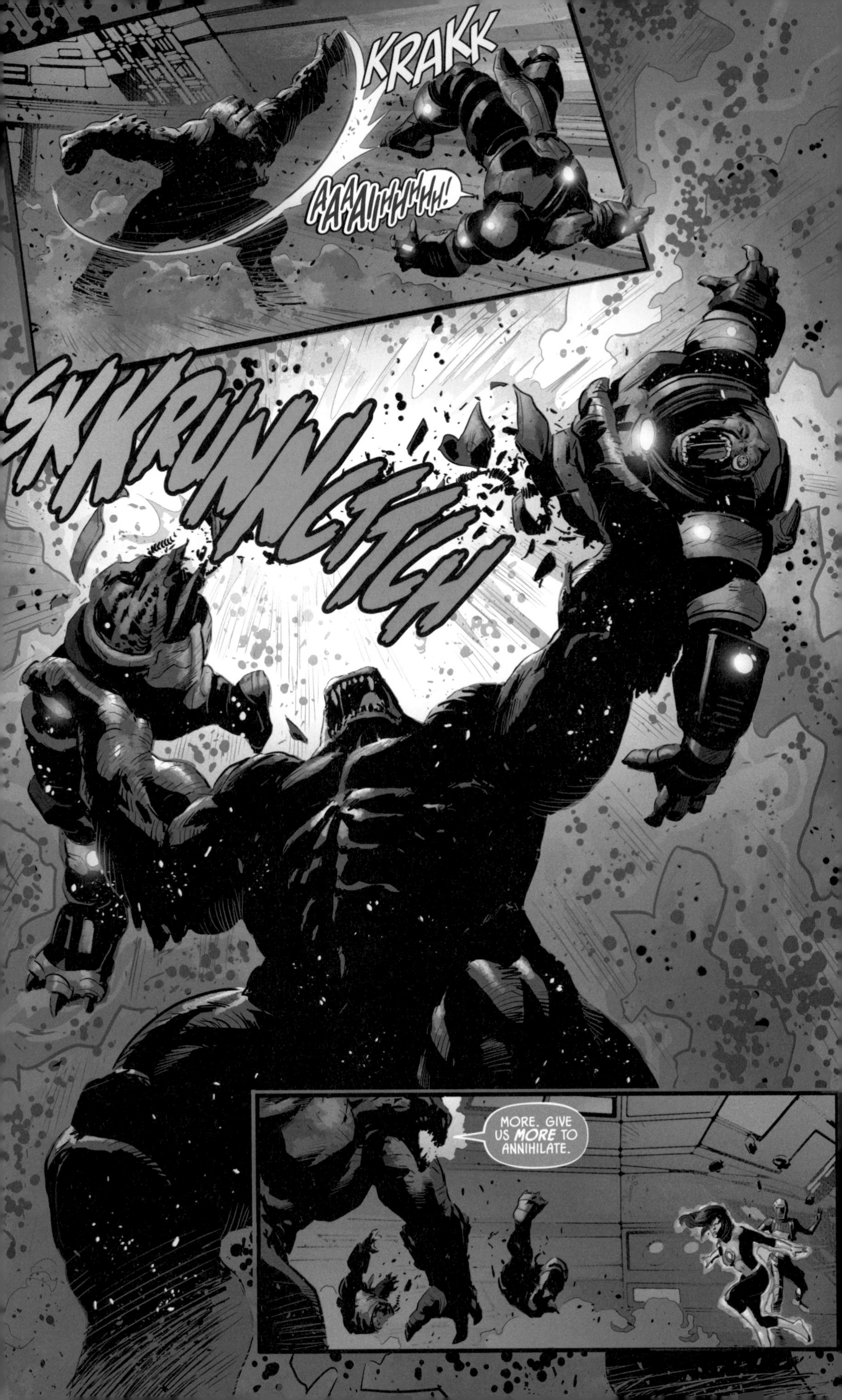

KRAKK
AAAIIHHHH!
SKKRUNNCTCH
MORE. GIVE US MORE TO ANNIHILATE.

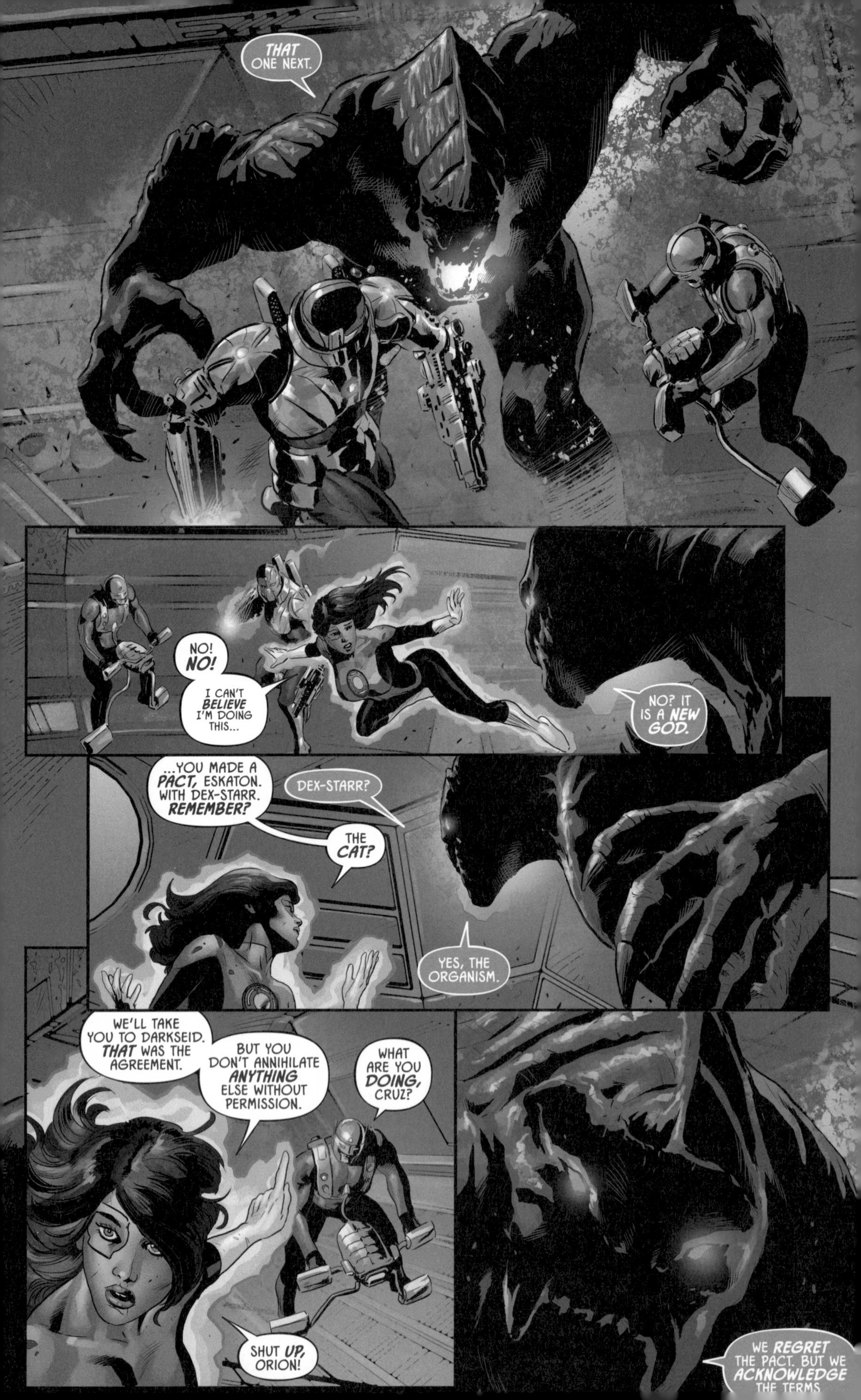
THAT ONE NEXT.
NO! NO!
I CAN'T BELIEVE I'M DOING THIS...
NO? IT IS A NEW GOD.
...YOU MADE A PACT, ESKATON. WITH DEX-STARR. REMEMBER?
DEX-STARR?
THE CAT?
YES, THE ORGANISM.
WE'LL TAKE YOU TO DARKSEID. THAT WAS THE AGREEMENT.
BUT YOU DON'T ANNIHILATE ANYTHING ELSE WITHOUT PERMISSION.
WHAT ARE YOU DOING, CRUZ?
SHUT UP, ORION!
WE REGRET THE PACT. BUT WE ACKNOWLEDGE THE TERMS

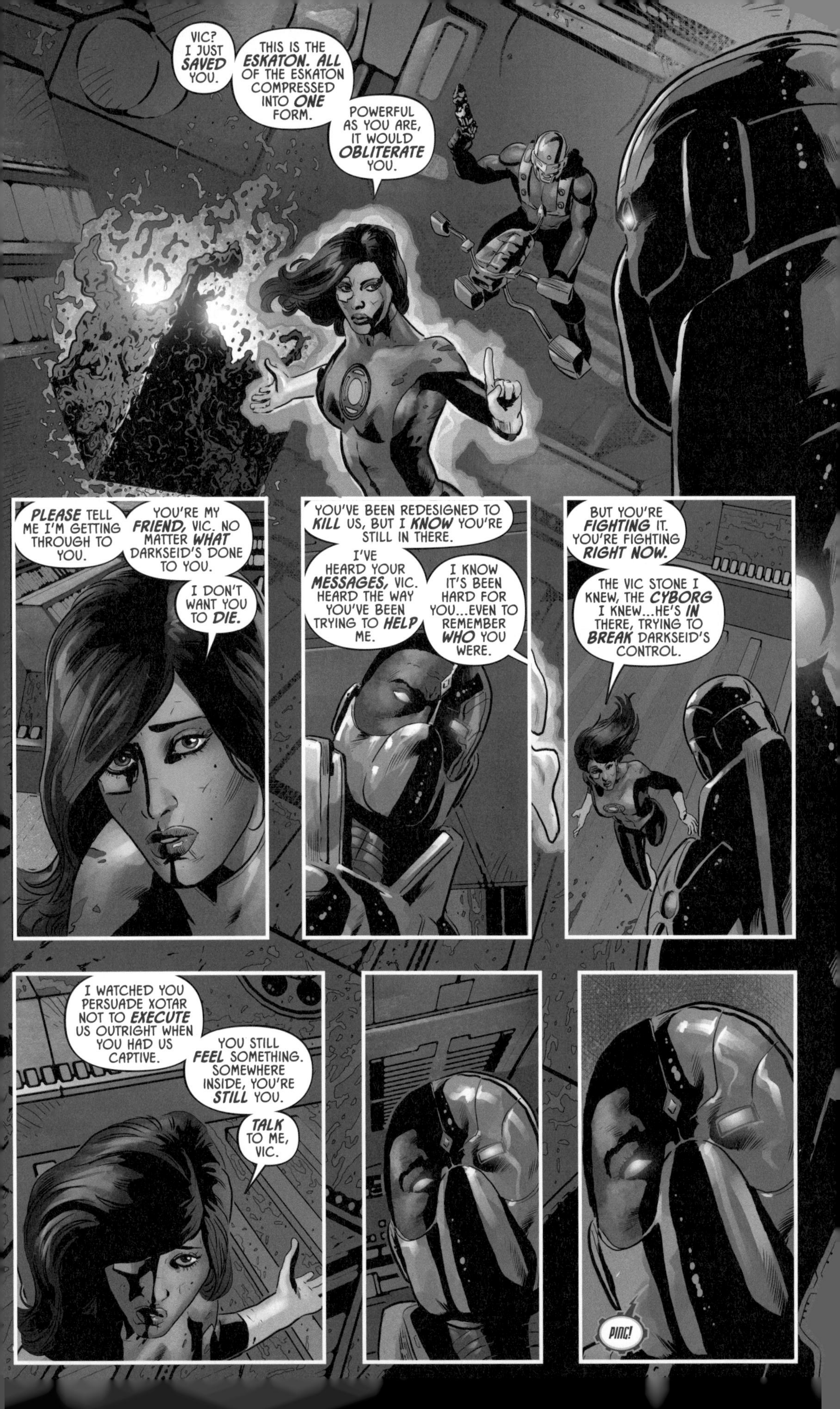
VIC? I JUST SAVED YOU.
THIS IS THE ESKATON. ALL OF THE ESKATON COMPRESSED INTO ONE FORM.
POWERFUL AS YOU ARE, IT WOULD OBLITERATE YOU.
PLEASE TELL ME I'M GETTING THROUGH TO YOU.
YOU'RE MY FRIEND, VIC. NO MATTER WHAT DARKSEID'S DONE TO YOU.
I DON'T WANT YOU TO DIE.
YOU'VE BEEN REDESIGNED TO KILL US, BUT I KNOW YOU'RE STILL IN THERE.
I'VE HEARD YOUR MESSAGES, VIC. HEARD THE WAY YOU'VE BEEN TRYING TO HELP ME.
I KNOW IT'S BEEN HARD FOR YOU...EVEN TO REMEMBER WHO YOU WERE.
BUT YOU'RE FIGHTING IT. YOU'RE FIGHTING RIGHT NOW.
THE VIC STONE I KNEW, THE CYBORG I KNEW...HE'S IN THERE, TRYING TO BREAK DARKSEID'S CONTROL.
I WATCHED YOU PERSUADE XOTAR NOT TO EXECUTE US OUTRIGHT WHEN YOU HAD US CAPTIVE.
YOU STILL FEEL SOMETHING. SOMEWHERE INSIDE, YOU'RE STILL YOU.
TALK TO ME, VIC.
PING!

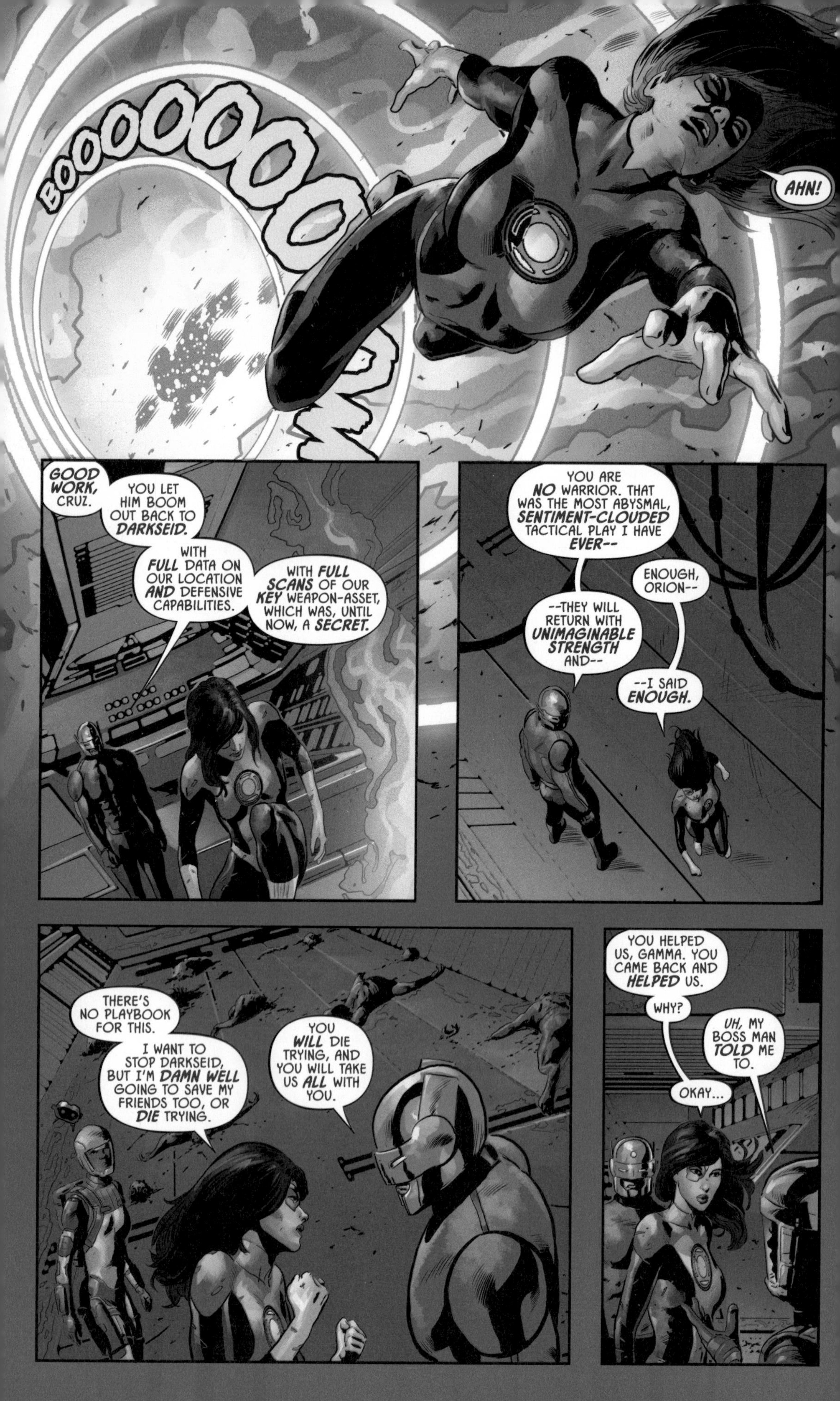
BOOOOOOOOOM
AHN!
GOOD WORK, CRUZ.
YOU LET HIM BOOM OUT BACK TO DARKSEID.
WITH FULL DATA ON OUR LOCATION AND DEFENSIVE CAPABILITIES.
WITH FULL SCANS OF OUR KEY WEAPON-ASSET, WHICH WAS, UNTIL NOW, A SECRET.
YOU ARE NO WARRIOR. THAT WAS THE MOST ABYSMAL, SENTIMENT-CLOUDED TACTICAL PLAY I HAVE EVER--
--THEY WILL RETURN WITH UNIMAGINABLE STRENGTH AND--
ENOUGH, ORION--
--I SAID ENOUGH.
THERE'S NO PLAYBOOK FOR THIS.
I WANT TO STOP DARKSEID, BUT I'M DAMN WELL GOING TO SAVE MY FRIENDS TOO, OR DIE TRYING.
YOU WILL DIE TRYING, AND YOU WILL TAKE US ALL WITH YOU.
YOU HELPED US, GAMMA. YOU CAME BACK AND HELPED US.
WHY?
UH, MY BOSS MAN TOLD ME TO.
OKAY...

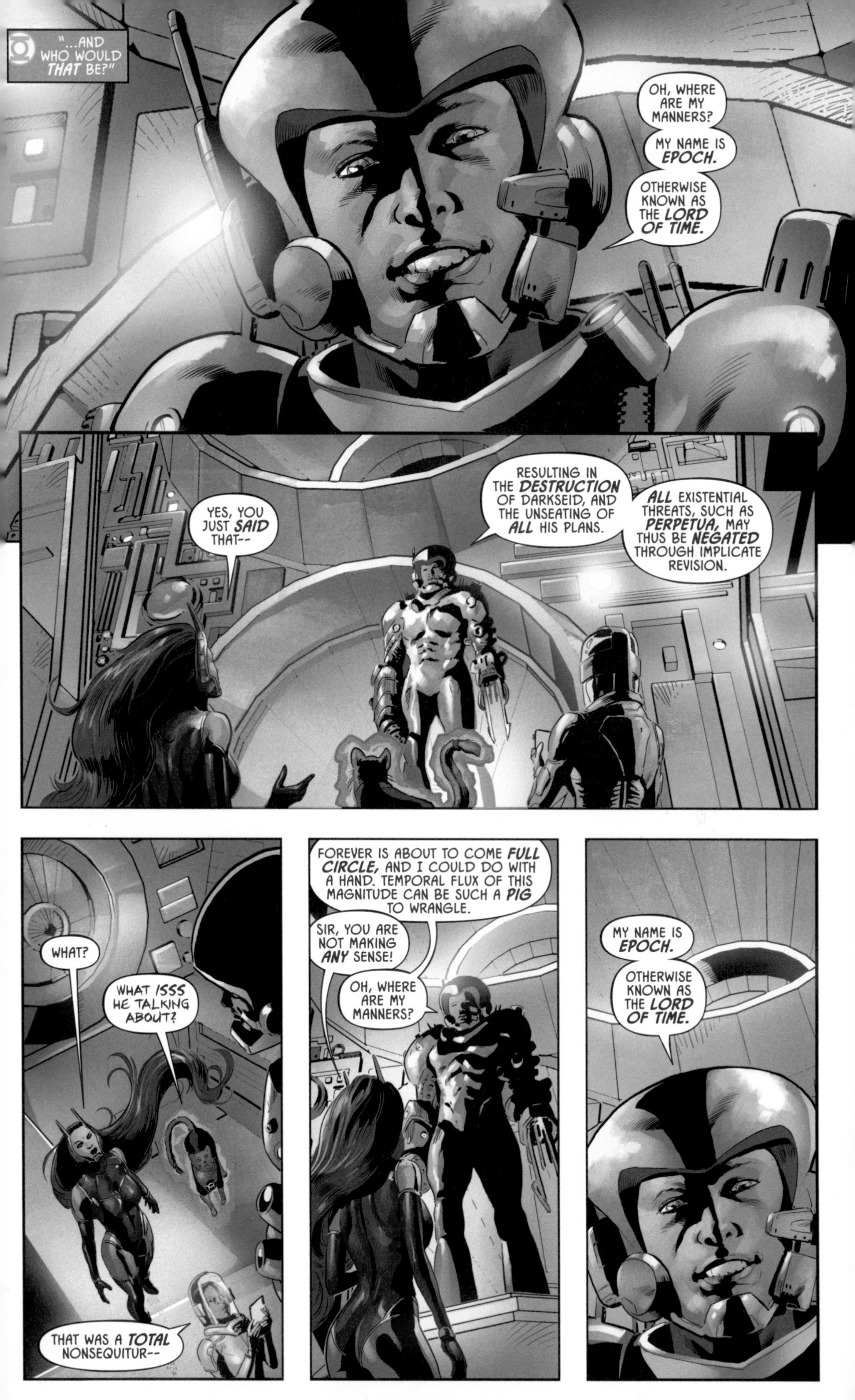
"...AND WHO WOULD THAT BE?"
OH, WHERE ARE MY MANNERS?
MY NAME IS EPOCH.
OTHERWISE KNOWN AS THE LORD OF TIME.
YES, YOU JUST SAID THAT--
RESULTING IN THE DESTRUCTION OF DARKSEID, AND THE UNSEATING OF ALL HIS PLANS.
ALL EXISTENTIAL THREATS, SUCH AS PERPETUA, MAY THUS BE NEGATED THROUGH IMPLICATE REVISION.
WHAT?
WHAT ISSS HE TALKING ABOUT?
THAT WAS A TOTAL NONSEQUITUR--
FOREVER IS ABOUT TO COME FULL CIRCLE, AND I COULD DO WITH A HAND. TEMPORAL FLUX OF THIS MAGNITUDE CAN BE SUCH A PIG TO WRANGLE.
SIR, YOU ARE NOT MAKING ANY SENSE!
OH, WHERE ARE MY MANNERS?
MY NAME IS EPOCH.
OTHERWISE KNOWN AS THE LORD OF TIME.

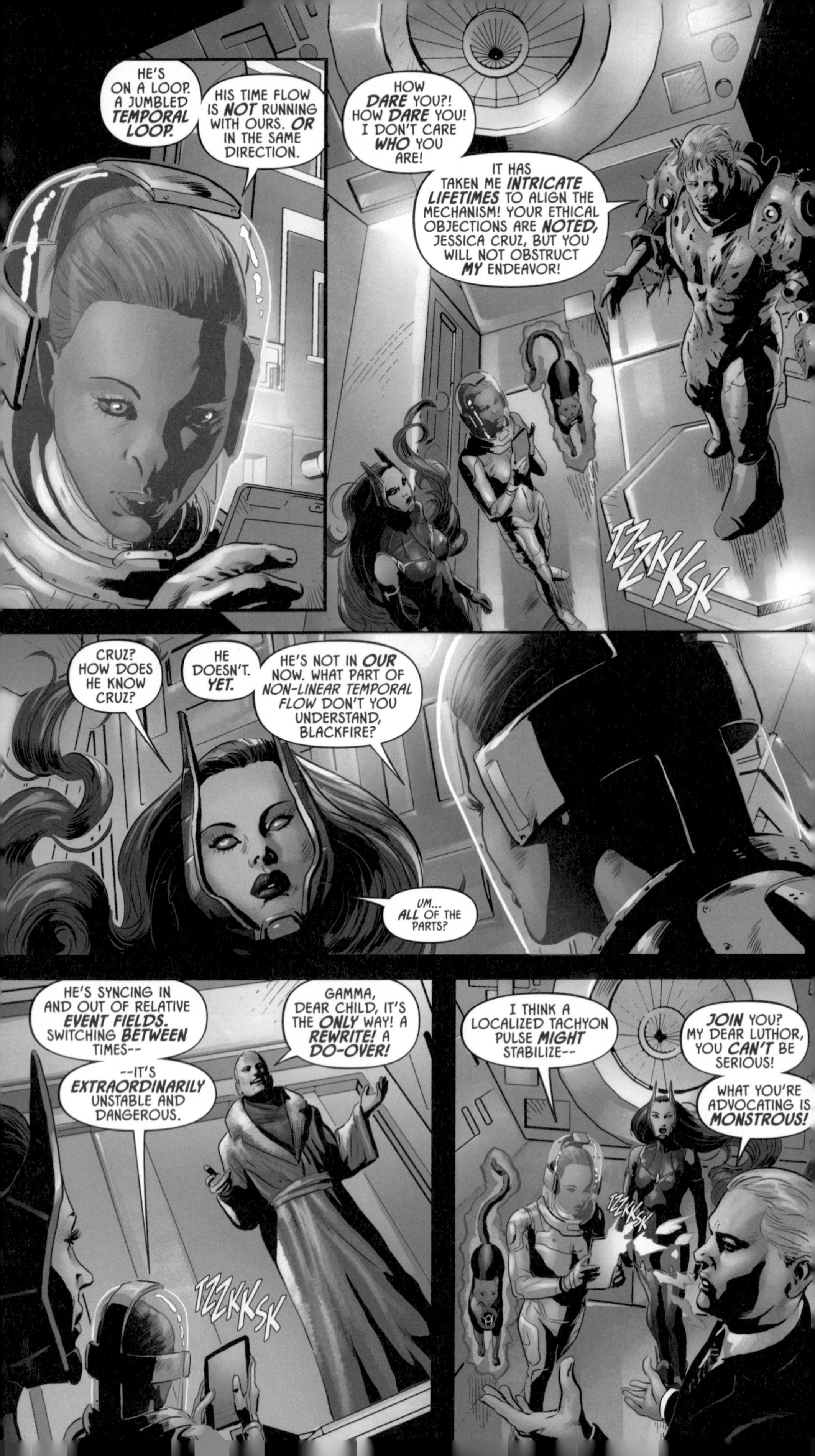

HE'S ON A LOOP. A JUMBLED TEMPORAL LOOP.
HIS TIME FLOW IS NOT RUNNING WITH OURS. OR IN THE SAME DIRECTION.
HOW DARE YOU?! HOW DARE YOU! I DON'T CARE WHO YOU ARE!
IT HAS TAKEN ME INTRICATE LIFETIMES TO ALIGN THE MECHANISM! YOUR ETHICAL OBJECTIONS ARE NOTED, JESSICA CRUZ, BUT YOU WILL NOT OBSTRUCT MY ENDEAVOR!
TZZKKSK
CRUZ? HOW DOES HE KNOW CRUZ?
HE DOESN'T. YET.
HE'S NOT IN OUR NOW. WHAT PART OF NON-LINEAR TEMPORAL FLOW DON'T YOU UNDERSTAND, BLACKFIRE?
UM... ALL OF THE PARTS?
HE'S SYNCING IN AND OUT OF RELATIVE EVENT FIELDS. SWITCHING BETWEEN TIMES--
--IT'S EXTRAORDINARILY UNSTABLE AND DANGEROUS.
GAMMA, DEAR CHILD, IT'S THE ONLY WAY! A REWRITE! A DO-OVER!
TZZKKSK
I THINK A LOCALIZED TACHYON PULSE MIGHT STABILIZE--
JOIN YOU? MY DEAR LUTHOR, YOU CAN'T BE SERIOUS!
WHAT YOU'RE ADVOCATING IS MONSTROUS!
TZZKKSK

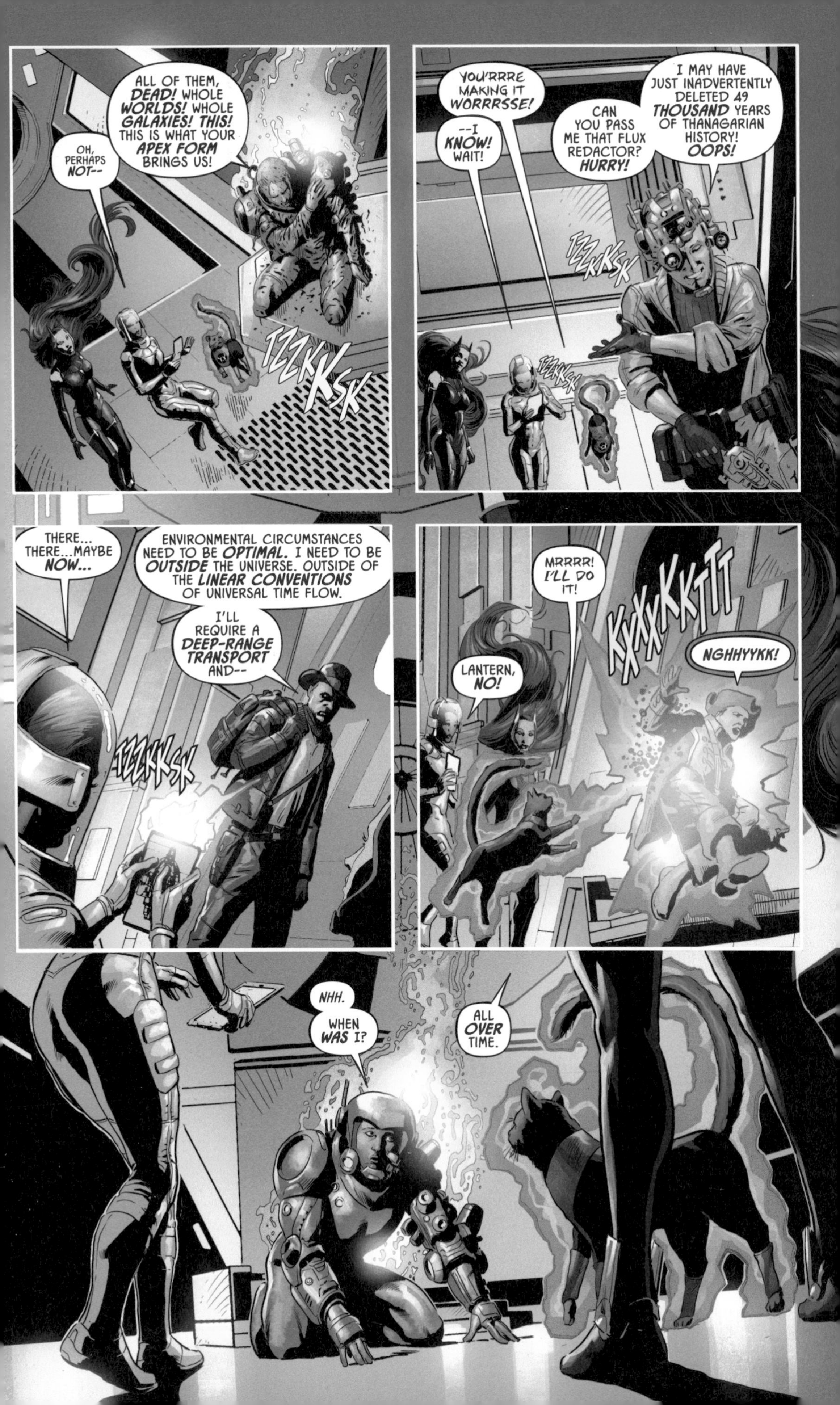
ALL OF THEM, DEAD! WHOLE WORLDS! WHOLE GALAXIES! THIS! THIS IS WHAT YOUR APEX FORM BRINGS US!
OH, PERHAPS NOT--
TZZKKKSK
YOU'RRRE MAKING IT WORRRSSE!
--I KNOW! WAIT!
CAN YOU PASS ME THAT FLUX REDACTOR? HURRY!
I MAY HAVE JUST INADVERTENTLY DELETED 49 THOUSAND YEARS OF THANAGARIAN HISTORY! OOPS!
TZZKKKSK
TZZKKKSK
THERE... THERE...MAYBE NOW...
ENVIRONMENTAL CIRCUMSTANCES NEED TO BE OPTIMAL. I NEED TO BE OUTSIDE THE UNIVERSE. OUTSIDE OF THE LINEAR CONVENTIONS OF UNIVERSAL TIME FLOW.
I'LL REQUIRE A DEEP-RANGE TRANSPORT AND--
TZZKKKSK
MRRRR! I'LL DO IT!
KXXXKKTTT
NGHHYYKK!
LANTERN, NO!
NHH.
WHEN WAS I?
ALL OVER TIME.

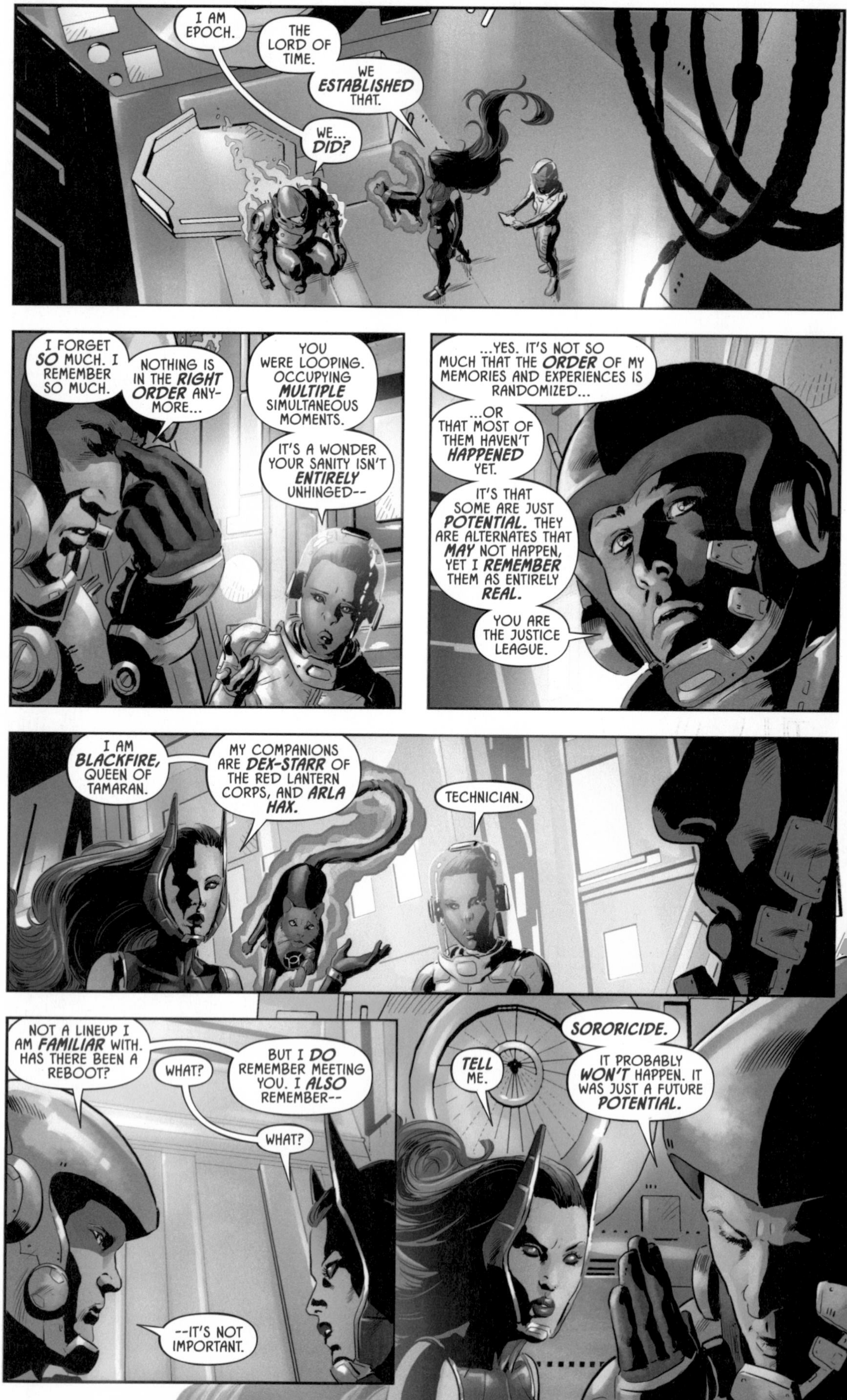
I AM EPOCH.
THE LORD OF TIME.
WE ESTABLISHED THAT.
WE... DID?
I FORGET SO MUCH. I REMEMBER SO MUCH.
NOTHING IS IN THE RIGHT ORDER ANY-MORE...
YOU WERE LOOPING. OCCUPYING MULTIPLE SIMULTANEOUS MOMENTS.
IT'S A WONDER YOUR SANITY ISN'T ENTIRELY UNHINGED--
...YES. IT'S NOT SO MUCH THAT THE ORDER OF MY MEMORIES AND EXPERIENCES IS RANDOMIZED...
...OR THAT MOST OF THEM HAVEN'T HAPPENED YET.
IT'S THAT SOME ARE JUST POTENTIAL. THEY ARE ALTERNATES THAT MAY NOT HAPPEN, YET I REMEMBER THEM AS ENTIRELY REAL.
YOU ARE THE JUSTICE LEAGUE.
I AM BLACKFIRE, QUEEN OF TAMARAN.
MY COMPANIONS ARE DEX-STARR OF THE RED LANTERN CORPS, AND ARLA HAX.
TECHNICIAN.
NOT A LINEUP I AM FAMILIAR WITH. HAS THERE BEEN A REBOOT?
WHAT?
BUT I DO REMEMBER MEETING YOU. I ALSO REMEMBER--
WHAT?
--IT'S NOT IMPORTANT.
TELL ME.
SORORICIDE.
IT PROBABLY WON'T HAPPEN. IT WAS JUST A FUTURE POTENTIAL.

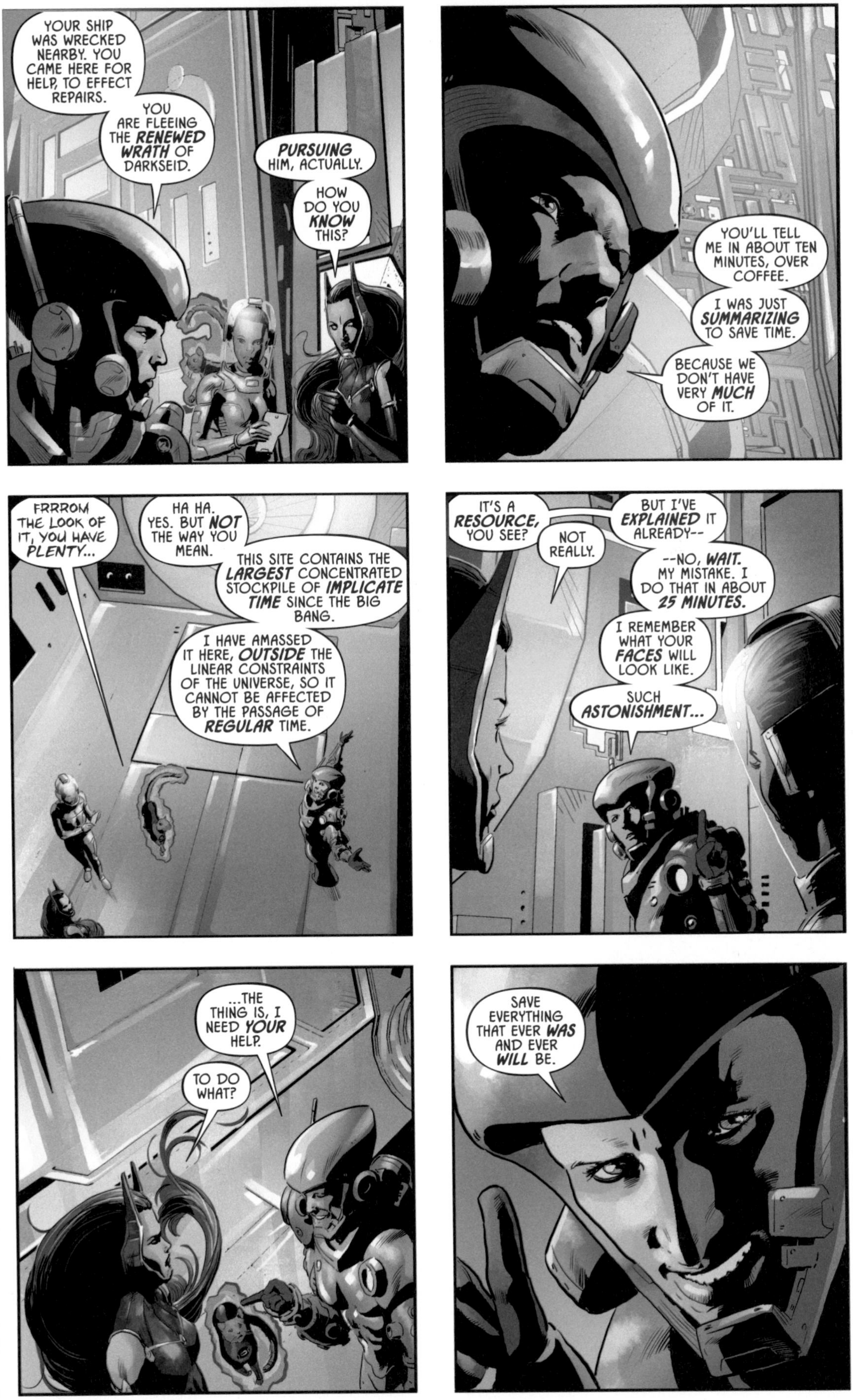

YOUR SHIP WAS WRECKED NEARBY. YOU CAME HERE FOR HELP, TO EFFECT REPAIRS.
YOU ARE FLEEING THE RENEWED WRATH OF DARKSEID.
PURSUING HIM, ACTUALLY.
HOW DO YOU KNOW THIS?
YOU'LL TELL ME IN ABOUT TEN MINUTES, OVER COFFEE.
I WAS JUST SUMMARIZING TO SAVE TIME.
BECAUSE WE DON'T HAVE VERY MUCH OF IT.
FRRROM THE LOOK OF IT, YOU HAVE PLENTY...
HA HA. YES. BUT NOT THE WAY YOU MEAN.
THIS SITE CONTAINS THE LARGEST CONCENTRATED STOCKPILE OF IMPLICATE TIME SINCE THE BIG BANG.
I HAVE AMASSED IT HERE, OUTSIDE THE LINEAR CONSTRAINTS OF THE UNIVERSE, SO IT CANNOT BE AFFECTED BY THE PASSAGE OF REGULAR TIME.
IT'S A RESOURCE, YOU SEE?
BUT I'VE EXPLAINED IT ALREADY--
NOT REALLY.
--NO, WAIT. MY MISTAKE. I DO THAT IN ABOUT 25 MINUTES.
I REMEMBER WHAT YOUR FACES WILL LOOK LIKE.
SUCH ASTONISHMENT...
...THE THING IS, I NEED YOUR HELP.
TO DO WHAT?
SAVE EVERYTHING THAT EVER WAS AND EVER WILL BE.

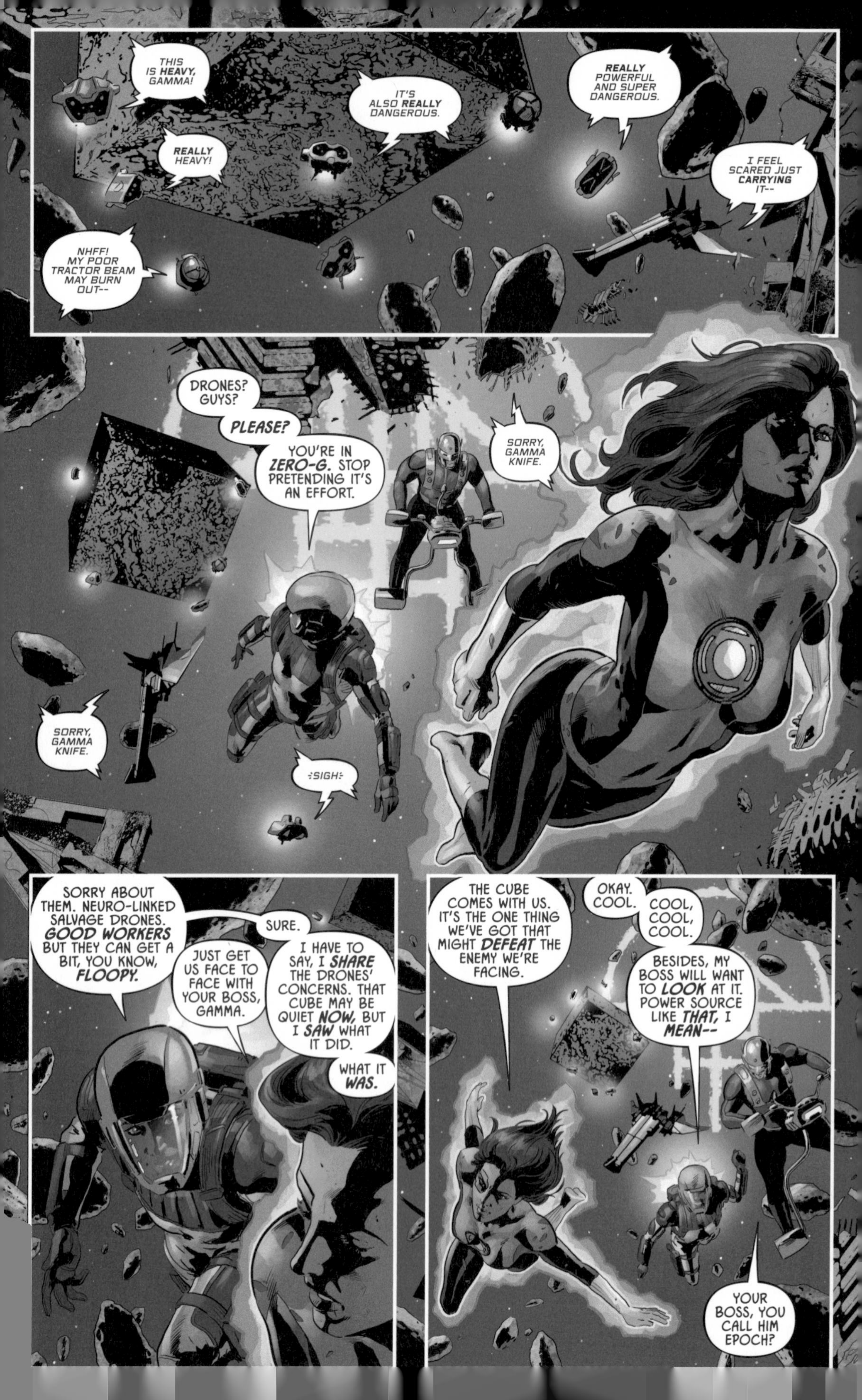
THIS IS **HEAVY,** GAMMA!
REALLY HEAVY!
IT'S ALSO **REALLY** DANGEROUS.
REALLY POWERFUL AND SUPER DANGEROUS.
I FEEL SCARED JUST **CARRYING** IT--
NHFF! MY POOR TRACTOR BEAM MAY BURN OUT--
DRONES? GUYS?
PLEASE?
YOU'RE IN ***ZERO-G.*** STOP PRETENDING IT'S AN EFFORT.
SORRY, GAMMA KNIFE.
SORRY, GAMMA KNIFE.
:SIGH:
SORRY ABOUT THEM. NEURO-LINKED SALVAGE DRONES. ***GOOD WORKERS*** BUT THEY CAN GET A BIT, YOU KNOW, ***FLOOPY.***
SURE.
JUST GET US FACE TO FACE WITH YOUR BOSS, GAMMA.
I HAVE TO SAY, I ***SHARE*** THE DRONES' CONCERNS. THAT CUBE MAY BE QUIET ***NOW,*** BUT I ***SAW*** WHAT IT DID.
WHAT IT ***WAS.***
THE CUBE COMES WITH US. IT'S THE ONE THING WE'VE GOT THAT MIGHT ***DEFEAT*** THE ENEMY WE'RE FACING.
OKAY. COOL.
COOL, COOL, COOL.
BESIDES, MY BOSS WILL WANT TO ***LOOK*** AT IT. POWER SOURCE LIKE ***THAT,*** I ***MEAN--***
YOUR BOSS, YOU CALL HIM EPOCH?

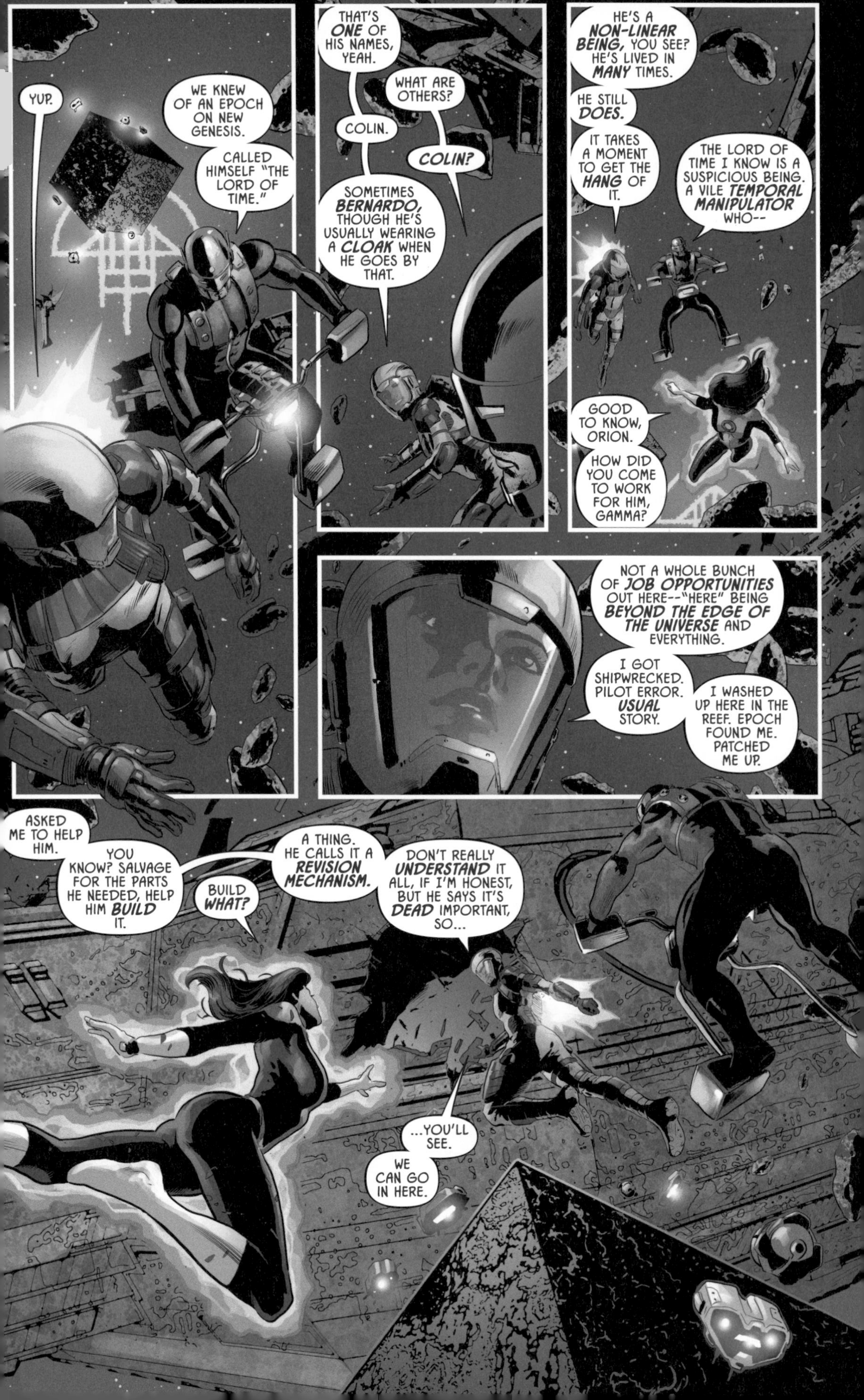

YUP.
WE KNEW OF AN EPOCH ON NEW GENESIS.
CALLED HIMSELF "THE LORD OF TIME."
THAT'S ONE OF HIS NAMES, YEAH.
WHAT ARE OTHERS?
COLIN.
COLIN?
SOMETIMES BERNARDO, THOUGH HE'S USUALLY WEARING A CLOAK WHEN HE GOES BY THAT.
HE'S A NON-LINEAR BEING, YOU SEE? HE'S LIVED IN MANY TIMES.
HE STILL DOES.
IT TAKES A MOMENT TO GET THE HANG OF IT.
THE LORD OF TIME I KNOW IS A SUSPICIOUS BEING. A VILE TEMPORAL MANIPULATOR WHO--
GOOD TO KNOW, ORION.
HOW DID YOU COME TO WORK FOR HIM, GAMMA?
NOT A WHOLE BUNCH OF JOB OPPORTUNITIES OUT HERE--"HERE" BEING BEYOND THE EDGE OF THE UNIVERSE AND EVERYTHING.
I GOT SHIPWRECKED. PILOT ERROR. USUAL STORY.
I WASHED UP HERE IN THE REEF. EPOCH FOUND ME. PATCHED ME UP.
ASKED ME TO HELP HIM.
YOU KNOW? SALVAGE FOR THE PARTS HE NEEDED, HELP HIM BUILD IT.
BUILD WHAT?
A THING. HE CALLS IT A REVISION MECHANISM.
DON'T REALLY UNDERSTAND IT ALL, IF I'M HONEST, BUT HE SAYS IT'S DEAD IMPORTANT, SO...
...YOU'LL SEE.
WE CAN GO IN HERE.

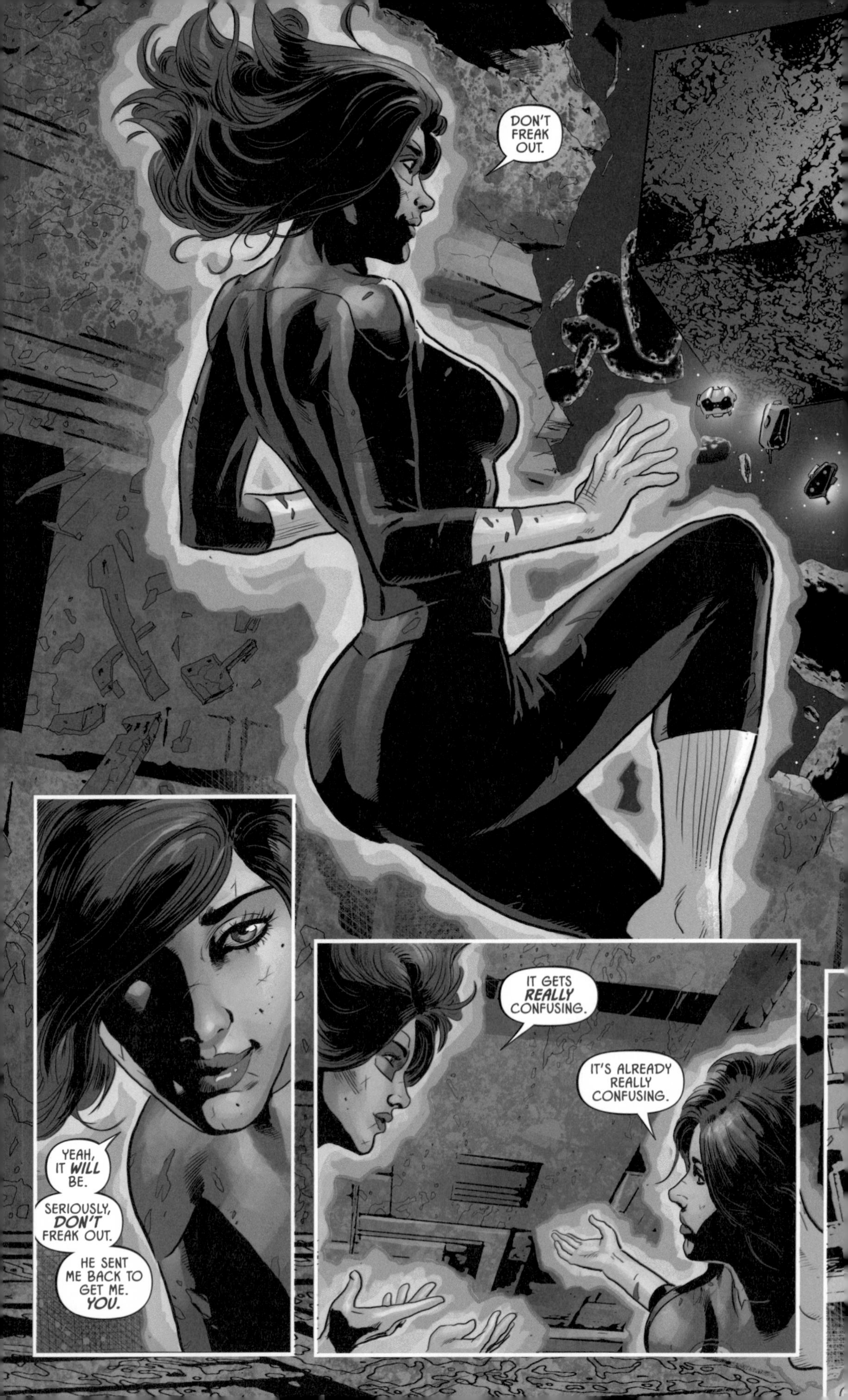
DON'T FREAK OUT.
YEAH, IT WILL BE.
SERIOUSLY, DON'T FREAK OUT.
HE SENT ME BACK TO GET ME. YOU.
IT GETS REALLY CONFUSING.
IT'S ALREADY REALLY CONFUSING.

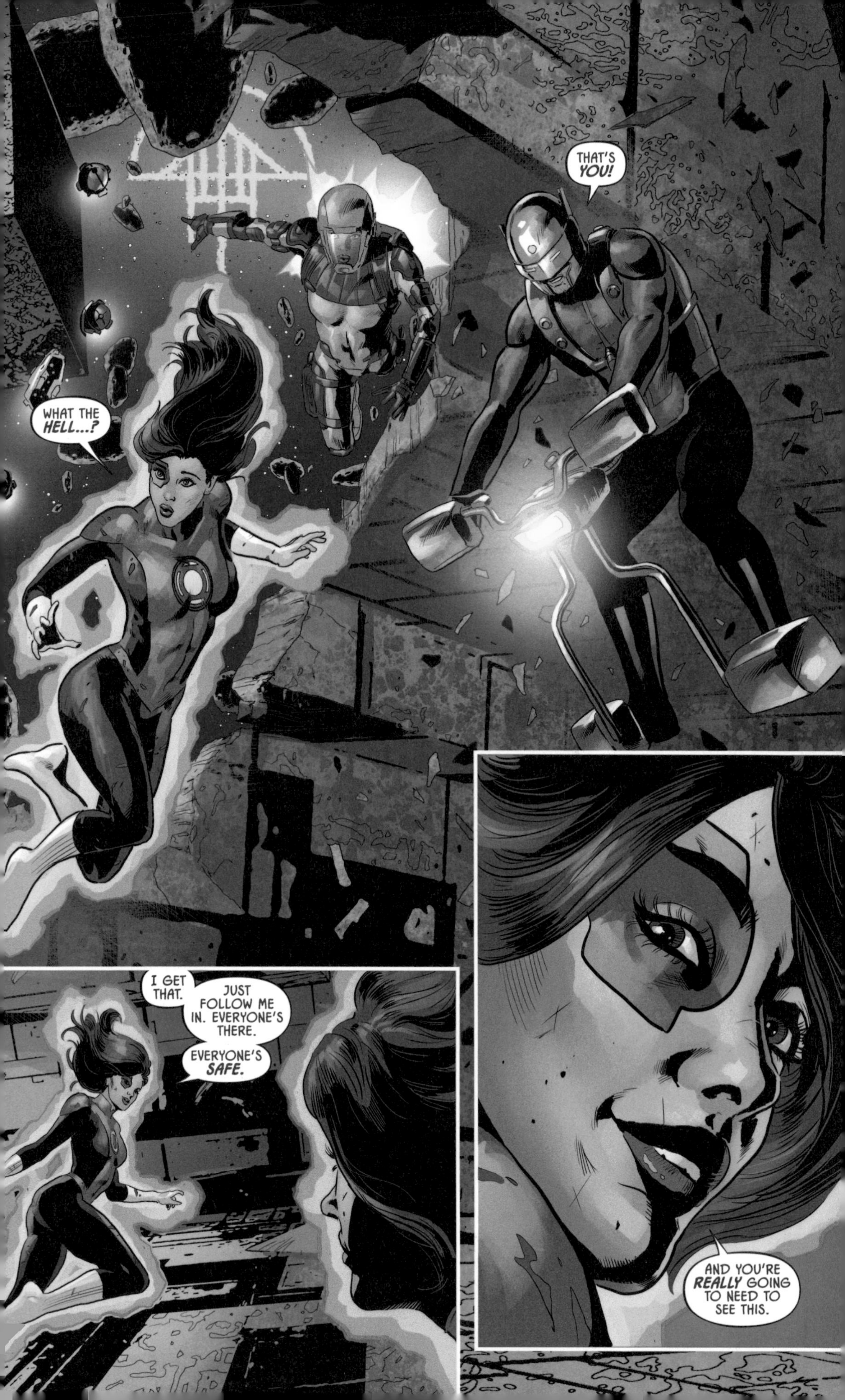
THAT'S YOU!
WHAT THE HELL...?
I GET THAT.
JUST FOLLOW ME IN. EVERYONE'S THERE.
EVERYONE'S SAFE.
AND YOU'RE REALLY GOING TO NEED TO SEE THIS.

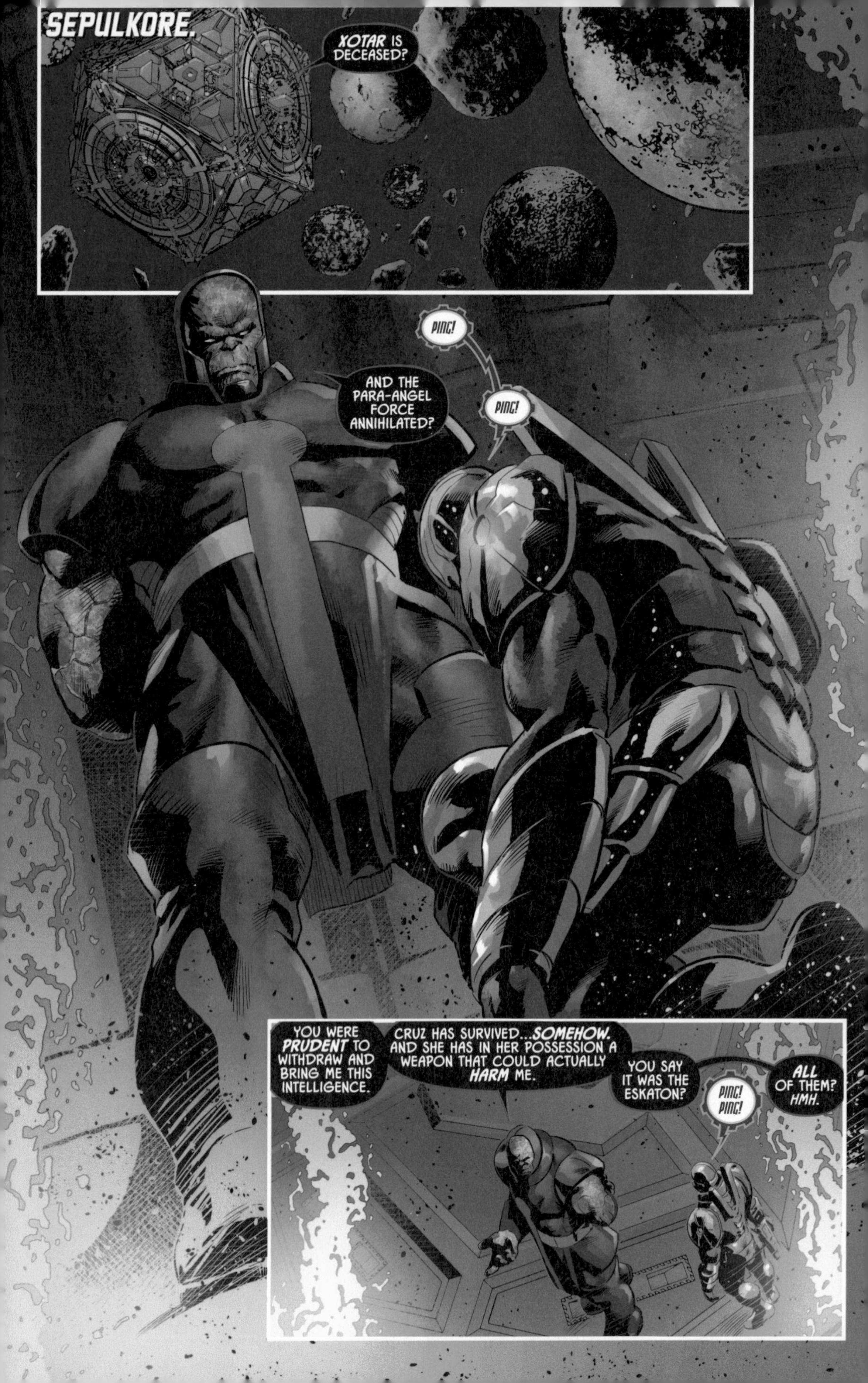
SEPULKORE.
XOTAR IS DECEASED?
AND THE PARA-ANGEL FORCE ANNIHILATED?
PING!
PING!
YOU WERE PRUDENT TO WITHDRAW AND BRING ME THIS INTELLIGENCE.
CRUZ HAS SURVIVED...SOMEHOW. AND SHE HAS IN HER POSSESSION A WEAPON THAT COULD ACTUALLY HARM ME.
YOU SAY IT WAS THE ESKATON?
PING! PING!
ALL OF THEM? HMH.

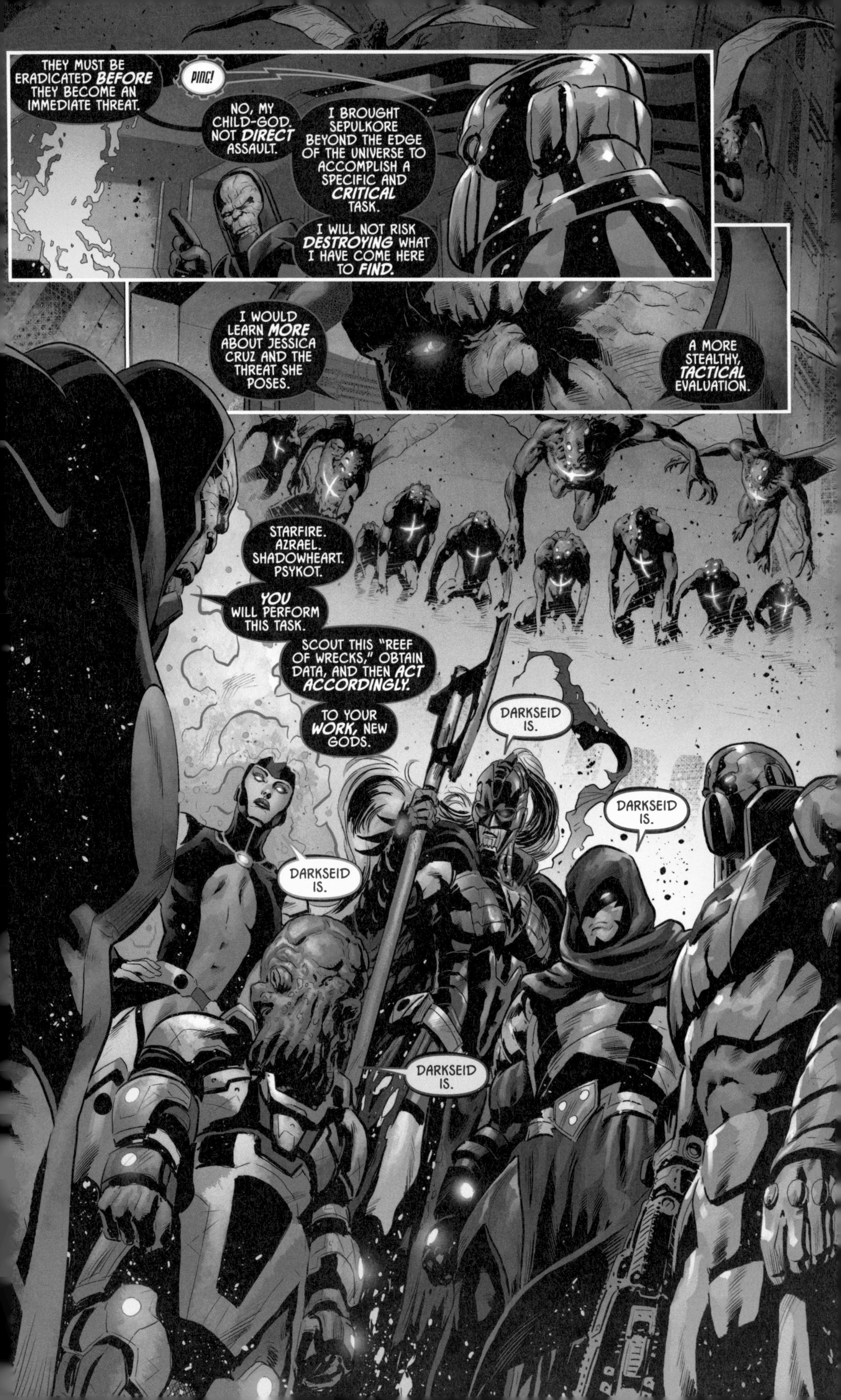

THEY MUST BE ERADICATED BEFORE THEY BECOME AN IMMEDIATE THREAT.
PING!
NO, MY CHILD-GOD. NOT DIRECT ASSAULT.
I BROUGHT SEPULKORE BEYOND THE EDGE OF THE UNIVERSE TO ACCOMPLISH A SPECIFIC AND CRITICAL TASK.
I WILL NOT RISK DESTROYING WHAT I HAVE COME HERE TO FIND.
I WOULD LEARN MORE ABOUT JESSICA CRUZ AND THE THREAT SHE POSES.
A MORE STEALTHY, TACTICAL EVALUATION.
STARFIRE. AZRAEL. SHADOWHEART. PSYKOT.
YOU WILL PERFORM THIS TASK.
SCOUT THIS "REEF OF WRECKS," OBTAIN DATA, AND THEN ACT ACCORDINGLY.
TO YOUR WORK, NEW GODS.
DARKSEID IS.
DARKSEID IS.
DARKSEID IS.
DARKSEID IS.

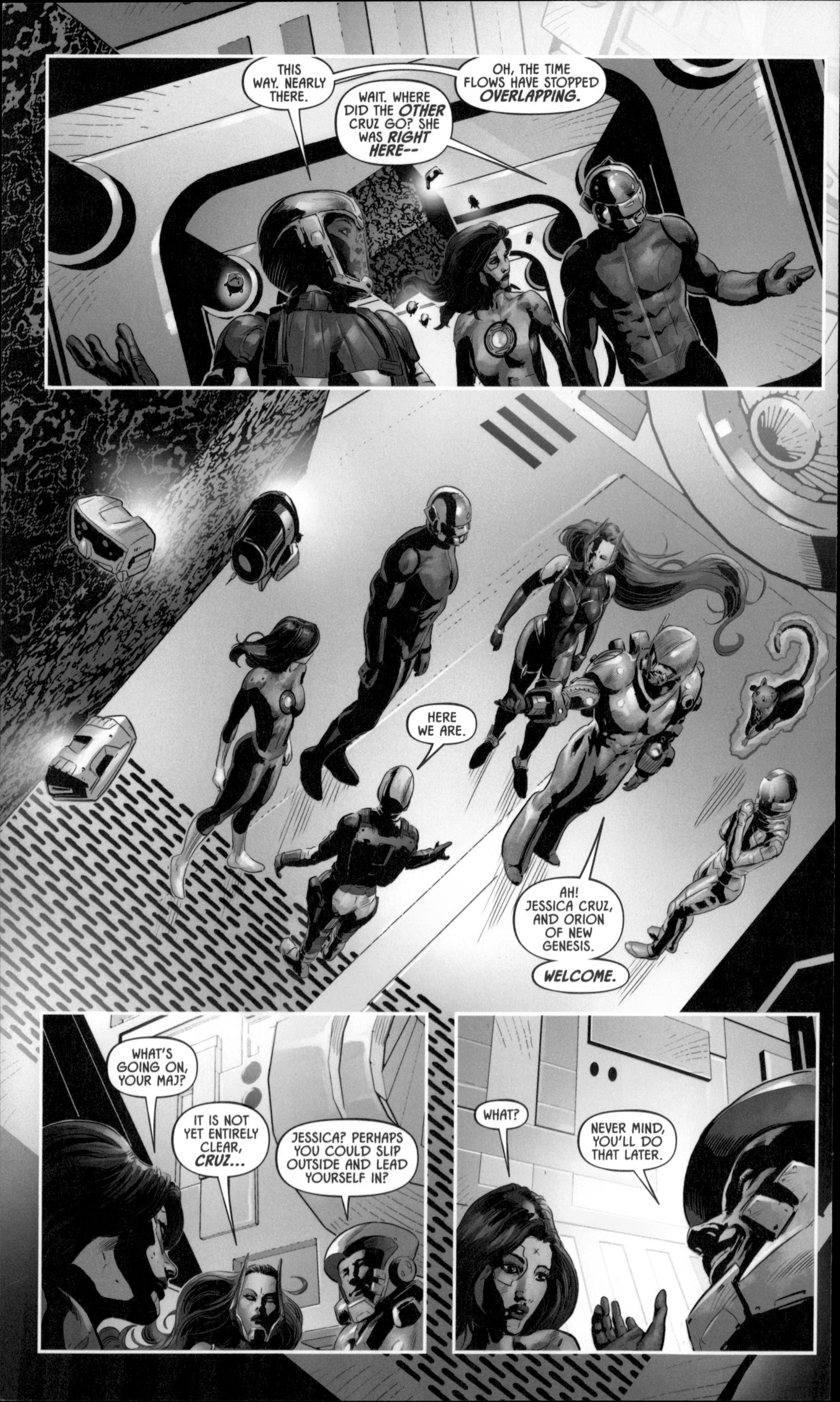
THIS WAY. NEARLY THERE.
WAIT. WHERE DID THE OTHER CRUZ GO? SHE WAS RIGHT HERE--
OH, THE TIME FLOWS HAVE STOPPED OVERLAPPING.
HERE WE ARE.
AH! JESSICA CRUZ, AND ORION OF NEW GENESIS.
WELCOME.
WHAT'S GOING ON, YOUR MAJ?
IT IS NOT YET ENTIRELY CLEAR, CRUZ...
JESSICA? PERHAPS YOU COULD SLIP OUTSIDE AND LEAD YOURSELF IN?
WHAT?
NEVER MIND, YOU'LL DO THAT LATER.

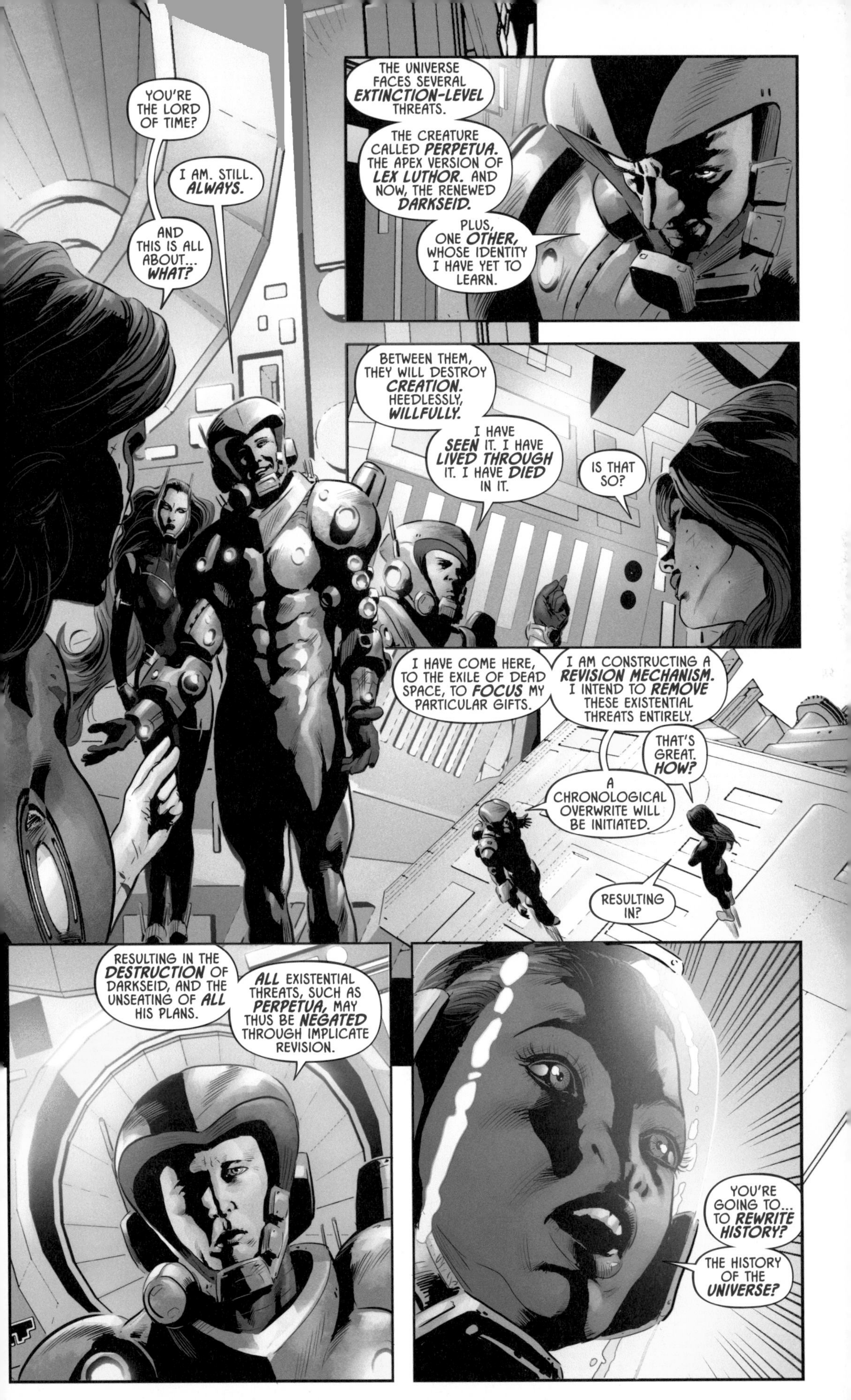
YOU'RE THE LORD OF TIME?
I AM. STILL. ALWAYS.
AND THIS IS ALL ABOUT... WHAT?
THE UNIVERSE FACES SEVERAL EXTINCTION-LEVEL THREATS.
THE CREATURE CALLED PERPETUA. THE APEX VERSION OF LEX LUTHOR. AND NOW, THE RENEWED DARKSEID.
PLUS, ONE OTHER, WHOSE IDENTITY I HAVE YET TO LEARN.
BETWEEN THEM, THEY WILL DESTROY CREATION. HEEDLESSLY, WILLFULLY.
I HAVE SEEN IT. I HAVE LIVED THROUGH IT. I HAVE DIED IN IT.
IS THAT SO?
I HAVE COME HERE, TO THE EXILE OF DEAD SPACE, TO FOCUS MY PARTICULAR GIFTS.
I AM CONSTRUCTING A REVISION MECHANISM. I INTEND TO REMOVE THESE EXISTENTIAL THREATS ENTIRELY.
THAT'S GREAT. HOW?
A CHRONOLOGICAL OVERWRITE WILL BE INITIATED.
RESULTING IN?
RESULTING IN THE DESTRUCTION OF DARKSEID, AND THE UNSEATING OF ALL HIS PLANS.
ALL EXISTENTIAL THREATS, SUCH AS PERPETUA, MAY THUS BE NEGATED THROUGH IMPLICATE REVISION.
YOU'RE GOING TO... TO REWRITE HISTORY?
THE HISTORY OF THE UNIVERSE?

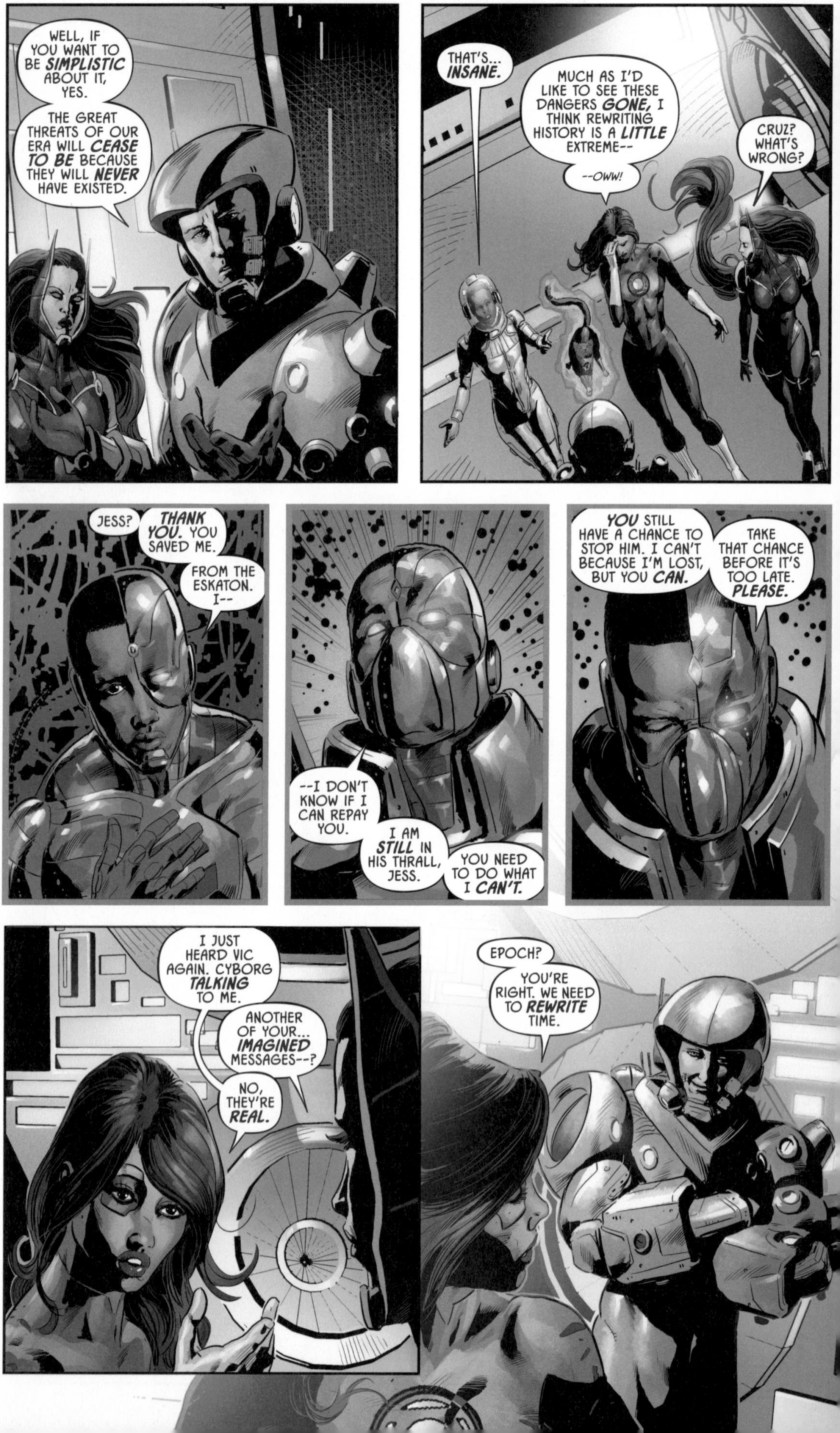
WELL, IF YOU WANT TO BE SIMPLISTIC ABOUT IT, YES.
THE GREAT THREATS OF OUR ERA WILL CEASE TO BE BECAUSE THEY WILL NEVER HAVE EXISTED.
THAT'S... INSANE.
MUCH AS I'D LIKE TO SEE THESE DANGERS GONE, I THINK REWRITING HISTORY IS A LITTLE EXTREME--
--OWW!
CRUZ? WHAT'S WRONG?
JESS?
THANK YOU. YOU SAVED ME.
FROM THE ESKATON. I--
--I DON'T KNOW IF I CAN REPAY YOU.
I AM STILL IN HIS THRALL, JESS.
YOU NEED TO DO WHAT I CAN'T.
YOU STILL HAVE A CHANCE TO STOP HIM. I CAN'T BECAUSE I'M LOST, BUT YOU CAN.
TAKE THAT CHANCE BEFORE IT'S TOO LATE. PLEASE.
I JUST HEARD VIC AGAIN. CYBORG TALKING TO ME.
ANOTHER OF YOUR... IMAGINED MESSAGES--?
NO, THEY'RE REAL.
EPOCH?
YOU'RE RIGHT. WE NEED TO REWRITE TIME.

Justice League Odyssey **#15** under acetate cover by
NEIL GOOGE

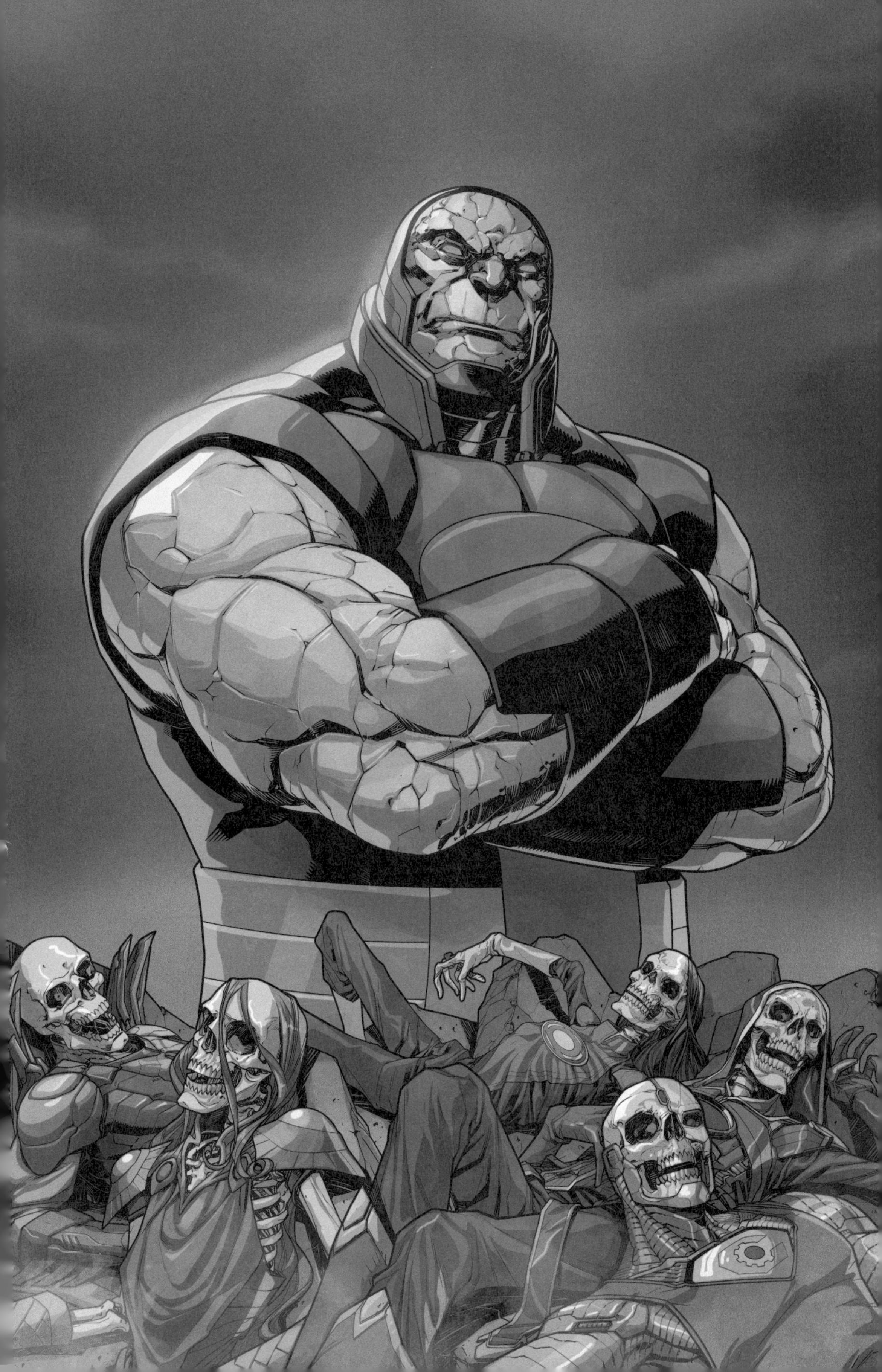

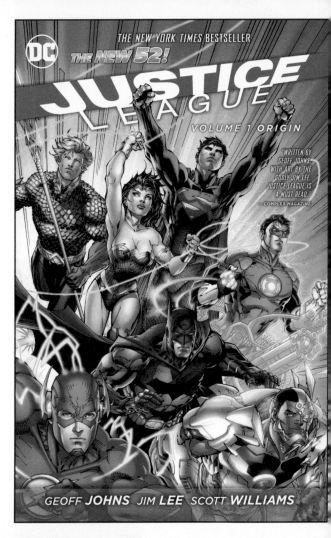

"Welcoming to new fans looking to get into superhero comics for the first time and old fans who gave up on the funny-books long ago."
– SCRIPPS HOWARD NEWS SERVICE

JUSTICE LEAGUE
VOL. 1: ORIGIN
GEOFF JOHNS
and JIM LEE

**JUSTICE LEAGUE
VOL. 2: THE VILLAIN'S JOURNEY**

**JUSTICE LEAGUE
VOL. 3: THRONE OF ATLANTIS**

READ THE ENTIRE EPIC!

JUSTICE LEAGUE VOL. 4:
THE GRID

JUSTICE LEAGUE VOL. 5:
FOREVER HEROES

JUSTICE LEAGUE VOL. 6:
INJUSTICE LEAGUE

JUSTICE LEAGUE VOL. 7:
DARKSEID WAR PART 1

JUSTICE LEAGUE VOL. 8:
DARKSEID WAR PART 2

Read more adventures of the World's Greatest Super Heroes in these graphic novels!

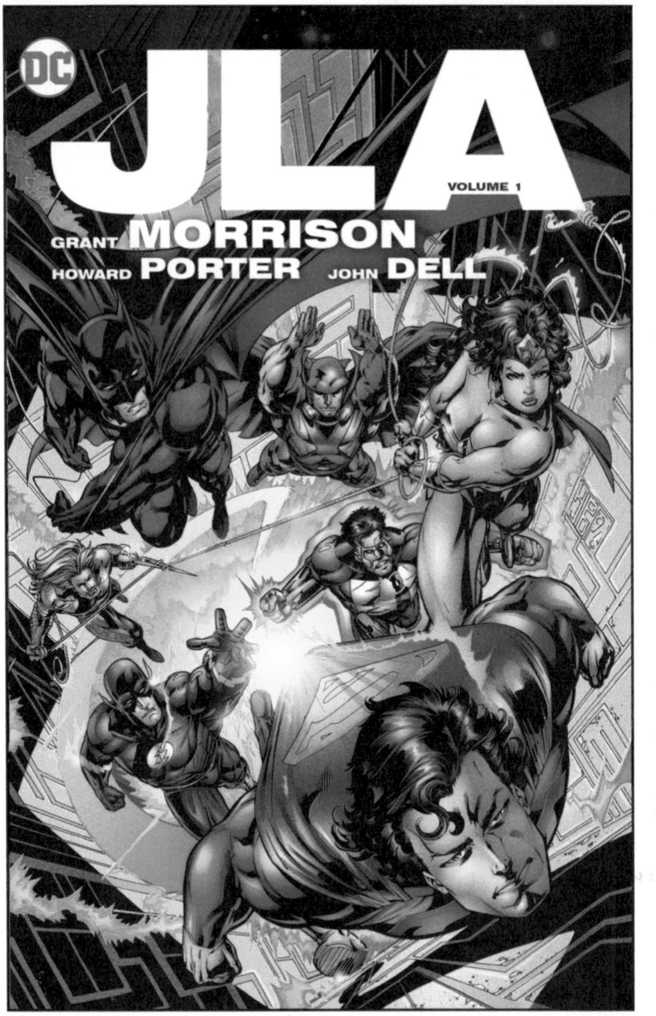

JLA
VOLUME 1
GRANT MORRISON
HOWARD PORTER JOHN DELL

JLA VOL. 1

GRANT MORRISON and HOWARD PORTER

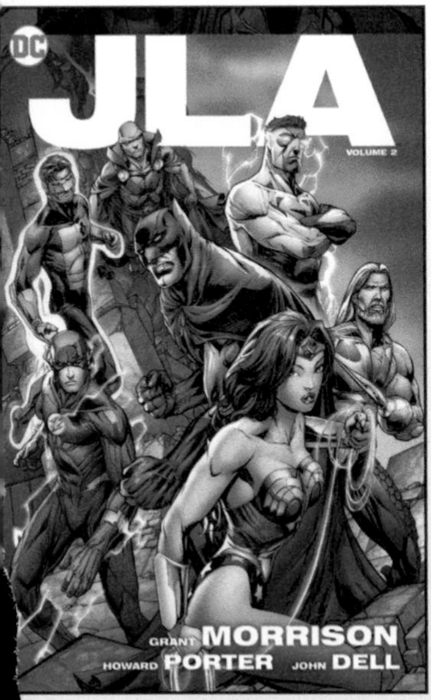

JLA
VOLUME 2
GRANT MORRISON
HOWARD PORTER JOHN DELL

JLA VOL. 2

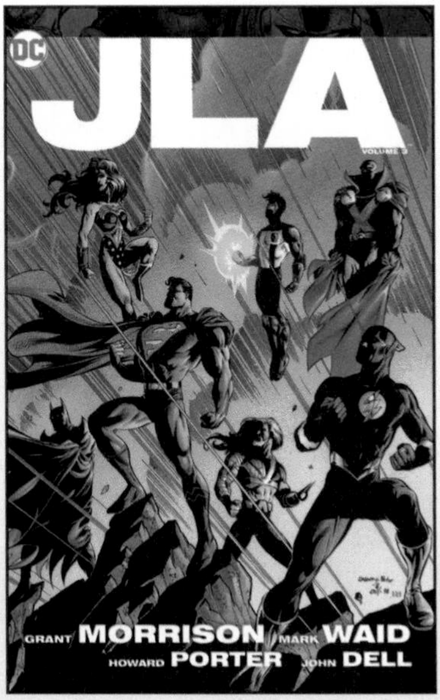

JLA
GRANT MORRISON MARK WAID
HOWARD PORTER JOHN DELL

JLA VOL. 3

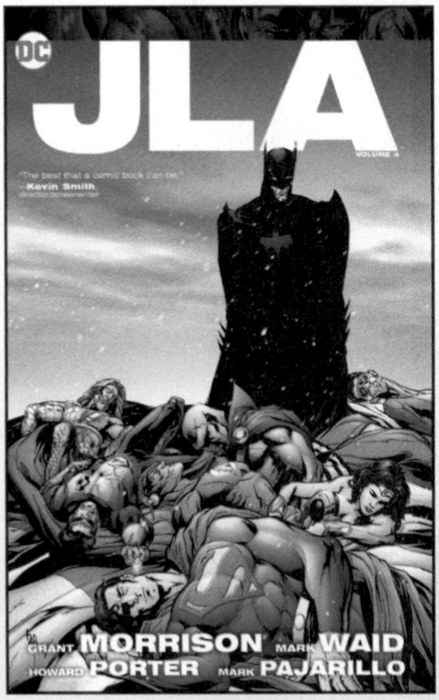

JLA
VOLUME 4
—Kevin Smith
GRANT MORRISON MARK WAID
HOWARD PORTER MARK PAJARILLO

JLA VOL. 4

Get more DC graphic novels wherever comics and books are sold!

Read more adventures of the World's Greatest Super Heroes in these graphic novels!

JUSTICE LEAGUE INTERNATIONAL: BOOK ONE–BORN AGAIN

JUSTICE LEAGUE: CORPORATE MANEUVERS

BOOSTER GOLD: THE BIG FALL